E-Education Applications: Human Factors and Innovative Approaches

Claude Ghaoui
Liverpool John Moores University, UK

Information Science Publishing

Hershey • London • Melbourne • Singapore

Acquisition Editor: Mehdi Khosrow-Pour
Senior Managing Editor: Jan Travers
Managing Editor: Amanda Appicello
Development Editor: Michele Rossi
Copy Editor: Alana Bubnis
Typesetter: Jennifer Wetzel
Cover Design: Jennifer Jones
Printed at: Yurchak Printing, Inc.

Published in the United States of America by
          Information Science Publishing (an imprint of Idea Group Inc.)
          701 E. Chocolate Avenue, Suite 200
          Hershey PA 17033
          Tel: 717-533-8845
          Fax: 717-533-8661
          E-mail: cust@idea-group.com
          Web site: http://www.idea-group.com

and in the United Kingdom by
          Information Science Publishing (an imprint of Idea Group Inc.)
          3 Henrietta Street
          Covent Garden
          London WC2E 8LU
          Tel: 44 20 7240 0856
          Fax: 44 20 7379 3313
          Web site: http://www.eurospan.co.uk

Library of Congress Cataloging-in-Publication Data

E-education applications : human factors and innovative approaches /
Claude Ghaoui, editor.
       p. cm.
Includes bibliographical references and index.
  ISBN 1-931777-92-6 (h/c) -- ISBN 1-59140-292-1 (s/c) -- ISBN
1-931777-93-4 (ebook)
  1. Internet in education. 2. Computer-assisted instruction. 3.
Instructional systems--Design. 4. Human-computer interaction. I.
Ghaoui, Claude.
LB1044.87.E36 2004
371.33'4678--dc22
                                2003017706

British Cataloguing in Publication Data
A Cataloguing in Publication record for this book is available from the British Library.

All work contributed to this book is new, previously-unpublished material. The views expressed in this book are those of the authors, but not necessarily of the publisher.

Dedication

This book is dedicated to the memory of my beloved Mum and Dad.

Fifty percent of the editor's royalty will be donated to an international charity, to support orphan children.

E-Education Applications: Human Factors and Innovative Approaches

Table of Contents

SECTION II: MORE ON INTUITIVE, SOCIAL AND INTERNATIONAL ISSUES

Preface

OVERVIEW AND MOTIVATION

There is compelling scientific, social and economic evidence for the need to widen access to education for everyone who wishes it. The consideration of people with diverse needs, capabilities and cultural differences must direct scientists and education stakeholders to look at the world in a new light. Widening access requires reducing disabling conditions under which users of education work.

We humans are amazingly innovative and inventive, and the proof is everywhere. If necessity is the mother of invention, then diverse necessities must lead to diverse, good innovation and inventions, which are human-orientated and user-centered.

The advances in Information and Communication Technology (ICT) have made it possible to reach out to a wider audience around the globe. However, even with a low cost technology, this is not always satisfactory. Reaching out successfully, to a wide range of people, requires care in employing user-centered approaches that are derived from human computer interaction (HCI) research and principles; *this issue remains a big challenge*. Motivated by this challenge, the book aims to emphasize the need to take multi-disciplinary and/or inter-disciplinary views on this issue, by marrying solutions from HCI, education, artificial intelligence, interactive multimedia technology and the WWW to benefit innovation in education.

The book focuses on "E-Education" (also known as online- or e-learning). In pursuing this motivation, the book promotes the continuous need to push for technology which serve people, instead of the other way round. Facilitating e-education requires technology that is usable and a new thinking of teaching and learning. This requires a technology and innovative solutions that can adapt to support many different groups of users and, most importantly, a passion to know who the users of education are so that they or their needs are not overlooked.

MAIN OBJECTIVE

The primary objective of this book is to enforce the need to take multi-disciplinary and/or inter-disciplinary approaches; when solutions for e-education (or online-, e-learning) are introduced. This makes innovative solutions that are user-centered possible and more effective. By focusing on the issues that have impact on the usability of e-learning, the book specifically fills-in a gap in this area, which is particularly invaluable to practitioners. The book is aimed at researchers and practitioners from academia, industry, and government, for an in-depth coverage of a broad range of issues, ideas and practical experiences on this subject. It aims to raise more awareness in this important subject, promote good practice, and share and evaluate experiences (advantages, disadvantages, problems faced and lessons learned).

DESCRIPTION OF CHAPTERS

This book includes 20 chapters, grouped into two sections. The following presents a brief overview of each chapter:

Section I: Models, Systems and Courses

Chapter I, *Engineering of a Virtual Community Platform: Realization of a Socialware with Integration of the 'User as Editor' Concept*, is written by Kerstin Röse, Leon Urbas, Alexander Künzer, Martin Christof Kindsmüller and Sandro Leuchter. This chapter describes "UseWorld.net," which smoothly integrates different information services with components for collaboration and personalization into an open user adaptive scientific portal. It presents an interdisciplinary approach to software engineering, incorporating the social aspects of virtual communities.

Chapter II, *Innovative Approach to Teaching Database Design through WWW: A Case Study and Usability Evaluation*, is by Joanna Jedrzejowicz. This chapter describes the "Postcourse" project, which is an e-course on database design. The innovative part of this project is in the interactive tools created and offered to the users of this course; a usability evaluation is discussed in the chapter.

Chapter III, *A Model-Driven Approach for Synchronous Dynamic Collaborative E-Learning*, by Véronique Baudin, Khalil Drira, Thierry Villemur and Saïd Tazi, describes a graph-based collaboration model that represents the structure of synchronous groups with their dynamic evolving. The model defines an advanced and distributed e-learning scenario involving three user groups: Teachers, Students and Coordinators. Two experiments are discussed detailing this work.

Chapter IV, *Smart ProFlexLearn: An Intuitive Approach to Virtual Learning Environment*," is by Claude Ghaoui and W.A. Janvier. This chapter provides an overview of distance learning and e-learning, and describes a Managed Virtual Learning environment prototype system called "ProFlexLearn," which was developed to support flexible e-learning. Further developments on this system, to add intuitive features were carried out; these are described and assessed in the chapter.

Chapter V, *An Expert-Based Evaluation Concerning Human Factors in ODL Programs: A Preliminary Investigation*, by Athanasis Karoulis, Ioannis Tarnanas and Andreas Pombortsis, presents a holistic evaluation approach to ODL, taking into account HCI and human factors, especially principles on collaboration and distributed cognition. The authors discuss lessons learned, with useful insights and suggestions.

Chapter VI, *Integrated E-Learning System and Its Practice*, by Toshio Okamoto and Mizue Kayama, describes an intelligent media oriented e-learning system. This system includes collaborative tools, as part of a learning management system, to facilitate interaction. Also, it offers an innovative educational method to link industry and university. This work has been tested, and analysis of the results are presented and used to inform further improvements.

Chapter VII, *SEGODON: Learning Support System that can be Applied to Various Forms*, Takashi Yoshino and Jun Munemori, describes learning support systems, which the authors developed, called SEGODON and SEGODON-PDA. The first consists of personal computers and local area network (LAN), and the second consists of Personal Digital Assistants (PDAs) and wireless LAN. An evaluation study is discussed to assess if this new system may have had an impact on improving students' results.

Chapter VIII, *Creative E-Transitions*, by Lynne Hunt, describes a pilot, online transition to a university project titled "Click Around Edith Cowan University," and an online, generic skills and career planning project called "Careering Ahead in Health Promotion". The author explains that both projects are informed by authentic learning pedagogy, which proved to be effective for e-learning.

Chapter IX, *Distributed Constructionism through Participatory Design*, is by Panayiotis Zaphiris, Giorgos Zacharia and Meenakshi Sundaram Rajasekaran. This chapter presents the implementation of Distributed Constructionism through a participatory design methodology for an online learning community, using a Modern Greek language course. Different aspects of participatory design were explored and quantitative analysis was carried out to evaluate its effectiveness in supporting users.

Chapter X, *Fast Track: School Based Student Software Design*, by Philip Duggan, Claude Ghaoui and Mike Simco, describes a pilot study, which explores the effectiveness of using participatory design in the learning of students. Students were involved in the design and development process of a software in a school environment. Preliminary results are encouraging and further usability evaluations on a larger scale are planned.

Chapter XI, *E-Learning as a Catalyst for Educational Innovation*, by Petek Askar and Ugur Halici, describes initiatives regarding e-learning and its impact on instructional design, management and the wider community. Experiences from Turkey were discussed by the authors.

Section II: More on Intuitive, Social and International Issues

Chapter XII, *Employing Intelligent and Adaptive Methods for Online Learning*, by Bernard Mark Garrett and George Roberts, discusses strategies for using intelligent and adaptive methods for online learning. It also gives an overview of representation of knowledge and intelligent agents, using a simulation application as an example. Future directions on the use of this technology in online learning are discussed.

Chapter XIII, *Toward Predictive Models for E-Learning: What Have We Learned So Far?*, is written by Maria Alexandra Rentroia-Bonito and Joaquim Armando Pires Jorge. This chapter raises an important concern of working and developing e-learning without taking a multidisciplinary and interdisciplinary approaches to the problem. In an effort to address this issue, the authors propose a holistic framework to e-learning.

Chapter XIV, *Supporting Informal Interaction in Online Courses*, by Juan Contreras-Castillo, Jesús Favela and Carmen Pérez-Fragoso, describes a system called CENTRES, which the authors developed to provide informal communications through instant messaging and presence awareness. A socio-academic based evaluation study was carried out to assess the usability of this system in an online learning environment.

Chapter XV, *The Orientation and Disorientation of E-Learners*, by Bernard Mark Garrett and Richard Francis, explores how students may be orientated and disorientated to online learning, examining some of the methods that can be employed to reduce some of the pitfalls, which come with this mode. The authors argue that disorientation experienced by students in this mode is part of the learning process to become better independent learners.

Chapter XVI, *Ensuring Usability in International Web-Based E-Learning Systems*, is written by Andy Smith. This chapter provides a summary of the main issues within cross-cultural usability with an emphasis on web-based systems. It discusses the application of generic models and theories to the field of e-learning systems and provides some future directions to ensure usability in the international context of e-learning.

Chapter XVII, *Knowledge Spaces: Cultural Education in the Media Age*, by Wolfgang Strauss, Monika Fleischmann, Jochen Denzinger, Michael Wolf and Yinlin Li, describes the work on e-learning carried out in the field of art and culture by the MARS research group. New forms of knowledge retrieval were investigated and discussed.

Chapter XVIII, *Development and Evaluation of a New HTML Browser Method of Presenting Reading Material for Students with Low Vision*, is by Kazuhito Ujima and Koichi Oda. This chapter describes a novel method, using both web technology and vision science, to predict the vision needs of individual students, and produce the appropriate reading material. Evaluation with students showed very encouraging results, which are presented.

Chapter XIX, *A Sign Language Teaching System Using Sign Language Recognition and Generation Methods*, by Hirohiko Sagawa and Masaru Takeuchi, describes a sign language teaching system that was developed, using sign language recognition and generation methods, to overcome three problems: lack of information about non-manual gestures, display of gestures and feedback given to learners on the correctness of their learned gestures. Evaluation showed positive results, which are discussed.

Chapter XX, *Precursors to Web-Based Methodologies: Lessons We Can Learn from Teaching Machines, Automatic Tutoring Devices and Learning Hierarchies*, is written by Robert S. Owen and Bosede Aworuwa. This chapter reviews the original methods on automatic teaching and tutoring machines, and compares these to hypermedia methods that are now enabled via the Web. Usability issues are explored in both contexts, with a greater emphasis on the educational aspects in an online learning mode.

CONCLUSION

The 20 chapters included in this book cover a wide range of important issues on the subject of "E-Education Applications: Human Factors and Innovative Approaches," representing experiences from 12 countries. It was really pleasing to have representations from the following 12 countries: UK, Greece, France, Germany, Portugal, Turkey, Poland, USA, Canada, Australia, Japan and Mexico. The chapters report on research, development and real experiences, including theory, practice, techniques, analysis, design and work in progress. Authors present new insights and views, by reflecting on the inter- and multi-disciplinary nature of this topic, addressing it from different perspectives, e.g., Computer Science/IT, Engineering, Psychology, Sociology, Cognitive Science, Art, and Design. The main contribution of this book is in its focus on "innovation and HCI-based" solutions for the benefit of e-education. This theme fills in a gap in literature, and particularly benefits practitioners who are working in different capacities in IT and the education sector.

Acknowledgments

I would like to specially thank Dr. Mehdi Khosrow-Pour, Editor-in-Chief, for inviting me to publish this book. Thanks and appreciation go to the authors who helped in the reviewing process. Many thanks go to the publishing team, in particular to Michele Rossi and Amanda Appicello, for their support and help. Finally, I would like to warmly thank all authors for their excellent and generous contributions, cooperation, and for sharing their invaluable experiences and insights. It has truly been a great privilege to work with international professionals like you. Thank you very much for helping me complete this project.

Claude Ghaoui, PhD
c.ghaoui@livjm.ac.

SECTION I:

MODELS, SYSTEMS AND COURSES

Chapter I

Engineering of a Virtual Community Platform:
Realization of a Socialware with Integration of the 'User as Editor' Concept

Kerstin Röse, University of Kaiserslautern, Germany

Leon Urbas, Technische Universität Berlin, Germany

Alexander Künzer, Aachen University, Germany

Martin Christof Kindsmüller, Technische Universität Berlin, Germany

Sandro Leuchter, Technische Universität Berlin, Germany

ABSTRACT

UseWorld.net is a federated user adaptive Internet portal that supports information exchange and cooperation in research and development in the area of human machine interaction. It has been jointly developed with members of Center of Human-Machine-Systems (ZMMS, TU Berlin), Chair of Industrial Engineering and Ergonomics (RWTH Aachen), Chair for Industrial Design (University of Essen) and Center for Human-Machine-Interaction (ZMMI, University of Kaiserslautern). The portal is operated by an independent open incorporated society. It integrates manifold information services (online journal, different thematic link collections, conference database, expert database) and a sophisticated cooperation component to support distributed teams by providing shared workspaces. Software agents for community awareness tasks and a clean and consistent interaction design complete the solution and support the portal's innovative operation concept, which intends to activate the users to become editors.

WHAT IS UseWorld.net?

Design Goals

Today, cooperative work is a common practice in research and development but it is done mostly "offline" so far. However, it is typical for both teams of developers in industry and scientists of different research organizations to work together as a virtual and interdisciplinary team. The goal of the described project is the development of a portal called "UseWorld.net." UseWorld.net smoothly integrates different information services with components for collaboration and personalization into an open user adaptive scientific portal. It was jointly developed by a distributed interdisciplinary team at four German universities to support information exchange and cooperation within the research area of human-machine-interaction. Scientific information services (electronic online journal, conference announcements, link list, job postings, pre-print server, bibliographic references, mailing lists, and expert database) are integrated, and structured by means of the metaphor of a browse-able web-catalogue. The integrated search engine of the portal does not only index the internal catalogue. It also considers the external content, which is connected to the portal by links. Registered users can establish and administrate mailing lists for particular interest groups. A shared workspace component enables file-based cooperation in working groups. Once again, registered users can easily form such groups and invite other portal users to take part in this working group.

UseWorld.net

The portal is operated by a non-profit organization. Except for the journal that is published by an editorial board, the operational concept does not require an editorial office for supplying new content. Instead, we applied the idea from several successful online communities and participative e-learning projects that all registered users can act as editors.

With this operational concept in mind, two main objectives have to be met by the engineering process: quality assurance of content and online community building. First of all, the community success relies on the activity of the community members. They will only take active part if they gain an individual benefit. Their avail is the content offered by other users, so they have to accept it and thus have to trust the content. Quality assurance is central because every registered user is allowed to place new information in public readable areas of the portal. To introduce quality assurance we provide registered users the possibility to rate content. Ratings are used in the portal's catalogue to filter and sort listing views. Thus low rated content will not displayed at a prominent place. Since the target group of UseWorld.net is interdisciplinary (psychologists, computer scientists, engineers, graphic designers), the interests and needs of the single portal user greatly differs. This results in a heterogeneous content and ratings. To qualify other users' ratings we apply (user adaptive) relevance information inferred from different sources: use of same workspaces, profile information (in means of catalogue

Figure 1: Components of UseWorld.net

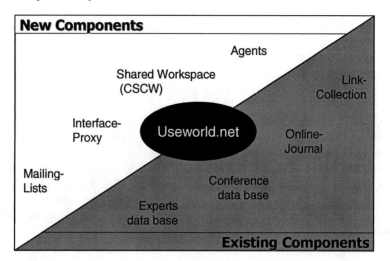

categories), activities in the catalogue, and adoption of certain roles within the community.

Users as Editors

As the operational concept of UseWorld.net does not include an editorial board (except for the journal), "growing up" an online community is a crucial factor for getting UseWorld.net to work as intended. The UseWorld.net online community is responsible for supplying new content and quality assurance of existing content, as well as creating and maintaining the etiquette of the community. This underlying basic principle of the community, which is also known as the "users as editors"-approach, has already been successfully applied in various online communities (Razi, 2002).

The likelihood of taking an active part in a community increases with the potential personal benefit that could be gained within that community. As the attention economy debate (i.e., Aigrain, 1997; Ghosh, 1997; Goldhaber, 1997a, 1997b) however shows personal benefit is a quite complex entity if one relates it to online activities in the World Wide Web. This applies notably to online communities like UseWorld.net.

The conditions in pure online communities highly differ from a computer mediated communication situation within a company. Whereas employees in a computer supported cooperative work (CSCW) context usually meet online as well as face-to-face, members of online communities have — as a general rule — never met personally. Working in a highly standardized company context, employees have to focus on task fulfillment mostly within a certain time frame. Their achievements are evaluated by superiors and they are accordingly paid by the company (Boos, Jonas, & Sassenberg, 2000). Online communities are primarily based on volunteers. Usually none of the community members can be forced to do something and there are no tangible incentives. Basic research in motivation psychology (Franken, 2001; Mook, 1996) even shows that incentives tend to be counterproductive. Furthermore, online communities have to deal with concerns of data security and protection of data privacy, as well as a lack of computer literacy and, especially with scientific online communities, copyright problems. Community members need a high degree of intrinsic motivation to participate actively in the development of an online community. Owing these circumstances it is not that surprising that a great deal of all online community building projects fail even though much effort has been put into these projects, due to the high profit opportunities within the field as, for example, Hagel and Armstrong (1997) predicted.

Taking into account all the problems mentioned in the last section it seems astonishing that there are some well running online communities at all. After analysing numerous well working online community-run portal sites, Kollock (1999) came to the conclusion that there are basically two states of motivation: self-interest (what seems to be the common motivation found) and altruism. Self-interest as a motivational state is linked to expectation of reciprocity: people are willing to help or cooperate with others if they can expect a future quid pro quo. According to Kollock (1999) and respectively, Kollock and Smith (1996), cooperation within an online community can only be successful if individuals:

- can recognize each other, i.e., they are not operating anonymously within the community;
- have access to each others' interaction history; and
- share the presumption of a high likelihood of a future encounter within the online community.

This leads to the conclusion that online communities have to offer possibilities of creating and managing relationships by supporting continuous interaction within their members. Therefore it is helpful to have some kind of archive to document and reconstruct the members' interactions. People tend to act from self-interest if they are aware that their actions have an effect on their reputations: high-quality contributions, impressive knowledge and the perception of being willing to help others enhances the prestige of the community member.

Although altruism as a motivational state for taking part in an online community is less common in comparison with self-interest, it is still frequent enough to be addressed if one thinks about community building. People with altruistic motivation try to meet the needs of the group or certain group members. This motivational state can be satisfied by establishing a public space where this need can be stated, communicated and discussed.

A widely discussed issue in the context of community building is the so-called public goods dilemma: if people can access public goods without restriction, they tend to benefit from those goods and therefore from others' contributions without contributing in the same way. If, on the other hand, most members of a community are led into temptation the public goods will vanish (Kollock & Smith, 1996), or as Kuwabara (1999) stated: "...but of course, if everyone free rides, the good is never produced." The main problem is to keep the balance between individual and common interest: an individually favorable and reasonable behavior turns out to be harmful for the others and — in the long run — disastrous for the community (Axelrod, 1984; Ostrom, 1990).

ENGINEERING OF A HOMOGENEOUS VIRTUAL COMMUNITY

While the above objective aimed at consumption of the portal's content, special efforts had to be made to motivate users to act as content producers. Online community building is addressed by social functions: registered users may adopt moderator roles; by design, rating is especially easy to fulfil and is graphically emphasized; by technical functions, an interface proxy permits for easy incorporation of new external web-information into the catalogue; by organization, privacy and security are important factors that we paid special attention to. With UseWorld.net we offer a system for both: direct cooperation in shared workspaces and for indirect cooperation through information sharing, discussing, and producing in the catalogue. An important community support for both is to enable change awareness implemented with agents that collect relevant information for its users and present it in emails and personalized portal pages.

Socialware means "systems which aim to support various social activities on network. Supports include linking people with others, smooth communications in a

Figure 2: Construction of Socialware for UseWorld.net

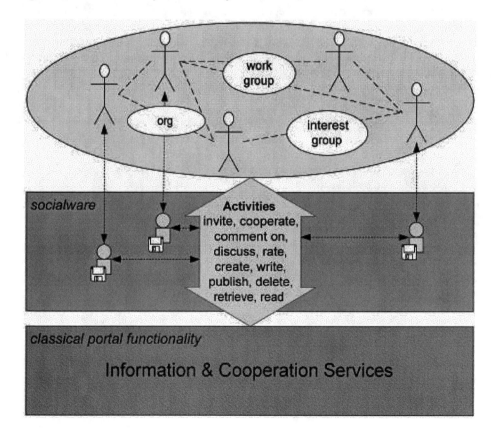

community and information integration for a community" (Hattori et al., 1999). Socialware focuses on the communicative aspect of software solutions. Such systems use the rules of interpersonal communication and transfer these structures into community software.

For UseWorld.net the implementation of a layered socialware architecture was chosen. (See Figure 2) The socialware functions are implemented by agents who listen to the stream of interactions. Their findings on the interests of the users and the relations between the actors are used in personalized information selection algorithms and are used to adapt the presentation of material. In consequence, it is possible to enhance the classical portal functionalities with new and already extant services with minimal changes at that level.

One question still remains: how to engineer socialware for heterogeneous communities? Unfortunately the approach is too young; that is general facts and best practices that could guide a prospective design of interaction principles are missing. In consequence, software development and engineering projects that are mainly assessed by means of user acceptance are in severe trouble: The established heavily pre-structured software engineering methodologies like the PSP/TSP (Radice et al., 1985), the Rational Unified Process (RUP) (Kruchten, 2000) or the V-Model (IABG, n.d.) are not sufficient for developing innovative collaboration platforms that meet the needs of heterogeneous communities. The main advantage of these methods — the definition of a straightforward engineering task with the ability to scale to very complex systems which makes them rather predictable if user requirements are clearly definable — is the main disadvantage in engineering where flexibility is necessary due to only weakly prior definable user requirements. On the other hand, the flexible user-centered software engineering process models that can be found in the literature, for instance the spiral models (Boehm, 1986) are emphasized to give too little support for planning and quality control in complex real world applications (in particular by members of the technical engineering disciplines).

Because of shortcomings or lack of acceptance of the above-mentioned well known software engineering approaches, we adapted and applied a parallel iterative engineering (PIE) approach that has, in particular, proven to be helpful for innovative industrial automation engineering tasks in human-machine systems (Urbas & Timpe, 2002; Timpe, Jürgensohn, & Kolrep, 2000) to structure our engineering problem. PIE has some unique features that make it highly attractive and suitable for innovative software engineering challenges (see also Figure 3):

- PIE divides the process into clearly separable and planable stages.
- PIE allows user participation in all phases.
- PIE parallels technological-functional and human factors activities.
- PIE foresees evaluation & assessment driven iterations during each stage.
- PIE is able to integrate locally established best practices and engineering know-how.

Not only to meet time-to-market requirements, but also to efficiently support the coordination and communication of the man-machine-interaction aspects, the process allows integration of the needs of human machine operators or software users with the engineering of the technical functions of the intended human machine system in a parallel fashion. The technology developers work parallel to human factors specialists in defined phases. After first defining the system's boundaries (e.g., target group and objectives),

Figure 3: Parallel Iterative Engineering Approach (PIE)

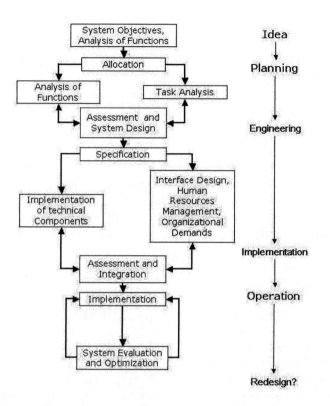

in the second phase technical functions (features) on one hand and user needs, expectations and abilities on the other are collected to guide the design of function and interaction principles. The result is a specification of use cases and corresponding technical functions. The next parallel step is to implement the technical system and to develop interface designs and organizational embedding. This process phase is accompanied with formative evaluations of mock-ups and prototypes supporting design decisions in early phases of software development. Finally, usability evaluation cycles help to optimize the software. This approach significantly reduces the risks of software development in innovative interaction oriented software projects. The systems engineering view on software development guides usability evaluation: Scenarios are defined on the basis of the use cases. Results are interpreted and weighted with objectives and target group in mind.

As PIE defines a universal (macro) process it needs (and allows!) to be concretized with and adopted to available engineering knowledge and best practices to set up a real world working structured and controllable software engineering process. For instance, it is possible to structure the stage specific evaluation and assessment driven iterations according to ISO 13407, which describes a cycle of four basic design activities:

- Understand and specify the context of use;
- Specify the user and organizational requirements;

- Produce design solutions;
- Evaluate designs against requirements.

The main advantage of this approach is that the phase transitions can be used as "quality gates," which are explicitly controlled by user requirements. To be able to react flexible on technology changes and new intermediate results, we have chosen to adopt an agile process model for the engineering and implementation stages. The members of the agile process model family have the following characteristics and rationale in common:

- Continuous attention to technical excellence and good design enhances agility;
- Simplicity — the art of maximizing the amount of work not being done — is essential;
- The best architectures, requirements, and designs emerge from self-organizing teams;
- At regular intervals, the team reflects on how to become more effective, then tunes and adjusts its behavior accordingly.

Among a set of well-described processes (ETVX — Radice et al., 1985; Extreme Programming (XP) — C3 Team, 1998), we have chosen to adapt the Feature Driven Development (FDD) concept of Coad et al. (1999) to our needs. FDD was first used with a team of 16-20 developers of varying abilities, cultural backgrounds and experience: four chief programmers (CP's) and 16 class owners split into User Interaction (UI), Problem Domain (PD) and Data Management (DM) teams. FDD is designed to scale to much larger team sizes. The limiting factor is the number of available CP's. Chief Programmer teams have proven, in practice, to scale well to much larger project teams (by the authors of FDD and independently by Brooks, 1995). The main objectives, which guided the choice, were:

- FDD enables fast iteration cycles.
- FDD provides high transparency for result oriented process management.
- FDD gives guidance for a rational selection of the task granularity level.
- FDD is communicable within all team members, not only computer scientists.

The main structuring elements of FDD are Features, Feature-Sets and Major Feature-Sets (see Table 1 "Features and Feature-Sets"). The enormous difference between XP and FDD is FDD's additional development of an overall domain object model. As developers learn of requirements they start forming mental images of the system, making assumptions and estimating on that basis. Developing an overall domain object model forces those assumptions out into the open, misunderstandings are resolved and a more complete, common understanding is formed. Features can be derived directly from the use cases documents. In addition we prioritized them according to the results of the evaluation of users' needs. Tracking by Feature in FDD describes a low-overhead, highly accurate means of measuring progress and provides the data to construct a large variety of practical, useful progress charts and graphs. The implementation of the core functions (basic servlets and classes) was paralleled by testing different designs and interaction principles on paper mockups and click models. Intermediate results of both streams were assessed and fed back into each of the parallel engineering tasks.

Table 1: Features and Feature-Sets

Entity	Attributes
Feature	• Rationale: client valued function • Granularity: implemented in less than two weeks • Pattern: **<action> the <result> <by|for|of|to> a(n) <object>**
Feature-Set	• Rationale: structuring on client interaction level • Pattern: **<action><-ing> a(n) <object>**
Major Feature-Set	• Rationale: structuring on module/component/object level • Pattern: <object> management

User Requirements

To learn the various requirements, needs and wishes of the potential members of the virtual community, a user analysis was conducted during the planning stage (Leuchter et al., 2002).

Analysis of user needs. To develop a successful and accepted portal, the user needs must be integrated. The first step is the analysis of user requirements, followed from different parallel-iterative evaluation steps.

Based on the idea and focus of the scenario "user as editor" of Kindsmüller et al. (2002), the former (further) user was interviewed with a questionnaire, sent via email. The aim of this questionnaire was the analysis of user requirements. The analysis was carried out as a two-part questionnaire and the participants were assigned coincidental to one of the parts. The first part was designed as a rating of the user-own working and cooperation behavior with online media, and shows quantitative results about kind and volume/limit of cooperation and experiences and problems in www-handling. The second part was carried out a while after the first as qualitative detail analysis. The participants were asked with open questions in the first part and therefore results from this the qualitative data for the analysis, which has enabled us to clarify and interpret the results of the second questionnaire part.

The participants were selected from the circle of interested readers of the online journal "MMI-interaktiv," which was the starting point and first activity of this community. The expected users of the UseWorld.net portal will be these community-members of "MMI-interaktiv" and other new usability interested users. Therefore the participants of the email questionnaire represent the further user of the developed community portal very well. Overall there were 72 participants: 45% engineers, 40% social and human sciences, and 15% from other relevant sciences. Selected results of this requirement analysis will be presented in the following:

Results of the requirement analysis. The results are distinguished between aspects of information processing, online experiences and cooperation behavior.

Information processing: Participants need 24% of their working time to search for "relevant information and content" in the context of their professional work. A really interesting aspect is the balance between input/output of information for and from the "net" (net as synonym for inter- and intranet). The results have shown that the user takes 25% of relevant working information from the net, but place only 8% into the net. The philosophy of the community portal is the scenario "user as editor." If currently less than 10% of the users accept sharing their work with other net-members, how does the scenario work and what are the fundamental basics to support a healthy balance between input and output?

Because we have used the two-part questionnaire method, we asked the participants of the second part: which conditions/support did they need to increase their output into the net? What are the barriers for a higher rate of adjustments? The main reason the participants named was the high technical and time effort for electronic publishing and adjusting into the net. To make net-publishing easier, they wish for a standardized method to support integrating existent content into the net with an easy transformation into a nice presentation format. Other barriers are unknown or unclear legal situation and lower reputation of online publication, as well as the pressure of actuality on the net (e.g., preprints, white papers, etc.).

Online experiences: The participants work nearly 70% of their working time in front of a computer based system. During this time they are 25% conscious online or work with the net. The working procedures are: 44% research, 37% communication, 7% cooperation, 4% planning, and 3% publication. This result shows the excellent potentials of a MMI-portal to support the online work and the possibilities to make them efficient.

Cooperation behavior: The results of the email questionnaire show that the participants use 37% of their working time for cooperation with other people: 24% for internal and 13% for external cooperation partners. More than 50% of the external cooperation is in the context of existent projects or informal contact. For this cooperation they use often email (39%) but very seldom the net (4%).

To understand the reasons for the low usage of the "net," the participants of the email questionnaire were asked — with closed rating questions — for the problems of usage. They should assess at a five-point rating scale (5 being "very problematic") the current problems. Problems with information search in the net are:

- With actuality (2.5),
- Search time (2.9),
- Quality (3.6),
- Completeness (3.8),
- Quantity (4.1).

These results are not really surprising. Most net-users know the problem of "lost in information." There are endless depots of information with high actuality and unproblematic search time, but the time to filter the relevant information for the individual and current focus of the user is the real problem. A corresponding problem is the low user knowledge about the handling of web tools, e.g., search tools. The results have shown that more than 50% of the participants have never worked with a shared workspace and 38.3% do not know for what they can use it. Software archives, mailing lists and newsgroups were activities and offers with a low usage rating. All participants reported the most experiences with search engines, but feel not well informed about the handling of this opportunity.

The participants expect from a further tool a support for: concentrated information search, support with information filtering for a specific task and support of professional cooperation with colleagues. Other aspects are: easy working in a new topic (e.g., research field) and self-presentation in professional context.

Requirements for the portal-development. After all, the following requirements for the MMI-portal were derived:

- There is a misbalance between the input and output of information. To balance this relationship, the UAE concept should be analyzed and usable information extracted for their integration into the portal.
- The user analysis has shown that there is a great need for better quality observation to reduce the information flood. To realize this: for the information of the portal a rating should be introduced and the rating results must be presented recognizably.
- To support the information filtering: The ratings are to be used to filter information for the user. The presentation of search results must be configurable, e.g., presentation via time or author criterion.
- The benefits of the portal must be well presented to support user participation, especially with the assessing of information. Offering of training documents, online-help, etc., could be useful for the novice user of the portal.
- One current problem is the limited availability of research papers. A preprint server could be an interesting offer to support current work in a non-conforming academic format and the early prepublication of book chapters (e.g., white papers).

Net-cooperation in working context is still rare. Nevertheless, the participants of our analysis expect better support for the handling of such cooperations. The interest for online cooperation is high, but the current offers have technical and handling barriers. Therefore, the integration of an easy-to-handle and well documented shared workspace into the portal is necessary.

Requirements for a CSCW-Part

To satisfy the users' cooperative needs, a web-based shared workspace was integrated into the portal. By the smooth integration an additional benefit could be achieved, as compared to other separated solutions, and should be both: flexible and easy to use (Künzer & Schmidt, 2001). A shared workspace is a kind of an Internet/World Wide Web (WWW) based groupware system. Users share workspaces (e.g., for different projects) with each other or have their own private ones (e.g., for personal documents).

A shared workspace can contain different kinds of information such as documents, pictures, URL links to other web pages, threaded discussions, information about other users and more. The use of shared workspaces is becoming increasingly popular today (Appelt, 2001). Many systems have problems and so the acceptance is often very low, e.g., the usability is usually not good, caused by the technical restrictions given by the Internet standards HTTP and HTML. Nevertheless, the requirements of the users are not considered adequately. But the aspect of usability is very important for such shared workspaces and often underestimated. The criteria for electronic workspaces in Figure 4 (Herel, 2000) form the basis for the requirement analysis.

Figure 4: Criteria for Shared Workspace (based on Herel, 2000)

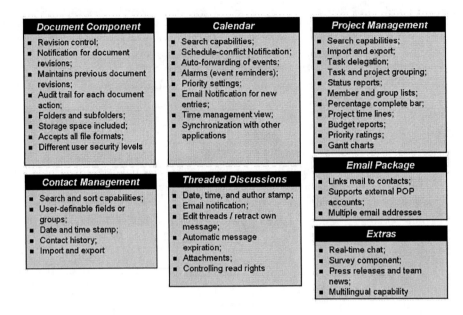

A survey should show how and to what extent people are using existing shared workspaces in their work. For this 28 persons were asked. Eighteen of these interviewees belonged to the university field. Figure 5 shows the results for the main features for those interviewees having at least a medium skill in working with shared workspaces (altogether 15 interviewees, thereof 10 of the university field).

Furthermore, the people who are involved in HMI were questioned for their requirement priorities according to the main features (Figure 5). This information was used for a detailed requirement list, which has formed the basis for the new shared workspace component of UseWorld.net.

Additional to these more technical requirements, the needs of the users have to be regarded, too. This covers the usability aspects (according to the ISO 92141-10) as well as the social aspects of the cooperative behavior: the requirements on socialware.

ENGINEERING OF AN PLATFORM FOR AN HETEROGENEOUS VIRTUAL COMMUNITY
The Portal Part

The realization of the UAE concept. Recipe based fabrication of online communities are at least bold ventures if not illusionary enterprises. Social relationships and group momentum are particularly hard to predict. As Rheingold (2000) explicates, online communities grow organically and tend to follow their own rules. Therefore controlling efforts always have to be adjusted to the current group context. Nevertheless, some well-approved principles could be derived from findings that were discussed in the last paragraph.

Figure 5: Users' Usage and Requirements for Shared Workspaces (5 = High, 0 = None)

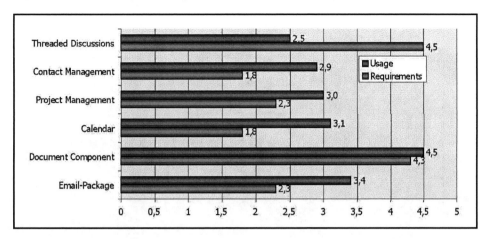

Introducing a dedicated and active moderator seems to be the most important step to nourish motivation of the community members. Moderators can enhance group activities and increase the efficiency of the group. They are responsible to communicate the group standards (etiquette), act as confessors for new community members and help in preserving continuity. Rojo (1995) even shows that an active moderator can — to some extent — compensate the lack of active members in an online community. Hence there was some effort put in the implementation of a graded moderation concept, which is part of an encompassing role concept (see Figure 6).

To realize this concept in UseWorld.net, we constructed a moderator concept, shown in Figure 6. There are four different user groups: (1) the anonymous user, (2) the pseudonymous user (or user with known identity), (3) the category moderator, and the (4) super moderator. The aims of this moderator concept are: protection of personal data privacy, generation of content, quality assurance, motivation and trust.

Basically, every user can become a moderator and being a moderator can be well adjusted to personal involvement, time resources and current interest. The moderation scope usually matches the user's interest: CaMos (Category Moderators) are responsible for one or more categories within the portal; SuMos (Super Moderators) are responsible for the whole portal. They can moderate every category, revoke moderation rights from other moderators and are able as well to chuck out uncooperative users. The moderators' mission statement can be paraphrased as: "the good host." A UseWorld.net moderator acts like a good host: new members are welcomed and encouraged to take active part, they start new topics and keep the discussion going.

Considering the public goods dilemma, we decided to introduce a role concept to clearly communicate the borderline between being in group and out of group. To get full access to all group resources one has to join the group. Several functionalities are only accessible for registered and authorised users. The commitment that is required to join the group leads to a comprehensible demarcation between members and non-members who in turn facilitate the togetherness of the group and the identification of the members with the group.

Three further selective measures address the public goods dilemma: personal presence, personal responsibility and personal history. Anonymity and lack of continu-

Figure 6: Moderator Concept in UseWorld.net

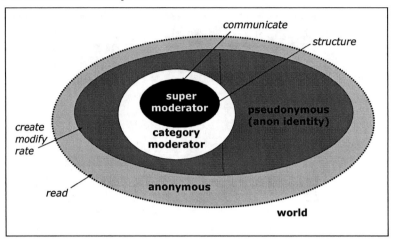

ity among the members promotes egoistic behavior. Therefore all modifying actions within the portal are tagged with the users' login name, which in turn is associated with a record of further personal data. Tagging entries and actions with user login names makes it easy to recognise people and enhances the constitution of personal relationships and online cooperation among the community members. Seeing all modifying actions supports the actors' personal responsibility. The portals memory of every action gives every community member as well as every information object a personal history. Information about past interactions of the members again increases the personal responsibility, whereas information about interaction with the portals' information objects facilitates getting up-to-date within a new area of interest and the familiarization of new members with the UseWorld.net-etiquette and the UseWorld.net who-is-who.

"Content is king" is the commonplace for virtually all web-based efforts. This is notably true for online communities like UseWorld.net. As Utz (2000) states, the likelihood of submitting high quality contributions increases with the quality and the manifoldness of the already existing entries. To implement a reasonable quality assurance we apply technical as well as social means. Technically UseWorld.net provides a highly sophisticated rating system in which each information object is rated towards the user's personal interest profile. On the other hand, a team of highly motivated volunteers from the contributing organizations bears the brunt of work. Most of them are domain experts for the categories they are moderating.

As mentioned before self-interest is a strong motivating factor. Therefore people can easily be convinced to contribute to a community if their contribution generates immediate benefit. If one can create a system where this is the case — even without anyone else contributing — it is very likely to succeed in the online community building process. Within UseWorld.net registered users gain as soon as they start inserting content. They not only have ubiquitous access to their information collection but are able as well to maintain it ubiquitously. As additional benefit they get the chance that others contribute to and comment on their information collection and they are informed if related information is available.

Design of Interaction Principles

The design purpose, which has to be followed during the development of the portal, is like any other complex system: to compress a high amount of information into a user-friendly structure. It is very important to decide how deep and how widespread information can be laid down. That means how much information can be placed on one single page or must be spread on additional pages. Furthermore it is very important to organize the amount of information that the user gets to only a focus on the information he or she needs during a process.

The fundamental part during the development is the difference between the non-registered and the registered user. Only the registered user has access to all of the functions the portal offers. That means for instance that only the registered user can go deeper into the structure of the portal and has the ability to publish and rate content. These system restrictions must be visible for the user and will be shown with graphical support in the navigation line. Non-usable parts are showed in a lighter color for non-registered user.

One of the challenges of the UAE concept is to show the user his or her possibilities with the portal by means of the graphic interface. The user must know at any place and time what he can do with the content as a publisher. Furthermore, he must know all the consequences that his editing can have to the portal. The possibilities the user has to edit some content are shown in a "dropdown box." After the users' decision to perform an action to some content, a formal dialog will appear to show the user that he has from now on the ability to create active the portal. To focus the work on the dialog, the navigation will be limited down to the portal logo, so the user can only perform steps that are important for his process. During this process the user gets the information on what kind of action he selected and how many steps he has to perform before his action can be finished successfully.

All content changing actions of all users will be transparent to the whole community, i.e., the community will know who performed the content editing. With this feature the sense of the individual responsibility for the portal shall be raised. This is very important for the UAE concept. The basic condition for this concept is a responsible and engaged attitude of all users!

Table 2: Advantages and Disadvantages for the Portal-Part

Advantages	Disadvantages
• Usable for anonymous and registered user • High flexibility • Easy handling of extension and structuring • Individualized information filtering • Pre-knowledge with handling of communities and internet services is not necessary	• There was only a limited basic structure for the user • Extension of basic use cases and structure only possible for the super moderator; no code-free adding • Only offering for the German HMI-community; no English version
Practical problems	
• Coordination of the interdisciplinary development work with different approaches. • Internet usage offers the service world-wide; cultural differences are not taken into account (at the moment)	

Figure 7: Model-View-Controller Design Pattern

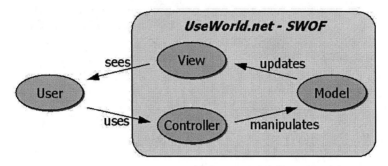

To raise the attitude of users, the navigation will show a status of the current portal activity through a graphical brain. This symbol represents the cumulated knowledge of the portal and is used to visualize the current quantitative overall participation index. This measure is defined as the balance between active and passive activities — that is publishing and editing vs. downloading and reading of content. Furthermore the user has access to a history of the individual participation index as an immediate activity reward or a reminder to become more active.

The CSCW Part

The architecture of SWOF uses an application server and is based on Java Servlet Pages. The free, available and widely used open source solution Tomcat has been chosen due to its JSP reference implementation. In order to derive an open architecture that can be easily extended, the Model-View-Controller (MVC) design pattern has been chosen (see Figure 7).

- As a model, basic object types for SWOF were implemented; this supports the basic features like database persistence, presentation and modification.
- The controller distributes user requests and forwards these to the referring objects and methods. If necessary, the controller can also be extended.
- The view component is responsible for the presentation in SWOF and can be tailored completely to support other layouts or user interfaces.

The possibilities to extend SWOF are shown schematically in Figure 8. Beginning on the lowest database level, where the used database can be changed, the class structure of SWOF allows changing features and objects. In most cases this is quite easy because the existing Java classes can be super classed to achieve the wanted functionality.

On the top level, SWOF can use a complete different presentation layer (e.g., for mobile devices, see Figure 9a) or just have a different layout according to a special corporate design (like a skin, see Figure 9b).

SWOF and UseWorld.net. The primary goal for developing SWOF was to extend UseWorld.net with a shared workspace. To achieve a smooth integration for this purpose several new object classes were created. On the one hand, the user's habits have to be supported in a more natural way. Thus, for example, tailored workspaces are used that can be recognized by the visual appearance and the different functionality according to

Figure 8: Possibilities to Extend SWOF

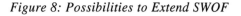

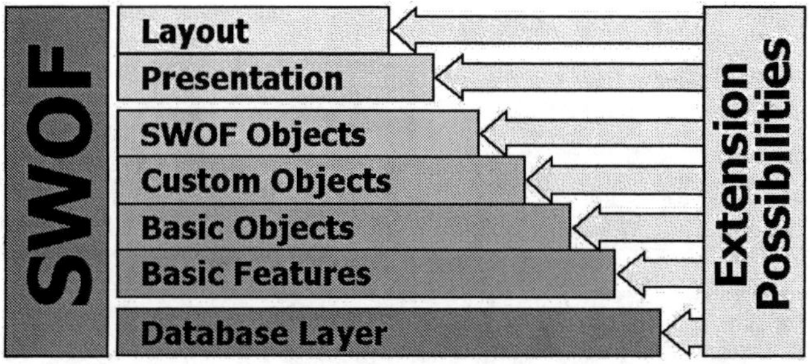

the natural habits of the users. In this way the self-descriptiveness of the object types is supported by:

- **Private Space:** Allows the user to store information objects of interest in a hierarchical file system, like links to the portal or documents he or she found. Privacy is especially important here and therefore the access for other users is not possible.

- **Workgroup:** Emphasizes the common interests of the members by showing their activities (last access, number of online-times) and so increasing their self-confidence. This is one possible way for user motivation (Kindsmüller et al., 2002).

- **Project Space:** Focused on solving a special project together with other users and contains additional project data (start/ finish date, project status).

On the other hand, new object classes were created corresponding to the objects in the portal like articles, categories, conferences, experts, etc. Moreover a new workspace will be developed to support the distributed review and publishing processes of an online journal (Röse et al., 2002).

Advantages. SWOF can be used for different cooperation tasks. The users of a shared workspace based on SWOF are supported by the high usability and the pre-structuring way the information can be organized in SWOF. Because the framework

Figure 9: SWOF with (a) Different Presentation Structure (left) and (b) Two Different Layouts (middle, right)

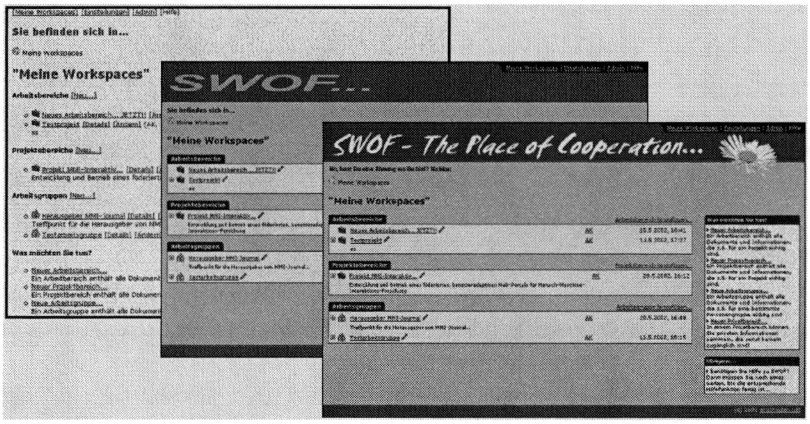

Table 3: Advantages and Disadvantages for the CSCW-Part

Advantages	Disadvantages
• Usable for different cooperation tasks • High usability • Easy adaptation and extension • Pre-structuring of information organization • Easy integration into other web-based portals	• There was no usable basic structure, e.g., Open Space; because all approaches were too specific or not developed in JSP • Users can not use an unlimited variety of their own applications; actually oriented on integration of standard applications like MS
Practical problems	
• Technical restriction given by the internet standards HTTP and HTML • Internet usage offers the service world-wide; cultural differences are not taken into account (at the moment)	

focuses on an easy adaptation and extension, other developers are able to integrate it smoothly into web-based portals like UseWorld.net.

Disadvantages. Nevertheless, the requirements of the users are not considered adequately. But, the aspect of usability is very important for such shared workspaces and often underestimated, especially for future use. Because of the cooperative idea of a shared workspace it is not possible for users to work with their favorite applications in every project they are involved in (rather the selection for a special tool depends on the companies' or the project strategy).

Unlike today, most users are using a small set of standard applications, e.g., they can deal with their preferred word processing tool well. This situation could change so that users have to do their work with several different shared workspaces. These characteristics dealing with the software aspects can be found similar in parts of the working fields, or the company, or even cultural aspects.

Practical Problems. Many systems have problems and so the acceptance is often very low, e.g., the usability is usually not good, caused by the technical restrictions given by the Internet standards HTTP and HTML when developers are looking for the smallest agreement and systems are realized without secondary techniques on the client server (like ActiveX, Java, etc.).

Evaluation of UseWorld.net

UseWorld.net was implemented as a prototype (see Figure 10) and the first evaluation steps are finished. The first evaluation of the prototype was carried out with 20 testers mostly from university background (engineers, computer scientists, psychologists). Some background information about the participants:

- *Computer experience/usage in average:* 12 years, approx. five hours daily, mostly professional
- *Internet usage in average:* six years, approx. two hours daily, mostly professional
- *Search engines in average:* five years, approx. 20 minutes daily, mostly professional
- *Participation in online communities:* most less than five communities, mostly private

Figure 10: Prototype of UseWorld.net

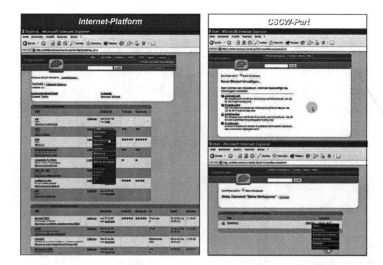

Typical use-cases were tested with a scenario-based-approach. For example, the task "Invite the member 'eva' into your workgroup and check the successful sending of your invitation to 'eva.'" The participants of the evaluation were expected future users of the UseWorld.net, but not the same individuals as in the requirement analysis, therefore users on the novice level of UseWorld.net-usage. The evaluation situation was structured with a short pre-questionnaire about experiences with online-cooperation and internet-usage, followed by a scenario-based testing of selected use-cases with UseWorld.net, followed by a post-questionnaire about subjective satisfaction with the usage of the system and finished by an open feedback discussion.

The items of the post-questionnaire were structured into two categories: "joy of use" and "ease of use," used a rating with five steps (see Figures 11 and 12). In the following some selected results of this evaluation are shown.

Figure 11: Score for the "Joy of Use"

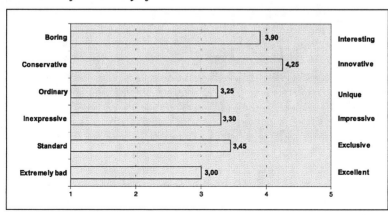

Figure 12: Score for the "Ease of Use"

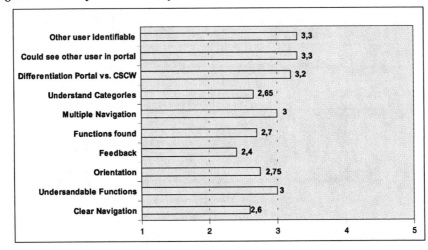

Overall, the user-satisfaction was appropriate for a prototype. In total the median for "joy of use" (using the hedonistic differential) was 3.45 and for "ease of use" 3.07. These results are not bad but show a potential for redesign. Interesting is the higher score for "joy of use."

The explanation of the participants in the feedback discussion was: UseWorld.net was obviously an innovative and interesting approach for them and they accentuated the high degree of freedom in structuring ones own workspace. During the feedback discussion some interesting problems and requirements were found (e.g., the problem with the usage of "Alias" as user name and the missed overview of all participants of the community). Other points were: different main-navigation-points in the navigation-strip on the bottom in the Portal- and CSCW-Area. The participants did not understand the difference and therefore they had problems with the understanding of the complete system structure of the whole system (Portal and CSCW). Only 56.3% have indicated in the post-questionnaire that the border between UseWorld.net-CSCW and UseWorld.net-Portal was at all times clear to understand for them. That indicates that the same navigation principles are useful and support the building of a homogenous navigation model. The separation with graphical design elements — different colors for different parts — are not transparent for all users.

On the other hand, all users emphasize the good correspondence of navigation (interaction design) between the Portal- and the CSCW-Area. The main actions in both areas were realized with pop-up menus (which include context-dependent main functions), and the users have indicated that it was easy to learn and use and comfortable for both Mac- and PC-users (no left mouse button functions). This was helpful, because the structure of both systems shows some differences in structure and action.

However, the participants were all pleased by the variety of the possibilities the community-portal offered for cooperation. In the scenario-based testing part, 90% of all participants have executed the CSCW-tasks successfully without any instructions. 77.7% of the participants could see that other users are also active (logged in) in the community. 78.5% of the participants have indicated in the post-questionnaire that they "would use this system again," and 60% would like to integrate their documents and information into the system. An important advantage for the user to participate in the community was the aspect of workplace-independent usage of the cooperation. The offer of global access (independent of location or used system) to the community was for all participants a really important aspect, in combination with the possibility to create the own "internet-workplace" and a private "sub-community" integrated in a comfortable portal-community.

ADAPTATION OF THE UseWorld.net-CONCEPT

A major advantage of the UseWorld.net framework is that it could be used in different virtual communities and cooperation cases without many modifications. If the community focuses on engineering, some additional object types can support the engineers, e.g., by previewing CAD files. Additionally the SWOF framework can be used in non-cooperation scenarios, e.g., it can be used to develop an electronic quality management (QM) system. This can be done by implementing a new interface and new object types for agreements and processes. The history function is helpful to log the document modifications. The development of special views supports the quality managers by showing important information, e.g., responsibilities and audit agreements, etc. (Oehme et al., 2002).

Socialware for school and learning communities. The adaptation of the UseWorld.net concept is also possible for learning communities. A concept for the adaptation of this concept is already developed. The name of the concept is "Virtual School 2005." Target is the most realistic virtual version of the infrastructure at school, including the interpersonal contacts and a flexible, time-independent and mobile usage via Internet. The Internet has the disadvantage of limited face-to-face interaction, but it offers the advantage of new interaction possibilities like CSCW-parts. CSCW as standard interaction strategy builds the basis for the foundation of a new social network

Figure 13: The Adaptation of the UseWorld.net Idea to "Virtual School 2005"

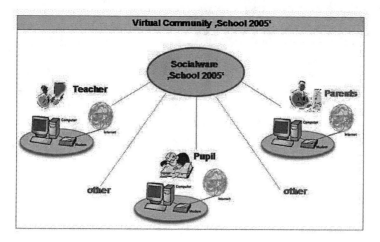

and the establishment of existing real network structures in school and learning context. With "Virtual School 2005" the Internet goes to the point of interest for all participants of school context and should become a normal medium for learning, communicating and socializing in the next years. However, the target is a socialware "school."

To realize the concept of a virtual school the UseWorld.net concept could be adopted. The presented concept with the object-oriented approach (based on use cases and standard vs. non-standard scenarios), PIE and FDD allowed the developer to reuse or "recycle" concept components. Therefore, the following usage aspects/components of UseWorld.net are integrated into the concept "Virtual School 2005":

- Laying out and managing of user profiles;
- Agent-based information filtering and presentation;
- Collection and managing of information from the Internet (www) like links, documents, references, events, jobs, journals;
- Lounge/chat area;
- CSCW-component for self-managing with work groups, project area (usable for limited time), work area, private area for discussion and data collection;
- User-as-editor principle with rating of content, comments on person and data, moderator concept.

Socialware should support the communicative and social abilities of a user and offer a global and flexible usage context. One important point for the realization of the concept "Virtual School 2005" is the analysis of the user context (which differs from the UseWorld.net) and the system adaptation on the specific user behavior. Short descriptions of four usage scenarios are shown in the following:

- *Individual Information Enquiry.* The agents' functionalities allowed the registration of an individual profile for each user. That could be structuring items like class, performance step, current courses, etc., and individual items like personal interests, membership of special sub-groups, favorite music, etc. These items could be used for information filtering, e.g., if a teacher inserts homework for a special course, all members will be informed. The user profiles are adaptable by the users themselves to react on changing interests and very specific information filtering.
- *Teamwork via CSCW (work area).* The CSCW component offers the establishment of closed work groups, e.g., for specific courses or teams. As an example: a team of five pupils got the task to work on a presentation about a historic event, like "French revolution." The pupils could create/establish a work space within two minutes and insert all digital or digitalized information around this topic (found via Internet search or scanned from books...). They could also create their own email information agent to inform each other about new information inserts. The information could be used to start a long-term collection for several years (for teachers or to start a long term project) or used only for one class. By the integration of standard software, the pupil or teacher could also use the information for a quick construction of PowerPoint slides for a presentation in front of the class. The system offers also the integration of all data presentation formats (slides, video, music, simulation). This kind of working procedure supports decentralized teamwork (current standard in many companies) and trains the pupils in typical working procedures for the future working period.

- *Class as Team in CSCW (project area).* It is the same principle of teamwork, via CSCW, added with the special offer for limited time group work. A class could use the project area-modus of UseWorld.net for the administration of information and communication areas. All relevant administration tasks for Class 8A could be accessed by the pupil, teacher, parents, and school psychologists independent of the specific profile and user right. Such tasks are: home work, digital class book, birthday lists, addresses and telephone numbers of all classmates, presentation of lesson contents (useful for ill pupils or to inform parents), and discussion forums for different groups like parents or teacher, official events and appointments, digital "black board," etc. The aim is a higher transparency of the school for all participants: pupils, parents, and teachers, and an offer to build up a time-independent, flexible, mobile network between school and home. Both should support the learning via Internet and the usage of the Internet as medium for flexible infrastructure.

- *Parents' Forum.* The Internet offers a lot of newsgroups and forums. Why not use the Internet for an information exchange between parents of kids from the same class? Sometimes there are not only age-specific behavior problems; there are often regional-specific or class-specific problems. A parents' forum offers the possibilities to discuss or organize: driving pools for school transport, planning of class excursions, etc. The development in the area of home devices shows that there will be microwaves and refrigerators with Internet access. However, it is time to start (or even support) the integration of the Internet medium into the personal area like: family-oriented communication, education and organization of the daily life.

Other use cases are: individual learning support for the pupil (where they can influence the learning speed and performance level), global school exchange and many more. The system "Virtual School 2005" offers a lot of possibilities for all participants and supports the networking and social structure with the "User as Editor" concept and the advantage of socialware. Therefore, this system would be able to transfer real structures into a virtual community "school" and add the advantages of Internet usage with a higher connecting potential and flexible usage.

The following effects are expected from the system "Virtual School 2005":

- Discussion with the medium "Internet" and acceptance as normal/standard working tool.
- Learning successes in accordance to Bandura's "model learning" (the usage and confrontation with the medium Internet at school and home and daily use support a kind of naturalness; all participants see each other in Internet-usage context and learn from each other; adopting usage strategies).
- Social abilities and understanding of the pupils, teachers and parents increase with permanent role changing (the role of pupil and teacher/parents change from one usage context to the other with the role change of novice and expert).
- The refreshment of the social abilities to support the personality development of the pupil; therefore, the Internet could also be an educational element.

The rating of content and people support the transfer of a real social structure into the socialware of a virtual community. Other aspects of the "User as Editor" concept are also usable in school environment, e.g., expert modus, moderator concept (independent from pupils or teacher position). All of these aspects support the growth of the virtual learning community "School 2005." The UseWorld.net concepts are used to offer the infrastructure for new learning methods and structures. The orientation of information handling is in adaptation of pupils' daily life requirements: flexible handling of learning context and learning environment as well as individual support.

INTERDISCIPLINARY CAPACITIES FOR THE ENGINEERING OF VIRTUAL COMMUNITIES

Interdisciplinary software engineering process approaches, as described in ISO 13407 and presented within this paper, are enablers for innovative software development, in particular for heterogeneous user groups with a priori only partially definable requirements. Paralleling the development activities does not only reduce the development time, but also helps to generate a common understanding due to direct task and goal-centered communication and cooperation.

Nevertheless, the high coordination effort in interdisciplinary teams might be somewhat limiting. Calling for disciplined practices on all involved parties solves only part of the problem. Further enablers for interdisciplinary work are necessary and have to be considered in planning and managing such projects:

- Meta-knowledge about engineering and development process is necessary for all developers involved. This knowledge must be communicated and developed for the specific problem, e.g., via internal project newsletter.
- Understanding of differences in partners objectives, accepted quality aspects of their home disciplines (pragmatic quality, scientific standards, emotional, formally superior).
- Integration of persons with good emotional intelligence to influence the working climate and support creative team discussions. Nevertheless, a coordinator with strong timetable orientation is necessary to find practical solutions in programming meetings.

Over all, with a good team spirit, each interdisciplinary work is soluble for a good technical exchange and personal experience. The transferability of the concept is also a result of multi-disciplinary views on the topic and make the systems much more valuable.

ACKNOWLEDGMENTS

We kindly acknowledge financial support by the DFN and BMBF under grant number VA/I-110 within the programme *Einsatz von Netzdiensten im wissenschaftlichen Informationswesen*. The user adaptive algorithms are jointly developed with the MoDyS Research Group which is sponsored by VolkswagenStiftung within the programme "Junior Research Groups at German Universities."

REFERENCES

Aigrain, P. (1997). Attention, media, value and economics. *First Monday*, 2(9). Retrieved November 17, 2002 from the World Wide Web: http://www.firstmonday.dk/issues/issue2_9/aigrain/.

Appelt, W. (1999). WWW-Based collaboration with the BSCW System. In *Proceedings of SOFSEM'99* (November 26-December 4, pp. 66-78), Milovy (Czech Republic), Springer Lecture Notes in Computer Science 1725.

Appelt, W. (2001). What groupware functionality do users really use? In *Proceedings of the 9th Euromicro Workshop on PDP 2001*, Mantua (February 7-9). IEEE Computer Society, Los Alamitos.

Augustin, G. (2002). Kids im Web: Nichts dichten, nichts denken? *Stern, Computer & Netze*. Retrieved October 19, 2002 from the World Wide Web: http://www.stern.de/computer-netze/readme/pflichtlektüre/neulich-im-netz/artikel/.

Axelrod, R. (1984). *The Evolution of Cooperation*. New York: Basic Books.

Boehm, B.W. (1986). A spiral model of software development and enhancement. *ACM SIGSOFT Software Engineering Notes*, 11(4), 22-32.

Boos, M., Jonas, K.J., & Sassenberg, K. (2000). Sozial- und organisationspsychologische Aspekte computervermittelter Kommunikation. In M. Boos, K.J. Jonas & K. Sassenberg (Eds.), *Computervermittelte Kommunikation in Organisationen* (S. 1-7). Göttingen: Hogrefe.

Brooks, F. P. (1995). *The Mythical Man-Month*. Addison-Wesley Longman.

Bruder, R., Hemmerling, S., Leuchter, S., Röse, K., & Rötting, M. (2000). Die Planung zur Weiterentwicklung von MMI-interaktiv. *MMI-Interaktiv*, 4.

C3 Team. (1998). Chrysler goes to "extremes." *Distributed Computing*, (10), 24-28. Retrieved February 21, 2002 from the World Wide Web: http://xprogramming.com/publications/dc9810cs.pdf.

Coad, P. (2000). Feature driven development and extreme programming. In S. Palmer (Hrsg.), *coadLetter*. Retrieved February 20, 2002 from the World Wide Web: http://www.togethercommunity.com/coad-letter/Coad-Letter-0070.html.

Coad, P., Lefebvre, E., & De Luca, J. (1999). *Java Modeling in Color with UML: Enterprise Components and Process*. Upper Saddle River, NJ: Prentice Hall.

Franken, R. E. (2001). *Human Motivation* (5th ed.). Pacific Grove, CA: Brooks/Cole.

Ghosh, R.A. (1997). Economics is dead. Long live economics! A commentary on Michael Goldhaber's "The Attention Economy," *First Monday*, 2(5). Retrieved November 17, 2002 from the World Wide Web: http://www.firstmonday.dk/issues/issue2_5/ghosh/.

Goldhaber, M. H. (1997a). The attention economy and the Net. *First Monday*, 2(4). Retrieved November 17, 2002 from the World Wide Web: http://www.firstmonday.dk/issues/issue2_4/goldhaber/.

Goldhaber, M. H. (1997b). What's the right economy for cyberspace? *First Monday*, 2(7). Retrieved November 17, 2002 from the World Wide Web: http://www.firstmonday.org/issues/issue2_7/goldhaber/.

Hagel, J., & Armstrong, A. G. (1997). *Net Gain: Expanding Markets Through Virtual Communities*. Boston, MA: Harvard Business School Press.

Hattori, F., Ohguro, T., Yokoo, M., Matsubara, S., & Yoshida, S. (1999). *Socialware: Multi-agent systems for supporting network communities*. Preprint of an official

ACM Version. Retrieved September 9, 2002 from the World Wide Web: http://citeseer.nj.nec.com/hattori99socialware.html.

Herel, H. (2000, August). Choosing a digital workplace. *ZDNet PC Magazine Reviews*. Available on the World Wide Web: http://agilemanifesto.org/.

IABG. (n.d.). *Das V-Modell - Planung und Durchführung von IT-Vorhaben: Entwicklungsstandard für IT-Systeme des Bundes.* Retrieved October 10, 2002 from the World Wide Web: http://www.v-modell.iabg.de/.

ISO 13407. (1999). Human-centred design processes for interactive systems.

Kindsmüller, M. C., Razi, N., Leuchter, S., & Urbas, L. (2002, February 20-22). Zur Realisierung des Konzepts "Nutzer als Redakteure" für einen Online-Dienst zur Unterstützung der MMI-Forschung im deutschsprachigen Raum. In GFA (Eds.), *Arbeitswissenschaft im Zeichen gesellschaftlicher Vielfalt* (pp. 133-137). 48. Kongress der Gesellschaft für Arbeitswissenschaft. Johannes Keppler Universität Linz. Düsseldorf: GfA-Press.

Kollock, P. (1999). The economies of online cooperation. Gifts and public goods in cyberspace. In M. A. Smith & P. Kollock (Eds.), *Communities in Cyberspace.* London: Routledge.

Kollok, P., & Smith, M.A. (1996). Managing the virtual commons: Cooperation and conflict in computer communities. In S. Herring (Hrsg.), *Computer-Mediated Communication: Linguistic, Social, and Cross-Cultural Perspectives* (pp. 109-128). Amsterdam: John Benjamins.

Kruchten, Ph. (2000). *The Rational Unified Process: An Introduction* (2nd ed.). Reading, MA: Addison-Wesley-Longman.

Künzer, A., & Schmidt, L. (2001). "MMI-Interaktiv" entwirft Netzdienste für das wissenschaftliche Informationswesen. In *Unternehmen der Zukunft*, Aachen, 2(3), 9.

Künzer, A., & Schmidt, L. (2002b). An open framework for shared workspaces to support different cooperation tasks. In *Proceedings of World Wide Work, Work With Display Units* (pp. 217-219). Berchtesgaden, Germany.

Kuwabara, K. (1999). *Bazaar at the edge of chaos: Software engineering from the bottom-up.* Honors Thesis in Sociology. Cornell University. Retrieved December 29, 2002 from the World Wide Web: http://www.cukezone.com/kk49/linux/contents.html.

Leuchter, S., Rothmund, T., & Kindsmüller, M. C. (2002, February 20-22). Ergebnisse einer Tätigkeitsbefragung zur Vorbereitung der Entwicklung eines Web-Portals für Mensch-Maschine-Interaktion. In GfA (Eds.), *Arbeitswissenschaft im Zeichen gesellschaftlicher Vielfalt* (pp. 129-132). 48. Kongress der Gesellschaft für Arbeitswissenschaft. Johannes Keppler Universität Linz. Düsseldorf: GfA-Press.

Meyer, F. (2000). SchulWeb-Schulen im WWW: Schüler und Lehrer nutzen Internet und World-Wide-Web. DFN-Mitteilungen. Retrieved October 9, 2002 from the World Wide Web: http://www.rtb-nord.uni-hannover.de/dfn/mitteilungen/html/heft40/D9/D9.html.

Mook, D. G. (1997). *Motivation: The Organization of Action* (2nd ed.). New York: W. W. Norton.

N.N. (2002). Schulen ans Internet. *Projekt der Swisscom.* Retrieved October 9, 2002 from the World Wide Web: http://www.swisscom.com/pr/content/public/schulenansinternet2/index_DE.html.

Oehme, O., Künzer, A., Kabel, D., & Mackau, D. (2001). Entwicklung eines intranetbasierten Wissens- und Qualitätsmanagementsystems. *VDI-Zeitung*, 4/2001.

Ostrom, E. (1990). *Governing the Commons: The Evolution of Institutions for Collective Action*. New York: Cambridge University Press.

Radice, R. A., Roth, N. K., O'Hara, Jr., A. C., & Ciarfella, W. A. (1985). A programming process architecture. *IBM Systems Journal*, 24(2), 79-90.

Razi, N. (2002). *Nutzer als Redakteure: Zur Problematik der Motivation bei Online-Arbeitsgemeinschaften*. Unpublished Thesis. Center for Media Research, Dept. of Psychology, Freie Universität Berlin.

Rheingold, H. (2000). *The Virtual Community: Homesteading on the Electronic Frontier* (rev. ed.). Cambridge, MA: MIT Press. Online version available on the World Wide Web: http://www.rheingold.com/vc/book/.

Rieger, S. (2000). *Schulen ans Netz: Internet spielt im Unterricht Nebenrolle*. ZDNet. Retrieved October 9, 2002 from the World Wide Web: http://news.zdnet.de/story/0,,s2090956,00.html.

Rojo, A. (1995). *Participation in scholarly electronic forums*. Unpublished Ph.D. Thesis, Ontario Institute for Studies in Education, University of Toronto. Toronto: Canada. Retrieved November 17, 2001 from the World Wide Web: http://www.digitaltempo.com/e-forums/tabcont.html.

Röse, K., Urbas, L., Gersch, P., Noss, C., Künzer, A., & Leuchter, S. (2002). Interdisciplinary development of a collaborative portal for a heterogeneous scientific community. In *Proceedings of the IADIS International Conference* (November 13-15, pp. 385-392). WWW / Internet 2002, Lisbon, Portugal.

Stangl. (2000). Das Internet im Unterricht an Österreichs Schulen. *Langzeitstudie zur Internetnutzung*. Zielstellungen. Retrieved October 9, 2002 from the World Wide Web: http://www.stangl-taller.at/INTERNETSCHULE/NETSCHULE2000/ziele.html.

Stangl. (2000a). Das Internet im Unterricht an Österreichs Schulen. *Langzeitstudie zur Internetnutzung*. Diskussion der Ergebnisse. Retrieved October 9, 2002 from the World Wide Web: http://stangl-taller.at/INTERNETSCHULE/NETSCHULE2000/diskussion.html.

Timpe, K.P., Jürgensohn, T., & Kolrep, H. (eds.). (2000). *Mensch-Maschine-Systemtechnik*, Düsseldorf: Symposion Publishing.

Urbas, L., & Timpe, K.P. (2002). Competence as a design goal. In H. Luczak, A. E. Çakir & G. Çakir (Eds.), *Proceedings of the 6th Int. Sci. Conf on Work with Display Units* (pp. 566-568). *WWDU 2002. Kongresshaus Berchtesgaden, 22-25. 5. 2002*. Berlin: ERGONOMIC Institut für Arbeits- und Sozialforschung.

Utz, S. (2000). Identifikation mit virtuellen Arbeitsgruppen und Organisationen. In M. Boos, K. J. Jonas & K. Sassenberg (Eds.), *Computervermittelte Kommunikation in Organisationen* (S. 41-55). Göttingen: Hogrefe.

Wilkens, A. (2001). *Die Kids stürmen das Netz. Heise online*. Retrieved October 9, 2002 from theWorld Wide Web: http://www.heise.de/newsticker/data/anw-26.10.01-005/.

Chapter II

Innovative Approach to Teaching Database Design through WWW:
A Case Study and Usability Evaluation

Joanna Jedrzejowicz, University of Gdansk, Poland

ABSTRACT

The objective of this chapter is to describe the Postcourse project, which is an e-course on database design. It can be reached via the World Wide Web and allows authorized students to create and work with their own databases placed on the university server. The system has been created from scratch, as no authoring package offered tools to interact with databases, which is the innovative feature of the project. The evaluation performed after the system had been used for two years proved that it is a valuable material for self-paced work.

INTRODUCTION

The World Wide Web has considerable potential for improving delivery and quality of education programs, and the benefits in re-engineering higher education are widely recognized. Educators have been quick to spot this potential and thousands of web-based courses and other educational applications have been made available on the Web. Unfortunately, according to many researchers, the currently available web-based courses and other innovative approaches based on Internet technologies are often poor in educational content. The e-education is a relatively new technology and the online courses are often developed by computer-enthusiastic staff who are not necessarily knowledgeable about educational concepts, or by educators who lack the computer knowledge.

The objective of the chapter is to describe, analyse and, possibly, learn the lesson from the experience of creating a web-based course on database design, which makes full use of the interactivity offered by the Internet. The first version of the course was reported in (Jedrzejowicz et al., 2001). The core part of the course, called the Postcourse, is exercises, which require creating and updating the databases stored on the university server. Thus the Postcourse makes use of the educational model of teaching by doing. This paradigm, translated into the fully implemented solution, means that students can interactively design, develop, and test their database projects through Internet. The described feature can be considered as an innovative approach extending the existing range of e-education models.

The chapter is organised as follows. We describe the context of use of the course — that is, the subject, the students who enrol for the subject and the online part that is the Postcourse. We give a general description of the Postcourse, comment briefly on the implementation issues and concentrate our attention on usability analysis and evaluation. The latter is based on ideas and methodology proposed in Nielsen (1993). Using Nielsen's approach, heuristic evaluation of the Postcourse usability was performed and its results are duly reported. Evaluation process has been supported by data obtained from a questionnaire, which is placed on the web site of the course. In the last part of the chapter, the plans for future developments are sketched and some general conclusions are presented.

Our experience of using the Postcourse to train groups of teachers gaining further education on post-graduate courses is limited since it has only been available for two academic years. However, our initial observations are encouraging. Students appreciated the enhanced access to support materials and information. Because they had access to exam questions and answers they were able to test their own understanding and learn more deeply. Most students have gained a better understanding of the subject compared to previous years and got better results during the exams.

The observations confirm that students largely had positive perception of the interactive features, self-testing and monitoring facilities and appreciated the ready access to online information.

CONTEXT OF USE — STUDY SITE AND THE STUDENTS

The starting point for developing an e-learning course, from the pedagogic point of view, is to identify the target group of recipients. The target group is characterised by describing their learning situation. In this case the target group are students who take part in three-semester, post-graduate courses for teachers aimed at further education in computer science. Usually around 70 teachers enrol for the course. The teachers spend five weekends in each semester at the university having lectures and tutorials in a traditional format. The majority of the work has to be undertaken by students in between the teaching weekends. To ease the task, varied materials are being prepared by the teaching staff. An introduction to database systems is an important component in the curriculum of the course. The course is based on one textbook (Ullman & Widom, 1997). When teaching this subject, a common belief of tutors was that some form of online teaching would be particularly useful in assisting students since they are of differing abilities and background in computer science. Some of them work as computer science teachers and their knowledge of the subject is often impressive, and some have never had anything to do with computers and have to struggle to keep pace with the rest. Besides, they are mature learners comfortable with independent learning, thus well prepared for online learning. An online course allows them to set their own pace of work, choose the time when they want to use it and decide which parts of the syllabus they want and need to study.

During the past two years the Postcourse has been well integrated with the course on databases and established its role as a valuable supplement for the students.

There are four groups of users of the Postcourse:

- "anyone,"
- learner-student,
- tutor,
- course administrator.

We distinguished the group of students from "anyone" since some parts of the course; that is exercises and online questionnaires, are available only for those users who were given passwords and their access to the course has been authorised.

Tutors are responsible for managing the course; that is deciding which materials should be included within it.

The course administrator maintains the course on the web server; that is loads any changes and modifications, as well as authorises the access of the students, as was already noted.

Students register for using the Postcourse when they first login; they enter the name, suggested login and password. Once they are authorised they have full use of all the parts of the course.

The access to exercises has to be limited since exercises require creating databases, inserting and modifying data in tables — and all this is performed on the server. Thus each user with a password is allowed some personal space on the server.

The role of the tutor and course administrator are separated since the tasks of the course administrator are of a technical character while those of tutors are of an academic nature — answering students' questions that are sent in as emails, grading assignments and designing the final version of the course. It is worth noting that the administration of a web-based course on technology implies a number of tasks and challenges that are not typical of conventional approaches.

THE TEACHING METHOD

The term "online courses" is used to apply to nearly any course which makes even a passing use of the Internet, as well as to those where every aspect of the course is only accessible electronically. The described course lies just between those two boundaries.

The teaching method designed for the database course was aimed at solving the problems of differing abilities by using online teaching approach. Presently the database course is organised as follows:

- students have on-campus lectures and laboratories,
- they have assignments in between the teaching weekends which are sent by email,
- all learning material is distributed via the WWW, and
- the Postcourse is an online part of the course, which can be used as an additional material; the students are free to choose the parts which they want to work with depending on their learning strategy.

Awarding marks for online work is a concern since it is difficult to be sure who is actually doing the tests and exercises. Therefore, before introducing the Postcourse it was decided that its use will not be obligatory and just offered as an additional help for those students who want to use it.

The three varieties of presentation styles supported by the Postcourse are *narrative* (tell), *example* (show) and *exercise* (do) with a strong emphasis on the last one. Learners have different preferences in the manner they learn best. Some learners like to learn by reading a narrative of new information. Some need examples, which is similar to the way crafts are learned from an expert in the field. The third view of learning is by doing quizzes, or tests and exercises.

Interactive tutorials are meant to be a repetition and extension of the knowledge already acquired. Students can review the lectures and, with the help of illustrative accompanying exercises, observe how the contents of the database are changed by appropriate instructions.

Tests, which are usually multiple-choice questions, cover most of the subjects of the fundamental course on databases. After a student completes a test the system recapitulates the results and shows, if necessary, the mistakes.

Figure 1: Students' Menu

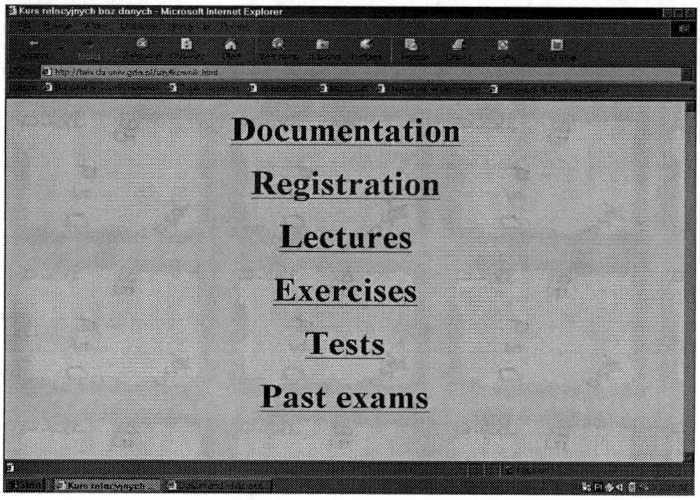

Figure 2: The Postcourse Login Screen

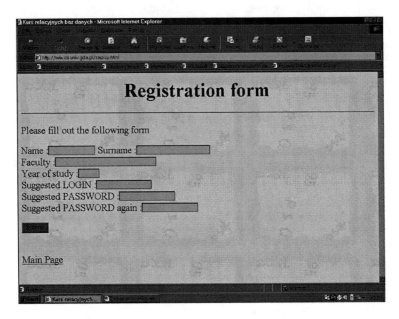

Online exercises are an essential part of the system. They make full use of computer-aided learning. They allow users to work with their own databases. To ensure security this is allowed only for users with passwords. Each user has a personal area on the server identified by the login, so that there is no intruding and interference; besides, the tasks can be solved gradually at each login session, as the data is always there, at the server.

Exercises are the main module of the course. This module has an activity based approach and introduces students to common applications of SQL (Structured Query Language).

The discussed module offers an innovative feature of providing each student with a possibility of developing her/his own learning case and gaining experience with working with it.

A typical student's session consists of the following steps:
(1) the student enters the name, login and password and the Postcourse performs authorisation,
(2) the Postcourse displays the exercise, for example:

The tables CUSTOMERS, ORDERS were created by the following SQL commands:
CREATE TABLE Customers
(c-number   char(10),
lname   char(20),
fname   char(20),
addr   char(20),
town   char(10)
)
CREATE TABLE Orders

```
(c-number        char(10),
number           integer,
amt              money,
date             date,
descript         char(30),
paid             money
)
```

You may check the current contents of the tables CUSTOMERS, ORDERS (selecting any name will produce the current contents)

1. *Create the table DRIVERS that inherits all the attributes from CUSTOMERS and contains one additional attribute **driving licence** of type char(10).*

    - write your command here –

2. *Create the view CUST_GDA consisting of all the customers from Gdansk.*

    - write your command here –

3. *Create the view, which has two attributes, a **customer number** (c-number from CUSTOMERS) and an **order description** (descript from ORDERS), for those customers who have at least one tuple in the ORDERS table.*

    - write your command here –

(1) the student's answers submitted to the Postcourse are checked, and if syntactically correct, then are sent to Postgres which performs the queries, otherwise the error message is displayed,

(2) the student has the possibility of checking the contents of the database by sending a query to dictionary tables pg_database, pg_user.

Observe that this type of exercises makes use of these features of online teaching, which cannot be replaced by a manual, CD-ROM or any other form of a teaching material. The user can observe the dynamic changes in the database performed by his queries.

Another important part of the Postcourse is past exams together with the answers. Usually 40% of the course final mark is based on the assignments and work in the computer laboratory during the teaching weekends and the rest, 60%, is the exam. The exam question usually follows the pattern: we describe some situation from every day life and ask students to design a relational database schema so that the required information can be kept. The rest of the question concerns defining constraints, triggers queries in SQL for the schema.

Below we list the important parts of a typical exam question:

Consider the following set of requirements for a university database that is used to keep track of students' transcripts:

• *the university keeps track of each student's name, student number, current address and phone, permanent address and phone, birthdate, sex, class, department, degree program. Student number has a unique value for each student,*

- *each department is described by a name, department code, office number, office phone, and address. Both name and code have unique values for each department,*

  ...

  Design an entity-relationship schema for this application and draw an ER diagram for that schema. Specify key attributes for each entity type and structural constraints on each relational type. Note any unspecified requirements, and make appropriate assumptions to make the specification complete.
  Specify the following queries in relational algebra:
- *list the names of students who will be 21 on January 1, 2001,*
- *retrieve the departments based in Gdansk which have more than 50 Ph.D. students,*

  ...

  Define the following queries in SQL:
- *retrieve the name and transcript of each senior student; a transcript includes course name, course number, credit hours, semester, year, and grade for each course completed by the student.*

  ...

Since there are several possible ways of designing a database satisfying the above requirements of the exam question, we put on the web site one solution which we consider the most appropriate, pointing out those parts which are often most difficult or neglected by students (for example in the above case — the structural constraints for each relation).

The past exams with answers allow students to test their understanding, receive feedback (for example, via email) and then retest their understanding. Thus students can observe that memorizing is insufficient and deep understanding is required.

In Mason (1998) it was observed that there are three elements which form the backbone of what continues to constitute the world of online courses. They are: asynchronous group and individual messaging, web access to course materials, and real-time interactive events. As follows from the above description of our course it contains all of the mentioned elements except the possibility of asynchronous group messaging, which in fact could be a valuable component and can be added in future.

SOFTWARE DESCRIPTION AND IMPLEMENTATION

Currently, the existing authoring systems like, for example, ToolBook (ToolBook, 2001), WebCT (WebCT, 2001), and TopClass (TopClass, 2001), provide a limited set of templates for developers. These tools provide significant file management and some limited HTML assistance so that one can create web-based course content without the need for a deeper knowledge of the Internet technology. They allow to present knowledge and data. However a major weakness of these systems is that they do not provide assistance to create learning content, which would teach by doing. The course on databases has a very practical aspect. We wanted to make the full use of the interactivity offered by online teaching as the student interest in the learning process is drastically increased when the level of interactivity is high. As we did not find an authoring system suitable for our purposes, the Postcourse was designed and then implemented from scratch.

When designing the Postcourse it was decided to make it simple and platform independent — so that it can be used by any of the popular browsers, not necessarily the latest version. Our students, who are mainly working teachers, have access to all kinds of equipment. It is not always a state-of-the-art teaching laboratory, which can be used for their studies and exercises as well. Sometimes they can access only a stand-alone, modem-connected PC at home. Besides, transmission speeds are a constant issue for the designers and programmers of web pages. Therefore in our project it was agreed that web page design should be driven by the needs of students with slower connections. For this reason, it was decided that all pages should be created in basic HTML with limited (or fast loading) graphics.

The Postcourse makes use of the following software tools:

- operating system — Linux,
- web server — Apache,
- database management system — Postgres,
- user's interface — HTML and PHP.

Apache is one of the most popular WWW servers for the Unix environment. It has a modular structure, which allowed us to incorporate modules needed for the system, that is PHP (Personal Home Page Tool) and the PostgreSql module. The first one is responsible for performing authorisation and interpreting students' answers to tests — checking and displaying incorrect information, if any. In case of online exercises, PHP module is performing the following actions:

- syntax analysis of the text filled-in by a student,
- if the text is syntactically correct then PHP sends a suitable statement to the PostgreSql module,
- PostgreSql module performs the action on the appropriate database (that is the one identified by login of the user) and sends back to PHP the information on the result, and
- PHP interprets the result, which is either the acknowledgment of a database transaction or information on encountered errors.

USABILITY ANALYSIS OF THE POSTCOURSE AS A SOFTWARE PRODUCT

Following Nielsen (1993), by usability we understand the sum of characteristics, which make software productive and also easy to understand, learn and use. In other words, usability of a software product is the extent to which the product is convenient and practical to use. The intuitive view of usability is sometimes called *user-friendliness*. Usability perception is subjective, it depends heavily on the context of use of the product — that is, the specific circumstances when and where the software is used. Several methods of analysing and assessing software usability have been proposed in the literature. For example, multi-criteria analysis described in Fenton and Pfleeger (1997), and AHP methodology (Analytic Hierarchy Process) introduced in Saaty (1990). It seems that so far there does not exist a consistent methodology tailored to meet the needs of the educational software, an interesting proposition was recently introduced in Maurer (2002).

To perform the usability analysis it is important to distinguish the groups of users because each group has its own priorities and expectations concerning the future use of the software product.

In case of web-based education software the following groups are important:

- learner-student, for whom the following factors are the most important: functionality, reliability, user friendliness and time effectiveness;
- teacher-tutor, for whom learning effectiveness, knowledge gains and satisfaction of students is of importance;
- software administrator-considers mainly how difficult it is to configure the system, what other tools are needed, also considers security issues and error-resistance; and
- education manager, responsible for buying suitable software for an educational institution takes under the consideration the following aspects: costs, expected advantages for students and teaching staff, improvement of teaching methods.

So far the Postcourse is not a commercial product; one university on experimental basis has used it for two academic years. Therefore in our analysis below we omit two groups and concentrate our attention on users-learners, who are the target recipients, and teachers-tutors.

System design process, which was iterative and followed the pattern design-test-redesign, included a heuristic evaluation of software usability. It is a usability engineering method defined in Nielsen and Mollich (1990) for solving usability problems during the user interface design. The approach involves up to 10 usability heuristics:

Visibility of system status: The system should always keep users informed about what is going on, through appropriate feedback within reasonable time.

Match between system and the real world: The system should speak the users' language, with words, phrases and concepts familiar to the user, rather than system-oriented terms. Follow real-world conventions, making information appear in a natural and logical order.

User control and freedom: Users often choose system functions by mistake and will need a clearly marked "emergency exit" to leave the unwanted state without having to go through an extended dialogue. Support, undo and redo.

Consistency and standards: Users should not have to wonder whether different words, situations, or actions mean the same thing. Follow platform conventions.

Error prevention: Even better than good error messages is a careful design, which prevents a problem from occurring in the first place.

Recognition rather than recall: Make objects, actions, and options visible. The user should not have to remember information from one part of the dialogue to another. Instructions for use of the system should be visible or easily retrievable whenever appropriate.

Flexibility and efficiency of use: Accelerators — unseen by the novice user — may often speed up the interaction for the expert user such that the system can cater to both inexperienced and experienced users. Allow users to tailor frequent actions.

Aesthetic and minimalist design: Dialogues should not contain information which is irrelevant or rarely needed. Every extra unit of information in a dialogue competes with the relevant units of information and diminishes their relative visibility.

Help users recognise, diagnose, and recover from errors: Error messages should be expressed in plain language (no codes), precisely indicate the problem, and constructively suggest a solution.

Help and documentation: Even though it is better if the system can be used without documentation, it may be necessary to provide help and documentation. Any such information should be easy to search, focused on the user's task, list concrete steps to be carried out, and not be too large.

It is recommended (Nielsen & Mollich, 1990) to use three to five evaluators since one does not gain much additional information by using larger number. In our case three evaluators from the department performed the evaluation. From our previous experience with designing educational software, we realised that a successful adoption of a computer-based teaching tool can follow only a well-planned pilot development that included consultation across all parties involved or likely to be involved in the future. A tool developed by an individual working in isolation without input from colleagues is very unlikely to be adopted by the rest of the academic unit. The evaluation helped to eliminate at least some problems in the final version. For example, it appeared that some users were lost in the authorisation process. They were astonished that after introducing their login they still could not use the Postcourse, forgetting that the authorisation of the course administrator is needed as well, which usually takes a day or two. Evidently, some information for the user was missing, violating the first usability heuristic. As a result, an additional message was placed on the login screen.

What is more, after the Postcourse was introduced into teaching and was available for the first time, four students, all experienced computer science teachers, agreed to repeat the process of heuristic evaluation. It was performed after they had completed the subject and passed the exam. Each individual evaluator inspected the interface alone without communicating with other evaluators. During each evaluation session there was an observer present who could listen to comments of the evaluators and then prepare a written report. The team working on the project then discussed the report.

To ease the task we asked each evaluator to evaluate each of the ten heuristics using a five-point scale (1-strongly disagree, 2-disagree, 3-neutral, 4-agree, 5-strongly agree). The obtained average scores are shown in Table 1.

Table 1 summarises the overall positive perception of the interface. Lower values for H9, H10 can be explained as follows. Some error messages are independent from the Postcourse and are drawn from Postgres; that is the database management system that works in the background. Its messages are meant for database professionals and are

Table 1

Heuristic	Mean
H1: the system keeps users well informed of what is going on	3.8
H2: the language is natural and familiar to the user	4.2
H3: it is easy to leave the unwanted state	4.8
H4: the system is consistent	4.5
H5: the system prevents errors	4.4
H6: all the objects are well visible	3.8
H7: accelerators are efficiently used	3.3
H8: dialogues are well tailored	4.2
H9: error messages are meaningful and helpful	3.1
H10: well defined help system and documentation	2.3

shortened to a minimal possible length. For some tasks the help system and documentation is not present online — this is a feature which needs to be worked on in the future version, if prepared.

A few words on the usability analysis by teachers-tutors should be said. In fact, it was performed at each stage of the work on the project since tutors developed it. For this group of users the important issue is the productivity and effectiveness of the educational software. From a short experience of using the system it appears that students who used the Postcourse had better final results (the details are explained in the next section). We realise that the Postcourse is not user-friendly enough for tutors, and to encourage more teaching staff to use it there is an urgent need to develop tools to enable them to add their own materials, tests, exercises etc. The extension of the project based on XML technology has just been started.

POSTCOURSE TEACHING TRIAL

The Postcourse was used for the first time in the winter semester 1999 and then in the summer semester 2000. The number of students taking part in the survey is given in Table 2.

It is worth noting that prior to this trial students had little or no experience with the Internet as shown in Table 3's survey performed with students of 1999 trial.

To encourage the students to use the Postcourse as an additional material, they had a presentation of the system during their first visit to the database laboratory. Then their

Table 2

Year	Total number of students	Students using Postcourse
1999	75	10
2000	68	22

Table 3

Experience	Email	Web-browsers
expert	9	9
some competence	25	29
little experience	19	23
no experience	10	7
no information	2	2

access was authorised so that they could make the full use of all the parts of the online course. The use of the Postcourse was on voluntary basis. It was stressed that the information whether a student used it or not, will have no effect on the final marks awarded for the course. The rather low number of students of 1999 group using this software was caused by their little experience with World Wide Web and/or no Internet connection at home or at school. This number doubled during the next semester, which is partly due to more students having Internet as well as the encouragement they have received from the students in the first group. We compared the final results in the exam of those students who had the opportunity of using the Postcourse with those who had never really used it (except having it shown at the university). It seems that the Postcourse was valuable, since the average result of those from the first group was 4.21 (on the scale 2-5 used in Poland, with 5 the best) versus 3.67 in the second group, which makes a 15% increase. There is also another possible explanation of this result — simply those who had decided to use the Postcourse had more experience with WWW and generally broader knowledge in computer science. So they would have had better results anyhow!

STUDENTS' EVALUATION
OF THE POSTCOURSE

To gather opinions from the students three different methodologies were used: observation, interview and document review. First, the observations were conducted at the university computer labs. We observed human-computer interaction and asked them to "think aloud" while they used the Postcourse. Second, we conducted an interview with some students immediately after they had finished their tasks. The interview following the observation lasted about half an hour for each student. Moreover, data were collected from an informal conversation with two students and one teaching assistant. Third, we examined various types of documents including the written report of the already described heuristic evaluation, assignments and students answers to the questionnaire.

The questionnaire is placed on the course web site. It helps to evaluate the course and get information to what extent the users found the Postcourse valuable as an additional teaching material. We received the questionnaire back from almost all the users (see Table 4).

In the first part of the questionnaire we asked some general questions on the course and in the second part they were connected with the Postcourse. Below we list all the

Table 4

Year	Number of Postcourse users	Number of received questionnaire
1999	10	9
2000	22	19

questions and in brackets we give mean of answers for $9 + 19 = 28$ questionnaires' returns, received from users — on the five-point scale as before, for all except Q1, Q7, Q8, Q9, Q13, Q14:

Q1: How much time do you spend working on the database course monthly?
     (6.8 hours)
Q2: The subject was relevant to the requirements of my profession.
     (4.8)
Q3: I find the subject difficult.
     (3.7)
Q4: The aims of the subject were clearly stated.
     (4.0)
Q5: The assignments could be completed within the allocated time.
     (3.6)
Q6: The feedback on assignments I received was well explained.
     (3.7)
Q7: Do you have access to the Internet at home?
     (35% yes)
Q8: How many times did you log on the Postcourse site?
     (6.7 times)
Q9: Which parts of the Postcourse did you find most useful? (choose one)
     (see Table 5)

Table 5

Part of Postcourse	Number of students	Percentage
tutorials and examples	2	7%
interactive exercises	13	46%
multiple choice questions	2	7%
email consultations	6	21%
past exams	5	18%

Q10: I found the Postcourse friendly to use.
      (3.8)
Q11: The questions and exercises were clearly formulated.
      (4.2)
Q12: I found the Postcourse helpful.
      (4.4)

Q13:   Please comment on those features, which were most useful.

Q14:   Please comment what changes would you expect in future versions.

The responses confirmed that some students found the course on databases difficult. They commented positively about having an extra source of materials. As was expected, interactive exercises proved to be useful for students who appreciated yet another opportunity to work on SQL queries and the possibility of email consultations in case of any doubts. This is especially important for students on this course who do not have an everyday contact with academics and have less chance of accessing materials in the library or working in the university computer labs. The responses to the open questions prove that the Postcourse aided the development of their understanding of databases. For example, because students had access to exam questions as well as answers they were able to test their own understanding, receive feedback and then subsequently retest their understanding. Some people pointed out that using the Postcourse encouraged them to use Internet, which they have never done before.

Of course there were some negative aspects pointed out as well. From the observations, interviews and questionnaire responses we found two kinds of students' distress. The first one was technological problems. Unfortunately, due to the breakdown of the university server, which happened twice in those two semesters, students had no possibility of using the Postcourse for some time. Besides, even when it worked often the transmission was slow. As expected, the majority of students accessed the Internet via a modem and were charged by the hour. As a result, working online was not only slow but also it could also be expensive. Some people indicated that these negative aspects caused them to lose interest in using the Postcourse. For some people, working online meant a change of study habits that they could not cope with. They were frustrated when something went wrong and could not get support or guidance from the tutor (or a colleague) at once. This feature was surprising since we expected that people with some experience in professional life would not have frustrations of that kind. It seems that the introduction of a discussion list could at least partially solve this problem.

Obviously, there is another negative impact of online learning as a whole that is disfranchising those students who lack web access. We believe that this problem will be gone in the very near future.

FUTURE WORK

Since our experience with using the Postcourse is quite encouraging, further developments of the system are planned:

- Develop software tools to enable tutors to prepare new tests and exercises, as well as create new pages.
- Extend the group of tutors willing to use the Postcourse as supplementary material for database courses; this requires picking the right people — those who are enthusiastic and willing to spend some time to get acquainted with the system.
- Increase access for students to ensure efficient, seven-days-a week access to the server — so far the Postcourse is placed on an experimental server working on predetermined days only.

- Introduce discussion lists – there is an agreement in literature that collaborative learning (Wright, 1999) provides clear educational advantages.
- Monitor students' experience with using the Postcourse.

After further development, we plan for more evaluation — this time not only by students but also by professionals who are tutors and had never used the system before, and also to measure the usability. Although usability has received widespread attention within the software community there are few agreed measures that capture the intuitive meaning. User performance measures defined in the MUSiC project (Bevan, 1995), for example, task effectiveness, temporal efficiency, productive period, and relative user efficiency, seem useful for our educational software. The plans are to perform the usability study of the Postcourse with the help of the above measures.

CONCLUSION

Although the data regarding the usefulness and effectiveness of using the Postcourse are limited due to the relative newness of this software and a rather limited number of users, the reactions of those who have used it are positive. Obviously, there is an initial effort for students in becoming familiar with the software. However, in the longer run, Postcourse features are of help in better organising a self-paced work of the student, realising which parts of the syllabus need to be worked upon and choosing the most appropriate time for studying.

The most valuable and innovative feature of the approach is the combination of the online interactivity and underlying Internet technologies with the learning-by-doing paradigm. In computer science courses (as the one discussed) such combination seems natural. In other areas of education the approach would require more effort for interface development and, especially, for design and implementation of virtual models of respective domains. Nevertheless, looking at various innovations brought about by Internet technologies, their ability to provide a virtual space to learning by doing solutions seems to be the most important one in terms of enhancing and re-engineering the education process.

In the last years, online education has attracted much attention and seems well on its way to becoming a standard feature of a modern university. The literature (Blackhurst & Hales, 1997; Hartwig et al., 2002; Janicki & Liegle, 2001; Mason, 1998; Schutte, 2000) shows that innovations in online learning and pedagogy offer a range of advantages and can supply a number of significant improvements to teaching and learning. A study (Schutte, 2000) reports an average of 20% higher test scores for students randomly assigned to a web-learning environment, in relation to those assigned to a traditional classroom. Our experience with the Postcourse confirms those facts widely.

REFERENCES

Bevan, N. (1995). Measuring usability as quality of use. *Software Quality Journal, 4*(2), 115-130.

Blackhurst, A.E, & Hales, R.M. (1997). *Using an education server software system to deliver special education coursework via the World Wide Web.* Retrieved July 11, 2001 on the World Wide Web: http://serc.gws.uky.edu/www/ukat/TopClass/tc.html.

Fenton, N. E., & Pfleeger, S. L. (1997). *Software Metrics.* Boston, MA: PWS Publishing.

Hartwig, R., Triebe, J.K., & Herczeg, M. (2002). *Usability engineering as an important part of quality management for a virtual university.* Networked Learning in a Global Environment World Congress, NL2002, Technical University of Berlin.

Janicki, T., & Liegle, J.O. (2001). *Development and evaluation of a framework for creating web-based learning modules: A pedagogical and system perspective.* Retrieved September 3, 2001 on the World Wide Web: http://www.aln.org/alnweb/journal/vol5_issue1/janicki/janicki.htm.

Jedrzejowicz, J., Kwapulinski, M., & Kwapulinski, P. (2001). Postcourse - WWW-based course on databases. In G.H. Chapman (Ed.), *Proceedings of the Conference on Computer Based Learning in Science,* CBLIS'01 (paper E4), Brno, Czech Republic.

Mason, R. (1998). *Models of online courses.* Retrieved November 24, 2000 on the World Wide Web: http://www.aln.org/alnweb/magazine/vol2_issue2/masonfinal.htm.

Maurer, H. (2002). *New aspects of e-learning.* Networked Learning in a Global Environment World Congress, NL'2002, Technical University of Berlin.

Nielsen, J. (1993). *Usability engineering.* New York: Academic Press.

Nielsen, J., & Mollich, R. (1990). Heuristic evaluation of user interfaces. In *Proceedings CHI'90 Conference of human factors in computing systems* (pp. 249-256). New York: ACM Press.

Saaty, T.L. (1990). *How to Make a Decision: The Analytic Hierarchy Process.* Pittsburgh: RWS Publications.

Schutte, J.G. (2000). *Virtual teaching in higher education.* Retrieved July 30, 2001 on the World Wide Web: http://www.csun.edu/sociology/virexp.htm.

ToolBook. Retrieved July 30, 2001 on the World Wide Web: http://www.asymetrix.com.

Ullman, J.D, & Widom, J. (1997). *A First Course on Database Systems.* Englewood Cliffs, NJ: Prentice-Hall.

WBT Systems Topclass. Retrieved July 30, 2001 on the World Wide Web: http://www.wbtsystems.com.

WebCT. Retrieved July 30, 2001 on the World Wide Web: http://www.webct.com.

Wright, P.W. (1999). Use of information and communication technology in education, some emerging areas of interest and related issues. In G.H. Chapman (Ed.), *Proceedings of the Conference on Computer Based Learning in Science,* CBLIS'99 (paper A2), University of Twente, Enschede, The Netherlands.

Chapter III

A Model-Driven Approach for Synchronous Dynamic Collaborative E-Learning

Véronique Baudin, LAAS-CNRS, France

Khalil Drira, LAAS-CNRS, France

Thierry Villemur, LAAS-CNRS, France

Saïd Tazi, Université Toulouse 1, France

ABSTRACT

This chapter describes a recent experience in the development of a model-driven approach. We present architecture foundations, model features, implementation characteristics and assessment scenarios.

A graph-based collaboration model has been proposed to represent the structure of synchronous groups, with their dynamic evolving. The model is used to define an advanced and distributed e-learning scenario involving three types of users: teachers, students and coordinators. Work of the synchronous group is supported by the PLATINE software platform composed of a multipoint videoconference, an application-sharing tool, a shared whiteboard and a session manager, developed in JAVA. The high-level scenario has been instantiated and tested in relation with two experiments: the first one related to a Cyberlicence training, the second to professional training.

INTRODUCTION

Rapid changes of the technological systems with the faster progression of the scientific domains require more frequent training periods during the professional career. These training periods are compulsory to bring up-to-date the knowledge required for working, interleaved with more operational work phases. In our opinion, adapted digital interactive and virtual campuses are a good solution to anticipate such particular training needs (Multimedia Technologies Portal for French Education, 2002).

E-learning systems, with integration of information and communication technologies, support training accesses in space (near or distant rooms from the trainer intervention site) but also in time (during the time periods chosen by the student and compatible with his other activities). Such systems must be able to organize consortium-based campus to strengthen information quality and quantity of the presented knowledge, as well as the services proposed to the students. The focus is made on training individualization and direct communication with personal relationships between trainer and trainees through adequate tools as discussion forums, chats, audio or videoconferences, usable according to the available resources. This augments student autonomy and increases their responsibility because each one manages himself his progress with flexible evaluation choice, either autonomously (self-evaluation) or with help (trainer evaluation). Finally, e-learning systems must facilitate access to complex knowledge such as business process experiments through web-based simulations, available locally or remotely with university distant servers.

During requirements analysis, the end-users, represented by different representatives of distance learning from French Centre National de la Recherche Scientifique and University institutes, stress the importance of a particular coordination function that manages data sharing and tools distribution between the involved participants during synchronous collaborative e-learning sessions. Managing these dependencies can be efficiently and correctly automated by using a formal model we introduce in this chapter, namely, the collaboration graphs. The defined model allows evolution of collaboration structures as required by the Distance Learning collaboration scenarios.

Most online environments that attempt to use collaboration as a learning strategy incorporate a set of communication technologies that are not structured according to theories and results published in social and cognitive sciences research fields concerning collaborative learning (South et al., 2000). Furthermore, the applications included in these systems (such as email, discussions forum, teleconferencing, etc.) don't generally take into account pedagogical aspects of communication between students and between students and learners. The paradigms that scaffold these systems are relied to classical applications paradigms. Miao et al. (1999) said " … Specifically, the weakness of these approaches is their primary reliance on a document-based paradigm, (…) conferencing-based paradigm (…), or room-based paradigm (…)." We postulate that these environments must, in addition, support cognitive and pedagogical rule-based collaboration. Indeed, the cognitive and social approaches will be helpful to capture complex collaboration scenarios, realizing the link and translation between user needs and processable models.

This chapter introduces first a model-driven approach for a synchronous collaborative e-learning environment. The model proposes a multi-tier architecture that is used to manage both communication channels and the collaboration space. These two functions are basic for collaborative environments and have to be explicitly handled for many collaboration situations. They involve optimizing communication paths: users that interact only using a text-based conferencing tool need not to have a large bandwidth contrarily to those that communicate using audio-video while simultaneously and heavily using CAD tools. Moreover, communication paths may have different properties for the same participant connected to different partners. Each communication path may also have asymmetric properties for the pair of participants it connects together, in a manner that is compliant with the data producer/consumer relationship. The management of the collaboration space is the second service that may rely on the formal description of collaboration graphs. The functions involved in this service include a valid distribution of the collaboration tools among the collaboration participants. This may be automatically and correctly deduced from the formal structure of coordination diagrams.

From the implementation point of view, this model is used to control the online session structure and its evolution in time. The collaboration graph is associated with the synchronous relationships between the members currently present in the e-learning session. Change events that appear in the e-learning group (i.e., role change events) induce modifications of the collaboration graph structure. These graph modifications will be taken into account by the session management layer that (de)activates the collaboration tools used during the e-learning session. The programmable model can be automatically processed by a session management software layer. It avoids a fully manual online session management from the connected users and creates a parameterable-model session layer usable to command and control the tools of the e-learning platform.

The e-learning PLATINE platform (Baudin et al., 2001) is composed of the basic tools and modules to support the remote interactions between the distributed group members.

This chapter will be composed of the following parts: the second section gives some definitions and requirements of the e-learning process. The third portion presents collaborative tools and existing e-learning platforms. Next, it emphasizes the proposed modeling approach to describe dynamic coordinated e-learning organizations. Following that, the basic e-learning prototype tools and modules that have been developed are presented. Finally, the last section defines the two chosen scenarios retained to validate the proposed approach.

E-LEARNING REQUIREMENTS

Collaborative Learning

To ease the work understanding, we define what is called collaborative learning in the literature. According to Johnson and Johnson (1978), we examine some features of collaborative learning and propose some high-level principles that could be applied to enforce collaborative learning situations.

There are three basic behaviours students can have to interact with each other as they learn. They can work in an individualistic way toward a goal without paying attention to other students, they can work in a competitive way to see who is "best," or they can work in a collaborative way with a vested interest in each other's learning as well as their own. Johnson et al. (1988) reported that even though these three behaviours in interaction are not equally effective in helping the learning process, students need to learn to be effective in each, because they will face situations in individualistic, competitive or collaborative patterns.

The collaborative learning that implies collaborative structures and techniques has many benefits to the learning process for students and teachers (Sapon-Shevin, 1990). The individualistic and competitive behaviours are characterized by negative goal interdependence where the gain of one person is seen as a waste for the others.

A collaborative e-learning environment should offer tools that allow teachers to have to apply positive interdependence. In the positive interdependence principle, students perceive that they can achieve their learning goals if, and only if, all the members of their group also attain their goals — the group goal always has to be part of the lesson. A collaborative e-learning environment has to facilitate special communication that applies the positive interdependence principle. Among specific elements that could help to apply this principle, we propose the following ones:

- Rewards: individual ones (each group member receives the same reward when the group achieves its goals) or collective ones (reward when the group goal is 90% achieved).
- Teachers may wish to highlight the collaborative relationships by giving students limited resources that must be shared (one copy of the problem or task per group) or giving each student part of the required resources that the group must then fit together.
- Teachers create role interdependence among students when they assign them complementary roles such as reader, recorder, checker of understanding, encourager of participation, and elaborator of knowledge. The environment must be adapted to help in defining these roles. Each member must be aware of his proper role and of the roles of the rest of the group.

E-Learning Benefits

The e-learning's environment today supply a whole outfit of utilities for the registration of a trainee, the definition of his training content path, some question tests validating the acquired knowledges, and tools of dialogues allowing the exchanges between teacher(s) and trainees, or between trainees. These basic tools that support dialogues start from forums where questions and answers are posted by the system users, "chats" (tools of textual dialogue, requiring a low bandwidth) until audio/video conferences. Most of the audio/video conference tools are used between participants connected on local area networks or offering at least enough bandwidth.

Content Learning Improvement

The first goal of these technological environments is not to suppress the traditional classroom training that they will substitute. In a first case, e-learning position is more dedicated to complementary ways of learning. These complementary lectures are made after classical lectures, where training domain has been first tackled and roughly presented. Such information complements can be made with e-learning systems; this is merely true if trainees are far away from the training center.

In a second case, for very specialized training, where specialists are few and not available in a sufficient way for many classrooms of students, e-learning systems boost this specialized knowledge diffusion.

In a third case, during traditional trainings, according to the themes or the learned subjects, specific business applications can be handled. Such applications require costly specific hardware or expensive licenses that cannot be bought for each participant. Remote access through e-learning systems is a good way to ease the access to such specific applications; it contributes and facilitates the circulation of highly specialized contents and tools.

So, e-learning systems improve the quality of the learning process, with supplementary, complementary, and sometimes highly specialized lessons.

Distance Reduction

These environments improve the procedures of traditional training. Their use increases because they offer other advantages in term of distance reduction. In several scenarios, a trainee or a student cannot move to hear a lecture, because of one of the following reasons:

- No mobility: inability for a geographic movement (some physical handicap, faraway of the training's site, costs of travels...)
- No good training/travel ratio: ratio duration between the training period and the travel duration low

Use of distance learning environments solves these problems by permitting remote participants to hear the lectures.

Dynamic Architecture for Generic Collaboration

As described by the upper part of Figure 1, most traditional e-learning approaches try to mimic conventional learning organization. Each student belongs to a unique classroom during the whole learning process. A unique teacher is inside his own classroom, attributed in advance. At the opposite of this scenario, our approach is dynamically coordinated. According to their learning requirements at a given step of their training, students may request assistance or advice from any teacher. For this, they use the mediation of the coordinator who connects them to the appropriate workspace dedicated to the learning topic (lower part of Figure 1).

The coordinated solution is useful for different situations:

- Mediated learning scenarios. This category corresponds to industrial training where a number of experts are requested during the same period to give targeted answers to complex multi-domains systems studied by a trainee;
- Adaptive distant communication media. Different students are connected from different remote locations and use communication media with sufficient quality of service. The coordinated cooperation between students and teachers allows each student to access remotely the learning center for short training periods in comparison to the necessary travelling time. Dynamic solutions with distant access for complementary studies are then useful to adapt to the trainer requirements.

Figure 1: Distance Learning Architectures

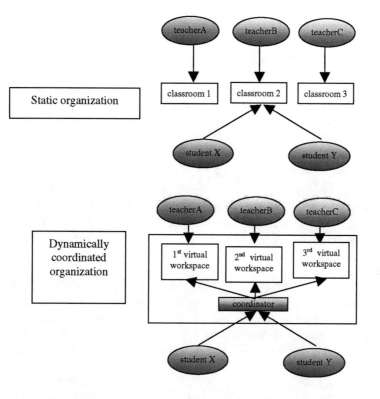

In order to handle these different situations, we adopt a graph-based model detailed in the sequel, capable of representing cooperation flows between the different actors involved in the collaborative learning process.

STATE OF ART E-LEARNING PLATFORMS

E-learning tools can be roughly decomposed in two categories: (1) Content Management Systems (CMS) and (2) Learning Management Systems (LMS) (AICC, 2002). Pure CMS environments are used for the off-line course creation and management, whereas pure LMS systems support online lectures with remote accesses. Nowadays, a lot of e-learning systems are supporting the two functions: they are grouped in Learning Content Management Systems (LCMS).

Pure CMS platforms are devoted to the course content development and are composed of authoring tools. As an illustrative example, the Serpolet platform (Serpolet Tool, 2002) can be cited. This platform links the basic multimedia documents and assembles them in a coherent way to compose the complete lecture. Other environments, such as WebCT (WebCT platform, 2002) and Learning space (LearningSpace, 2002), are good tools for authoring lectures. As these two last platforms own their communication functionalities to support the lecture performing (LMS functions), their detailed characteristics will be presented within the communication tool section. Indeed, as the

PLATINE prototype platform presented in this chapter is related to support distant lecture performing, the state of the art has been centered to e-learning communication tools.

Tools designed to ease communication exchanges between people, within Learning Management Systems (LMS), must be able to support collective intelligence, i.e., the results of the group communication process are better than the one of each individual person (Turoff, 1993). One of the main elements for the success of e-learning is its support of active collaboration between users (Paloff et al., 1999). E-learning LMS communication tools can be based on synchronous or asynchronous communication technologies: several existing advanced realizations are then presented in the sequel.

Asynchronous Approaches

Many portals propose information or lectures on specific domains or thematics. The lecture broadcast is made from sites on which the information is stored in HTML format, possibly enriched by audio and/or video information. From those dedicated sites or portals, courses can be downloaded or consulted freely or with paid access. Interactions between students and teacher are made with asynchronous communication tools: email, Frequently Asked Questions Forums.

The Digital Learning Program (McClelland, 2000) is one of the most advanced in Europe: all the lectures support are digitized and are available for the students in HTML format, according to the modules they have to learn. Classical students use them through synchronized web browsers when they are in co-presence with the teacher in the same room. But distant students can access lectures asynchronously when they are studying in an autonomous mode.

The Scolastance tool (Scolastance, 2002) is another improved web portal to manage educational and administrative documents between teachers, students and administrative staff. People connect to the web site with an identifier and a password. According to their pre-defined and static role, they can access several documents. For instance, students can access their notes, the time schedule, and the documents related to the lectures.

The WebCT environment (WebCT Platform, 2002) is first used in author mode to create classical or multimedia courses. Mechanisms to evaluate the learner studies, with the amount and the quality of the knowledge acquired by them, are included. To support the lecture performing, each learner uses a classic web interface. The Albi French university proposes courses about civil and European laws, in a Cyberlicence context through the WebCT platform (Campus de France Portal, 2002).

Pure Asynchronous Approaches Limits

The characteristics of the current Internet, with a low bandwidth, strongly maintain use of asynchronous approaches. But the distance learning support has to be adapted to be handled by the students in an autonomous mode. However, trainers often need to do numerous tasks: they are not available all the time to help or to answer students. In such case, asynchronous communications, with email-based systems, are efficient to assist students in their work.

At the opposite side, e-learning systems based on asynchronous technologies lack spontaneous interactions between participants: documents are downloaded and people are working autonomously. They do not encourage informal dialogues or direct people-to-people interactions; sometimes important when students encounter difficulties or problems that could stop them from advancing their studying. Such interactions must be supported by synchronous collaboration tools, presented below.

Synchronous Approaches

In the majority of cases, asynchronous interactions are supported by e-learning systems. However, we can observe a stronger demand for synchronous interactions. Such synchronous environments must at least include the following functionalities:

- Direct communication between members
- Ways of interactive information exchange (documents and applications)
- Management functions (role of the participants and dynamic entries and exits for synchronous sessions in particular)

Indeed, in a traditional class with the presence of the trainer, dialogues and information exchanges can take place between the participants. A trainee asks a question and the trainer answers, so the whole group takes advantage of the explanation. It is then necessary to associate the lecture support with communication tools to avoid participants being isolated with only lecture slides or HTML pages.

Synchronous distance learning systems create virtual classrooms, where people are teaching/studying in a distributed way, but in co-presence. Such systems include videoconferences and information-sharing spaces to support the interactive display of documents required for synchronous dialogues in a distributed way.

Management functions are required to control and synchronize the dynamic interactive dialogues.

General Traditional Solutions

Multimedia teleconferencing is gaining maturity through the definition and the implementation of two key standards, namely H.323 and T.120 promoted by the ITU (Drira et al., 2001). H.323 standard defines parameters and rules for enabling processing, formatting, and synchronization of audio and video signals over the communication links. The T.120 standard is a family of specifications and application protocols that completes H.323 for synchronous collaborative work. It provides real-time data conferencing standards that allow people at multiple locations to conduct a voice conference call and create and manipulate still images such as documents, spreadsheets, color graphics, and photographs. Although the driving market force behind T.120 was teleconferencing, it can satisfy a much broader range of applications including interactive gaming, virtual reality on the Internet, real-time news feeds, and process control applications.

In 1996, Microsoft introduced NetMeeting (NetMeeting, 2002), a collection of T.120 dataconferencing applications for use on Windows platforms. This product is available from Microsoft for free and highly participates in the gain of popularity of this kind of applications. The desktop NetMeeting standard suite includes a point-to-point audio/video conference, an application-sharing tool and a chat tool.

Customized Distance Learning Solutions

Numerous distance-learning environments are being integrated and built on top of the Microsoft NetMeeting Technology. As the most popular ones, we can cite the LAVAC tool (Toma, 2002) and the Speaker tool (Speaker Tool, 2002). These distributed systems are supporting multimedia authoring modules, used in real-time by the students to learn English language. The teacher can interact with them to correct any mistakes during practice. Evaluation functions are included within such systems.

The LearningSpace tool (LearningSpace, 2002) is a complete platform to develop course contents, and also to manage the content path of the learners. Several facilities of dialogue are available for the participants (forum, chat and videoconference in a virtual classroom). These tools are used in a free mode, where rights of speaking, roles and discussions are not supervised by the system.

Another trend is the tight integration of all the synchronous collaboration tools as elementary components and plugs-ins into web-based interfaces. The WebEx meeting center is a good example of this approach. The web interface is used to connect to the WebEx conference room. Once connected, the classical collaborative tools are automatically activated, with the list of connected members. In addition, WebEx gives co-browsing facilities to share and synchronize web documents (Webex, 2002; Drira et al., 2001).

THE COLLABORATION GRAPH MODEL
Model for Collaboration

To represent the way people of the synchronous collaborative session are exchanging information between them, a formal model, based on graphs, has been introduced (Villemur, 1995). This model appears simple enough to be handled in a natural way by the application layer, and general enough to be adapted to numerous and various collaborative configurations. Moreover, this model can be used with different data type, classical or multimedia.

Knowledge Relationships Between Members

A collaborative group is composed of a set of users whose relationship defines the way the members are organized. The structure of the collaboration is represented by a directed graph, the collaboration graph, as shown in Figure 2. Vertices represent users, edges represent relations between users. Each user has a set of data. An edge from user "U1" to user "U2" means that "U1" owns data transmitted to "U2" when their value changes. It is important to note that an edge does not represent data ownership, given by the vertices, but represent the relation of information exchange between members. With this approach, user "U1" collaborates with user "U2" if he sends some information to him.

The proposed collaboration model is based on data producer/consumer relationships, to represent and process data exchanges for synchronous and interactive work sessions. Such sessions handle interactive dataflows (e.g., video, real-time audio), which are described in a natural way by the labeled edges of the model. To avoid proposing a too complex and complicated model, not easy to handle, other types of possible data (such as shared data) are not taken into account. Such data is directly processed by the active applications during synchronous sessions.

Dynamic Groups

The collaborative work can be conducted when an adequate subset of members exists. The conceptual model is then extended to define which members must collaborate at the same time and how they must collaborate.

The application associated with the collaborative group has to define the subsets of users that have a meaning for the implementation and the realization of the collaborative work. Among all subgraphs of the collaboration graph, the application chooses those that are semantically possible with a set of rules or predicates that depend on the collaborative work to be realized. The retained subgraphs represent the subgroups of users who are present simultaneously. They are called *valid instantaneous graphs*; their structure directly comes from the one of the initial collaboration graph (Figure 2).

The current group configuration evolves in time when entries and exits of group members are considered. In the same way, role and function changes (for instance a passive student becomes active by making a comment) from the members already present in the collaborative group introduce modifications of the current valid instantaneous graph. At any time, the current configuration corresponds to a valid graph.

Distance Learning Application Scenario

The previous collaboration model is used to characterize the relationship and data exchanges between the members of the distance-learning group. The first functional analysis has been made with a model-based approach to be automatically taken into account by the whole e-learning platform. Moreover, the collaboration graph model fits well to numerous and different collaborative scenarios. It guarantees certain genericity to the proposed platform: although it is first devoted to distance learning situations, it can easily be adapted to other collaborative domains.

Figure 2: A Collaborative Group

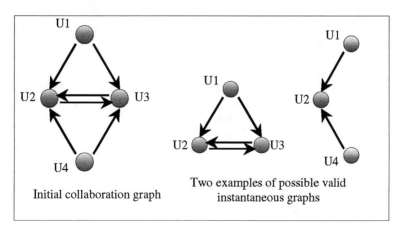

Initial collaboration graph

Two examples of possible valid instantaneous graphs

Figure 3: Collaborative Scenarios for Distance Learning

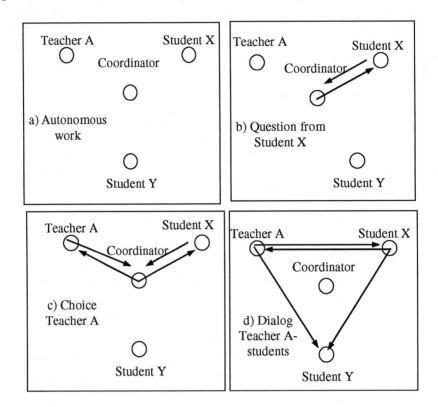

Configuration Presentation

Figure 3 describes part of an e-learning scenario with the graph-based collaboration model. The data flows represented are supporting the required interactions between students, the coordinator and the chosen teacher. In the (a) configuration, each group member is working in an autonomous way. When Student X encounters a problem, he asks the Coordinator ((b) configuration). According to the student problem, the coordinator selects the most suitable teacher. In the (c) configuration, Teacher A has been chosen. Then, the dialogue established between Teacher A and Student X is broadcasted to the whole distributed classroom.

The data exchange relationships between the members of the collaborative group are defined by the collaboration graphs. They serve to identify and model the various information streams required for the application scenarios, in order to integrate them into the remote-help collaborative platform. So, this latter model is able to handle the data exchanges between the group's members in an automatic way. Afterwards, this model can be refined by adding a set of attributes to each edge, which defines in a more precise way the group member features (display of the session, broadcasting of information, remote-control...). Every feature is represented as a set of data stream, which describes the transmitted data flow as exactly as possible, with potentially an associated quality of service. The identified features are implemented by specialized tools described in the next section.

COLLABORATION TOOLS AND MODULES: THE PLATINE PLATFORM

This section presents the characteristics of the PLATINE platform that supports the presented dynamic e-learning scenarios. Four main components have been identified. To maintain a good consciousness of the distributed e-learning community, some of them are based on good quality video and audio streams, adapted for interactive communications by the way of personal computers.

PLATINE Tools

Jvisio Multipoint Videoconference

The member visualization is carried out using an adaptable videoconferencing system, called Jvisio. Jvisio manages all the video and audio data required for viewing the different distributed members. It is concerned with the capture, compression, transmission, decompression and presentation of the multimedia data through multipoint communications.

The Jvisio interface consists of two types of video windows: a local video, captured by the local video camera, monitors the images sent to the other members; this window can be hidden to save space. The other video window displays the images of the distant members.

A videoconference control panel is added to select the local parameters of each member (networking parameters, choice of the multicast group configuration, input device selection...).

The distant video windows are dynamically modified, according to the changes of the group structure.

To ensure compatibility with other current videoconference systems, the video and audio flows are based on the H.263 standard format. Each computer is equipped with a H.263 digital video card to process the digitized images. To manage the media hardware heterogeneity, the Java Media Framework extensions (JMF) software layer has been retained as the implementation base of the videoconference.

AST Application Sharing

The application-sharing tool (AST) is a general tool for sharing any application including video-based ones. It gives remote views of the shared applications and supports the remote control of these applications. Each member's interface is composed of a video window area that grabs the images of the shared applications of a chosen member and displays their video images to the screens of some or all the other members. AST periodically samples the images of the shared applications.

AST design is based on top of the Virtual Network Computing tool (VNC, 2002). This tool is built using the client/server paradigm. A single member can propose to share his environment by launching an AST server. He becomes the group manager and authorizes other group members to remote control his local environment. The other members launch an AST client to connect to the AST server. The group member shared environment is then remotely viewed and accessed by all the other client members. In that way, AST is a synchronous multi-user tool.

When a group member is authorized by the shared context owner, all the remote commands coming from the authorized participant are forwarded to the shared environment, leading to remote action on his shared applications. Concretely, the authorized member remotely controls the shared applications through his accessible video copy. The other client members see the effects of the remote actions on their displayed video copies in real time. The main advantage of this system is that any application (multimedia or not) can be shared through AST, because only video samples of the application windows are sent. This choice guarantees that AST is a generic tool that can be used for very different applications on top of various platforms.

SW Shared Whiteboard

The shared whiteboard (SW) tool reproduces the behaviour of a classical whiteboard in a distributed way by using client/server architecture. The interface of the shared whiteboard is composed of a graphical window for each member. A selected group member (the server member) displays slides written in GIF or JPEG format and writes annotations upon them. His slides and annotations are sent to the other connected group members (the client ones) who can add personal private annotations not seen by the other members. These annotations are saved in association with the appropriate slides. Only graphical data are exchanged between group members. SW is fully developed in JAVA.

SM Session Manager Module

The session management (SM) provides the two following services: user coordination (membership management) and cooperation tools coordination (tool floor control).

The group membership management service is in charge of controlling the evolution of the session with respect to time. It aims, when possible, to pass from an on-session configuration to another one by considering the requests of entry and exits from the participants.

The tool coordination service manages the different tools, giving them all the information required for their individual configuration. It controls their reconfiguration, according to the floor control changes. Then, it maintains tool awareness by displaying their current state.

In the current implementation, SM is composed of a graphical window owned and piloted by the session chair. According to the previous e-learning scenario, the chair's role is held by the Coordinator. The other group members consist of trainers and trainees. The floor control and group management is made by hand, and the graph-based session model is used as a formal analysis of the communication requirements between the group members. But the next step is to use them within a programmable online session management layer in charge of automatically processing session management changes that occur when group-change events are generated by the users (Drira et al., 1999; Rodriguez Peralta et al., 2001). This layer will avoid many manual changes actually made

Figure 4: Off-Line Session Preparation

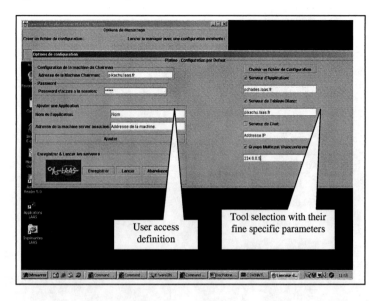

by the coordinator. The latter can concentrate more on the group work. For the e-training domain, he focuses his effort on supervising learning and providing help.

Before automatic processing, the e-learning session must be prepared by a human session manager who selects the available and required e-learning tools, creates the user access rights, and saves them in a configuration file. This off-session preparation is nowadays possible with the graphical panel of Figure 4.

Implementation Technologies

The JAVA language supports the programming of the PLATINE platform components. With its more and more important number of reusable classes, it has been retained as a unified technology for the development of the diverse parts of the platform and as general glue for their integration.

Networking communications are based on IP Multicast for the multipoint unreliable multicast exchanges.

RTP/RTCP communications are retained for the audio/video transmissions through the JMF Java devices.

The reliable multicast required for small control message exchanges is implemented with N Client/Server TCP connections.

Figure 5 shows a screendump of the Coordinator workstation, with the previous described tools and the session manager panel.

Figure 6 presents the tool look of a current group member, either trainer or trainee. The main difference with the Coordinator screen is the absence of session manager panel. The other tools (videoconference, application sharing and shared whiteboard) are always active.

Figure 5: Coordinator Screen

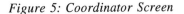
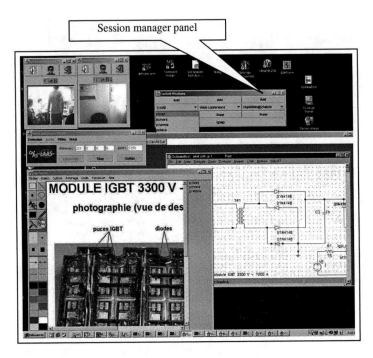

Figure 6: Participant Screen

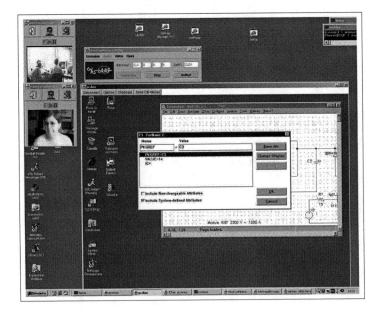

Figure 7: Model-Driven Approach for E-Learning Software Support

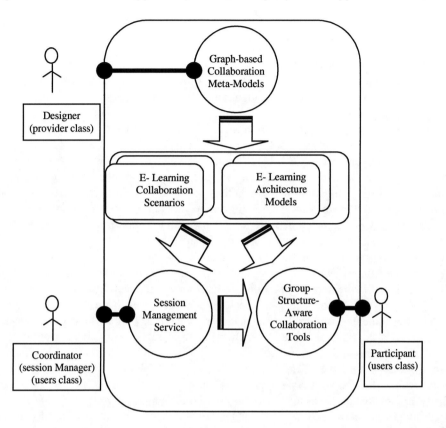

PLATINE Synthesis

Figure 7 summarizes the modeling approach retained for the design of our e-learning platform. The modeling level is used to capture in a formal and unified way all the requirements coming from e-learning architectures and collaboration scenarios. This level is first managed by the session designer that produces them with dynamic collaboration graphs.

These graph structures are inputs for the operational level composed of the PLATINE modules. In a more precise way, the SM Session Manager module uses them to pilot and synchronize the session. With them, it controls the group structure-aware collaboration tools (Jvisio, AST, SW) and configures them according to the retained graph structures. This level is under the control of the Coordinator.

SCENARIOS AND EXPERIMENTS

The two scenarios are supported by two different physical configurations:
- All the participants are geographically distributed. The teacher speaks from his office, and the students hear the course from their personal workstation.

- The trainees are structured in several groups distributed in different geographic places. The teacher and a first group of students are located in a same classroom, and the other groups of students are distributed in several other rooms.

Cyberlicence Scenario

The first selected application scenario of our study concerns the training in complex domains, with a wide range of knowledges and know-hows. It is situated in the context of a French bachelor of law ("licence en droit" with studies about civil, labour, administrative, European community, and public liberties laws), called Cyberlicence, already organized at the University of Toulouse 1 (Baudin et al., 2001).

The course contents are developed using the WebCT platform (WebCT platform, 2002). They are created by the teachers in law, helped by an engineer (having the double competence of jurist and computer specialist) who plays a coordinator's role between the professors and the students. These coordinators have a central role in managing the lectures. They have the responsibility to manage course support and to teach teachers in law how to use these advanced communication technologies.

The students living near Albi live in the premises of the university campus located in downtown Albi. They have exclusive access to the distant courses from Albi campus with sessions of dedicated workstations. Synchronous videoconferences are regularly organized with ISDN connections. These videoconferences are transmitted at some predefined moments from the Toulouse university campus to the Albi campus. During these sessions the trainers (called e-teachers) answer questions in a synchronous way (interactive distributed co-presence). Other questions can also be handled in an asynchronous way through the discussion forums managed by WebCT. The WebCT platform contains an additional whiteboard, but it is seldom used by the e-teachers and trainees, that limits them to the forum and videoconference handling. This whiteboard has limited capabilities and cannot take into account display of remote applications, such as tax law simulations.

Our contribution consists of improving the previous current synchronous approach to implement a larger interactivity between the trainees, the e-teachers, and the engineer team. With regard to the environment used in an operational way today, other useful functionalities are added, allowing:

- The various participants to share the complete work contexts (static documents of courses, business-specific applications),
- A coordination facility to manage the participants, and to control their turn of speaking,
- Every participant to have a multicast dialogue tool on his workstation.

Every domain or speciality is under the responsibility of an expert, who can help a trainee if he encounters some domain-specific problem. When the scenario is instantiated in the "Cyberlicence" context, the expert group is composed of the e-teachers belonging to the "Cyberlicence." Their targeted knowledge (in subjects such as constitutional, labour, European community laws) are the different topics required for any expert.

The coordinator belongs to the engineer team: he is a computer specialist and a non-specialized jurist at the same time. These two roles induce his two main functions:

(1) Firstly, the coordinator must technically assist the trainees. When a technical problem is encountered, his advanced knowledge in computer science is required to help the participants who encounter difficulties.

(2) Secondly, he intervenes at a first level of help when any student has a question about law. Thanks to his jurist knowledge, according to the domain-specific problem raised by a trainee, he selects a competent and available expert and directs the student to the selected expert.

Direction of Information Systems (DSI) Scenario

The models, mechanisms and tools implemented for our digital campus are used in a second scenario for professional training by the Direction of Information Systems (DSI) department of the French National Centre for Scientific Research. The DSI department is located in two distant geographic sites: Labège near Toulouse and Meudon near Paris.

This service periodically organizes internal training, according to the agents' needs. The training sessions can be led by an inside trainer (a member of the DSI staff) or an outside one. PowerPoint slides compose the training scenario documents, but use of specific application software is also required. In this case, the DSI staffs must be grouped in the same place for training the specific tools and techniques. The current choice to attend the training consists of grouping the trainees in a single classroom, located either in Labège or Meudon. The training is led in a classical way.

The work sessions have short durations, from one to four hours.

The travelling time of the staff involved in these meetings is high in comparison with the duration of the training sessions: it is about the same value. The travelling cost is not negligible too. Furthermore, a great number of DSI people are unavailable during their travel and training session meeting; it creates important perturbations in the DSI department running. These three main reasons fully justify the use of e-learning solutions between Meudon and Labège.

The identified training physical configurations are represented in Figure 8.

Tool Adequacy with the E-Learning Scenarios

The dynamic previous collaborative e-learning scenarios require a set of basic functionalities to be fully developed as follows.

High-Level Interaction Mode

The communication conventions of the dynamic e-learning scenarios are first based on the questioning/answering interaction model. Such interaction appears first between a requested student and the coordinator, then, at a second level, between a student and a teacher. In the two cases, they begin with a videoconference call system included within JVisio. They are firstly supported by audio-video communications of the JVisio conference and secondly by the two sharing tools, the SW Shared Whiteboard and the AST Application Sharing tool of the PLATINE platform.

Collaboration Functions

The *viewing document* function is used to share different documents. It is the basic function required to access a common context for any group work.

Figure 8: DSI E-Learning Configurations

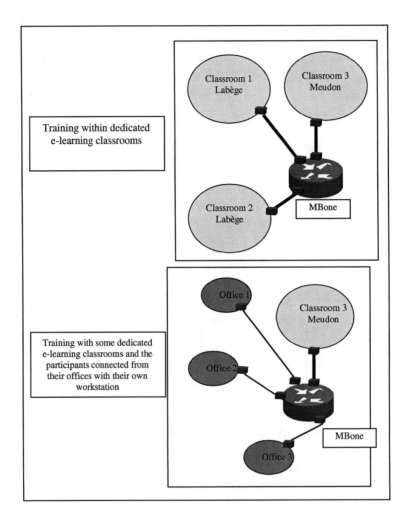

In a conference room, the group members can add handwritten notes to achieve more interactivity for any discussion or explanation. It is identified as the *viewing annotation function.*

People use the *writing annotation* function to take personal or global annotations associated with the presented documents.

All these three high-level functions are supported by the SW Shared Whiteboard of the PLATINE platform.

In the same way, the *viewing function* can be extended for the display and sharing of dynamic multimedia applications. It is guaranteed by the AST Application Sharing tool.

During explanations, lecturers use a pointer to focus on an important part of the displayed document and to highlight some particular or difficult points. The *mouse-*

pointing function is included in the two sharing tools of the PLATINE platform; the SW Shared Whiteboard and the AST Application Sharing tool both support remote pointing.

Control and Coordination Functions

The group members have access to the video and to the voice of the other members. This functionality has to be reproduced in any distributed classroom to maintain a group consciousness. This *group visualization function* is now supported by the JVisio videoconference tool.

The *trainee supervision function* means having a look at the personal documents of another participant, to supervise the members of a group: for instance, in a trainer-trainee context as a glance function. The AST Application Sharing tool guarantees this function.

The Coordinator can give the floor to a selected trainee, if the latter encounters difficulties or asks questions that require pointing or writing on the documents displayed. This *floor control function*, now under the responsibility of the Coordinator, is supported by the SM Session Manager module.

Sharing a common collaboration space is useful when several users want to discuss on a same subject. This function is required when many users try to access and handle documents synchronously in common. The *sharing document function* is implemented by the SW Shared Whiteboard.

CONCLUSION

Unlike many other e-learning platforms that try to reproduce the classical learning scenarios and configurations in a distributed way, the focus of our work is to extend the classical learning scenarios in a complementary post-lecture direction: supporting dynamic interactions (as questions/answers) for complementary or highly-specialized lectures.

This extension has been achieved by the development of a prototype e-learning platform, PLATINE that supports the following essential characteristics:

(1)   Dynamic coordinated access for interactive and synchronous trainer-trainee dialogues
(2)   Remote access to online shared documents or applications, including highly specialized business applications
(3)   Group member visualization to maintain learning as a real group.

The next step of our work is the e-learning platform evaluation within the two retained scenarios. The feedback obtained by these evaluations will allow us to tune the collaboration models. This way, we can improve the degree of acceptance of the PLATINE dynamic e-learning platform and take benefits from the results of this experimental approach.

REFERENCES

AICC. (2002). Aviation Industry CBT (Computer-Based Training) Committee. Available on the World Wide Web: http://www.aicc.org.

Baudin, V., Drira, K., Villemur, T., & Tazi, S. (2001, May 21-23). Une approche synchrone pour une télé-expertise distribuée. *1ères Journées Francophones des Modèles Formels de l'Interaction (MFI'01)*, 3, 363-377.

Campus de France portal. (2002). Available on the World Wide Web: http://www.campusdefrance.prd.fr.

Drira, K., Gouezec, F., & Diaz, M. (1999). Design and implementation of coordination protocols for distributed cooperating objects. A general graph-based technique applied to CORBA. In *Proccedings of the Third IFIP International Conference on Formal Methods for Open Object-based Distributed Systems* (FMOODS'99), Florence, Italy (February 15-18).

Drira, K., Martelli, A., & Villemur T. (eds.). (2001). Cooperative environments for distributed systems engineering. *Lecture Notes in Computer Science*. Springer.

Johnson, D.W., & Johnson, R.T. (1978). Cooperative, competitive, and individualistic learning. *Journal of Research and Development in Education*, 12, 8-15.

Johnson, R.T., & Johnson, D.W. (1988). Cooperative Learning. *'In Context' Review #18* (Special number on Transforming Education). Available on the World Wide Web : http://www.context.org/ICLIB/IC18/Johnson.htm.

LearningSpace. (2002). Lotus – IBM. Available on the World Wide Web: http://www.lotus.com/home.nsf/welcome/learnspace.

McClelland, B. (2000). Digital Learning and program supports: An examination of developments for students in higher education. In *Proceedings of the 26th Euromicro Conference*, Maastricht (September 5-7, 2, 43-49).

Miao, Y., Fleschutz, J.M., & Zentel, P. (1999). Enriching learning contexts to support communities of practice. In *Proceedings of Computer Support for Collaborative Learning* (pp. 391-397).

Multimedia Technologies Portal for French Education. (2002). Available on the World Wide Web: http://www.educnet.education.fr.

NetMeeting. (2002). Microsoft. Available on the World Wide Web : http://www.microsoft.com/netmeeting.

Paloff, R., & Pratt, K. (1999). *Building Learning Communities in Cyberspace: Effective Strategies for the Online Classroom*. San Francisco, CA: Jossez-Bass Publishers.

Rodriguez Peralta, L.M., Villemur, T., & Drira, K. (2001). *An XML on-line session model based on graphs for synchronous cooperative groups*. International Conference on Parallel and Distributed Processing Techniques and Applications (PDPTA'2001), Las Vegas, USA (June).

Sapon-Shevin, M. (1990). *Student support through cooperative learning. Support networks for inclusive schooling* (W. Stainback & S. Stainback, eds.). Paul Brookes Publishing Co. Available on the World Wide Web : http://www.quasar.ualberta.ca/ddc/inclusion/schoolcaring/cooplrn.htm.

Scolastance. (2002). *Infostance*. Available on the World Wide Web: http://www.scolastance.com.

Serpolet tool. (2002). *A6 – MediaGuide*. Available on the World Wide Web: http://www.a6.fr.

South, J.B., & Miller Nelson, L. (2000). An online environment that scaffolds moving from novice to expert collaborative learners. *Proceedings of EDMEDIA 2000*.

Speaker tool. (2002). Neuroconcept. Available on the World Wide Web : http://www.neuroconcept.com.

Toma, T. (2002). Lavac Presentation. Available on the World Wide Web: http://www.lairdil.iut-tlse3.fr/ftp/Toma/LAVAC/PRESENTATION/PRESENTATION.htm#_English_Summary.

Turoff, M. (1993). Computer-mediated-communication requirements for group support. In *Reading in Groupware and Computer Supported Cooperative Work* (pp. 407-417). Morgan Kaufman.

VNC. (2002). *Virtual Network Computing application.* Available on the World Wide Web: http://www.uk.research.att.com/vnc.

Villemur, T. (1995). *Conception de Services et de Protocoles pour la Gestion de Groupes Coopératifs.* Ph.D. Thesis, Université Paul Sabatier, Toulouse III.

WebCT platform. (2002). United Learning Technologies. Available on the World Wide Web: http://www.webct.com/products.

Webex. (2002). WebEx Communications. Available on the World Wide Web: http://www.webex.com.

Chapter IV

Smart ProFlexLearn:
An Intuitive Approach to Virtual Learning Environment

Claude Ghaoui, Liverpool John Moores University, UK

W.A. Janvier, Liverpool John Moores University, UK

ABSTRACT

This chapter is based on the authors' vision that "A virtual university should be, to the learner, a distance or online learning environment that can be transmitted via the World Wide Web by an intelligent tool that is intuitive to use, a simulation of the real-world learning experience and, at all stages, interacts with the learner's changing profile."

INTRODUCTION

The chapter looks at the background of Distance Learning Tools (DLT), the development of "Promoting Flexible Learning" (ProFlexLearn) as a DLT, the background of Intelligent Tutoring Systems (ITS), introduces Learner Profiling (Communication Preference {CP}, Learning Styles {LS} and motivational factors), the development of ProFlexLearn into a Web Intelligent Student Distance-education Model (WISDeM), and its architecture and future improvement as a generic Intelligent Tutoring System (ITS).

DISTANCE LEARNING TOOLS

Computer Assisted Learning has been developing since the 1950s' simple Linear Programs (English & Yazdani, 1999). The current vogue is to offer so-called Virtual Universities with many institutions recycling material, creating web sites and claiming delivery through a Virtual University: in reality, learning in a university relies not only on the official modular content, but on the inter-personal communication between student-student-tutor and the way the module is presented. The general accepted standard is that a learner must be able to experience Self-Directed Learning, Asynchronous and Synchronous communication (Ryan et al., 2000). Bouras and Philopulos (2000) consider in their paper that the "Distributed Virtual Learning Environment," using a combination of HTML, Java and VRML (Virtual Reality Modelling Language), providing Virtual chat rooms, lectures using announcement boards, slide presentations and links to WWW pages, makes learning easier. Cooper's (2000) research shows that post-secondary institutions want to offer online facilities to meet the educational needs of a fast-paced, computer literate society. Hegarty et al. (1998) provide a step-by-step guide for setting up distance learning classrooms using telecommunications technology. Marshall-University (1999) reports that most DLTs combine, to a greater or lesser extent: *Authentication* for access, *Communication* — asynchronous/synchronous, *Course Control, Help, Manuals* — student and tutor, *Questions & Answers,* and *Students* presentation areas. JCUs' (2000) research indicates that the two most popular academic DTLs are Blackboard™ and WebCT™ following in-depth research they purchased Blackboard™— neither *allow full customisation nor do they include artificial intelligence (AI) or profiling.*

PROMOTING FLEXIBLE LEARNING

ProFlexLearn interactive MLE System was developed in 1995/1996 under the guidance of Dr. Claude Ghaoui of Liverpool John Moores University (Ghaoui, 1996/1997). Further developments of the system and the creation of online learning material continued from 1995 and linked into a composite site: it developed into a fully functional DLT offering all of the usual DLT components (see Cooper, 2000; Hegarty et al., 1998; IsaBelle & Nkambou, 1998; JCU, 2000, for a detailed listing of components offered in DLTs). During 1998/1999 these were amalgamated onto a Unix server linking some fifty-seven separate web sites with a common front page. Interactive tutorials and other facilities, such as forum, feedback and search were added using CGI/Perl scripting. ProFlexLearn contains circa 760MB of information and various tools/facilities that are designed to assist a student to benefit from self-directed, asynchronous and synchronous learning (see Ryan et al., 2000, for a discussion on these). The site is designed in three sections:
(i)   *"Learning Materials of Modules"* which provides all the materials required for the six HCI related modules (Human Computer Interface — HND, Human Computer Interaction — M.Sc., Introduction to HCI — B.Sc., Multimedia Applications Workshop — M.Sc., Multimedia Authoring — B.Sc., and User Interface Design — B.Sc.).
(ii)   *"Other Courses"* which provides additional relevant information to the Modules. This contains the main bulk of additional information being, as mentioned above, a conglomeration of student web sites that have been specifically prepared over

a period of years to cover a wide rage of topics, set as coursework, and included where the quality and content reached the HCI and knowledge subject matter required.

(iii)   *"A set of interactive educational tools"* to facilitate learning, communication and collaboration.

With development, the ProFlexLearn web browser (client-server) was changed to use a Windows2000 Server Pack, and FrontPage Administration Service Pack running Active Server Pages (ASP) and FrontPage using JavaScript, Java Applets, Dynamic Hyper-Text Mark-up Language (DHTML), ODBC, Access linking, Excel linking, Style Sheets and Password control. For synchronous communication it uses Microsoft Windows NetMeeting for an audio video conference between two people or I-Visit for multi-users: the former includes a whiteboard server and data files. It supports administration, author and learner and can link to external files using normal web hyperlinks, thus accessing files created by any normal e-communication package (e.g., MS Word, Excel, Access, Word, Adobe PDF files, Images, RealPlayer, SMIL, Text files {Notepad, TextPad}).

The first prototype of ProFlexLearn requires restructuring to allow for easy replication of tutorials by creating a more generic model. It offers limited tracking facilities; there is no statistical package, no reporting facilities have been developed, assessment only offers self-marking multi-choice question and answer revision and short tutorial questions (tutor marked), and it offers no Artificial Intelligence (AI) and limited assistance to the author.

Changing ProFlexLearn to the Generic Model

In essence the "Module System" files, where rewritten in ASP linking to the tutorial files, provided that they are "saved-as" the template HTML or PPT (PowerPoint file) as designated in the module folder. Links to PDF files can be created using the Access database facility. Folders can be saved in "Other Course" as a self-contained web site or by directly editing the new Module using (D)HTML, XML, etc., Interactive Multi-choice Question/Answers are added, amended or deleted using the Access Administration front-end.

Learning with ProFlexLearn

ProFlexLearn allows the potential user to preview Module and Course content. Each module's specification and the "Other Courses" content are contained in the public part of the web site. To gain access to the actual content requires the learner to be registered. In particular, the screen is well planned and assists the student (Figure 1) — the ✓'s indicate existing functionality.

Registration

The learner can register as an external user or a student user. The former has limited access to "Short Courses" as requested at registration, the latter has full access to authorised module pages and all the content in "Short Courses."

Figure 1: ProFlexLearn — Screen Usability

LEARNING - ProFlexLearn Screen Usability			
Screen Layouts		Navigational Images	
Amount of information displayed	✓	Use appropriate	✓
Arrangement of information	✓	Use consistent	✓
Display always on screen	✓	Use clearly understood	✓
Screen Colours		Sequence of Screens	
Use of colour appropriate	✓	Next screen predictable	✓
Colour use consistent	✓	Going back easy	✓
Colour useful	✓	Progression clearly understood	✓
Screen Highlighting		Informative Images	
Hyperlink colour use understandable	✓	Use appropriate	✓
Use of bolding	✓	Aided understanding	✓
Use of reverse video	✓	Aided learning	✓
New Windows		Alphanumeric characters	
Aided navigation	✓	Easy to read	✓
Aided learning experience	✓	Font usage	✓
New Windows opened when required	✓		

Learning Support Materials Facilities

Modules contains various sections:

- *Overview* — this provides the student with a brief synopsis of the whole module: it is of particular use when a student is choosing which modules to take towards his/her degree
- *Specification* — this provides precise details of the module requirements and provisions: staff details, time to be spent on lectures/tutorials/seminars/laboratory work/field work/other times/exam and private study, course pre-requisites, recommended prior study, co-requisites and barred combinations
- *Main Topics* — this including links to all lecture/lab session notes and exercises: the semester week, lecture title, lecture notes, presentation materials (slides, PowerPoint, video, audio), additional information pertinent to the lecture, link to the multi-choice questions/answers for the specific week, tutorial questions to be pre-prepared before the tutorial, and full details of the lab session exercises with notes and explanation where relevant
- *Coursework* — this provides all assignments and coursework that will be used to assess the student module grading pertinent to his/her degree
- *Past Exam* — this provides copies of all relevant past exam papers to enable the student to gain incite to exam style and requirements
- *Downloads* — provides a link to all relevant online materials/programs that the student will need to complete the module

- *Resources* — this provides links to all relevant resources that the student is expected to read (books, literature, etc.) and web sites of particular interest that contain pertinent information
- *Revision* — provides a basic interactive self-marking multi-choice question and answer facility that allows the student to conduct personal testing, thereby ensuring that what "is needed to be known" is known

Other Courses: contains more than 60 tutorials in nine sections HCI relevant information: sections on Computer Hardware and Programming, Computer Networks, HCI-Related Topics, International Languages, Medical Multimedia, Multimedia in Education and Training, Miscellaneous Topics, Virtual Reality and WWW and Multimedia.

Links: Liverpool John Moores University's (LJMU) Lion Library and other student facilities, and external resources.

Site Search: allows a student to search the web site's contents.

Video Conferencing: uses MS Netmeeting.

WWW Search: links to the most popular web search engines.

Communication Tools

Email: this links the user to the LJMU email server.

Discussion Forums: each module has its own discussion forum with threaded links created by either the tutor or student. The forums allow Posting, Search and Reply: all entries are both user and time stamped.

Feedback: this facility allows users to post feedback to their own module area: entries are both user and time stamped.

MS Netmeeting: includes synchronous group audio/video communication/tutoring (Whiteboard, chat, audio and video-conferencing).

Student Web Sites: Students have the use of their web space both for individual and group work.

Group Pages: Students have shared folder facilities enabling them to collaborate asynchronously.

Thus the student has a wide variety of facilities that cover all potential requirements within the module data and facilities.

Authoring and Administration

Figure 2 shows the authoring and administrative functionality — the ✓'s indicate existing functionality and the 'x' indicates functionality that it is not available.

Technical Admin — Hardware/Software Requirements — ProFlexLearn

On the server-side, ProFlexLearn uses a Windows NT/2000 server and an Access database using ODBC linking with ASP (Active Server Pages) for interactivity. If the Windows NT is used, NT service pack 4 is required with ASP service pack facilities and

Figure 2: ProFlexLearn Software and Module Administration

Software and Module ADMINISTRATION			
Technical		*Module*	
Plug-and-Play Installation	x	Installing required parts - easy	x
Maintenance easy and time efficient	✓	Access authorisation - easy	✓
Can use Windows 2000/NT server	✓	Access maintenance - easy	✓
Can use SQL server	✓	Assessment reporting	x
Runs on Windows 2000/NT	✓	Statistical reporting	x
Runs on UNIX	x	Grade Book facility	x
System supports Active Server Pages (ASP)	✓	Student/Group Homepage facility	✓
System supports MS FrontPage server	✓	Student/Group Folder facility	✓
Database Administration by Web	some	Student/Group web site facility	✓

MS FrontPage 98/2000 Information Services enabled. Windows 2000 Server pack automatically includes all ASP APIs. MS FrontPage 2000 server administration is also required.

Requirements for Course/Module Delivery

The following minimum specifications are required: 100 MHz CPU, RAM 32 MB, screen resolution 640x480 pixels, image enabled, JavaScript enabled, plug-in RealPlayer v 8. Any client-side v.4 or greater browser can be used. Scripting should be enabled and RealPlayer needs to be set to recognise SMIL applications (see http://www.helio.org).

Authoring

Module Specification: authored by the database front end.

Main Topics: Lecture Slides authored in HTML or PDF, *Additional Information* authored by Word, *Lab session* notes and exercises authored by Word, *Coursework* authored using Word or Excel, *Exam Papers* authored using Word or Excel, *Download* authored by the database front end, *Resources* authored by the database front end, and *Revision & Tutorial* authored via the database front end.

Scenario

A new user, John, enters the system and selects his school and course group — this opens the course group front-page. He now selects the list of modules and enters the one he wishes to use. The logon screen opens and he enters his student registration number and password: the module front-page opens. He now checks the syllabus and notes that 25% is assessed by exam and 75% is assessed by coursework, he also makes a list of the books he will need to use for study. He has a quick look at the resources facility and finds that not only are required reading books listed but also further links that are likely to be of use. He opens the Main Topics page and notes the time and title of his first lecture. He opens the lecture notes, these provide him with information and links to pre-lecture reading that will be of use. He opens the lecture slides and downloads these so that he can look at them before the lecture. He now opens the forum and sees that, as yet, no threads have been posted. At the lecture, his tutor sets the tutorial study for the next session and tells the class that coursework will be posted during the coming week.

During the coming week he opens the Tutorial link and finds that the tutor has posted some questions to be answered, part of which includes the request for the students to have an open forum discussion about a particular question to be discussed at the next tutorial. One of the questions is not clear so he opens the email connection and asks his tutor about it. When he opens the forum again he finds that a thread has been posted by the tutor and there is already a discussion ongoing. He joins in and launches a new thread about one of the topics being discussed. Having read these comments and read the required book chapters, he opens the Revision Question and Answer and attempts the multi-choice Q&As. The running total tells him that he has 55% for the questions attempted: he leaves the session for now. Later he opens the Q&As again and finds that the questions that he has already answered and the results are stored, he resets the revision and does it again. This time he scores 88%, which gives him some confidence; however, he feels that he could improve and uses the search facility to look for some ideas about what to read. He notes that some additional material is available in "Other Courses" and opens this section…

Conclusion

This may seem to be an ideal student, nevertheless, it does provide an insight to what can be achieved; however, this whole interaction, whilst being an effective DLT, lacks human-human inter-personnel interaction and may well not be able to offer the student the best interaction available — it is human-computer interaction where all interaction has been pre-decided, it contains no real-time motivational feedback nor direction or interaction specifically designed for this particular student. This is where the introduction of appropriate AI embodied in an Intelligent Tutoring System needs to be incorporated, including Communication Preference, Learning Styles and Teaching Styles interaction — the rational for WISDeM's development (Janvier & Ghaoui, 2001). Djian et al.'s (1999) research indicates that the union of a DLT with an ITS, producing a generic Human-Centred ITS tool for the World Wide Web has a lot to offer to the different users concerned.

INTELLIGENT TUTORING SYSTEMS (ITS)

ITS originated in the AI movement of the late 1950s and early 1960s, when researchers such as Alan Turing, Marvin Minsky, John McCarthy and Allen Newell thought that computers that could "think" as humans do were just around the corner; however, researchers and developers found that the practicality of creating a generic system was "too hard" (Urban-Lurain, 1999).

1950s - 1960s: Computer Assisted Learning has developed from the 1950s with simple Linear Programs (Yazdanir & Lawler, 1987). Urban-Lurain (1999) reports that by the late 1960s and early 1970s, many researchers now considered the learner — they were the first to "model" learners: they modelled learners' behaviour not knowledge states.

1970s - 1980s: Urban-Lurain (1999) reports that the dominant paradigm in the late 1970s and early 1980s was Information Processing: researchers envisaged human cognition as set of black-box-processes as opposed to responses to external stimuli, and anticipated that precision models could be described by computer programs. In the 1980s, ITS evolved in several directions: as single reproductions of a super-teacher using multiple knowledge sources (learner-pedagogical-subject models), and as simplified models able to complete precise tasks mirroring tutor-knowledge. By 1989, the AI community had concluded that intelligence should finally result from a joint construction between the human and the computer (cooperative tutoring systems, social learning systems, collaborative systems) (Aimeur et al., 2001).

1990s - 2000s: There was a flurry of activity during this decade, the following are symptomatic:

- 1995 *"Andes."* a Physics/Maths AI system (Gertner & VanLehn, 2000; Schulze et al., 2000; VanLehn, 2000)
- 1996 Lieberman (1997) reports that the *Remembrance Agent* is an *"Autonomous interface agent"* similar to COACH
- Nkambou et al.'s (1996) CREAM (Curriculum Representation and Acquisition Model) was launched
- Urban-Lurain (1999) reports that learner modelling remains at the core of ITS research, and Wær (1997) reports that research and development are being concentrated on two main areas: System User Modelling and Natural Language Dialogue
- Lieberman (1997) considers that the educational market requires a combination of DLT and ITS in order to achieve real success
- Murray (1999), in common with many other researchers, believes that ITSs are too complex for the untrained user and that *"we should expect users to have a reasonable degree of training in how to use them, on the order of database programming, CAD-CAM authoring, 3-D modelling, or spreadsheet macro scripting."*

LEARNER PROFILING

This section describes Communication Preferences, Neuro-Linguistic Programming, Learning Styles — Myers-Briggs Type Indicator® (MBTI)®, VARK, and Learning Styles: Teaching Styles mapping.

Communication Preference

People use their own preferred technique(s) to exchange ideas with others, acquire knowledge and pass knowledge to a third party. These preferences have been the basis of much research (Borchert et al., 1999; Fleming, 2001; Robotham, 1999). Catania (1992) reports that almost all learning is external to the body, being introduced by one of the five senses, with the input using the Iconic (60% sight), Echoic (30% hearing) and Haptic (10% touch) cortex of the memory (Olfactory {smell} and Gustatory {taste} use proportionally little). Sadowski and Stanney (1999) report that there is a tendency to prefer one sensory input over another in a given context (**v**isual, **a**uditory or **k**inaesthetic {tactile and haptic} instances), and Pasztor (1997) reports that rapport with a partner is key to effective communication and that incorporating Neuro-Linguistic Programming (NLP) language patterns and eye-gaze in intelligent agents will allow customisation of the (virtual) personal assistant to the particular habits and interests of the user thus, making the user more comfortable with the system. Pasztor (1998) also confirms that introducing the correct sub-modality (**v**isual, **a**uditory, **k**inaesthetic) will enable the subject to more easily remember and recall instances.

VARK Learning Style Preferences

A well-respected psychometric model is VARK (Fleming, 2001). A student's VARK descriptor is formed as a combination of up to five different modes of information input: **V**isually, **A**uditory, **R**ead/write, **K**inaesthetic and Multi-modality, the last is a recent addition (Borchert et al., 1999). Driscoll and Garcia's (2000) research is interesting in that results, obtained for student class profiles using VARK, indicate that their learning styles are firmly in place by the time a student goes to a university and may well differ substantially from what their tutors perceive and/or assume.

Learning Styles

Students have preferred learning styles that directly impact their ability to assimilate and retain course content (Borchert et al., 1999).

Myers-Briggs Type Indicator® (MBTI)® — Learning Styles

One of the most successful models to establish personality types/learning styles is the Myers-Briggs Type Indicator® (Murphy et al., 2002; Myers & Myers, 1995). MBTI® is a self-report personality inventory designed to provide information about your Jungian psychological type preferences (Carl G. Jung was a Swiss psychiatrist {1875-1961} who identified certain psychological types {Extroversion/Introversion — Judgment/Perception}). Murphy et al. (2002) reports that it is more widely used by educators in the USA than any other model. There are 16 types (**ESTJ** — Extrovert : Sensing : Thinking : Judgment ‖ **ESTP** — Extrovert : Sensing : Thinking : Perception ‖ **ESFJ** — Extrovert : Sensing : Feeling : Judgment ‖ **ESFP** — Extrovert : Sensing : Feeling : Perception ‖ **ENTJ** — Extrovert : Intuition : Thinking : Judgment ‖ **ENTP** — Extrovert : Intuition : Thinking : Perception ‖ **ENFJ** — Extrovert : Intuition : Feeling : Judgment ‖ **ENFP**

— Extrovert : Intuition : Feeling : Perception || **ISTJ** — Introvert : Sensing : Thinking : Judgment || **ISTP** — Introvert : Sensing : Thinking : Perception || **ISFJ** — Introvert : Sensing : Feeling : Judgment || **ISFP** — Introvert : Sensing : Feeling : Perception || **INTJ** — Introvert : Intuition : Thinking : Judgment || **INTP** — Introvert : Intuition : Thinking : Perception || **INFJ** — Introvert : Intuition : Feeling : Judgment || **INFP** — Introvert : Intuition : Feeling : Perception) made up from the four preference categories: (i) Interpersonal Communication, (ii) Information Processing, (iii) Information Evaluation, and (iv) Decision Style. Most researchers see Information Processing as the most important in terms of implications for education (Borchert et al., 1999). These sixteen preference styles relate to eight Jungian functions and to four classes (Dominant, Auxiliary, Tertiary or Inferior). For example, the ISFJ type (Introvert - Sensing - Feeling - Judgement) tends to exhibit to the real world the type shown by either an ESFJ (Extrovert - Sensing - Feeling - Judgement) or ENFJ (Extrovert - Intuition - Feeling - Judgment) by using their Auxiliary functionality. Larkin-Hein and Budny (2000) consider that, while extroverts' learning preferences are shown, the *"cardinal precaution in dealing with introverts is not to assume that they have revealed what really matters to them."*

Student Learning Styles to Teaching Styles

Hoover and Connor (2001) report that matching your learning style to teaching style can result in more effective learning and greater academic achievement. Fuller et al. (2000) outlined the Teaching Styles preferences for the MBTI® styles and provided suggestions for faculty development for seven of the sixteen MBTI® types. Montgomery and Groat (1998) point out that *"matching teaching styles to learning styles is not a panacea that solves all classroom conflicts,"* that other factors such as the student's motivation, pre-conceptions, and multicultural issues also impinge on the student's quality of learning; nonetheless, understanding and reacting to learning styles in teaching enhances the quality of learning and rewards teaching.

Summary

IT STARTS WITH THE LEARNER — the development of the initial Student Learning Styles Profile (Communication Preference, Learning Styles and Motivational Feedback Style), and its mapping to the system's Teaching Styles, BEFORE module content is accessed.

WISDeM

This section introduces WISDeM, both as a DLT and its components and as an ITS, its current state and development. A useful simile is to say that WISDeM is starting at Everest's "Base Camp" and that its later development can go through various camps whilst approaching the "Holy Grail" of the summit Including (Janvier & Ghaoui, 2001), for example, Avatars, Natural Language (NL), Multi-modality, Autonomous Hyperlink Searching, linking and using other ITS, or indeed any other development that will further the ability of a DLT to effectively and efficiently interact with every learner who uses the system.

WISDeM — The Distance Learning Tool

WISDeM has been developed as a generic DLT including all normal DLT components using ProFlexLearn as the basis.

WISDeM — The Intelligent Tutoring System

This section expands on the various parts of the ITS development, the Architecture, Student Profiling - Communication Preference, Learning Styles, Motivation, providing detailed Dialogue Network Diagrams and textual description.

The Architecture

WISDeM's architecture's basic design (Figure 3) allows for inter-disciplinary reuse of module content with two global servers (master and AI) and individual servers for tutor module groups (module administration and content). The *Master Server* is used to store School/Department and module details linking both the student to his/her relevant module server and provides inter-disciplinary reusability of module content. The *Module Servers* contain all module material required for a normal DLT interaction with the learner and the administration front-end facilities. The global *AI Server* serves all University module servers, storing *Learner Profiles, Communication Preferences, Motivational Data,* and *Pedagogical Data.*

When a learner uses the system for the first time, his/her Communication Preference and Learning Styles are stored in the learner profile data table: the learner profile is updated as the system is used, enabling the system to interact in real-time with the learner

Figure 3: WISDeM — Architecture

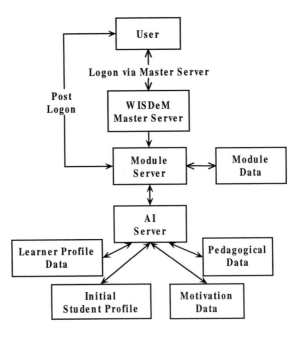

— either autonomously or by request — by providing feedback and links to relevant module materials. This system allows a student to log on to any authorized module and use the module content.

Scenario

This section describes a typical scenario that outlines WISDeM's functions and provides a detailed model (Figure 4). A new learner connects to WISDeM and selects his/her school and module: the master-server handles this request routing the learner to the module-server running his/her module. The learner uses his/her University Registration ID, password and Module selection to log on. The system checks for *userNew* or *userExisting*, if the former, the CP question/answer screen is opened following completion of which the LS question/answer screens are activated with questions/answers designed to match the learner's Language Pattern as ascertained from the CP answers. The full Learner Profile is saved in the Learner Profile Repository and the module front page is opened.

Figure 4: WISDeM Detailed Data Flow

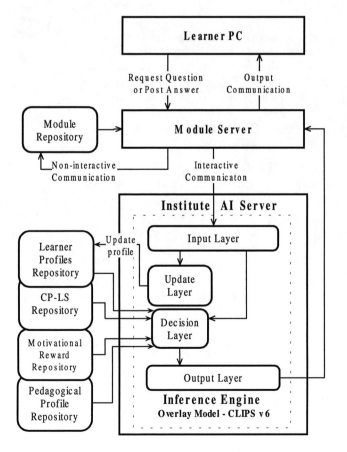

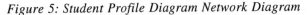

Figure 5: Student Profile Diagram Network Diagram

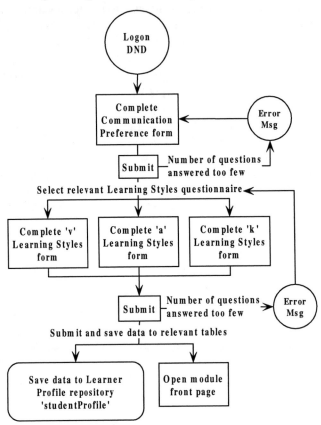

Student Profiling

The Diagram Network Diagram (DND) (Figure 5) outlines the flow to establish a student's profile: Communication Preference (CP). Following learner identity validation, 21 questions are output, seven questions covering each of the three main sensory memory input: (i) **V**isual memory, (ii) **A**uditory memory, and (iii) **K**inaesthetic (feelings) memory, that are specifically related to the student's sensory perception. For example, for (V) *"I prefer a lecture to be illustrated with slides,"* for (A), *"I like music more than art,"* and for (K), *"When I recall an experience, I usually remember how I felt about it."* The answers are evaluated and a link opens a Learning Styles questionnaire.

Learning Styles (LS)

This questionnaire outputs questions couched in the language pattern relevant to the learner's CP. The LS questions were developed using the MBTI® principles and style with five pairs for each LS. The LS questionnaire asks 10 questions, split into couplets, on the four sections — Inter-personnel Communication, Information Processing, Information Evaluation, and Decision Style. Each set of questions has been replicated using the three language patterns (VAK): for example for (V), *"I notice that I tend to talk more than I listen,"* for (A), *"I tend to talk more than I listen,"* and for (K), *"I feel that I tend to talk more than I listen,"* and presented to the student according to his/her CP. Provided all sections are answered, the resulting computer analysis selects one LS profile out of the sixteen possible profiles. The CP and LS are logged in the Learner Profile database. Fuller et al.'s (2000) research results show the following LS type testing results over a small sampling: **Extrovert** = 53%, **Introvert** = 47%, **Sensing** = 24%, **iNtuition** = 76%, **Thinking** = 41%, **Feeling** = 59%, **Judgement** = 53% and **Perception** = 47%. The LS combination scores were ENFP and INTP = 18%, ENFJ, INFJ, ENTJ and ISFJ = 12% and INFP 6%. If we look at the highest (ENFP:INTP) examples, we could extract an idea of a typical Teaching Style that is required:

- **ENFP** = "Use friendly statements interacting quickly, using 'What-if' questions with motivational friendly positive feedback which do not interrupt with tutorial flow using conceptual ideas not too detailed."

- **INTP** = "Ask for written answers using 'What-if' questions and brief motivational objective feedback, designed to give support, autonomously interposed with the tutorial, using conceptual ideas not too detailed."

Defining Relationships between Learning Styles and Teaching Styles

In WISDeM the relationships between Personality Types and Learning/Teaching Styles and Motivational factors have been developed using these with each of the 16 personality types plotted on a scale of: 1) *Measured : Quick* (MQ), and 2) *Friendly : Reserved* (FR) (Figure 6). The feedback requirements have also been listed for each scale together with Novice/Expert factors: the novice learner tends to require more time and support, whereas the expert learner tends to require less time and support (Handley,

Figure 6: Plotting Personality Types

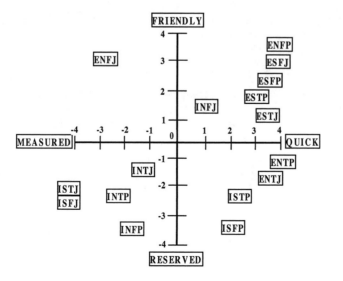

2002). Thus each personality type receives interaction based on the initial psychometric test results. This type is NOT "locked in stone," each learner has the facility to affect the way the system reacts by being able to change the amount and timing of support, interruption and feedback.

The Novice/Expert factors are changed as the learner progresses through the tutorial Q&A according to the depth of knowledge exhibited. The test system allocates a non-AI marker to 50% of the learners who are not able to change the interaction factors to enable controlled evaluation (Janvier & Ghaoui, 2002).

Using Interactive Questions and Answers

After using the tutorial facilities, the learner opens the multi-choice Question/ Answer "Revision" section, which is offered either as weekly or course revision, and starts to use the facility. All answers are logged and the learner's knowledge state is updated in his/her Learner Profile data table, these are retained to enable the learner to return at a later time to pick up his/her work. The facility offers: *Analysis Report, Answer Feedback, Correct Answer, Help, Hints, Next Question, Question Bibliography* and *Restart current/all Topic/s.*

WISDeM Current Position

WISDeM is still being developed. The DLT section has been operative for some time and has successfully been used by three modules, the generic structure is complete. The database administration section for authoring is nearing completion: the front-end allows a tutor to enter staff and student authorization and make basic screen presentation changes. MS Word, Excel and PowerPoint are used to create module content: HTML authoring is not required though can be used if required. Of the ITS section, the initial Student Profiler has been built and is currently being evaluated, initial replies from students indicate that this is working well and provides accurate profiles. The multi-choice question and answer section is part of the current DLT facility that has been used by the three modules; however, work is now underway to change this facility to include the AI and Motivational aspects discussed in this chapter. Thus the "Base Camp" of WISDeM is nearing completion.

FUTURE TRENDS

The "Base Camp" phase will be completed with a scientific evaluation to prove whether or not the research hypothesis that *"When a DLT-ITS interacts with the learner using his/her Communication Preference Language Patterns, Learning Styles and Motivational requirements, it increases Human Computer Interaction (HCI) communication capability and, thus, enhances learning experience and effectiveness"* is valid. A user-evaluation study will be designed and carried out soon. Research shows that most students prefer multi-modal communication (Fleming, 2001); thus use of AI in linking multi-modality will also be considered. Avatars aid learning (Colburn et al., 2000; Shaw, Ganeshan et al., 2000), for example ADELE, is a Bayesian Student Modelling expert centric animated pedagogical agent where development is now looking into eye gaze

(Colburn et al., 2000; Ganeshan et al., 2000; Mayo, 2001; Shaw et al., 2000); thus, the development of an interactive intelligent Avatar using eye-gaze must be considered for WISDeM, always taking into consideration the student's profile.

CONCLUSION

This chapter looked at the development of DLTs and ITSs and the fact that merging the two in a generic tool is preferable to independent development. It introduced the concept of using psychometric tests to pre-determine a student's profile, continued to demonstrate how this could be done and the requirement to match this initial profile with teaching styles BEFORE the student instigates modular learning, and also introduced the initial steps WISDeM is going through to reach the "Base Camp."

REFERENCES

Aimeur, E., Frasson, C., & Lalonde, M. (2001, March). The role of conflicts in the learning process. *SIGUE OUTLOOK, 27*(2), 12-27.

Borchert, R., Jensen, D., & Yates, D. (1999). *Hands-on and visualization modules for enhancement of learning in mechanics: Development and assessment in the context of Myers Briggs Types and VARK Learning Styles.* Paper presented at the ASEE Annual Conference, Charlotte, North Carolina, USA.

Bouras, C., & Philopulos, A. (2000). *Distributed virtual learning environment: A Web-based approach.* Paper presented at the 26th EUROMICRO Conference (EUROMICRO'00), Maastricht, The Netherlands.

Catania, A. C. (1992). *Learning - Remembering* (3rd ed.). Prentice-Hall International Editions.

Colburn, R. A., Cohen, M. F., & Drucker, S. M. (2000). *The role of eye gaze in Avatar Mediated Conversational Interfaces.* Microsoft Research, Microsoft Corporation, 1 Microsoft Way. Available on the World Wide Web: http://www.itpapers.com/cgi/PSummaryIT.pl?paperid=10265&scid=431.

Cooper, L. (2000). On-line courses: Tips for making them work. *Electronic Journal of Instructional Science and Technology (E-Jist), 3,* 20-25.

Djian, D., Azarmi, N., Azvine, B., Tsui, K. C., & Wobcke, W. (1999). *Towards human-centred intelligent systems: The intelligent assistant.* Available on the World Wide Web: http://www.bt.com/bttj/vol18no1/today/papers/d_djian/contents.htm.

Driscoll, S. A., & Garcia, C. E. (2000). *Preferred learning styles for engineering students.* Paper presented at the ASEE Annual Conference, St. Louis, Missouri, USA.

English, E., & Yazdani, M. (1999). Computer-supported cooperative learning in a Virtual University. *Journal of Computer Assisted Learning, 15 (An invited paper),* 2-13.

Fleming, N. (2001). *Teaching and Learning Styles: VARK Strategies.* Neil Fleming.

Fuller, D., Norby, R. F., Pearce, K., & Strand, S. (2000). Internet teaching by style: Profiling the on-line professor. *Educational Technology & Society, 3*(2), 71-85.

Ganeshan, R., Johnson, W. L., Shaw, E., & Wood, B. P. (2000). *Tutoring diagnostic problem solving.* Paper presented at the 5th International Conference, ITS 2000, Montreal, Canada, June.

Gertner, A. S., & VanLehn, K. (2000). *Andes: A coached problem solving environment for physics.* Paper presented at the Intelligent Tutoring Systems Conference, Montreal, Canada.

Ghaoui, C. (1996/1997). *A prototype system for the support of online flexible learning: Admin, Tutor and Student modes.* Two Internal Reports: Liverpool JMU [Published by a tertiary fellowship].

Handley, K. (2002, September 26-27). *Comparison of novice and expert learner's perception of instructional feedback in computer-based training to develop managerial problem-solving skills.* Paper presented at the HCT2002 Workshop, "Tools for Thought: Communication and Learning Through Digital Technology," Brighton, UK.

Hegarty, M., Phelan, A., & Kilbride, L. (1998). *Classrooms for Distance Teaching and Learning: A Blueprint.* Leuven, Belgium: Leuven University Press.

Hoover, T., & Connor, N. J. (2001). Preferred learning styles of Florida Association for Family and Community Education Volunteers: Implications for professional development. *Extension Journal, 39. Available on the World Wide Web: http:// www.joe.org/joe/2001june/a3.html.*

IsaBelle, C., & Nkambou, R. (1998). *A Framework for web-based Distance Learning Environments.* Universite de Moncton, Faculte des science de l'education, Moncton, Nouveau-Brunswick, Canada. Available on the World Wide Web: http:// citeseer.nj.nec.com/408083.html.

Janvier, W. A., & Ghaoui, C. (2001, September). *Searching for WISDeM, the Holy Grail of intelligent distance education.* Paper presented at the HCT2001 Workshop, "Information Technologies and Knowledge Construction: Bringing Together the Best of Two Worlds." University of Sussex, Brighton.

Janvier, W. A., & Ghaoui, C. (2002, November 1-4). *WISDeM: Student Profiling using Communication Preference and Learning Styles mapping to Teaching Styles.* Paper presented at the APCHI 2002, 5th Asia Pacific Conference on Computer Human Interaction, Beijing, China.

JCU. (2000). *Online Systems: Research and Evaluation* (Teaching and Learning Development project). James Cook University. Available on the World Wide Web: http:/ /www.tld.jcu.edu.au/general/syrvey_re/recs.html.

Larkin-Hein, T., & D. Budny, D. (2000). *Why bother learning about learning styles and psychological types?* Paper presented at ASEE Annual Conference, St. Louis, Missouri, USA.

Lieberman, H. (1997). *Autonomous interface agents.* Paper presented at the ACM Conference on Human-Computer Interface, Atlanta, Georgia, USA.

Marshall-University. (1999). *Comparison of online course delivery software products.* Marshall University. Available on the World Wide Web: http://www.marshall.edu/.

Mayo, M. J. (2001). *Bayesian student modelling and decision: Theoretic selection of tutorial actions in intelligent tutoring systems.* Ph.D. Thesis, University of Canterbury, New Zealand.

Montgomery, S. M., & Groat, L. N. (1998). *Student learning styles and their implications for teaching.* Centre for Research on Learning and Teaching, University of Michigan, USA. Available on the World Wide Web: http://www.crlt.umich.edu/ occ10.html.

Murphy, E., Newman, J., Jolosky, T., & Swank, P. (2002). *What is the Myers-Briggs Type Indicator (MBTI)®*. Association of Psychological Type. Available on the World Wide Web: http://www.aptcentral.org/.

Murray, T. (1999). Authoring intelligent tutoring systems: An analysis of the state of the art. *International Journal of Artificial Intelligence in Education, 10*, 98-129.

Myers, I. B., & Myers, P. B. (1995). *Gifts Differing: Understanding Personality Type*. Palo Alto, CA, USA: Consulting Psychologists Press (CPP Inc.), Financial Times, Prentice Hall.

Nkambou, R., Lefebvre, B., & Gauthier, G. (1996, January). *A curriculum-based student model for intelligent tutoring systems*. Paper presented at the Proceedings of the Fifth International Conference on User Modeling, Kailua-Kona, Hawaii.

Pasztor, A. (1997, August 7-10). *Intelligent agents with subjective experience*. Paper presented at the 19th Annual Conference of the Cognitive Science Society, Stanford University, Stanford, CA, USA.

Pasztor, A. (1998). Subjective experience divided and conquered, communication and cognition. In E. Myin (Ed.), *Approaching Consciousness, Part II* (pp. 73-102). Available on the World Wide Web: http://citeseer.nj.nec.com/pasztor98subjective.html.

Robotham, D. D. (1999). The application of learning style theory in higher education teaching. *GDN Discussion Papers*. Cheltenham, UK: Geography Discipline Network. Available on the World Wide Web: http://www.chelt.ac.uk/el/philg/gdn/discuss/index.htm.

Ryan, S., Scott, B., Freeman, H., & Patel, D. (2000). *The Virtual University: The Internet and Resource-Based Learning (open and distance learning)*. London: Kogan Page.

Sadowski, W., & Stanney, K. (1999). *Measuring and managing presence in virtual environments*. Lawrence Erlbaum Associates, Inc. Available on the World Wide Web: http://vehand.engr.ucf.edu/handbook/Chapters/Chapter45.html.

Schulze, K. G., Shelby, R. N., Treacy, D. J., Wintersgill, M. C., VanLehn, K., & Gertner, A. (2000). Andes: An intelligent tutor for classical physics. *The Journal of Electronic Publishing*, 1-6.

Shaw, E., Ganeshan, R., Johnson, W. L., & Millar, D. (2000). *Building a case for agent-assisted learning as a catalyst for curriculum reform in medical education*. Paper presented at the SSGRR 2000 Computer & e-Business Conference, International Conference on Advances in Infrastructure for Electronic Business, Science, and Education on the Internet, L'Aquila, Rome, Italy.

Urban-Lurain, M. (1999). *Intelligent tutoring systems: An historic review in the context of the development of Artificial Intelligence and educational psychology*. Available on the World Wide Web: http://aral.cse.msu.edu/Publications/ITS/its.htm.

VanLehn, K. (2000). *ANDES: An intelligent tutoring system for physics*. Available on the World Wide Web: http://www.pitt.edu/~vanlehn/andes.html.

Wær, A. (1997). *What is an Intelligent Interface? Introduction seminar*. Available on the World Wide Web: http://www.sics.se/~annika/papers/intint.html.

Yazdanir, M., & Lawler, R. W. (1987). Intelligent tutoring systems: An overview. In *Learning Environments and Tutoring Systems* (Vol. 1). Bristol, UK: Intellect Books.

Chapter V

An Expert-Based Evaluation Concerning Human Factors in ODL Programs:

A Preliminary Investigation

Athanasis Karoulis, Aristotle University of Thessaloniki, Greece

Ioannis Tarnanas, Aristotle University of Thessaloniki, Greece

Andreas Pombortsis, Aristotle University of Thessaloniki, Greece

ABSTRACT

In this chapter we describe the expert-based approach in evaluating Open and Distance Learning (ODL) environments. Our study is mainly concerned with the domains of Human-Computer Interaction (HCI) and Human Factors (HF), and the synergy between them in the field of ODL. The most promising approach to evaluating ODL is one which attempts to frame the ideas from distributed cognition research in a way that is more usable by HCI designers. Though the distributed cognition framework acknowledges a vast majority of cases suited to HCI designers and evaluators, it has never been tried before as a framework for the evaluation of the cognitive work that is distributed *among people, between persons and artifacts, across time and between abstract resources of information in the ODL domain. So, the main contribution of this chapter is on one hand to present the contemporary research on the domain, and, on the other hand to pinpoint the main concerns and to propose trends for further research on this complicated field that combines ODL, HCI and HF in such a holistic manner.*

INTRODUCTION

Most contemporary organizations spend enormous amounts on education and training in order to enhance the abilities of their human resources. A clear tendency in this direction is to utilize some alternative educational approaches, like Computer Based Training (CBT), distance learning or another technology-enhanced variation that better suits the needs of the particular organization.

Contemporary research on Human Factors has been concerned with participation and skill in the design and use of computer-based systems. Collaboration between researchers and users on this theme, starting with the pioneering work of Donald Norman (Norman, 1986) and Alan Newel (Card et al., 1983), has created a shift from the idea that Human Factors is a passive observation of users to the idea of Human Actors, where you create models for the interactions between actors, artifacts and the settings in which interaction occurs (Preece et al., 1994).

THE COMMUNICATION CHANNEL

Apart from its theoretical foundation as a research field, Open and Distance Learning still carries its "childhood diseases": the isolation of the student and the subsequent inactivity and loss of interest. Many solutions have been proposed, with varying levels of success, however, we believe the roots of this problem lie with an issue that almost any researcher of the field pinpoints: the transition of the traditional class to its distant counterpart breaks the personal contact between the participating parts and leads to the isolation of the student. However, the interaction between the members of the class has been proven to be of paramount importance in every educational environment and must not be underestimated. In terms of the scientific domains involved, the communication channel described here is the fusion of Human Factors, ODL and HCI. Rogers and Ellis (1994) argue that traditional task analysis is ineffective for modeling open distance learning and instead argue that a more appropriate unit of analysis is the network of people and technological artifacts involved in the work. In this approach, analysis focuses on the transformation of information representations as they are propagated around the network, and also how shared representations are used to coordinate learning through the communication channel. This so-called distributed cognition (DC) perspective has been used to describe a range of activities from navigating warships to solving children's puzzles, and DC has been discussed as one component of a theory to bridge research in CSCW, ODL and HCI (Nardi, 1996). Yet, despite this claim and despite the fact that the DC perspective is so obviously relevant to HCI theory and design, the ideas from distributed cognition research have not really gained visibility in the HCI community. So, we can argue that similarities and differentiations of traditional education and ODL emerge from the *fact* of granting knowledge, and from the *method* of granting it as well. The definition we prefer to follow here is that *"the communication channel is the modes, the methods and the tools that realize the communicative interaction between the participants and the instructional environment."*

To clarify this definition, we also attempt to describe it schematically. In the following diagrams, the whole set of arrowed lines constitutes the communication channel. The thickness of the line indicates the potential of the interaction, i.e., a thicker line indicates a stronger interaction, while a dotted line means a weaker interaction.

In the traditional approach, we experience the pattern in Figure 1.

Figure 1: The Traditional Communication Channel

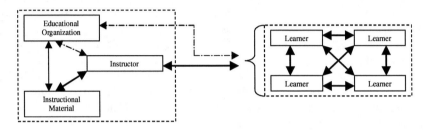

The instructor belongs to the educational organization and has a strong interaction with the educational material, which is produced by him/her (lectures, exercises, etc.) and by the educational organization (printed material, etc.). The "class" comes into contact with the educational material via the instructor, while the students maintain a strong social relationship amongst themselves, thus facilitating the exchange of knowledge and meta-knowledge. However, in the case where physical distance is experienced between the participants, as in the case of distance learning environments, the above pattern alters to that shown in Figure 2.

Figure 2: The ODL Communication Channel

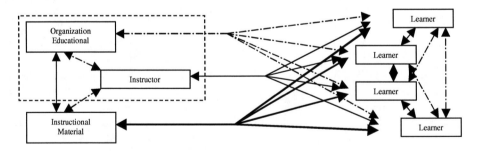

The notion of the class is no longer apparent, due to the individualization effect that occurs in all forms of distance learning. In addition, the notion of the teacher is much weaker as well, who is in this case often called the "tutor" because the learners mainly come into direct contact with the educational material, while the tutor fades out to a more supporting role. In this context the role of the tutor alters to a manager and facilitator of learning, rather than a director (Squires & McDougall, 1994). At the same time, the breaking up of the class in its parts (the students) leads to an individualised interaction between the tutor and every student, which however is also weaker.

It is now commonly advocated that cognition and learning are situated in specific learning contexts (e.g., Brown et al., 1989). A situated view of learning implies that effects on learning of using information and communication technology will depend on the context in which it is used, with all the components of a learning environment (people and artifacts) interacting and contributing to the learning process. According to this point of view, the attempt of third generation ODL systems has long been to upgrade the interaction between tutor and learners and learners themselves to a level that will be of advantage over the present situation. So, the communication channel seems to be a very substantial component of ODL, and its presence must be maintained at every cost. The first signs in this direction are positive. Indeed, an applicable solution seems to be telematics, which is based on ICT. For many providers of distance education, telematics (all forms of electronic communication) has stepped in and is often portrayed as a viable substitute for face-to-face contact, if not indeed a panacea for distance education in particular and education in general (Mugler & Landbeck, 2000).

THE EDUCATIONAL EVALUATION

Many writers have expressed their hope that constructivism will lead to better educational software and better learning (e.g., Brown et al., 1989; Papert, 1993). They stress the need for open-ended exploratory authentic learning environments in which learners can develop personally meaningful and transferable knowledge and understanding. The lead provided by these writers has resulted in the proposition of guidelines and criteria for the development of constructivist software and the identification of new pedagogies.

A recurrent theme of these guidelines, software developments and suggestions for use is that learning should be authentic, on a cognitive and contextual level. A tenet of constructivism is that learning is a personal, idiosyncratic process, characterised by individuals developing knowledge and understanding by forming and refining concepts (Piaget, 1952), which finally leads to the five main socio-constructive learning criteria (Squires & Preece, 1999) that must be met in order to characterize an educational piece as socio-constructive: credibility, complexity, ownership, collaboration and curriculum.

Human Factors research in the educational domain is investigating the visual search of computer menus and screen layouts. These models provide detailed empirically validated explanations of the perceptual, cognitive and motor processing involved (Kieras, 1988). However, there are certain known difficulties in the evaluation of educational environments in general, such as the difficulty to anticipate the instructional path every student will follow during the use of the software (Tselios et al., 2002), or the fact that such environments usually expand as they are used by the students (Hoyles, 1993). Nevertheless, in general, it is acclaimed to study the usability of an educational piece in relation to its educational value (Squires & Preece, 1999; Tselios et al., 2002).

However, the problem of evaluating educational software in terms of Human Factors is one shared by many HCI practitioners. It is important to know if a design is being used as it was intended. When a design is being used differently than intended, then it is important to discover if that use is compatible with current domain practice. The most promising approach to evaluating educational HF (Human Factors) is one which attempts to frame the ideas from DC (Distributed Cognition) research in a way that is more usable by HCI designers. This approach is described as the Distributed Information Resources Model (or Resources Model for short). The Resources Model takes seriously the idea introduced to HCI by Suchman (1987) that various types of information can serve as resources for action and a set of abstract information structures can be distributed between people and technological artifacts. The Resources Model also introduces the concept of interaction strategy and describes the way in which different interaction strategies exploit different information structures as resources for action. In this sense the Resources Model is an HCI model in the DC tradition. The aim of the continuing work on the domain is to apply the Resources Model to collaborative distance educational settings where resources are shared between individuals. In this way it is hoped to explore the value of the Resources Model as a framework for bridging between HCI, ODL and CSCW research.

Apart from Zhang's work on ODL (Zhang & Norman, 1994), there have been few explicit attempts to use the ideas of distributed cognition to account for HCI phenomena. Scaife and Rogers (1996) analyse graphical representations as forms of external cognition and emphasise the importance of considering how the properties of such representations can affect thinking and reasoning. However, they do not provide an account of action or interaction. Monk (1999) has pointed out that these models of display-based interaction represent only one kind of interaction. By developing a framework for classifying different interaction models, Monk demonstrates that graphical representation models are unable to model certain types of interaction, such as interaction with moded interfaces. Since control of action is entirely relegated to the display in these models, they would be unable to model error-free interaction with an interface possessing hidden modes. In order to avoid mode errors in these kinds of interfaces, the user's internal memory for the effects of previous actions must also play a role in controlling interaction. In order to capture a broader range of interaction styles, a more generic approach to the role of display information in supporting interaction is required, one which is capable of spanning a range of interaction styles. The resources model described earlier aims to achieve this by a more considered use of the ideas from distributed cognition described above.

EXPERT-BASED VS.
USER-BASED EVALUATIONS

The most commonly applied evaluation methodologies are the expert-based and the empirical (user-based) evaluation ones, according to the taxonomy of most researchers on the field (e.g., Preece et al., 1994; Lewis & Rieman, 1994). Expert-based evaluation is a relatively cheap and efficient formative evaluation method applied even on system prototypes or design specifications up to the almost ready-to-ship product. The main idea is to present the tasks supported by the interface to an interdisciplinary group of experts who will play as professional users and try to identify possible deficiencies in the interface design.

However, according to Lewis and Rieman (1994), "you can't really tell how good or bad your interface is going to be without getting people to use it." This phrase expresses the broad belief that user testing is inevitable in order to assess an interface. Why then, don't we just use empirical evaluations and continue to research expert-based approaches as well? This is because the efficiency of these methods is strongly diminished by the required resources and by various psychological restrictions of the participating subjects. On the other hand, expert-based approaches have meanwhile matured enough to provide a good alternative. Nowadays, expert-based evaluation approaches are well established in the domain of HCI. Cognitive Walkthrough (Polson et al., 1992) and its variations (Rowley & Rhoades, 1992; Karoulis et al., 2000), Heuristic Evaluation (Nielsen & Molich, 1990) and its variations (Nielsen, 1993) and Formal Usability Inspection (Kahn & Prail, 1994) are the most encountered approaches in the field.

An expert-based approach to Human Factors evaluation for educational software is primarily performed by using a distributed cognition approach and a multidisciplinary team of experts (Williams, 1993). A lot of the drawbacks to the application of this theory are shared with many other evaluation techniques used in HCI, particularly those relying on heuristics. One advantage of distributed cognition, with respect to too much data, is that the theory helps focus on where to look in the data by the emphasis on domain expertise and task relevant representational state. A second problem is that this method is time consuming, as with all analysis. Again, this is a problem that many analysis methods face, even those not video-based. It is a problem encountered in virtually all educational industries using HCI, where the pressure to "get the product out" is essential.

ADAPTATION TO THE WEB

According to Marchionini (1990), the use of hypermedia and the web allows the learners access to vast quantities of information of different types, control over the learning process, and interaction with the computer and other learners. A pilot study performed at Cornell University (Fitzelle & Trochim, 1996) had, as its primary research question, whether the web site enhanced student perceptions of learning. The research findings showed that students thought that the web site significantly enhanced their learning of course content. Student perceptions of performance in the course were also predicted by variables of enjoyment and control of the learning pace.

Every web-based instructional program is a collaborative environment on its own, allowing users to communicate and interact with all participating entities; therefore, in common with current thinking, cognition is "distributed" between users, the environment and learning artifacts, including computers, when learning takes place (Brown et al., 1989; Salomon, 1996). The distribution of cognition leads learners to construct their own concepts, which they use to learn.

In the domain of the evaluation of web-based courses, educational psychology provides many theoretical principles for application in the development and evaluation of online instructional technology. Milheim and Martin (1991), in studying learner control motivation, attribution and informational processing theory, identify learner control as an important variable in developing the pedagogy of web sites. It is beneficial to generally maximize learner control as it enhances the relevance of learning, expectations for success and general satisfaction, contributing to heightened motivation (Keller & Knopp, 1987). This research looked specifically at the control of pace by the student as a factor in building on existing theory. A tenet of constructivism is that learners direct their own learning either individually or through collaborative experiences. This implies that learners need to find their own pathways through learning; a philosophy that underpins hypertext and many web-based instructional systems (Murray, 1997). E-mail, listserves and web browsers also support this approach by enabling students to search for information and discuss issues with others around the world. So, one can infer that the collaborative and interactive nature of the web mainly supports learning by means of the augmented motivation of the student. On the other hand, it is common for students to make wrong assumptions or possess an incorrect mental model of the domain they study. However, HCI researchers are much better at understanding and augmenting the artifact. The artifact, in conjunction with the user, determines which operators users can apply to reach their goals and often plays a central role in maintaining state information for the task. It is time-consuming to evaluate sessions with users, and setting up a usability laboratory may cost a lot of money. There are researchers that suggest a way to overcome these problems, which is to move the usability laboratories to the users and experts (Catledge & Pitkow, 1995). By using the web as a usability laboratory, we are able to reach a wide range of users and experts. In order to achieve that, tools are needed that can monitor users' actions as well as allowing experts to send feedback about the interface. One environment suitable for the task at hand is the web itself. By creating interfaces in html and catching user events in the html pages, it also captures users' actions and cognitive states.

FROM HUMAN FACTORS TO HUMAN ACTORS

Computational cognitive modeling is emerging as an effective means to construct predictive engineering models of people interacting with computer systems (Preece et al., 1994). Cognitive models permit aspects of user interfaces to be evaluated for usability by making predictions based on task analysis and established principles of human performance. Cognitive models can predict aspects of performance, such as task execution time, based on a specification of the interface and task. Cognitive modeling can thus reduce the need for user testing early in the development cycle. Cognitive models can also reveal underlying processing that people use to accomplish a task, which can help designers to build interfaces and interaction techniques that better complement the actual processing that humans apply to a task. When built with an architecture such as EPIC (executive process-interactive control, Kieras, 1988), ACT-R/PM (atomic components of thought with rational analysis and perceptual/motor enhancements, Anderson & Garisson, 1995), or EPIC-Soar (the Soar architecture with enhancements from EPIC), cognitive models also contribute to Allen Newell's grand vision of a unified theory of cognition (Card et al., 1983). Methodologies for applying cognitive architectures to predict aspects of human performance and learnability are still evolving (Kirschenbaum et al., 1996).

On the other hand, Heuristic Evaluation (Nielsen & Molich, 1990) and Formal Usability Inspection (Kahn & Prail, 1994) are criteria- or heuristic-based methodologies. So, the next point of concern is the appropriate list of criteria or heuristics needed to assess the environment. As already stated, a good starting point provides the socio-constructivist view of instruction. Some studies in the field (e.g., Tselios et al., 2001) are based on the constructivist approach for open learning environments, sometimes also

Table 1: The Learnability Heuristic List, according to Tselios et al. (2001)

a1 Does the system facilitate the active interaction of the user?
a2 Is the development of personal problem solving strategies by the learners possible?
a3 Are tools available, corresponding to the way he learns and to his/her cognitive level?
a4 Are the available tools of alternating transparency, so that it is possible to express differentiations between students as well as intrinsic differentiations of every student?
a5 Does the environment afford experimentation with the acquired knowledge?
a6 Are there multiple representations and multiple solutions that students can explore?
a7 Is there adequate system feedback and progress feedback, so that the student can reconsider his/her strategies?
a8 Is there the possibility for the student to assess his/her activities on his/her own?

known as micro-worlds (Papert, 1980). Their study concludes by presenting a set of learnability heuristics (see Table 1).

Squires and Preece (1999) proceed one step further: they do not make a combination, but a fusion of Nielsen's heuristics with the five socio-constructivist learning criteria (credibility, complexity, ownership, collaboration and curriculum) thus providing a new list, which they claim to be a versatile tool in predictably evaluating educational pieces by their usability and simultaneous learnability. They state that the underlying socio-constructivist theory of nearly every contemporary educational environment is, to a high degree, compatible to the stated Nielsen-heuristics. The authors conclude with a list of "learning heuristics," as shown in Table 2 (Squires & Preece, 1999).

Finally, a study performed by Karoulis and Pombortsis (2003) regarding ODL environments concluded with a more comprehensive criteria list, containing 10 axes with 53 criteria, which is intended for a more holistic and detailed evaluation of the environment (see Table 3).

A different approach, with comparable goals, is to arrange for a cognitive HF model to interact directly with applications through their user interfaces. The main drawback is that the model must now address a new set of complexities dealing with visual processing, object manipulation, action planning, and so forth, to a greater level of detail than required by the approaches above. The potential advantages of extending a cognitive model in this way, however, are compelling:

- *Ecological validity*. By their nature, interface simulations and specifications are abstractions; they often pay attention to unimportant details of a real interface. Real user interfaces exhibit variations in timing, predictability and reliability of

Table 2: The Learning Heuristics, according to Squires and Preece (1999)

1. Match between designers' and learners' mental models.
2. Ensure navigational fidelity.
3. Provide appropriate levels of learner control.
4. Prevent peripheral cognitive errors.
5. Understandable and meaningful symbolic representation.
6. Support personally significant approaches to learning.
7. Build strategies for the cognitive error recognition, diagnosis and recovery cycle.
8. Match with the curriculum.

Table 3: The Holistic List, according to Karoulis and Pombortsis (2003) (the criteria are omitted)

```
1.  Content
2.  ODL adaptation and integration
3.  User interface
4.  Use of technologies
5.  Interactivity with the instructional material
6.  Student's support
7.  Communication channel
8.  Acquisition of knowledge
9.  Projects and "learning by doing"
10. Assessment and self-assessment
```

actions, as well as the occurrence of events uninitiated by the user, among other behavioral properties, which may or may not be relevant to the performance on a given task. Neglecting these subtleties, however, can bring the validity of empirical cognitive modeling results into question. We can forestall potential objections along these lines by reducing the distance between cognitive models and real environments.

- *Real-world problem relevance.* Cognitive modeling goals usually include a concern for solving problems of general interest, rather than focusing solely on problems for model calibration or benchmarking. Real user interfaces easily provide real-world problems; additional design and maintenance effort is required to replicate such problems in a simulation or specification.
- *External standards for comparison.* Progress in cognitive modeling often arises from comparisons of different models on the same problem. In some cases it is straightforward to determine whether two instances of a problem are directly comparable. However, as researchers take on more complex problems in richer environments, this determination can be more difficult, especially if the tested interfaces differ significantly (e.g., an active simulation in one case and a symbolic specification in another). This difficulty can be isolated if environmental information and interactions stem from a single independent source, a real user interface.
- *Development effort.* In some cognitive modeling efforts, considerable work is devoted to developing realistic user interface scenarios, either as static representations or device simulations. Ironically, much of this effort reproduces functionality that already exists in a form appropriate for human users, but is inaccessible (e.g., programmatically) to a cognitive model.

CONCERNS

The main question that remains unanswered with regards to the learnability of the environment is whether the experts are really able to predict the problems experienced by the learners and the cognitive domain of the environment. Some studies in the field (e.g., Tselios et al., 2001) argue that an expert evaluator cannot predict the students' performance, although he/she can assess heuristically the learnability of the environment, with mediocre results.

Another issue that needs further research is the protest stated by Spoole and Schröder (2001) regarding the optimal number of evaluators. The authors presented the results of some recent research that brings into question the long-standing rule of thumb put forth by Jakob Nielsen (Nielsen & Molich, 1990), concerning his description of Heuristic Evaluation. The point of contention is whether one can truly find the majority of usability problems in complex web sites by employing a very small number of testers. The Nielsen rule of thumb, referred to by the authors as the "parabola of optimism," states that five testers can find 85% of the problems in a web site regardless of its size. In contrast, Spoole and Schröder's research indicates that the number of testers needed increases linearly with the size of the web site. There are some objections to this statement, mainly because the heuristic methodology is not task-based and because simple test users have been proven not to perform well in heuristic approaches. However, the claim of Spoole and Schröder (2001) becomes too important to be ignored, because educational sites can expand greatly, users mainly perform tasks in such sites and ODL includes de facto the cognitive parameter of inexperienced users.

FUTURE TRENDS

The expert-based approach, as presented in this chapter, does not yet seem suitable for a holistic evaluation of the environment. We are entering the age of ubiquitous computing in which our environment is evolving to contain computing technology in a variety of forms. Such environments, also called "media spaces" (Stults, 1988) are developments in ubiquitous computing technology, involving a combination of audio, video and computer networking. They are the focus of an increasing amount of research and industrial interest into support for distributed collaborative work.

These concerns are of interest for ODL ubiquitous environments, as a large amount of educational and private data is circulating between the participating entities. The assessment of such an environment is a challenge for expert-based evaluation of Human Factors.

CONCLUSION

The two roles of expert-based evaluation in Human Computer Interaction (HCI) are to aid design and analysis. Distributed Cognition is a theoretical framework that differs from mainstream cognitive science by not concentrating on the individual human actor as the unit of analysis. Distributed Cognition acknowledges that in a vast majority of cases cognitive work is not being done in isolation inside our heads but is *distributed* among people, between persons and artifacts, and across time. This has a natural fit for ODL, where the behavior we are interested in is the interaction of all the involved entities through the communication channel, the system of people and artifacts. What makes a system cognitive is the presence of processes applied to representational states that result in cognitive work. Tracking the representational states can uncover the specific cognitive processes being employed. In a system, these representational states can be directly observable. While the movement of the boundary of the unit of analysis from individual to system facilitates observation, there is still the difficult task of deciding which observed representations are actually relevant representational states for a particular cognitive activity. Theory and domain expertise work together during observation to aid an analyst in determining these task relevant representational states. However, the method differs from these other fields by the pervasive influence of the distributed cognition theory.

Cognitive theory is far from sacrosanct. Indeed, in recent years the dynamicism of mainstream cognitive theory has been shown by its adaptation and incorporation of the connectionist challenge from below and its recent response to the challenge of situated action from above (e.g., Zhang & Norman, 1994). We firmly believe that applied cognition must be based upon cognitive theory.

REFERENCES

Anderson, T.D., & Garisson, D.R. (1995). Critical thinking in distance education: Developing critical communities in an audio teleconferencing context. *Higher Education, 29*, 183-199.

Brown, J.S., Collins, A. & Duguid, P. (1989). Situated cognition and the culture of learning. *Educational Researcher, 18*(1), 32-42.

Card, S.K., Moran, T.P., & Newell, A. (1983). *The Psychology of Human-Computer Interaction*. Hillsdale, NJ: Lawrence Erlbaum Associates.

Catledge L. D., & Pitkow J. E. (1995). Characterizing browsing strategies in the World Wide Web. *Computer Networks and ISDN Systems, 27*, 1065-1073.

Fitzelle, G., & Trochim, W. (1996). *Survey evaluation of web site instructional technology: Does it increase student learning?* Retrieved from the World Wide Web: http://trochim.human.cornell.edu/webeval/intro.htm.

Hoyles, C. (1993). Microworlds/schoolworlds: The transformation of an innovation. In C. Keitel & K. Ruthven (Eds.), *Learning from Computers: Mathematics Educational Technology* (pp. 1-7). Berlin: Springer-Verlag.

Kahn, M., & Prail, A. (1994). Formal usability inspections. In J. Nielsen & R. L. Mack (Eds.), *Usability Inspection Methods* (pp. 141-171). New York: John Wiley & Sons.

Karoulis, A., & Pombortsis, A. (2003). Heuristic evaluation of web-based ODL programs. In C. Ghaoui (Ed.), *Usability Evaluation of On-Line Learning Programs* (pp. 86-107). New York: IDEA.

Karoulis, A., Demetriades, S., & Pombortsis, A. (2000). The cognitive graphical jogthrough – An evaluation method with assessment capabilities. In *Applied Informatics 2000 Conference Proceedings* (pp. 369-373), February 2000, Innsbruck, Austria. Anaheim, CA: IASTED/ACTA.

Keller, J., & Knopp, T. (1987). *Instructional Theories in Action: Lessons Illustrating Theories and Models*. Hillsdale, NJ: Erlbaum Associates.

Kieras, D. E. (1988). Towards a practical GOMS model methodology for user interface design. In M. Helander (Ed.), *The Handbook of Human-Computer Interaction* (pp. 135-158). Amsterdam: North-Holland.

Kirschenbaum, S. A., Gray, W. D., & Young. (1996). Cognitive architectures for human-computer interaction. *SIGCHI Bulletin*.

Lewis, C., & Rieman, J. (1994). *Task-centered user interface design: A practical introduction*. Retrieved from the World Wide Web: ftp.cs.colorado.edu/pub/cs/distribs/HCI-Design-Book.

Marchionini, G. (1990). Evaluating hypermedia-based learning. In D. H. Jonassen & H. Mandl (Eds.), *Designing Hypermedia for Learning* (pp. 355-376). NATO ASI Series, 67. Springer Verlag.

Milheim, W.D., & Martin B.L. (1991). Theoretical bases for the use of learner control: Three different perspectives. *Journal of Computer-Based Instruction, 18*(3), 99-105.

Monk, A.F. (1999). Modeling cyclic interaction. *Behaviour & Information Technology, 18*(2), 127-139.

Mugler, Fr., & Landbeck, R. (2000). Learning, memorisation and understanding among distance learners in the South Pacific. *Learning and Instruction, 10*(2), 179-201.

Murray, J. H. (1997). *Hamlet on the Holodeck: The Future of Narrative in Cyberspace*. New York: The Free Press.

Nardi, B.A. (1996). *Context and Consciousness: Activity Theory and Human-Computer Interaction*. Cambridge: MIT Press.

Nielsen, J. (1993). *Usability Engineering*. San Diego: Academic Press.

Nielsen, J., & Molich, R. (1990). Heuristic evaluation of user interfaces. In *Proceedings of Computer-Human Interaction Conference* (CHI) (pp. 249-256). Seattle, WA.

Norman, D.A. (1986). Cognitive engineering. In D. Norman & S. Draper (Eds.), *User Centered System Design*. Hillsdale, NJ: Lawrence Erlbaum Associates.

Papert, S. (1980). *Mindstorm: Children, Computers and Powerful Ideas*. New York: Basic Books.

Papert, S. (1993). *The Children's Machine: Rethinking School in the Age of the Computer*. New York: Basic Books.

Piaget, J. (1952). *The Origins of Intelligence in Children*. New York: International University Press.

Polson, P.G., Lewis, C., Rieman, J., & Warton, C. (1992). Cognitive walkthroughs: A method for theory-based evaluation of user interfaces. *International Journal of Man-Machine Studies, 36*, 741-773.

Preece, J., Rogers, Y., Sharp, H., Benyon, D., Holland, S., & Carey, T. (1994). *Human-Computer Interaction*. Addison-Wesley.

Rogers, Y., & Ellis, J. (1994). Distributed Cognition: an alternative framework for analysing and explaining collaborative working. *Journal of Information Technology, 9*(2), 119-128.

Rowley, D., & Rhoades, D. (1992, May). The cognitive jogthrough: A fast-paced user interface evaluation procedure. In *Proceedings of the ACM, CHI '92* (pp. 389-395). Monterey, CA.

Salomon, G. (ed.). (1996). *Distributed Cognitions: Psychological and Educational Considerations*. Cambridge: Cambridge University Press.

Scaife, M., & Rogers, Y. (1996). External cognition: How do graphical representations work? *International Journal of Human-Computer Studies, 45*, 185-213.

Spoole, J., & Schröder, W. (2001). Testing web sites: Five users is nowhere near enough. In *Proceedings of the ACM - CHI 2001*.

Squires, D., & McDougall, A. (1994). *Choosing and Using Educational Software: A Teachers' Guide*. London: Falmer Press.

Squires, D., & Preece, J. (1999). Predicting quality in educational software: Evaluating for learning, usability, and the synergy between them. *Interacting with Computers, 11*(5) 467-483

Stults, R. (1988). The experimental use of video to support design activities. *Xerox PARC Technical Report SSL-89-19*. Palo Alto, California.

Suchman, L.A. (1987). *Plans and Situated Actions: The Problem of Human Computer Interaction*. Cambridge: Cambridge University Press.

Tselios, N., Avouris, N., & Kordaki, M. (2002). Student task modeling in design and evaluation of open problem-solving environments. *Education and Information Technologies, 7*(1) 19-42.

Tselios, N.K., Avouris, N.M., & Kordaki, M. (2001). A tool to model user interaction in open problem solving environments. In N. Avouris & N. Fakotakis (Eds.), *Advances in Human-Computer Interaction* (pp. 91-95). Patras, Greece: Typorama.

Williams, K. E. (1993). Automating the cognitive task modeling process: An extension to GOMS for HCI. In *Proceedings of the Fifth International Conference on Human-Computer Interaction Poster Sessions* (Vol 3., p. 182). Abridged Proceedings.

Zhang, J., & Norman, D.A. (1994). Representations in distributed cognitive tasks. *Cognitive Science, 18*, 87-122.

Chapter VI

Integrated E-Learning System and Its Practice

Toshio Okamoto, University of Electro-Communications, Japan

Mizue Kayama, Senshu University, Japan

ABSTRACT

In this chapter, we present an intelligent media oriented e-learning system. In this system, we have developed a LMS (Learning Management System), some learning control systems and some learning media, with a flexible framework. It is intended to provide a collaborative workplace to encourage interactions among lecturer/learners. Moreover, we propose an innovative educational method of a cooperative link between a university and an industry for higher education. We analyze these results and the problems we encountered, as well as offer constructive solutions. Furthermore, we have developed some intelligent media such as an analyzer/summarizer by the statistical natural language processing for data log of discussion process to encourage/aware discussion/negotiation between learners and an automatic reporting processor.

INTRODUCTION

One could never predict the explosive growth of the Internet. This growth is so close, tight and wide that everyone feels the power/magic of the information evolution. Education certainly is riding on its waves. The "Internet" is becoming the catch phrase in the world of school education, which makes distance education possible to anyone at anytime and from anywhere. As such, a new learning style called "e-learning" emerged under the new umbrella concept of "Learning Ecology," where the Internet raises the level of communications and collaborations among people via technology.

In retrospect, the traditional computer-assisted instruction (CAI) underpinning e-learning comprised early attempts to realize the environment of individual learning and assure a learner's fundamental competency. However, CAI was a closed system within a certain educational school. Therefore, it did not spread out widely/deeply into society. Nevertheless, it is quite valuable to review the various kinds of results taken from CAI research/development, such as authoring functions, learning support functions, supervising functions, delivering functions and so on.

Nowadays, the concept/system of e-learning is rapidly widespread with the advent and prevalence of the Internet. On one hand, via the Internet, people can communicate with each other at anytime and from anywhere. On the other hand, people can share, rebuild, stock and reuse the various kind of information. Here it is clear that e-learning gets the citizenship in the educational society instead of CAI. As a response to the social advance, it is necessary to construct a new learning society such as individual learning, learning organization and learning community. As mentioned above, we can say that the Internet is a kind of "Treasure Island" of educational resources worldwide, although it includes much harmful information.

To date, the need for an understanding of e-learning issues has not been met by a coherent set of principles for examining past work and plotting fruitful directions. Obviously, it would be difficult to document the many seeds sown now. However, it was not an accident that an early example in Japan was at the University of Electro-Communications, where my colleagues and I were the first, in the end of 1990s, to report on efforts to develop an e-learning system called RAPSODY. From our experience and a few other pioneering efforts in e-learning researches, we attempt to define/catalog the e-learning environment as follows:

- Individual learning environment with learning materials
- Group learning environment such as a collaborative learning
- Classroom learning (lecturing)

This learning ecology has the mixed mode of either synchronous or asynchronous by using any teaching/learning contents, audio/visual devices such as video-conference/meeting, and communications tools such as Chat/e-mail via the Internet.

In this chapter, we start by discussing the relationship between digital technologies and human learning. Secondly, we introduce the framework of "e-learning" in the Internet Era and propose a new learning ecology for broadband communication technologies. Then, we show the integrated e-learning system called RAPSODY, which has the learning management system (LMS) that consists of managing functions of learning materials/curriculum, learners' profile and information, learning log-data and guiding of learning objects. Moreover, we describe our educational practice/experience carried out between our university and companies as a cooperative linkage program. In addition, we introduce the architecture of the collaborative learning platform with knowledge management oriented shared memory in order to support participants' awareness and learning achievement. Finally, we propose the future direction of e-learning ecology and technologies in consideration of educational meanings.

BACKGROUND AND POTENTIALS OF E-LEARNING

When we think modality of the computerization education, it is generally categorized as follows:

1. Self-study entity through electronic information media-based (e.g., computer) materials/courseware
2. The learning entity with the electronic information media (e.g., computer) as learning tools/problem-solving/representation/transmission medium
3. The learning entity about information and communication technology/social problems/others
4. Computerizing entity of the education itself

The relationships among those entities are mutually compensated and an e-learning cycle is developed. Although the ideas here are in line with building the environment for "anybody" to learn something from "anywhere" and at "anytime" in the e-society, if classified roughly, there are two purposes of expansions: on one hand to enlarge the study opportunity, and on another to develop people's new competence.

The Significance of Digital Society

In the 21st century, the digitalized society makes time faster and space closer; moreover, the whole world is full of the swirl of a lump of huge information. It seems that we cannot distinguish between a natural occurrence and an artificial one.

Here, we specify the features of the digital/network society:

1. Based on digital technology, it is possible to represent and process various information/knowledge in the same environment/context. Multimedia, as one of the e-media, provides a platform to create some artificial matters with all kinds of virtues/value.
2. It provides a cyberspace for mutual communications from everywhere and at any time.
3. In this cyberspace, it is possible to keep track of all kinds of activities for data-sharing/reusing.
4. It supports all kinds of activities by employing reinforcement tools (e.g., representation/cognitive/creation action amplifier).
5. The information technology acts as a stimulus to the business growth (i.e., alter the business qualitatively) in all fields of politics and economics, enterprises, medical, education, welfare, environment, research activities, and others.

The development and widespread use of Internet technology provide four possibilities as follows:

1. Enable always-on connections (i.e., constant access to the Internet)
2. Enable obtaining high capacity content in a short time via the high-speed line/cable
3. Enable obtaining high-quality contents, e.g., high-definition images or clear voice
4. Allow interactive communications/interfaces smoothly

Based on the above communications underpinnings, the following e-learning needs/services emerged with development of digital technologies and media:

1. Multi-student-users can make and use one content via the Internet collaboratively, e.g., programming, music, novel, painting, and some other productions.
2. Students can get one-to-one/individualized instruction from expert, and thereby acquire expertise.
3. People can take part in activities in a virtual environment (e.g., field trip/sketching events/concert/role-play). These activities cannot be played easily in daily life.
4. It is possible to roam museums/libraries/beauty spots and historical landmarks around the world.
5. It is possible to execute the transmission of high-definition images/voice data and high-computation software simultaneously.

Absolutely, these possibilities break a new ground for the establishment of all kinds of educational environments. Therefore, we have to rebuild the new framework/ways of educational system, organization and management.

The Design of E-Learning and Educational Environment

Our educational environment, using broadband networks, is built on three dimensions: the first one is the pedagogical goal representing the capacities/knowledge to acquire, the second one is the subject content, and for the third axis the learning modes are defined by seven components:

1. Distance individual learning environment. This environment provides courseware for knowledge/skills acquisition (i.e., e-learning course like WBT/VOD systems).
2. Distance individual learning environment for the discovery learning using various search engines/VOD search/navigation mechanism.
3. Problem-solving learning in distance individual learning environment using simulations/support learning tools/others.
4. Videoconference system in collaborative learning environment, like instructional presentation/question-answer/multi-multi-sites telecommunications.
5. Collaborative learning in a small group/pairs, i.e., video-conference mechanism, accompanied with chat tool/other communication tools/various applications/a screen shared viewer/learning log mechanism.
6. Collaborative simulation learning type. Different learners perform different functions in teamwork learning pattern, and as such form a special skill in the learner's own domain, e.g., a collaborative activity within the huge jet plane's cockpit.
7. Linkage/coordination among different organizations/areas, e.g., access online school's library, online museum, etc.

In the establishment of education environments, the most important idea is to start by defining the instructional goal, and then the classifying of learning contents that are best equipped to build the learning environment; additionally, the research on the method is required to build the asynchronous collaborative learning contents. Further research directions should be put on the study of the learning environment with the virtues of individualized learning and collaborative learning as well. In this case, the transmission of the real images and voice data is required. The fundamental environment components for e-learning systems of the next century are shown in Figure 1, which demonstrates the whole information system related to e-learning environments. It consists of several management functions, such as curriculum/learning, materials management, learners' profile/log-data management, learning supporting, etc., as LMS. To construct those educational management systems, we need, technologically, several data/file-processing modules such as distributed file system, synchronous data communications and so on. If any applications and tools related to e-learning can be plugged in this platform, we would build a collaborative learning environment where learners can share/operate these software/data in real time. In addition, the total management system of e-learning is required for executing a real educational project/practice, which means research project management, learning schedule management, courseware developing and so on.

THE INTEGRATED E-LEARNING SYSTEM: RAPSODY

What is RAPSODY?

RAPSODY is an integrated guide system that can logically connect individual learning units. Its primary idea is "CELL" corresponding to the LOM proposed by IEEE-LTSC (IEEE-LTSC, 2000), and is intentionally focused on three primary aspects in order to represent educational meaning within the distance learning environment: learning goals, learning contents and learning media in order to share digital learning materials. We call this conceptual scheme the Distance Ecological Model (Okamoto, 2001). Each of the CELLs also has several other attributes (slots), such as features of the material,

Figure 1: The Concept of Framework for Media Mixed E-Learning Environment

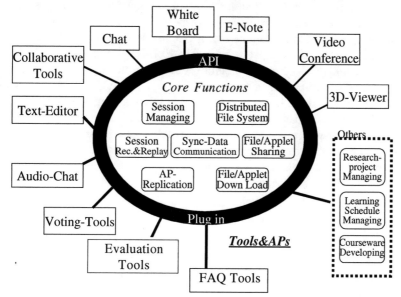

Table 1: The Frame Representation of the CELL

	Frame-name	Slot-value
Slot-name	Learning objectives for a learner	Subjects which should be understood Subjects which should be mastered
	Subject-contents	The unit topic
	Learning form	The prepared learning environment
	Evaluating method	The learners' evaluation method
	Useful tools	The software used for the learning activity
	Operational manual of tool	The software operation method used for the learning activity
	Prepared media	The learning media which can be utilized
	Guide-script	The file which specifies the dialog between learner and system

available tools, a related CELL, Guide-Script, etc., besides Table 1. From a user's (learner) point of view, this model seems to be quite transparent in order to identify/select his/her learning conditions, and the system can easily guide toward an adequate Learning Object according to his/her requirements. The phrase "Ecological Model" means multi-modal "learning environment." This concept means to assure free accessibility to learning goals, learning contents and learning media/environment according to a user's need anytime and anywhere. We use the ecological model in the wider sense of ecology.

This system can logically link the CELLs based on the Distance Ecological Model of RAPSODY, which provides the learning guide environment by taking into consideration each user's individual learning needs/conditions. The Distance Ecological Model is built on three aspects. The first one represents the learning goals or competency specification in terms of any curriculum. The second one stands for the aspect of the curriculum (subject-contents). From the third aspect, the favorite learning media (form) can be chosen, e.g., VOD, videoconference, or distance learning/education. By selecting a position on each of the three aspects, a certain CELL is determined. A CELL consists of several slots, which represent the features/characteristics of the Learning Object. Especially, the most important slot in the CELL is "Script," which describes the instruction guidelines of the learning contents, the self-learning procedure, and so on. In the following, we will explain the meaning of learning media in more details. Figure 2 shows the conceptual generated framework. The concept of the CELL in the Distance Ecological Model is quite important, because it generates the learning scenario, including the information to satisfy the learner's needs, the learning-flow of subject materials and the guidelines for self-learning navigation.

Operating Flow in RAPSODY

This system aims to support self-learning. The role of this system is first to identify a CELL in the model according to the learners' needs. Then, the system tries to set up an effective learning environment by retrieving the proper materials for the learner, along with the Guide-Script defined in the corresponding CELL. So, the system offers programs for both Retrieving and Interpreting. The system's executing steps are as follows:

Step 1: Record the learner's needs.

Step 2: Select a CELL in the Distance Ecological Model according to the learner's needs.

Step 3: Interpret the CELL in the guide WM (Working Memory).

Step 4: Develop interactive learning with the learner according to the Guide-Script in the guide WM.

Step 5: Store the log-data of the dialog. The log-data collects information on the learning histories and learners' needs and behaviors.

Step 6: Provide the needed and useful applications for the user's learning activities and set up an effective learning environment.

Step 7: Give guidance-information, according to the CELL script guidelines, and decide on the proper CELL for the next learning step.

The system architecture related to the process of learning guide/support is shown in Figure 3. It is necessary to explain the dialog mechanism (algorithm) between user and system. The interpreter controls and develops the dialog process between user and machine according to the information defined in Guide-Script description language. This Guide-Script description language (GSDL) consists of some tags and a simple grammar for interpreting a document, similar to the HTML (Hypertext Markup Language) on the WWW. The interpreter understands the meanings of the tags, and interprets the contents. The description form by GSDL is shown:

1.   <free> Definition: description of the text (instruction)
2.   <slot (num.)> Definition: a link to a slot value in the CELL
3.   <question> Definition: questions to a learner

Figure 2: The Conceptual Scheme of the Learning Ecological Model and RAPSODY

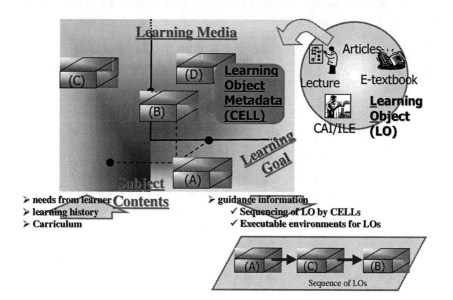

Figure 3: The System Architecture of RAPSODY

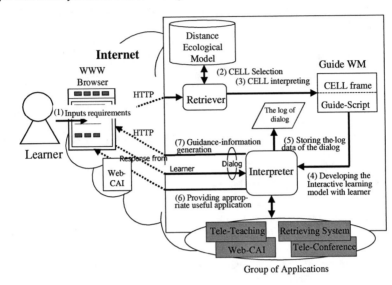

4.   <choice> Def.: branching control according to a learner's response
5.   <exe> Call: to relevant CELLs
6.   <app> Def.: applications for learning activities (Tele-Teaching, etc.)

COOPERATIVE LINKAGE BETWEEN UNIVERSITY AND INDUSTRY BY RAPSODY

The Industry and University cooperation program is the political project proposed by the Japanese Ministry of Education (MEXT). The objective of this program is not only the completion of an environment where upstanding members of the society with business, industry or university background can learn, but also to the connection and harmonization of university educational research and society practice and practical business. Specifically, the program aims at offering the university student access to the practical, business point of view and practical knowledge on one hand, and the industry and company employee an opportunity to improve oneself and an access to higher knowledge and education (Salvador, 1999). In this way, we are promoting an educational collaboration program that binds university and industry (Okamoto, 2001. The Ministry of Education has appointed the University of Electro-Communications (UEC) with the enacting of this cooperation program between Industry and University. The target learners are industry people as well as regular students of the university who wish to learn about the new Information Technology (IT) issues. The actual putting into practice involves the extension of the existing curriculum toward more flexibility (Rosenberg, 2001; Slomen, 2001; Nieminen, 2001; Chen, 2001).

In this section, we report on our experiences with introducing this program, about the framework, settings, actual implementation and first results. We analyze these results and the problems we encountered, as well as offer constructive solutions. Furthermore, we have developed the knowledge repository in an e-learning environment, such as an analyzer/summarizer by the statistical natural language processing for data log of discussion/communication process between learners and a teacher, though we can't introduce its details here.

The Program

The subject of career development involving acquisition of high experience and knowledge in the field of information communication technology is an important subject for the future information communication society. The starting courses of the program involve this discipline. The lectures were focused on high information technology, large-scale information system planning and application, and network technology. For the first year period, the courses involved the following topics:

* Multimedia Communication Technology
* Information Security

Moreover, the appointed lecturers for the industry and university cooperation program are not only researchers and professors from our graduate school, but also company researchers and implementers as well. This is due to the fact that it is important for students to acquire knowledge about not only the theoretical side related to information systems, but also about the practical side.

The lectures are held as collaborative lectures of the type called "omnibus" (each lecturer presents only one lecture). Although this new curriculum is of a flexible nature, with many evening hours (to ensure easy participation from far sites) and a relatively concentrated information contents given over a short time period (again, to ensure that company workers loose not too many hours with this program), the UEC graduate school has established a regular credit system for certification purposes. The level of certification is master level.

Experimental Situation

Here we report an example situation of a lecture entitled "multimedia communication science/technology and application." The syllabus of this lecture includes: multimedia and distributed cooperation, CSCL (collaborative system collaborative learning) and collaborative memory, multimedia communication technology, ATM networks, new Internet technology, media representation form and application, data mining, multimedia and distributed cooperation learning support systems, knowledge management, standardization and new business models. The total number of learners attending the lecture was 63, among who only 13 were curriculum students. This time, the distance company sites that cooperated were located near Tokyo, in Kanagawa prefecture. The distance companies were linked via Internet and ISDN circuit, therefore establishing a real time bi-directional information transmitting and receiving environment. Figure 4 displays the geographical distribution of the distance company sites.

From the distance company sites to the UEC, the needed round trip time of the closest site is two hours by public transportation, and for the furthermost the round trip is about six hours. Therefore, considering the hours of time saved and the convenience of the distance education method, the system presents evident merit for both learners from far company sites as well as company managers.

Figure 4: Location Map of Company Sites

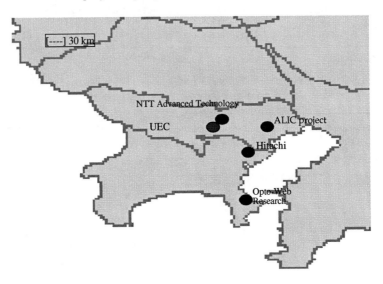

E-Learning System Configuration

It is necessary to provide a lecture environment that guarantees both the lecture movie, sound and lecture materials presentation distribution for attending students, as well as a dialogue function supporting the communication between lecturer and students. We have implemented these functions by using a VOD (Peltoniemi, 1995; Hui, 2000) server and a WWW (World Wide Web) server. Figure 5 shows the system configuration of the distance learning system.

Each site has to configure the transmission server and the viewer. Each distance lecture site establishes two dedicated channels: one for receiving only and one for sending only. By connecting respectively the lecture classroom transmission with the distance site reception and the distance site transmission with the lecture classroom reception, bi-directional communication is implemented. Each function is outlined:

1.   Transmission function of lecture's movie and sound: the movie and sound of the lecture is distributed to the attending sites with the help of the VOD server real time transmission function (Okamoto, 2000b). Moreover, in the case of some companies, their Internet access and therefore, the transmission/reception of lecture movie and sound is not free. To cope with such a network environment, we had to ensure a dedicated Proxy server that relays the distribution of lecture movie and sound between Internet sites, to ensure the data reception. Students at far sites attend lectures by viewing the lecture movie and sound data distributed by the VOD server.

2.   Lecture material presentation function: the lecture materials are formatted as HTML (Hyper Text Markup Language) sources and offered to students via the WWW server. Students use the WWW browser to access the lecture materials and to follow the lecture progress by referring the appropriate page.

3.   Dialogue (chat) function: the communication tool between lecturer and student: It is constructed by a CGI (Common Gateway Interface) program written in Perl

Figure 5: Network Structure Among Remote Sites

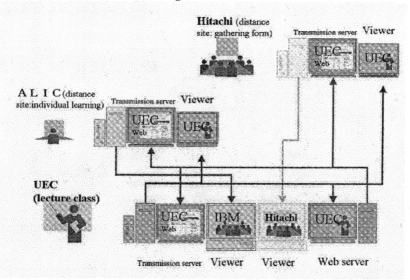

(Practical Extraction and Report Language). Lecturer and students access the CGI program via the WWW browser and perform Q&A sessions via the chat terminal screen.

One problem appearing is that the lecture movie and sound data sending and reception conditions depend on the network traffic conditions. Namely, if the reception data has a delay, far site students have difficulty in viewing the lecture, therefore failing to understand the lecture contents. Therefore, we have set up a bi-directional communication channel between lecture site and far sites. In this way the communication channel between lecturer and students is guaranteed, independent of the Internet

Figure 6: Hybrid E-Learning Environment System

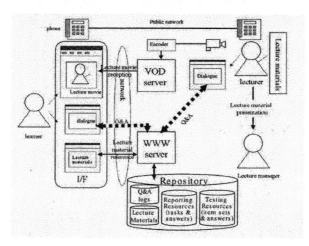

Figure 7: Registration Interface of Lectures and Learners

Main Menu
(1) lecture site/distance
     learning site
     registration
(2) lecture movie receiv-
     ing
(3) Lecture materials indi-
     cations
(4) dialogue tool startup

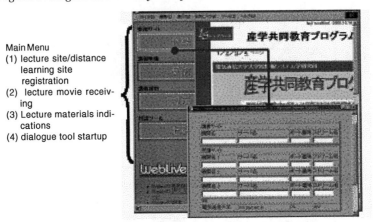

Lecturer/learner far sites registration:
[macine name I VOD server IP address I VOD server port number I
streaming identifiers] input

network conditions. Figure 6 shows the distance lecture environment structure (lecture site -> far sites) as well as the interface of both lecturer and students. As can be seen in the figure, the lecture manager transforms the lecture materials into HTML form and performs the registration into the lecture materials database.

Figure 7 displays the main menu lecture site and attending sites registration window. Concretely, data recorded are machine name (organization name), VOD server IP address and port number and VOD contents stream identifier. Students attend lectures (Figure 7) via our distance lecture environment interface. First, they select the lecture movie "reception" button from the main menu. The system than enquires for the movie to display.

The Environment for Distributed E-Learning Contents

We have developed web-based learning materials "Multimedia Communication Technology" by HTML, PERL, CGI, and Java, and VOD materials by Stream Authorware tools. The VOD materials consist of archive data of movies/sounds from live lectures in remote areas. According to the stream of movies, PowerPoint manuscript for each lecture is inserted with a synchronous signal in an appropriate position. This environment has three pull-down menus (i.e., a learning objective, a learning mode, and a contents-catalog) to enable learners to select and retrieve whatever they need. This distributing function has been implemented in our original Learning Management System (LMS) named RAPSODY (Okamoto, 2002).

The Collaborative Workplace for Q&A

We built a collaborative workplace to encourage interactions among lecturer/learners. In such a case, learners can exchange their knowledge and their way of thinking, furthermore they can refine/build the knowledge acquired via lectures. By a collaborative workplace, we mean a kind of BBS, nevertheless, in addition to Chat function, this workplace enables data/information sharing transmitted from different sites. Each student can drag/drop any data whatever they need from personal (individual) workplace

Figure 8: Instruction for Media Usage

movie viewing window
Characteristics: Lecturer
can view the far sites alter-
natively.

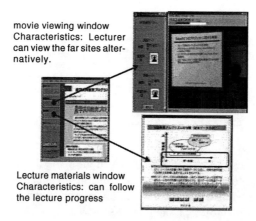

Lecture materials window
Characteristics: can follow
the lecture progress

to collaborative workplace and vice versa. In addition, they can transmit with attaching some annotations for arbitrary objects in the collaborative workplace. Those data are saved in the log-repository with the standardized record format through the collaborative memory. If somebody wants to refer/analyze those data for any purpose, such as knowledge mining/management and so on, s/he would reuse this repository under the lecturer's admission.

The Assessment Module for Learners

After lecture/web-learning, a test or reporting for learners as a summative evaluation is needed. In this environment, we have provided the repository of a set of test items and reporting tasks according to subjects (course-unit) matched with each learning objective. Students can pick up certain amount of test items or reporting tasks designated by a lecturer, and then reply/send back their answers to the digital pigeon box. As such, a lecturer can score and evaluate their achievements online. The simultaneous test is carried out in order to avoid a student's copying behavior from others. Moreover, the text analyzer was implemented to check the similarity of the reporting contents from the students automatically. This analyzer was built on the statistical natural language processing method, performing the following functions: picking up important keywords, its occurrence frequency, and co-occurrence of the related word for a certain word.

After pressing the button "lecture site -> lecture movie," the system pops up the "lecture movie playback" window and starts the playback (Figure 8). Moreover, when clicking the main menu's "lecture materials presentation" button, the system presents the lecture materials, too. Students can browse the lecture material via the buttons "advance" and "return." To enable the Q&A session, the lecturer has to select from the main menu the dialogue tool "startup," an action that will generate a "chat" window.

Lecturers attend lectures via a similar procedure to the students. Firstly, they select the lecture movie "reception" button from the main menu (Figure 7). If the students' far sites are equipped with VOD server, video camera, microphone and movie encoder, it is possible for lecturers to receive the image (and sound) of the students attending the

Figure 9: Time Series Movie Bit Rate

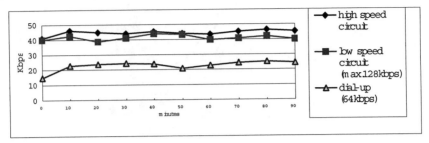

lectures. Similarly to the students, the lecturer can view the movie and sound and use the playback function. Moreover, in the case of multiple far sites, the lecturer can switch between them. Q&A sessions are possible as full movie and sound exchange, as chat (in text format) or via the regular telephone line.

EVALUATION OF "INDUSTRY AND UNIVERSITY" COOPERATIVE EDUCATION PROGRAM

Evaluation Procedure and Result

The evaluation of the program focuses on how many of the objectives stated in the introduction were actually achieved, and was performed from the two points of view enumerated below:

1. *Science and technology aspect:* Here we analyze the operations, functions and the lecture movie and sound data transmission and reception.
2. *Educational aspect:* Here we examine the meaning and significance of the distance education lecture in the frame of the industry and university collaboration project, via questionnaires filled in by the students.

The analysis of the lectures from the above-mentioned points of view is a continuous process.

Figure 10: Time Series of Movie Frame Rate

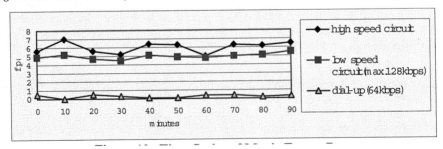

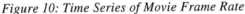

Figure 11: Time Series of Sound Bit Rate

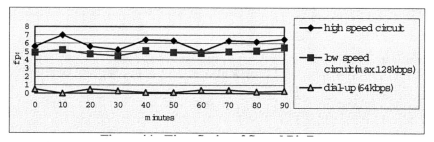

(1a) Science and technology aspects; evaluation 1: movie and sound data transmission and reception aspect

We have measured the delays, time-lapses and evolution of the lecture movie and sound data transmission. For this purpose, we have analyzed a situation with three sites exchanging VOD data. Each site was respectively connected to the Internet via either a high speed, low speed dedicated circuit (maximum rate 128 kbps), or via a business provider dial-up IP link. For the analysis of the transmission, we have collected data from each site on the movie bit rate (Figure 9), movie frame rate (Figure 10) and sound bit rate (Figure 11). As can be seen in the figures, the maximum real transmission values are, respectively, 48 kbps for the maximum real movie bit rate, 10 fps for the greatest real movie frame rate and 13.2 kbps for the highest real sound bit rate.

We will first discuss the movie transmission. For movie bit rates of 40 kbps and above, the lecture transmission is stable, with little interruptions, and the frame transmission is of about five frames per second. However, we have experienced that for the dial up connections, reception at the students' far sites is of about one frame per 10 to 20 seconds. At this rate, the lecture movie playback window often freezes into a still image for several seconds. Students attending lectures from such sites complained therefore that movie and sound reception is often asynchronous. Compared with the movie data reception, the sound reception was relatively stable for all participating sites. The above experimental result shows clearly that for such distance lectures the limitation is given by the movie reception, and that it is recommended to implement distance lecture environments on network circuits allowing maximum transmission capacity of 128 kbps or more. If a provider IP connection cannot be avoided, the distance lecture environment can be improved with a number of adjustments, as follows.

The first adjustment is related to the lecturer's actions. The VOD system used in our distance lecture environment complies with the H.261 standard, which bases the movie distribution on information compression via a frame prediction mechanism. Namely, the transmitted/ received information weight changes according to the movie data, movie complexity and details, movement intensity, etc. If the lecturer's actions are various, the transmission data weight grows. However, if the lecturer's actions during the lecture are moderate, the movie changes are reduced and therefore the lecture movie distribution can become a little more stable. As another adjustment, the creation of a dedicated low speed circuit for the VOD server is necessary.

Table 2: Problems and Solutions on Implementing Remote Site Learning Environment

Encountered Problems	Solutions/ Results
Web lecture materials are not synchronous with the lecturer indications. If the lecturer is browsing quickly through the material (as often in the second half of the lecture), the distance learners cannot keep up with the current page.	By using applications with share function, the synchronous display in both lecture room and far sites is possible. One drawback is that the lecturer's personal browsing through the material is not possible anymore.
The circuit speeds of the distance lecture sites differ. Reception is therefore difficult for some sites.	Multiple preparations are necessary for correct movie and sound transmission. The server setup should follow the various requirements of the distance sites.
During the Q&A session, the communication quality is reduced by the existent delay between lecture room and far sites.	There is no fundamental replacement scheme at present. New infrastructure and communication hardware is necessary. Rehearsal prior to the actual Q&A session is useful (or guidance of session by a chair person).
The phone line Q&A sound problems: 1)Noise, hauling; 2)Speaker volume and receiver volume differ.	1) Noise, hauling are caused by the using of a large combination of equipment; 2) The volume difference can be cancelled by the circuit resistance value.

If these adjustments are made, all sites can reach similar bit rate, and the distribution occurs according to the different frame rates: i.e., according to the network bandwidth of the access points, the distribution to high speed circuit students' far sites should be high rate, whereas the low speed circuit far sites should receive low rate movie and sound data.

(1b) Science and technology aspects; evaluation 2: distance education system operatively and functions

We have identified a few possible improvement points concerning lecturing via a distance education system, with focus on application result, operatively and function. Table 2 shows the recommended improvements for the distance lecture environment. Some items in the table point to proposed solutions, others to countermeasures, and again others just present situational examinations.

(2) Educational aspects evaluation: questionnaire survey

After each industry and university cooperation program lecture we have asked the learners to fill in a questionnaire. The questionnaire contains 21 questions that are a combination of both free description form questions and questions with a five-step assessment scale. For the latter, the students should choose the most appropriate of the five steps (5: I strongly think so, 4: I am inclined to think so, 3: Neither Nor, 2: I am inclined not to think so, 1: I definitely don't think so).

As the industry and university cooperation program lectures cycle is not yet finished, we could not aggregate all the questionnaire results yet, and therefore could not establish conclusive results. However, at present we have finished the first round

Figure 12: Average on the Result of Curriculum Questionnaire

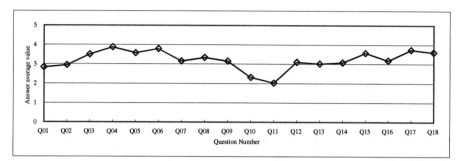

of lectures and it is possible to derive some suggestions and hints. Figure 12 shows the average answers of the first lecture. Questionnaires were anonymous and 38 questionnaires were returned from the 63 distributed. As the questionnaire (Table 3) average is in general around 3 or 4, the result can be called satisfactory. Questions Q4 through Q6 (about students interest in the subject, the motivating effect of the lecture and about the knowledge they acquired) showed high scores.

Students had an average of a 2.8 preliminary knowledge on the subject (Question Q1). This result possibly points to the fact that learners with no prior knowledge up to learners with some prior specialty knowledge all were interested in the lecture. As the acquisition of high-level specialty knowledge is the main object of the industry and university cooperation program, this is an extremely important pointer. A low result was noticeable especially for questions Q10 and Q11 (regarding the far site transmission situation). Therefore, an important sub-goal and improvement point for the next lectures is the harmonization of the transmission with the far sites. As these were the results of the first lesson in the series, such problems were perhaps unavoidable, and the

Table 3: Question Items

Q1. Did you have previous knowledge on the contents of this lecture?
Q2. Is there an important connection between today's lecture and your research/study field?
Q3. Do you think you will be able to use today's lecture contents in your future research/job?
Q4. Are you interested in the topics presented by today's lecture?
Q5. Do you feel that today's lecture has opened new perspectives?
Q6. Did today's lecture deepen your knowledge?
Q7. Was today's lecture according to your expectations?
Q8. Was today's lecture level appropriate?
Q9. Was today's presented subject of expertise of importance?
Q10. Was the cooperation with the far sites smooth?
Q11. Could you consider the far sites part integrated in the lecture environment?
Q12. Did the lecture materials offered with the lecture help you in understanding the lecture?
Q13. Did lecturing and lecture material presentation run smoothly?
Q14. Was question asking made easy by the offered environment?
Q15. Were today's sound and movie transmission clear?
Q16. Was today's lecture complete and sufficient for you, although designed as a distance education lecture?
Q17. Was the time distribution appropriate for today's lecture?
Q18. Was the time distribution appropriate for far sites, with regard to the Q&A session?

management and synchronization of lecturer, lecture manager, technical supporters, and teaching assistants was difficult to establish. Some of these problems have already been solved in the following lectures of the same cycle, but as the results were not yet analyzed, we present here our first experiences only to be of use and serve to guide other educators worldwide.

Considerations

In this chapter, we have presented our experience with the introducing of the industry and university education cooperation project at our graduate school to promote the future high level information communication society based on lifelong education. Especially, we have highlighted the following points.

1. The implementation method as well as possible problems of the distance lecture environment offering synchronous study possibility at the lecture site as well as far sites, based on bi-directional communication.

2. The issue of curriculum integration and certification/recognition of both on-site and far-site learners. Whole learners achieve credits according to the master course credit system.

3. We have discussed and presented our efforts in the direction of building the infrastructure necessary to support the lecturing within the industry and university education cooperation program. Specifically, we referred to the prior collecting of information, which is to be sent together with the lecture movie and sound transmission.

We hope to support and respond to the forecasted growing future learning demand, especially on advanced IT topics, and to create the chance and environment for a wide area high-level education. In the next section, we would like to take up "collaborative learning" and design issues for it from technological point of view.

COLLABORATIVE LEARNING AND ITS ENVIRONMENT

Collaborative learning is a participants' initiative learning form that has been more and more stressed with the paradigm shift from the teaching side to the learning side in the current learning technology. The object of collaborative learning is the group activity and the collaborative mutual interdependence-relations within the group(s). Simply put, in collaborative learning, each learner is accorded a sub-task and they try to accomplish it. As the result, the group goal is reached and collaborative mutual interdependent learning is achieved.

Distributed collaborative learning is a type of collaborative learning that can take place in the network environment, etc., with multiple learners geographically far from one another (O'Malley, 1994). Geographically, a distanced situation can mean remote or far physically, but this also covers cases where direct interaction and dialogue is not possible among participants due to other reasons. Distributed collaborative learning support is a research domain that tries to find out ways to support the collaboration of multiple learners on the network (CSCL - Computer Supported Collaborative Learning) (ISO/IEC JTC1 SC36), in problem solving or other cooperative curriculum activities, according to the used LT (Learning Technology) (ISO/IEC JTC1). Compared with CSCW (Computer Supported Cooperative Work) (Conklin, 1988; Malcolm, 1994; Winograd, 1986), CSCL has as a goal not so much the working efficiency, but the learning achievement efficiency, and the promotion of deep understanding of the subject field by the learner, combined with the recognition or meta-recognition of this achieved ability by other persons (Dillenboug, 1999).

The regular CSCL-management software implementation provides usually two types of activity space: a private working space and a collaborative working space, where the learners can exchange information in a synchronous or asynchronous manner. Many researches are studying these two types of activity spaces, the information exchange types that exist and those that are necessary (Synnes, 1999; Okamoto, 2000a).

Primitive Activities and Functionality of Collaborative Learning Environment

Here, we first describe primitive and interactive activities among participants in collaborative learning from macro point of view. As the technological functions, CSCL should provide any appropriate tools for those activities. To carry out those functions, the following resources are absolutely required in collaborative learning environments. Furthermore, more refined cognitive tools would be desired for facilitating group collaborative learning, corresponding to above enumerated activities as much as possible. So, we regard the common platform/infrastructure to have those resources built easily in the system as extremely essential conditions. The primitive activities that appear in collaborative learning are: Dialogue (with Interaction), Data/Idea sharing, Observing/Suggesting, Turn-taking, Coordinating/Control and Planning/Executing, and Initiative/Supervising. The resources required in collaborative learning are Dialogue Channel, Shared Workplace (shared object space), Personal Workplace, and Computer Mediated Communication Media.

Secondly, we describe functionality of Collaborative Learning Environment. Figure 13 displays the basic communication layers on the Collaborative Learning Environment

Figure 13: The Structural Layer Model of the Collaborative Learning Environment

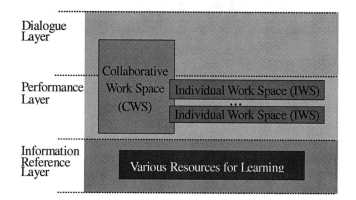

Figure 14: Components (Objects) of Collaborative Learning Environment

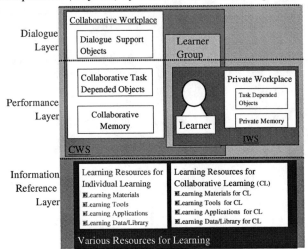

from a user's standpoint and usage of resources. We suppose to categorize "collaborative learning behavior" into learner-to-learner dialogue (communication) and other activities (problem solving, etc.). The figure shows the layers prepared for the collaborative learning goal and the collaborative work, as well as the layer containing the various learning resources to consult during collaborative learning.

In a collaborative learning situation, a learner could face a problem that s/he cannot solve, and by interactions with his/her learning companion(s), exchange meaningful information that can open up to him/her another person's ways of perception and help him/her find out the inconsistencies of his/her own judgment steps. Present research analyze situations as presented above, their coming into being, their catalysts and effects, and have as a goal to single out the triggering elements, in order to reproduce such situations. Moreover, as the learning efficiency has been shown to increase in such situations, many systems try to positively encourage them with the help of computer implementations.

Essential Elements (Components) of Collaborative Learning Environment

Essential Elements of the Collaborative Learning Model

Figure 14 shows the details and various essential elements for the conceptual configuration of the collaborative learning model. The working place and working subjects are brought together and labeled accordingly. Learners can belong to one or more groups and can be involved in projects or parts of projects together, sharing the particular space and a certain work for the rest personally.

The shared working place (collaborative workplace) contains the dialogue support objects for dialogue and information exchanging, the collaborative working objects for each member's activity and the collaborative memory itself for referencing and information accumulating, shown in Figure 14. On the other hand, the private working place contains the working depository of the private working objects, and the private memory to take log-data for each member's personal activity.

The information reference layer contains various kinds of information to satisfy personal needs or to achieve collaborative learning goals, such as learning materials, any educational data, applications, tools, and so on.

Essential and Structural Elements for Building the Collaborative Learning Environment

There are six essential structural/basic elements (objects) for building the collaborative learning environment:

a. Collaborative learning environment representation
b. Collaborative work space representation
c. Collaborative learning resource(s) representation
d. Collaborative workplace representation
e. Learner group model in collaborative learning
f. Collaborative memory structure representation

(a) Collaborative Learning Environment Representation. Many systems have already used the collaborative learning paradigm, and helped us comprehend the important structural points necessary for a collaborative learning environment. We have displayed these in Figure 13 and Figure 14 as the hierarchical structure of the collaborative learning environment, composed of a collaborative workspace, a private workspace and a space for various resources. Moreover, to define the collaborative learning environment, it is vital to define the four concepts below.

• Structural model of the collaborative learning environment

• Essential structural elements of the collaborative learning environment

• Attribute(s) of the essential structural elements of the collaborative learning environment

• Relation(s) of the essential structural elements of the collaborative learning environment

(b) Collaborative Working Space Representation. The collaborative workspace is an essential structural element of the collaborative learning environment that establishes a virtual space for collaborative activities for each group, and ensures the continuity of these collaborative activities within that space (by activity related information recording, etc.). The definition of the work-space requires also the definition of the following terms below.

• Structure of the collaborative learning space

• Essential elements of the collaborative learning space structure

• Attribute(s) of the essential elements of the collaborative learning space structure

• Relation(s) of the essential elements of the collaborative learning space structure

(c) Learning Resource(s) Representation. The collaborative learning resource(s) are the resources that have to be guaranteed for private activity or for collaboration (for all or a few members), such as screen sharing or operation sharing. For this definition, we need to clarify the term:

- Essential structural elements of the collaborative learning resource(s)
- Fundamental referencing model of resources

(d) Collaborative Workplace Representation. The collaborative workplace is an essential component in the collaborative working environment, used by the group members. Namely, the collaborative workplace is in a relation of "use_of" with respect to the group. The collaborative workplace is determined by the objects used for performing collaborative activities among the remote group members. These objects are important to achieve a certain collaborative work and the collaborative memory needs both objects of storage and retrieval. Moreover, the understanding and defining of the collaborative workplace requires the definition of the following terms:

- Collaborative workplace structure
- Essential elements of the collaborative workplace structure
- Attributes of the essential elements of the collaborative workplace structure
- Relation(s) of essential elements of the collaborative workplace structure

(e) Learners' Group Model for Collaborative Learning. The group is defined within the collaborative workspace of the collaborative learning environment. The group uses the collaborative workplace and pursues the collaborative learning goal. This goal is defined as a set of individual achievements expected from the multiple members of the group. To define the learner group model, the following elements and terms must be defined:

- Group model structure
- Essential elements of the group model structure
- Attribute(s) of the essential elements of the group model structure

(f) Collaborative Memory Structure Representation. The collaborative memory is included in the collaborative workplace of the collaborative workspace. The collaborative memory serves to store the objects used for dialogue support and the objects used and developed in collaborative working or problem solving. Moreover, it has the role to retrieve these objects and stored information at requests in relation with collaborative working. To define the collaborative memory structure, the definition of the following terms below is necessary:

- Collaborative memory structure
- Essential elements of the collaborative memory structure
- Attribute(s) of the essential elements of the collaborative memory structure
- Relation(s) of the essential elements of the collaborative memory structure

Data Transmission Model in Collaborative Learning Environment

Data Transmission Model in Collaborative Learning Environment

Figure 15 shows exclusively the data transmission model in collaborative learning environment populated with learners and group(s). The collaborative learning support system has to able to send and receive, at a learner's request, collaborative and private

Figure 15: Data Transmission Model of Collaborative Learning Environment

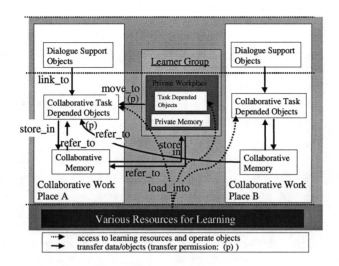

work space essential elements information. Figure 15 illustrates our hypotheses, and displays a minimum of required relations, as will be explained, e.g., there has to be ensured a function able to fetch collaborative/private work objects requested by the group or privately from various resource(s) (load_into relation). This relation is defined within the essential structural elements of the collaborative learning environment.

The figure shows also other essential relations between the essential structure elements of the collaborative workspace. A relation ensures the sending and receiving of problem solving communication data within the collaborative working place, between the dialogue support objects and the collaborative working objects (link_to relation). Another relation ensures the inserting/saving of objects, results and information from the private workplace of the private workspace as collaborative work objects of the collaborative workplace (insert_in relation). The relations between the collaborative work objects and the collaborative memory are "store_to," when it refers to storing work objects into the collaborative memory, and "refer_to" when it means referring objects already stored.

Common Objects for Interface

The common objects for building the interface means defining the five items below.
a.   Interface between learning resource(s) and collaborative work object(s)
b.   Interface between dialogue support object(s) and collaborative work object(s)
c.   Interface between the private work space and collaborative work object(s) of the collaborative workplace
d.   Interface between collaborative work object(s) of the collaborative workplace and the collaborative memory
e.   Interface between the collaborative memory and the group model

(a) Interface Between Learning Resource(s) and Collaborative Work Object(s). The group performs collaborative activities by loading the collaborative work object(s) of the collaborative workplace from the learning resources, for group and personal use.

Namely, multiple groups use the learning resource(s). By activating a group request, a memory image of the requested learning resource(s) is produced, and therefore the collaborative working object(s) of the group collaborative working place come into being. Moreover, after finishing the collaborative learning, or after a group request, the collaborative working object(s) are deleted. For defining these types of functionality and the interface and its regulations, the following items below must be defined.

- Learning resource(s) reference structure
- Essential elements of the learning resource(s) reference structure
- Attribute(s) of the essential elements of the learning resource(s) reference structure
- Relation(s) of the essential elements of the learning resource(s) reference structure
- Protocol between the learning resource(s) agent and the collaborative work object agent

(b) Interface Between Dialogue Support Object(s) and Collaborative Work Object(s). The dialogue support object enhances the information exchange between the learners and manages the communication activity history. The role of the communication among learners is to support the smooth proceeding of the various learning and work activities managed by collaborative work object(s). Namely, the communication that takes place in order to achieve the group-learning goal is closely related to the collaborative work for problem solving. Therefore, it is indispensable for the group portfolio creation and the group results report to attach links between the collaborative work for problem solving, as well as the communication related to it. For the computer to understand the meaning of the communication, it is necessary to link the output of the dialogue support object and the collaborative working object. For this purpose, the items below need to be defined.

- Dialogue support object and collaborative work object output data structure
- Essential elements of the dialogue support object and the collaborative work object output data structure
- Attribute(s) of the essential elements of the dialogue support object and the collaborative work object output data structure

(c) Interface Between the Private Working Space and Collaborative Work Object(s) of the Collaborative Workplace. Collaborative learning does not always take place in the collaborative workspace. A group member can bring in work results from the learner's private workplace to the collaborative workplace, or the work result from the collaborative workplace can be copied to the private workplace. The private workplace contains private work object(s) and a private memory. The above type of information exchange is our working hypothesis. For this purpose, together with the definition of the collaborative work object input data, the definition of the output data of the private workplace is also necessary.

- Private workplace output data structure
- Essential elements of the private workplace output data structure
- Attribute(s) of essential elements of the private workplace output data structure

- Relation(s) of the essential elements of the private workplace output data structure
- Protocol between the private workplace agent and the collaborative workplace agent
- Protocol between the collaborative workplace agent and the collaborative work object agent

(d) Interface Between Collaborative Work Object(s) of the Collaborative Workplace and the Collaborative Memory. The collaborative work object output data is the learning log data for problem solving via collaborative learning. The interface uniformity between the collaborative work object(s) and the collaborative (group) memory within the collaborative workplace is ensured by the collaborative learning log exchange and the collaborative work object addition/deletion. By establishing a uniform representation of the collaborative learning log, the accumulation in the collaborative (group) memory and the reference to the collaborative (group) memory can be implemented in an interoperable form. The technological issues to specify our hypothesis contain the nine items written below.

- Relation between the essential elements of the collaborative workplace structure and learning log structure
- Storage request structure of the learning log into the collaborative memory
- Essential elements of the storage request structure of the learning log into the collaborative memory
- Attribute(s) of the essential elements of the storage request structure of the learning log into the collaborative memory
- Relation(s) of the essential elements of the storage request structure of the learning log into the collaborative memory
- Reference request structure of the learning log from the collaborative memory
- Essential elements of the reference request structure of the learning log from the collaborative memory
- Attribute(s) of the essential elements of the reference request structure of the learning log from the collaborative memory
- Relation(s) of the essential elements of the reference request structure of the learning log from the collaborative memory

(e) Interface Between the Collaborative Memory and the Group Model. The collaborative memory of the collaborative workplace stores various data developed during the group curriculum activities. This information is the ordered and managed information of the group model. Thereafter, the group model is registered. In the case some new group activity commences, the previous activity history and results from the group model are referred. Therefore, the collaborative memory maintenance is necessary. In order to establish the correct reference to such information, the items below have to be defined and regulated.

- Relation between the collaborative memory attribute(s) and the group model attribute(s)
- Output data structure from the collaborative memory into the group model

- Essential elements of the output data structure from the collaborative memory into the group model
- Attribute(s) of the essential elements of the output data structure from the collaborative memory into the group model
- Relation(s) of the essential elements of the output data structure from the collaborative memory into the group model

Data Exchange in the Collaborative Learning Environment

Virtual Agent in the Collaborative Learning Environment

One of the essential structural elements of the collaborative learning environment is the virtual agent (Paiva, 1996). The information exchange between the other essential structural elements is done via agent(s). The attribute(s) of the appropriate essential elements are stored in the collaborative memory as well as the learning log developed during the collaborative learning curriculum. Furthermore, depending on the request from group member(s) and collaborative work object(s), agents refer the information in the collaborative memory and integrate the exchanged information into a defined form. The concrete function of agents is to cope with the behavioral differences of the essential structural elements. Moreover, the information exchange protocol content varies, according to the transmission source and reception destination, and according to the behavior or functions of the bi-directional structure of the essential elements. However, the basic functions and structure of the agents in the collaborative learning environment are defined simply as the exchange, deletion, and addition of essential structural elements.

Collaborative Learning Agent

The technological issues to specify for the agents delimited by the hypothesis is represented by the five items below:
1. Collaborative learning environment agent(s) structure
2. Collaborative learning environment agent type(s)
3. Essential elements of the collaborative learning environment agent(s) structure
4. Attribute(s) of the essential elements of the collaborative learning environment agent(s) structure
5. Relation(s) of the essential elements of the collaborative learning environment agent(s) structure

Considerations

The technological concept formation of the basic and common platform for building the collaborative learning environment needs a collective effort and is an ongoing process. We have outlined here some of the primitive considerations from our experiences, and the issues to specify toward future standardization. In addition, further required functions for the collaborative learning environment are as follows (Okamoto, 2000a):
- Coordination (constrained and mediated by external environment)
- Reification (material evidence in the external environment)
- Illustration (external representation)

- Storage (in later use, for the purpose of reflection)
- Examples of general tools for supporting collaboration are as follows.
- Concept Mapping tool
- Editors for argumentation network
- Work flow (planning tool)
- WYSIWIS (What You See Is What I See)

So far, we have integrated a few parallel projects that have related goals concentrated around distance-learning and lifelong learning, also under the name RAPSODY (Okamoto, 2002) and RAPSODY-EX (Kayama, 2001). In this chapter, from the academic point of view, we mentioned systematically the fundamentals about the common functions/components for building the platform of a collaborative learning environment through our research experiences for the future direction of the standardization. However, those considerations and issues are the first step for standardizing it. So, we need much more investigation and discussion to have a lot of people understand the importance of this matter.

NEW PLATFORM FOR SUPPORTING COLLABORATIVE LEARNING: RAPSODY-EX

Outline of RAPSODY-EX

We can implement various kinds of learning forms and design interactive and collaborative activities among learners. The extended version of the system is RAPSODY-EX. This system handles a collaborative learning support environment, and has an educational knowledge management (Davenport, 1997) function for both students and faculties. This function works for promoting and facilitating their learning tasks based on the collaborative learning process model. RAPSODY-EX can effectively carry out collaborative learning support in asynchronous/synchronous learning modes. Various information in the educational context is referred and reused as knowledge which oneself and others can practically utilize. We aim at the construction of an increasingly growing digital portfolio database.

A learner group, which guarantees the smooth transmission of knowledge, can form a community (the knowledge community) by sharing and reusing common knowledge learning activities that occur within this group are as follows: the achievement of learning objectives as a group; the achievement of the learning objectives of each learner; the achievement of the learning objectives of the learner group that consists of multiple learners. RAPSODY-EX supports the transmission of knowledge in the learner group and the promotion of the learning activity. Figure 16 shows an example of the collaborative learning with RAPSODY-EX. It is indispensable that RAPSODY-EX has the following functions:

- The function which controls learning information for the individual learner and the group.
- The function which manages learning information of the learner for mediation.

Figure 16: Collaborative Learning Form Based on RAPSODY-EX

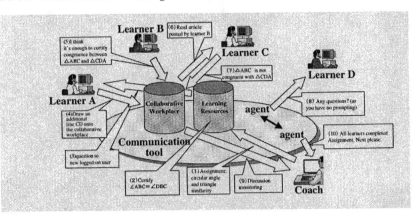

RAPSODY-EX is a collaborative learning environment which extends the functions of RAPSODY, in consideration of the concept "Intelligent Media Oriented." RAPSODY selects the assignment of the learning media to a student. The examples of the learning media are shown in Figure 17. One of the learning media for individual learning is the CBR system with short movies about classroom teaching process about "information" (Inoue, 1999). The learning medias for collaborative learning are an object_model editor, an action simulation tool and a communication tool. The student advances his/her study about "information," using these tools with RAPSODY and RAPSODY-EX. Based on the Guide-Script defined by the mentor, the learning media considered to be suitable for the learning state of a student are reasoned. At this time, RAPSODY uses a student's needs, a learning history of a student, the mentor's expertise and so on. The learning mode for a student is determined. RAPSODY has two learning modes, an individual learning mode and a collaborative learning mode. In the individual learning mode, the learning process within the given learning media is not dependent on RAPSODY. Only the result of learning is recorded by RAPSODY, and serves as his/her learning history. The results of learning are the study media, the learning date, the learning time, the result of the pretest and/or posttest, degree of comprehension, and so on. They are dependent on the learning media that registered with RAPSODY.

In the collaborative learning mode, the learning process within the given learning media is preceded in RAPSODY-EX. RAPSODY-EX provides the communication tool between learners/mentors, and the tool/application for collaborative and/or cooperative work. A learning history while using these tools is stored and managed by RAPSODY-EX.

The learner and group information are produced from the learning space. This information will be stored in the collaborative memory. This information is defined as the information of the learning entity. We also define the method of information management of such information and the structure of the collaborative memory.

Framework of Information Management on Learning Entity

The simple mechanism of the management of learning information developed in this study is shown in Figure 18. The processing mechanism consists of two components.

Figure 17: Examples of the Learning Media in RAPSODY

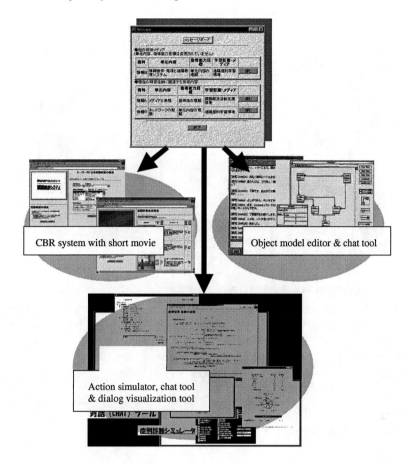

The first one is a module, which offers the learning environment. The second one is a collaborative memory, which controls various information and data produced from the learning environment. In the learning environment, two types of functions are offered. One is the monitoring function for the learning progress. The other is the tool/application for the collaborative learning. The former function controls the learning history/record of individual learners and the progress of the collaborative group learning. The latter tool/application becomes a space/workplace for collaborative synchronous/asynchronous learning. The information of learning entity, which emerged from such a learning environment, is handed to the collaborative memory. The collaborative memory offers two types of functions. One is the knowledge processing function, and the other is the knowledge storage function. In the former, input information of learning entity is shaped to the defined form. In the latter, for the formatted information, some attributes related to content are added. The complex information processing takes place in the collaborative memory.

Figure 18: Framework of Information Management Based on RAPSODY-EX

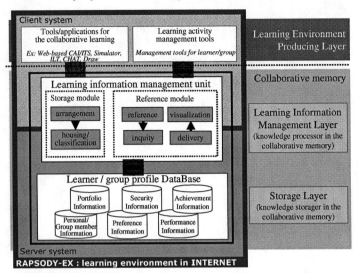

The Collaborative Memory

In the collaborative memory, the behaviors such as information generation/arrangement/housing/referencing/visualization appeared, and then the collaborative memory manages the expressed knowledge in the learning space. RAPSODY-EX is a learning environment, which possesses a knowledge management mechanism. In this environment, the following objects are executed during group learning.

- Review of the learning process,
- Summarization of the problem solving process, and
- Reference of other learners' problem solving method.

Learning information is expressed by a unified format. Then, that information is accumulated in the collaborative memory. This information becomes the reference object of the learner. The generation and the management of the information on the learning performance and the portfolio of the learner and group are the main objects of the knowledge management. In this study, learning information is obtained from the application tools for the collaborative learning. It is necessary to control the learning record, the reference log of the others' learning information and the log of problem solving and learning progress. To realize this control, not only techniques based on symbolic knowledge processing approach, but also techniques based on sub-symbolic knowledge processing approach are used.

The collaborative memory consists of two parts. One is the information storage unit. The other one is the management unit of the stored information. The information storage unit mainly processes four kinds of information.

- Learning information,
- Information on the learner,
- Information on the setting of the learning environment, and
- Information on the learning result.

The information management unit deals with the reference/arrangement/integration of learning information. The individual learner profile information is composed of information following the IEEE Profile information guidelines (IEEE, 2000). The group information is expressed by the expansion of the individual learner profile information. The conversion from the learning log data to learning information is necessary to develop this profile database. The information that should apply in learning information is as follows:

- Information and/or data on its learning context and/or learning situation
- Information about the sender and the receiver of the information
- Significance and/or outline in the educational context
- Information on the relation structure of the information of learning entity
- Reference pointer to individual learner and group who proposed or produced the information
- Relation with other material

By adding this information, the information of the learning entity is arranged into a unique form. If a learner requires some information related to his/her current learning, RAPSODY-EX shows the (estimated) desired information to the learner.

The Knowledge Management in RAPSODY-EX

In this study, the processing described in 1.4.3 is considered as a process of the knowledge management in the learning context. The concept of knowledge management is defined in Davenport (1997). Knowledge management is "the systematic process of finding, selecting, organizing, distilling and presenting information in a way that improves an employee's comprehension in a specific area of interest."

Nonaka arranged the process of knowledge management as a SECI model (1995). The SECI model is expressed as a conversion cycle between tacit knowledge and expressive knowledge. Tacit knowledge has a non-linguistic representation form. Expressive knowledge is a result of putting tacit knowledge into linguistic form. Tacit knowledge is shared with others by converting it into expressive knowledge. In the SECI model, socialization (S)/externalization (E)/combination (C)/internalization (I) of knowledge is expressed.

Knowledge management in an educational context is defined as follows:
"the systematic process of finding, selecting, organizing, distilling and presenting information in a way that improves a learner's comprehension and/or ability to fulfill his/her current learning objectives."

RAPSODY-EX aims to support participants' activities in the C (combination of knowledge) phase. Moreover, it affects not only the process of knowledge conversion from the C phase to the I (internalization of knowledge) phase, but also from the E (externalization of knowledge) phase to the C phase. The information of the learning entity contains the expressed knowledge by learners. This overt knowledge can be represented by natural language as verbal information. So, we can regard this knowledge as one that would be elicited from the learner's tacit knowledge.

In this situation, what we have to consider is as follows:

- *Who are the subjects of our knowledge management work?* Learners and the persons who support the learners are our subjects. The learners' task is to acquire the ability/skill for the problem solving. On the other hand, supporters' tasks are to support for acquisition of ability/skill of the learner, and support of the problem solving by the learner. Supporter means a facilitator/tutor/coach/organizer, etc.

- *What are the knowledge resources in the learning group?* For learners, the knowledge for the effective and efficient problem solving is their knowledge resource. On the other hand, for the supporters, the knowledge on problem setting and activity assessment is their knowledge source.

- *What is the gain for the learning group?* The gains for learners are to acquire the ability in which to effectively and efficiently solve the problem, and to acquire the meta-cognition ability. For supporters, the acquisition of the ability of supporting the ability acquisition of the learner is their gain.

- *How are the knowledge resources controlled to guarantee the maximum gain for the learning group?* By the information processing to relate common knowledge of collaborative memory and learning context, we try to manage the knowledge in the collaborative learning. To create the collaborative portfolio between individual and group learning, extension of acquired knowledge of learners, knowledge extraction from learning history under the problem solving and making outline of problem solving process.

The examples of knowledge management in the RAPSODY-EX are shown in Figure 19. A log data of a dialog is visualized by three kinds of methods.

Figure 19: Examples of Knowledge Management Based on RAPSODY-EX

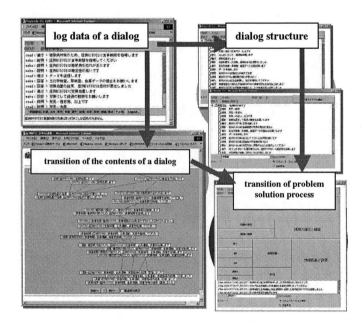

The first method is visualization of the dialog structure. The dialog layers are reasoned based on the dialog proceeding model (Inaba, 1997) and the utterance intention information that were given to the dialog log. The result is shown as tree structure. The second method is visualization of transition of the contents of a dialog. An appearance of the important term that is in a dialog is searched for using the term dictionary about the current discussion/learning domain (Chiku, 2001). This result and the timing connection of each utterance are considered to detect a transition of the contents of a dialog. The result is shown as graph structure.

The third method is visualization of transition of problem solution process. One utterance can be unified as meaningless unit for the problem solving process from the first and the second processing result and an educational mentor's expertise/educational intentions. The result reconstituted as problem solution process is shown with the structure that imitated the dendrogram.

SUMMARY AND CONCLUSION

The education retrospective of the 20th century portrays it as a time of classroom learning (in-lecture), group learning and individual learning in traditional styles (CAI), and e-learning styles. Education is evolving with technology advancement. The influence of the Internet extends beyond the learning/education itself. It is used as a place to seek information and realize self-development. Prospectively, technological innovation will increase the speed and capacity, moreover, the availability of access. In this chapter, we described the meaning of the e-learning world, moreover, we introduced the integrated e-learning system "RAPSODY" and its practical experience. Then, we presented the technological aspects (the functional relationship such as data flows between personal work–space and collaborative one) for supporting collaborative learning. Finally, we showed the new architecture of a platform for supporting collaborative learning.

In the coming broadband era, the prospects of e-learning are promising. Obviously, the learning needs are dynamic and various in a high-computerization age. As a response to this society advance, e-learning is here to stay, involving the methodology of instruction, cooperative and collaborative learning, self-study, and others; moreover, concerning all kinds of media; furthermore, engaging various evaluation ideas. Nevertheless, the most important is to form a sound academic capacity and to create/obtain a new ability toward the new era. In keeping with these purposes, we need to design a learning environment of great depth and extension, and expect the instructor's expertise to put this learning environment into educational practices. Especially, the method of group configuration, the preparation of the learning contents/media, and then the instructor's team-works are the most eloquent/meaningful parameters.

Finally, we would like to portray some essential matters in order to achieve real successes in the e-learning world:
1.   Quality of content based on well-examined curriculum (or competency library) reflecting the specified learning goals
2.   Quality of services from educational/technological perspective
3.   Involvement/commitment of human mentors
4.   Copying with technology changes

5. Seamless information flow and easy access
6. Knowledge repository for reusing resources
7. Integration of authoring and delivering
8. Sharing functions such as "plug-in" for applications and tools

These essential matters set the stage for the 21st century to host collaborative development of infrastructure for large-scale use by the profession, and research essential for education advancement.

ACKNOWLEDGMENT

We would like to appreciate my colleagues, Dr. T. Matsui, Mr. H. Inoue and Dr. A. I. Cristea. They have devoted themselves to make this project progress with sparing no effort.

REFERENCES

Chen, N. & Shin, Y. (2001). Stream-based lecturing system and its instructional design. *Proceedings of International Conference of Advanced Learning Technologies* (pp. 94-95).

Chiku, M., Yu, S., Kobayashi, Y., Inoue, H., & Okamoto, T. (2001). A dialog visualization tool. *Proceedings of the 62nd Annual Conference of the Information Processing Society of Japan* (pp. 241-244).

Conklin, J. & Begeman, M.L. (1988). gIBIS: A hypertext tool for exploratory policy discussion. *ACM Transaction on Office Information Systems, 6*(4), 303-331.

Davenport, T. (1997). *Working Knowledge.* Cambridge, MA: Harvard Business School Press.

Dillenboug, P. (1999). *Collaborative Learning, Cognitive and Computational Approaches* (Advances in learning and instruction series). Pergamon.

Hui, S. (2000). *Video-on-demand in education.* Retrieved from the World Wide Web: http://www.cityu.edu.hk/~ccncom/ net14/vod2.htm.

IEEE. (2000). *Draft standard for learning technology: Public and private information (PAPI) for learner.* IEEE P1484.2/D6. Retrieved from the World Wide Web: http://ltsc.ieee.org/.

IEEE-LTSC. (2000). *Draft Standard for Learning Object Metadata, IEEE P1484.12/ D4.0.* Retrieved from the World Wide Web: http://ltsc.ieee.org/.

Inaba, A. & Okamoto, T. (1997). Negotiation process model for intelligent discussion coordinating system on CSCL environment. *Proceedings of the International Conference of Artificial Intelligence in Education* (pp. 175-182).

Inoue, H. & Okamoto, T. (1999). Case base reasoning system for information technology education. *Proceedings of the 7th International Conference on Computer in Education* (pp. 1083-1086).

ISO/IEC JTC1 (Joint Technical Committee 1). Available on the World Wide Web: http://www.jtc1.org/.

ISO/IEC JTC1 SC36 (Standards for Information Technology for Learning, Education, and Training). Available on the World Wide Web: http://jtc1sc36.org/.

Japanese Ministry of Education, Culture Sports Science and Technology (MEXT). Available on the World Wide Web: http://www.mext.go.jp/.

Kayama, M., Okamoto, T., & Cristea, A.I. (2001). Collaborative learning support knowledge management for asynchronous learning networks. *Proceeding of International Conference on Advanced Learning Technology* (pp. 490-49).

Malcolm K.C. (1994). *Cooperative Work with Multimedia*. Berlin: Springer-Verlag.

Nieminen, P. (2001). Videolecturing for international students. *Proceedings of International PEG Conference* (pp. 162-168).

Nonoka, I. (1995). *The Knowledge-Creating Company*. London: Oxford University Press.

O'Malley, C. (ed.). (1994). *Computer Supported Collaborative Learning* (NATO ASI seriesv.F-128). Berlin: Springer-Verlag.

Okamoto, T. (2001). *Advanced information society: Synthetic research on the contents, system and form of teachers' education* (final report). Grant of the Ministry of Education:(A)(1)09308004.

Okamoto, T., Cristea, A.I., & Kayama, M. (2000a). Towards intelligent media-oriented distance learning and education environments. *Proceedings of the 8th International Conference on Computer in Education* (pp. 61-72).

Okamoto, T., Matsui, T., Inoue, H., & Cristea, AI.I. (2000b). A distance-education self-learning support system based on a VOD server. *Proceedings of International Workshop on Advanced Learning Technologies* (pp. 71-78).

Okamoto, T., Seki, K., Kayama, M., & Cristea, A.I. (2002). RAPSODY: A self/collaborative-learning multimedia based teacher training distance support model. *International Journal of Computers and Applications, 24*(2), 52-57.

Paiva, A. (1996). Communicating with learner modelling agents. *Proceedings of the ITS '96 Workshop on Architectures and Methods for Designing Cost-Effective and Reusable ITSs*. Available on the World Wide Web: http://www.cdl.leeds.ac.uk/~amp/MyPapers/its96ws.html.

Peltoniemi, J. (1995). *Video-on-demand overview*. Available on the World Wide Web: http://www.cs.tut.fi/tlt/stuff/vod/ VoDOverview/vod1.html.

Rosenberg, M.J. (2001). *E-learning: Strategies for Delivering Knowledge in the Digital Age*. New York: McGraw-Hill.

Salvador, L.G. (1999). Continuing education through distance training. *Proceedings of International Conference on Computer and Education* (pp. _512-515).

Slomen, M. (2001). The E-learning Revolution: From Propositions to Action. London: Chartered Institute of Personnel and Development.

Synnes, K., Parnes, P., Widen, J., & Schefstroem, D. (1999). Net-based learning for the next millennium. In *Proceedings of the 3rd World Multiconference on Systemetics, Cybernetics and Informatics/ The 5th Int. Conf. Information Systems Analysis and Synthesis*. Available from the World Wide Web: http://www.cdt.luth.se/~unicorn/papers/sciisas99/sciisas99.pdf.

Winograd, T. & Flores, F. (1986). *Understanding Computers and Cognition*. Addison-Wesley.

Chapter VII

SEGODON:
Learning Support System that can be Applied to Various Forms

Takashi Yoshino, Wakayama University, Japan

Jun Munemori, Wakayama University, Japan

ABSTRACT

We have developed learning support systems, named SEGODON and SEGODON-PDA. SEGODON consists of personal computers and a Local Area Network (LAN). SEGODON-PDA consists of Personal Digital Assistants (PDAs) and wireless LAN. We have applied them to classes, the results of which show that the class using SEGODON was not superior to the usual class which did not use digital equipment. The result of the end-term examination was almost the same regardless of the systems' used. The result of the evaluation using SEGODON-PDA was comparatively high. We analyzed the results and found that good results were derived from the curiosity of students in the class using new digital equipment like a PDA.

INTRODUCTION

In recent years, personal computers (PCs) have progressed amazingly and the Internet has spread widely. Many web-based learning support systems have been developed (Web-Based Training, 2002; Harasim, 1999). We have been developing learning support systems for about 10 years (Munemori et al., 1993; Yoshino et al., 1999a; Yoshino et al., 1999b; Yoshino et al., 2001; Munemori et al., 2002). In the early 1990s, we developed several information management systems for exercises of programming

(Munemori et al., 1993). In the mid-1990s we developed distance-learning systems for lecture-type classes and an exercise-type class because we can use audio and video communication via the Internet easily.

We show the learning support systems, which are named SEGODON (diStance lEarning support GrOupware for university eDucational envirONnment). SEGODON is a real time distance learning support system for PCs. SEGODON supports both lecture-type classes and exercise-type classes. Forty students can use their own PC, each of which has a CCD (Charged Coupled Device) camera and a microphone for audio and video communication. A shared pointer is attached for indicating in each PC, and the teacher teaches students with a shared pointer on the prepared contents. The shared temporal drawing function can also be used for teaching. SEGODON has two means of recording class content, which are named the Blackboard system and the Note system. The former is for the teacher and the latter is for students. The contents of the Blackboard system and the Note system are the same. Students can take their notes freely in the Note system.

SEGODON-PDA is a learning support system, which uses a Personal Digital Assistant (PDA) and a wireless LAN. Each student has a PDA with the wireless LAN. The teacher teaches students by writing the lecture notes on the Blackboard. In the latter half of the lecture, students download the exercise data using the PDA and the wireless LAN. Students solve the problem and then write the answer on the Blackboard, carrying and using the PDA. The class consists of a lecture-type class and an exercise-type class by the PDA and the wireless LAN.

We show our learning support systems and the results of its implementation and usage in the chapter.

SYSTEM DEVELOPMENT
SEGODON for Lecture

SEGODON is equipped with the fundamental functions for lectures and for exercises. Also, the system also has special functions for lecture and for exercise. This section shows the fundamental functions, and the special function for lecture.

Design Policy

The following items are fundamental policies required for distance education.
1. *Easy operation of the whole system by a teacher.* Conventional distance learning support systems do not take into account the importance of easy operation of the whole system by a teacher in classes. We thought that the easy operation functions of the whole system are required.
2. *Shared temporary drawing.* In conventional systems, a shared pointer is only a pointing method on a shared screen. Explanation with only a shared pointer is hard to understand for the receiving side. We have developed a new pointing method, named shared temporary drawing.

System Overview

Conventional systems use one PC for every site for audio and video communication (Maeda et al., 1997; Zaslavsky et al., 1998). In SEGODON, each participant uses one PC.

This system supports audio and video communication. The PC on the teacher's site continually displays the state of the classroom using a remote control camera. The upper half of the teacher's body is always seen on a screen in the classroom. A teacher in a remote location can give lectures to students in a classroom using this system. During Question and Answer (Q&A) sessions the teacher and one student can communicate through audio and video equipment. The students' PCs also displays lecture data. The audio and video channels between a teacher and students cannot be connected with a large amount of audio and video communication, due to limitations on network bandwidth, and computer throughput. Thus, after examining the necessary audio and video elements, we decided that the teacher and classroom computers should remain constantly connected. Three computers would be connected in Q&A sessions. SEGODON is also equipped with two shared pointers (one for the teacher, and another for students).

Hardware Configuration

An overall view of the distance learning support system is shown in Figure 1. This system uses the teacher's computer (PC), 40 students' computers (PC), two managing computers (PC), a file server computer (Work station), a remote camera control computer (PC), and a projection computer (PC). Additional equipment is a remote control camera, a multimedia projector and two speakers.

The hardware equipment for the students consists of the Power Macintosh 8100/100AV (Apple Computer) with a 15-inch monitor, a CCD camera, and a microphone. For the teacher's computer, any Power Macintosh will do. In addition, a CCD camera and a microphone are required.

Figure 1: Configuration of SEGODON

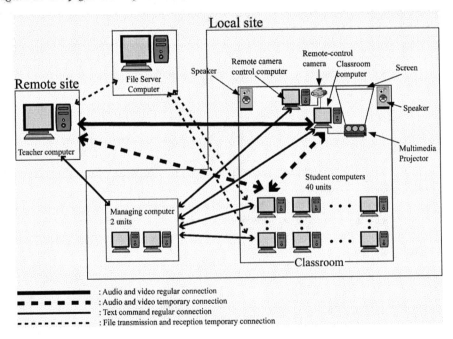

```
                                    : Audio and video regular connection
                                    : Audio and video temporary connection
                                    : Text command regular connection
                                    : File transmission and reception temporary connection
```

Software Configuration

The software for this system consists of the Blackboard system, the Note system, audio and video switching system, HyperQTC (Yoshino et al., 1999a) and NetGear (Yoshino et al., 2001). HyperQTC and NetGear are our original intercomputer multimedia communications software. The Blackboard system and the Note system, based on our card-type database software called Wadaman (Yoshino et al., 2001), has been developed and enhanced with additional functions.

The Blackboard system corresponds to the conventional blackboard on which a teacher writes lecture notes. The Blackboard system is displayed on the monitors of the teacher and all the students, and allows the teacher to show lecture notes to the students. The teacher can control the system.

The Note system is a subsystem for students to use for note taking. Its interface is almost the same as the Blackboard system. Students cannot control the Blackboard system, but they can freely use the Note system. The Note system uses exactly the same material as the Blackboard system. Table 1 shows the supporting functions of the system. A description of their functions follows.

Most conventional distance learning support systems are similar to ordinary electronic meeting systems. The support function for a lecture must be made easy, because complicated operation is difficult for a teacher during a class. The camera operation in the students' site is important to grasp the situation of a classroom. Thus, we have developed the function audio and video switching button and remote-control camera operating pointer shown in Table 1.

This system uses HyperQTC and NetGear for intercomputer communication. Both are communication applications that use QuickTime Conferencing (Apple Computer). Since TCP/IP (Transmission Control Protocol/Internet Protocol) is used for the text command communication, and UDP/IP (User Datagram Protocol/Internet Protocol) for the audio and video communication, this system can be used from anywhere as long as

Table 1: Supporting Functions of SEGODON

Supporting functions	Explanations
Shared temporary drawing function	• This function draws lines temporarily in freehand in real time on a shared lecture card for a lecture. Erasing by a teacher is unnecessary, since it is deleted automatically when the page is changed or a fixed time elapses.
Lecture data creation support function	• This function is used to organize data scanned as lecture data.
Audio and video switching button	• Students' name is displayed for audio and video connection. The list of names shows the seat number, and can be used as a seating list.
Remote-control camera operating pointer	• It enables a teacher to view specific spots in the classroom using a mouse pointer. It controls panning, angle of elevation and zooming.
Teacher's shared pointer	• The teacher's pointer is shown on the students' monitor as it is moved.
Students' shared pointer	• The student's pointer is displayed during Q&A sessions on the monitors of both teacher and student.
Question button	• When a student pushes the question button, the audio and video-switching button of his or her name is highlighted.
Text-based Q&A function	• This function performs text-based questions and answers between a teacher and a student. Anonymous questions are possible between student and teacher.
The acquisition function of student's pictures	• The function shows the still pictures of students' faces on the seating list with the names of students for a teacher.
The acquisition function of a student's monitor picture	• The function provides a snapshot of the screen of the student's PC.
Automatic installation function	• This function automatically distributes teaching materials to each student's PC before a class.

Internet connection is possible. With this system, HyperQTC is used for the text command communication, and NetGear for audio and video communication.

The Internet, the communication channel for this system, has the problem of not being able to guarantee sufficient bandwidth. Therefore, we used two computers for audio and video connections at most times, and three during Q&A sessions. As for the text command communication that controls teaching material synchronism, the system distributes text commands to individual computers via the managing computer to reduce the amount of online communication.

The fine line in Figure 1 indicates the configuration of the text command communication. Text command communication is achieved through the managing computer, and is sent and received between the teacher computer and all of the student computers. Because of this communication form, it is possible to send commands with a capacity of several-ten bytes per communication between computers. The communication form is used for the following purposes: to control the Blackboard system and the shared pointer synchronously, to control the data of Q&A sessions, to switch audio communications, and to control the remote-control camera.

The bold line and the broken bold line in Figure 1 indicate the configuration of the audio and video communication. Due to the large data amount of the audio and video communication, the limitations of the network, and the computer processing capabilities, the teacher and student computers cannot be connected at all times. Thus, after examining the necessary audio and video elements, we decided that the teacher computer and classroom computer should be constantly connected. Three computers would be connected in Q&A sessions. As a result, one-on-one communication between the teacher and any student is possible.

The teacher computer monitor during distance learning classes displays the upper part of the teacher's body, the view of the classroom by the remote-control camera, the Blackboard system, and the audio and video switching window. During Q&A sessions with a student, his or her image window is displayed as well. The student computer monitor displays the student, the Blackboard system, and the Note system. During Q&A sessions with the teacher, the teacher's image window is displayed as well. The Blackboard system, the image of the classroom, and the image of the teacher are displayed on the classroom screen.

Special Function for Lecture

We have developed the following functions for lecture.

1. *Shared temporary drawing function.* In conventional systems, a shared pointer is the only pointing method on a shared screen. Explanation with a shared pointer is difficult to understand, due to the teacher's gestures not being visible on a shared screen. An additional reason is the differences in the delay time of audio and video (AV) information and shared screen information. We have developed a new pointing method, called shared temporary drawing. This function leaves the loci (the locus which moved a mouse) of a shared pointer temporarily. Figure 2 shows the use image of the shared temporary drawing function. This function can draw lines on lecture data temporarily in real time. This function begins drawing when a mouse button is pushed, and ends when it is released. Erasing work by a teacher is unnecessary since it deletes automatically when the page is changed or a fixed time elapses.

Figure 2: Relation of the Mouse and Its Drawing on a Shared Temporary Drawing Function

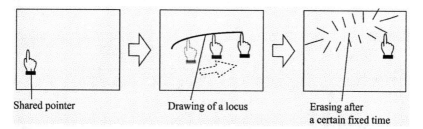

Shared pointer   Drawing of a locus   Erasing after
                                                                  a certain fixed time

2. *Lecture data creation support function.* Teachers complained that it time consuming to prepare the lecture data on PC for distance learning classes. In SEGODON, lecture notes written on paper are scanned into a PC using an image scanner. We developed an arrangement function of lecture data in order to arrange the scanner data. We developed the arrangement function to arrange lecture data from the scanner easily. We changed the size of the Blackboard system to A4 size (297mmx210mm), because most lecture notes are written in A4 size. From a limitation of a monitor's size, we developed a shared scroll function of lecture data.

Application of SEGODON for Lectures

The system has been continuously used for lectures on "High Frequency Engineering" 11 times. Table 2 shows the numbers of students who attended the distance learning classes. Students gathered in the computer exercise room on the second floor of the department of information and computer science. The students were in their third year at the department of information and computer science. A teacher was present in the room

Table 2: The Number of Attending Students in Every Class (Lecture Type)

Date	The number of attending students
10.19.99	13
10.26.99	11
11.02.99	10
11.09.99	6
11.30.99	6
12.07.99	7
12.14.99	6
12.21.99	6
01.11.00	8
01.18.00	3
01.25.00	6

Figure 3: An Example of a Screen on a Classroom

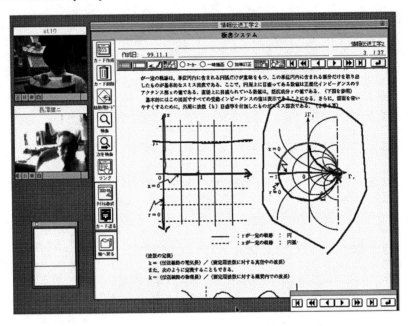

of the fifth floor of the same building. The lecture time was 90 minutes. This system was used 11 times in lectures out of 14 times. The usual classes were carried out three times (twice before the applications, and once after the applications). We carried out the questionnaire survey by students and the teacher after each class. Figure 3 shows the screen on a classroom. The handwritten lines in Figure 3 were drawn by the shared temporary drawing function.

Results of SEGODON for Lectures

The questionnaire results for students are shown in Table 3. A five-point scale was used (with the choices "1: very bad," "2: bad," "3: neutral," "4: good" and "5: very good") for students to evaluate each item on the questionnaire. The questionnaire results are the average values of 11 occasions. Figure 4 shows an example of the five-point scale on a questionnaire sheet.

The shared temporary drawing function on a shared screen was rated highly by students (Table 3, see (11)). We found that students relaxed during the lectures (Table 3, see (6)). Concerning overall evaluation of this system, the question "Would you like to participate in distance learning class again?" (Table 3, see (12)) — the average

Figure 4: An Example of the Five-Point Scale on a Questionnaire Sheet

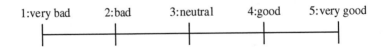

Table 3: The Questionnaire Results of Students in Lecture-Type Classes (Using SEGODON) and Regular Classes

Questionnaire items	Average value	
	Using SEGODON	Regular classes
(1) Did you understand the content of the lecture?	3.3	3.5
(2) Did you understand the content of the lecture from the teacher's facial expression and gestures?	3.1	3.2
(3) Did you understand the content of the lecture by the teacher's voice?	3.6	3.5
(4) Did you understand the content of the lecture by the card screen on the monitor (or by the blackboard)?	3.6	3.5
(5) Did you understand the content of the lecture by the teacher's shared pointer (or by the teacher's arm and finger)?	3.6	3.3
(6) Did you feel nervous during the lecture? (1: relaxed, 5: nervous)	2.1	2.3
(7) Were you satisfied with the lecture?	3.2	3.2
(8) Was the lecture interesting?	3.0	3.1
(9) Were the characters on the blackboard (the card screen) legible?	3.7	2.9
(10) Did you participate eagerly in the lecture?	3.0	3.1
(11) Was the shared temporary drawing function useful for understanding the lecture?	3.7	-
(12) Would you like to participate in the learning class again?	3.7	-
(13) Was it easy to operate this distance learning system?	3.5	-

was 3.7, "Was it easy to operate this distance learning system?" (Table 3, see (13)) — the average was 3.5. The students showed relatively positive evaluations of this system and the classes.

To use this system, a student need only turn on the computer and type in their login name and password. There is no need to operate the computer during class, which reduces the burden of operation for a student.

In order to compare regular classes with distance learning classes, the questionnaire surveys were carried out before applications of this system. The questionnaire results in regular classes are shown in Table 3. Concerning understanding of the content of a lecture, the difference of evaluation between regular classes and distance learning classes is small (Table 3, see (1) through (5)). Concerning the legibility of a character on the blackboard (regular classes) or the card screen (distance learning classes), evaluation of distance learning classes is higher than that of regular classes (Table 3, see (9)).

The questionnaire results for teachers are shown in Table 4. A five-point scale was used to evaluate each item on the questionnaire. Teachers could almost fully understand the situation in the classroom from the video information from the remote-control camera (Table 4, see (2)). Concerning the operation of the shared screen, both a shared pointer and the shared temporary drawing function were rated highly (Table 4, see (5), (10), (11)). The function for "deletion" was popular. Satisfaction with the system was evaluated comparatively highly (Table 4, see (6)). The teacher was able to operate this system alone during classes (Table 4, see (8)).

Table 4: The Questionnaire Results of the Teacher in Lecture-Type Classes (Using SEGODON)

	Questionnaire items	Average value
(1)	Were you able to do the lecture as planned?	3.8
(2)	Could you understand the situation in the classroom from the video from the remote-control camera?	3.8
(3)	Could you understand the situation in the classroom and students from the sound of the speaker?	3.3
(4)	Were you able to communicate the content of the lecture adequately using the card screen?	3.9
(5)	Were you able to communicate the content of the lecture adequately using the shared pointer?	4.0
(6)	Were you satisfied with the lecture?	3.7
(7)	Is this distance learning support system preferable?	3.0
(8)	Was it easy to operate this distance learning system?	3.7
(9)	Was it easy to operate the remote-control camera?	2.9
(10)	Was it easy to operate the shared temporary drawing function?	4.0
(11)	Was the shared temporary drawing function useful to the class?	4.2

We examined an end-term examination. The results of the end-term examination over a period of five years are shown in Table 5. The 1995 fiscal year and the 1996 fiscal year are the results of regular classes. The 1997, 1998 and 1999 fiscal years (this application) are the results of distance learning classes. All classes were taught by the same teacher. Although the 1999 fiscal year was higher than other fiscal years in the average score, no significant difference was found as a result of variance analysis test. It was deemed a good tendency that no difference was seen compared with the result of the examination by the regular classes.

We evaluated the lecture data creation support function. It took about 20 minutes to make per page of lecture data before using this function. In this application, the lecture data on paper was read using an image scanner, and the data were used as lecture data. It took about two minutes to make one page of lecture data using lecture data creation support system.

Table 5: Attending Students' Scores of the End-Term Examination

	Regular classes		Distance learning classes		
	1995 fiscal year	1996 fiscal year	1997 fiscal year (2 times)	1998 fiscal year (7 times)	1999 fiscal year (11 times)
Average score	69.4	65.8	67.5	66.5	74.2
Standard deviation	12.3	3.7	4.3	7.9	15.4

Table 6: The Part of Supporting Functions for Exercise

Supporting functions	Explanations
Report submission system	• The function supports report submission from students to a teacher.
Mail system	• The function supports an exchange of mail in this system using the Wadaman card.
Input support palettes for applied mathematics exercise	• The function eases inputting of expressions used in the "Applied Mathematics Exercise."
The operation support palette for applied mathematics exercise	• The palette collects the functions frequently used by students in the "Applied Mathematics Exercise."
The one-touch title creation function	• This function creates automatically a report title (a submission time a real name, a login name and an exercise name) by one-touch.

SEGODON for Exercise

Table 6 shows the functions developed for exercise. We describe the function related to exercise-type classes among the newly added functions. The report submission system supports report submissions from students to a teacher during class time. We developed this function to conduct exercise-type classes. We discovered that many students found drawing with a mouse to be a troublesome task. Thus, we developed input support palettes for applied mathematics exercises. The palettes support easy input of the expressions used in "Applied Mathematics Exercises." The one-touch title creation function automatically creates a report title with just one touch. This was developed because a teacher was bothered by untitled reports submitted by students at the time of marking and return.

Application of SEGODON for Exercise

SEGODON was used between buildings in Kagoshima University continuously four times. A teacher was in the teachers' room on the sixth floor of the department of electrical and electronics engineering. Students gathered in the computer exercise room on the second floor of the department of information and computer science. Table 7 shows the number of students who attended the distance learning classes. A questionnaire was carried out each time. From the results, we extracted the problems and improved the system. The students were second-year students of the department of bioengineering, and 29~32 students participated. The class was "Applied Mathematics Exercise" and the content of the classes concerned the Laplace transforms. The class time was 90 minutes, and followed this procedure:

Table 7: The Number of Attending Students in Every Class (Exercise Type)

Date	The number of attending students
6.3.98	32
6.17.98	28
6.24.98	31
6.30.98	30

1. The teacher lectured on the solutions to exercise problems using the Blackboard system. He explained the method using an exercise.
2. Each student solved a problem and submitted an answer report using the report submission function.
3. The teacher checked the submitted reports and returned the results to the students during the lecture. This was carried out from the second time the system was used.

We applied our system to these distance-learning classes four times following six normal classes. Moreover, in order to evaluate the application effect of the system, after the normal classes we examined the contents of the exercises. We did the same after the distance learning classes as well.

Result of SEGODON for Exercises

After each lecture, a questionnaire was given to students. We evaluated the students' degree of satisfaction of our system. A five-point scale was used (with answers "1: very bad," "2: bad," "3: neutral," "4: good" and "5: very good") for each item on the questionnaire. The questionnaire results are shown in Table 8.

The students had several questions during the performance of the four exercises in these applications. As an overall tendency, evaluations were critical compared with the lecture-type classes. We think this is because a student has to operate the system actively in an exercise-type class. A description item in the questionnaire, "How many times out of 15 would you want to take the lecture by distance learning?" showed that although after the 1st lecture the average was 5.8 times, it fell after the second lecture.

We examined a small test on the lecture range after six normal classes. Moreover, we examined a small test on the lecture range after four distance learning exercises. No difference was seen in the average or distribution by the results of the examinations (normal exercises: average of 50.5 points, distance learning exercises: average of 51.3 points). However, there is also the factor of the difference in the level of difficulty experienced by subjects. We think that the results of the test are good compared with the results of the test in normal exercises. This system allowed a teacher in a remote place to conduct an exercise-type class.

SEGODON-PDA

The conventional learning support system may reach large-scale, whereupon management of the system may be serious. The creation of electronic content for a lecture is also time-consuming for a teacher. A system is needed that can be used easily for both teachers and students. Recently, there has been an increase in simple lecture support systems, in which students use their own laptop computers connected to the Internet. That system did not use special software. They use a web browser to refer the content relating to the class. Laptop computers can be carried easily, but we cannot write something on the Blackboard while carrying and viewing a laptop computer. The computer may be too large and too heavy to use with one hand. As very small equipment that can be used with one hand is needed, we will give attention to the PDA and wireless LAN. A PDA is an electronic device for business basically, such as schedule management. There is no system that has effectively used PDAs for lectures. A PDA is very

Table 8: The Questionnaire Results of the Students in Exercise-Type Classes (Using SEGODON)

Questionnaire items	Average value
(1) Did you understand the content of the lecture?	3.1
(2) Did you understand the content of the lecture by the teacher's face and the expression on the screen?	2.7
(3) Did you understand the content of the lecture by the teacher's voice from the speaker?	2.9
(4) Did you understand the content of the lecture by the card screen of a monitor?	3.2
(5) Did you understand the content of the lecture by the teacher's shared pointer?	3.2
(6) Did you feel nervous during the lecture? (1: relaxed, 5: nervous)	1.9
(7) Were you satisfied with the lecture?	2.8
(8) Did you prefer this lecture to regular lectures?	2.8
(9) Would you like to participate in the learning class again?	3.2
(10) Was the lecture interesting?	3.3
(11) Did you find the process of this lecture adequate? (1: slow, 3: adequate, 5: fast)	2.8
(12) Did you participate eagerly in the lecture?	3.5
(13) Were the input support palettes useful?	3.3

compact and light, and the ability of PDAs has become sufficient to process data for a lecture. Wireless LAN can be used for all classrooms in our university. So, we have developed a lecture support system with PDAs and wireless LAN and can download data using PDAs and wireless LAN in lectures.

Design Policy
1. *Using PDA and Wireless LAN.* A PDA is very compact and light. The ability of PDAs has become sufficient to process data for a lecture. Wireless LAN is suitable for a network corresponding to the mobility of a PDA.
2. *Support for a part of regular lecture.* Most conventional learning support systems support an entire lecture. During a lecture, a teacher and student always use PCs. It was felt that a part of regular lectures was required.

System Overview
SEGODON-PDA is applied to lectures in two ways:
1. Students download exercise data using PDAs and wireless LAN in a lecture. Students answer exercises on their PDA.
2. The teacher distributes homework to each PDA, which students complete before the following class.

Figure 5: Configuration of SEGODON-PDA

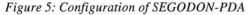
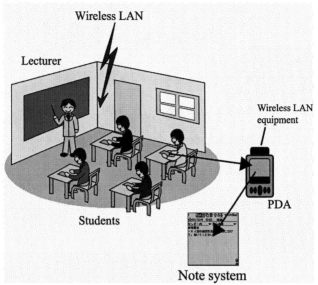

Hardware Configuration

SEGODON-PDA consists of PDAs (VisorEdge, Handspring), wireless LAN equipment (SpringPort Wireless Ethernet Module, Xircom), portable keyboard (Stowaway portable keyboards, TARGUS), and note software (Gmemo) (Munemori et al., 2001).

Figure 5 shows the configuration of SEGODON-PDA. The wireless LAN system can be used (IEEE802.11b) in any classroom in our university.

Software Configuration

Each student carries a PDA at all times and can review lectures anytime, anywhere. Students can download the exercise data using PDAs and wireless LAN in a class. The PDA has note software (GMemo), in order to paste the download data.

The system also has the function to distribute homework to PDAs and to collect completed homework from PDAs.

Application of SEGODON-PDA

We have applied the system to the "basic information engineering" class for third year students of the department of design and information sciences in our university. The content of the lecture concerns the basic concept of information processing, like logical circuits. Figure 6 shows the portable unit of the SEGODON-PDA. The unit consists of a PDA, a wireless LAN unit, and a portable keyboard. Each student carries the portable unit at all times.

The teacher writes lecture notes on the blackboard. In the latter half of the lecture, students download the exercise data using PDAs and wireless LAN. The PDA has the note software (GMemo), to paste the download data. Students solve the problem in GMemo and then write the answer on the blackboard, carrying and viewing the PDA.

Figure 6: Portable Unit of SEGODON-PDA

Figure 7 shows the example of the exercise in GMemo. The content of the exercise is to draw a Venn diagram. The student wrote the answer by free hand input and keyboard input. Writing situation (input time, name and location of writer) was inputted at the top part of the screen. The area of the screen is 160 dots x 160 dots. We can scroll three times (160 dots x 3) in length.

Figure 8 shows a portable unit of another student. The user in Figure 8 did not use the portable keyboard. The black part of the portable unit is the equipment for the wireless LAN. Figure 9 shows that the user of the portable unit in Figure 8 writes the answer on the blackboard while using the PDA simultaneously.

Figure 7: Example of Exercise Solutions in GMemo

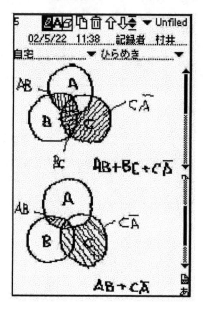

Figure 8: Example of Another Solution

Result of SEGODON-PDA

Five students took the class. One student had prior experience using the PDA. We performed the class with SEGODON-PDA two times. We carried out the questionnaire survey with the students after lectures. A five-point scale was used (with answers "1: very bad,"; "2: bad," "3: neutral," "4: good" and "5: very good") to evaluate each item on the questionnaire. The results of the questionnaire are shown in Table 9 and Table 10. We add the result of SEGODON in 1999 fiscal year to Table 10, which is one of a conventional type learning support system for reference. SEGODON supports the "High frequency engineering" course.

Students could understand the content of the lecture (4.2, 3.3) using SEGODON-PDA. Each value in the parentheses shows that "4.2" is the result of the lecture using SEGODON-PDA, and "3.3" is the results of the lecture using SEGODON. We use the same description method hereafter. They were satisfied with the course (3.8, 3.3) using SEGODON-PDA. Many students considered the course using SEGODON-PDA to be more desirable than regular lectures (4.4, 3.3). They wanted to participate in it again if possible (4.4, 3.7) using SEGODON-PDA (with wireless LAN). They rated the course as highly interesting (4.2, 3.0) using SEGODON-PDA. They felt that they could participate

Figure 9: Example of Using a Portable Unit

Table 9: The Questionnaire Results of Using SEGODON-PDA

- Merits with PDA
  - It is easy to carry.
  - We can input directly with a pen.
- Problems with PDA
  - It is difficult to use for a long time.
  - It became easy to input by the portable keyboard. But it is still difficult to input the data using the on-screen keyboard.
- Merits of wireless LAN
  - It is easy to connect to a network.
  - We can connect to a network anywhere.
- Merits of the class
  - It is interesting.
  - We can get the data in real-time from a network.
- Demerit of the class
  - We sometimes lose time in operating PDAs.
- What are the merits of using PDA for lectures?
  - We can connect to a network and download the data in the lecture.
  - In a regular lecture, the communication is mostly one way from a teacher. It is something new and interesting when we use the system.
- Do you think a PDA can be applied to other kinds of work?
  - I want to write a report using PDA.
  - I want to use our schedule control.
- What is your impression of the lecture?
  - I want to add some functions to the PDA.
  - You should do more lectures using PDA.

in the lecture very well (3.8, 3.0) using SEGODON-PDA. The total results of the comparison are shown below.

- Lectures using SEGODON-PDA were rated highly by students.
- Students felt that the lectures using SEGODON-PDA was interactive, because they could download the content of the lecture using wireless LAN in the class and they could write something on the blackboard while viewing the SEGODON-PDA.
- PDAs may not substitute laptop PCs at the present time, since much more business software is required.
- Portable keyboards were rated highly, but students felt that the on-screen keyboard of the PDA was difficult to use.

DISCUSSION

Table 11 shows the results of usage of SEGODON and SEGODON-PDA compared with the results of a regular class. The subjects were not the same in each application. Some classes, which were supported, were a different class. So, we cannot make definitive conclusions. But we can suggest the following:

Table 10: Comparison of SEGODON-PDA and SEGODON

Questionnaire items	Average value	
	SEGODON-PDA	**SEGODON**
(1) Did you understand the content of the lecture?	4.2	3.3
(2) Did you feel nervous during the lecture? (1: relaxed, 5: nervous)	2.2	2.1
(3) Were you satisfied with the lecture?	3.8	3.2
(4) Did you prefer this lecture to a regular lecture?	4.4	3.3
(5) Would you like to participate in the learning class again?	4.4	3.7
(6) Was the lecture interesting?	4.2	3.0
(7) Did you think the process of this lecture was adequate? (1: slow, 3: adequate, 5: fast)	3.2	3.2
(8) Did you participate eagerly in the lecture?	3.8	3.0
(9) Was the PDA useful for the lecture?	3.6	-
(10) Was it easy to input to the PDA?	3.4	-

1. The evaluation of the classes, which were supported by PCs, was almost the same with regular classes without the supporting system. The result of an end-term examination was almost the same. The learning support system might be effective for distance learning because a regular class cannot support it.
2. The results of evaluation using PDA (SEGODON-PDA) were high (Table 11, see (4) and (6)). Students want to participate in the class again (Table 11, see (5)). We analyzed the results and found that the good evaluation derived from the curiosity of the class (Table 11, see (6)), neither from understanding the class (Table 11, see (1)), nor satisfactoriness of the class (Table 11, see (3)).
3. Students participated eagerly in the exercise-type class (Table 11, see (6)). But if the supporting function for the exercise class was insufficient, the evaluation of it became low (Table 11, see (3) and (4)).
4. Students did not feel nervous in every type of class (Table 11, see (2)).
5. The process of each class was thought to be adequate.

The evaluation of the SEGODON-PDA was high because the class was partially an exercise-type and students were interested in PDAs.

RELATED WORK

There are many examples of collaboration systems available today. Most of Internet based educational systems are video teleconferencing systems, and web-based virtual auditorium or lecture room systems.

Table 11: Comparison Regarding Evaluation of the Students of SEGODON-PDA, SEGODON for Lecture, SEGODON for Exercise and Regular Classes

Questionnaire items	Average value			
	SEGODON-PDA	SEGODON (for lecture)	SEGODON (for exercise)	Regular class
(1) Did you understand the content of the lecture?	4.2	3.3	3.1	3.5
(2) Did you feel nervous during the lecture? (1: relaxed, 5: nervous)	2.2	2.1	1.9	2.3
(3) Were you satisfied with the lecture?	3.8	3.2	2.8	3.2
(4) Did you prefer this lecture to a regular lecture?	4.4	3.3	2.8	-
(5) Would you like to participate in the learning class again?	4.4	3.7	3.2	-
(6) Was the lecture interesting?	4.2	3.0	3.3	3.1
(7) Did you think the process of this lecture was adequate? (1: slow, 3: adequate, 5: fast)	3.2	3.2	2.8	3.0
(8) Did you participate eagerly in the lecture?	3.8	3.0	3.5	3.1

We compare our system with several other commercial and research activities briefly: Microsoft NetMeeting (Microsoft NetMeeting, 1999), TANGO (Beca et al., 1999; TANGO, 1999), Habanero (Jackson et al., 2002; Habanero, 1999), Centra (Centra, 1999), Placeware (Placeware, 1999), Kmi Stadium (Scott, 1998; KMi Stadium, 1999), and the system of Zaslavsky and Baker (Zaslavsky et al., 1998). Microsoft NetMeeting supports basic collaborative tools (audio-video conferencing, chat rooms and whiteboard). TANGO, Habanero, Centra, Placeware and KMi Stadium are web-based collaborative packages. TANGO and Habanero are written in Java and their application can be shared via exchange of API calls between the core and the application. Centra, Placeware and KMi Stadium can accommodate and allow many simultaneous participants. Their systems make available as a reusable resource. Centra supports up to 250 simultaneous users per event. Centra includes multi-way audio conferencing, yes/no responses and feedback, live application sharing, whiteboard, just-in-time content updates, text chat, and spontaneous polling. Placeware supports up to 1,000 people at the same time. The features of Placeware are almost the same as those of Centra. KMi Stadium is a Java-implemented system, allowing thousands of simultaneous participants, even over 28.8kbps dial-up modems. The features of KMi Stadium also look like those of Centra. Unlike Centra and Placeware, KMi Stadium can run live "streaming video" on higher-bandwidth clients.

The system of Zaslavsky and Baker resembles our system about an arrangement of an instructor and students, and the form of lectures. In their system, an instructor was at a distance site and students were in the lab. The demo computer in the lab was connected to an LCD panel and a projector. Audio was transmitted through speakers connected to the demo computer. Real-time video images were captured by the instructor's video cameras and demo computers. The pictures of both the instructor and the students were superimposed on Web-based lecture notes. Students could join the meeting between the instructor and TA from their client computers in the lab. They could gain access to shared textual and drawing windows (a shared whiteboard). Moreover their system has both web-based lecture notes and frequent email.

Comparisons between our system and the system devised by Zaslavsky and Baker are the following: Unlike their system, our system has a remote control camera for observing a classroom, a remote-control camera random operating function, one-on-one communication using audio and video for the students' direct Q&A sessions and interlocking marker function. Additionally, in the Zaslavsky and Baker system, the TA plays an essential role, for example, to control the organization of program windows in the demo computer. In our system, although TA has an important role, it is not indispensable. A teacher can operate our system alone.

CONCLUSION

There exist many learning support systems. We have developed the learning support systems, called SEGODON and SEGODON-PDA. SEGODON consists of PCs and LAN. SEGODON-PDA consists of PDAs and wireless LAN. We have applied them to the lecture-type class and the exercise type-class for several years.

The results of the application show that the class using the learning support system of PCs (SEGODON) was not superior to regular classes, which did not use digital equipment. If the supporting function was not sufficient, the evaluation of it may become low. The result of the end-term examination was almost the same regardless of classes.

Regular classes have been conducted for years and students seem to be familiar with them. Students also want to make notes in their notebooks in class, yet most learning support systems cannot accommodate that. However, if students use new digital equipment like PDAs, their motivation would undoubtedly greatly increase.

Our conclusion is that it is desirable to support distance learning because we cannot perform distance learning without digital equipment. We should support the exercise-type class by PDAs because the motivation of students would be high using new digital equipment.

In the future, we intend to apply the learning support systems to classes repeatedly and to further improve the system. The learning support system will become sufficient for a special class.

REFERENCES

Beca, L., Fox, G.C., & Podgorny, M. (1999). Component architecture for building web-based synchronous collaboration systems. *Proceedings of IEEE 8th International Workshops on Enabling Technologies: Infrastructure for Collaborative Enterprises* (WET ICE '99) (pp. 108-113).

Centra. (1999). Retrieved December 4, 2002 on the World Wide Web: http://www.centra.com/.

Habanero. (1999). *NCSA Habanero*. Retrieved December 4, 2002 on the World Wide Web: http://www.isrl.uiuc.edu/isaac/Habanero/.

Harasim, L. (1999). A framework for online learning: The Virtual-U. *IEEE Computer, 32*(9), 44-49.

Jackson, L. S., & Grossman, E. (1999). Integration of synchronous and asynchronous collaboration activities. *ACM Computing Surveys* (CSUR), *31*(2). ACM Press. Retrieved December 4, 2002 on the World Wide Web: http://portal.acm.org/citation.cfm?doid=323216.323359.

KMi Stadium (1999). Retrieved December 4, 2002 on the World Wide Web: http://cnm.kmi.open.ac.uk/projects/stadium/.

Maeda, K., Aibara, R., Kawamoto, K., Terauchi, M., & Otsuki, S. (1997). An environment for multimedia communication literacy. *Proceedings of ED-MEDIA/ED-TELECOM 97* (pp. 653-658).

Microsoft NetMeeting (1999). Retrieved December 4, 2002 on the World Wide Web: http://www.microsoft.com/windows/netmeeting/.

Munemori, J., Yoshino, T., & Nagasawa, Y. (1993). Development of a distributed multimedia platform and its application to intellectual cooperative works. *Transactions of Information Processing Society of Japan*, 34(6), 1385-1393.

Munemori, J., Yoshino, T., & Yoshida, A. (2002). Movable lecture support system using PDAs. *Proceedings of 2002 IEEE International Conference on Systems, Man, and Cybernetics* (SMC 2002), (vol. 1).

Munemori, J., Yoshino, T., & Yunokuchi, K. (2001). A spiral-type idea generation method support system for sharing and reusing ideas among a group. *Proceedings of 2001 IEEE International Conference on Systems, Man, and Cybernetics* (SMC 2001) (pp. 1898-1903).

Placeware (1999). Retrieved December 4, 2002 on the World Wide Web: http://www.placeware.com/.

Scott, P., & Eisenstadt, M. (1998). Exploring telepresence on the Internet: The KMi stadium webcast experience. In M. Eisenstadt & T. Vincent (Eds.), *The Knowledge Web*. London: Kogan Page.

TANGO (1999). *Tango - A Java/WWW-Based Internet Collaborative Software System*. Retrieved December 4, 2002 on the World Wide Web: http://trurl.npac.syr.edu/handout/tango.html.

Web-Based Training (2002). *Web-Based Training Information Center*. Retrieved December 4, 2002 on the World Wide Web: http://www.webbasedtraining.com/home.aspx.

Yoshino, T., Munemori, J., Nagasawa, Y., & Yunokuchi, K. (2001). Development and evaluation of a distance learning support system SEGODON. *Proceedings of 2001 IEEE International Conference on Systems, Man, and Cybernetics* (SMC2001) (pp. 1081-1086).

Yoshino, T., Munemori, J., Yuizono, T., Nagasawa, Y., Ito, S., & Yunokuchi, K. (1999a). Development and application of a distance learning support system using personal computers via the Internet. *Proceedings of the 1999 International Conference on Parallel Processing* (pp. 395-402).

Yoshino, T., Munemori, J., Yuizono, T., Nagasawa, Y., Ito, S., & Yunokuchi, K. (1999b). Application of distance learning support system SEGODON to exercise-type classes. *Transactions of Information Processing Society of Japan*, *40*(11), 3946-3956.

Zaslavsky, I., & Baker, K. (1998). The experimental web-based Interactive environment in distance teaching of GIS and geographic data handling. *Proceedings of the 1998 ACSM Annual Convention.*

Chapter VIII

Creative E-Transitions

Lynne Hunt, Edith Cowan University, Australia

ABSTRACT

The creative use of e-learning to facilitate the transition to and from university is the subject of this chapter. It describes a pilot, online transition to university project entitled Click Around ECU (Edith Cowan University) and an online, generic skills and career planning project called Careering Ahead in Health Promotion. Both projects are informed by authentic learning pedagogy that seeks to engage students in problem solving and learning by engaging in purposeful activities. The projects also seek to empower students to decide for themselves what they need to know about the transition process. Each project is described in the context of its implications for e-learning. The core thesis is that e-learning produces creative outcomes when embedded in appropriate pedagogy.

INTRODUCTION

'You can't teach creative writing,' said Lancaster. 'You provide the chance. The occasion. You encourage. You facilitate. You offer the window of opportunity.'
'I am a window cleaner, as it were,' said Dr. Bee. 'Or rather you are.'
'Exactly,' said Lancaster.

These lines from Michael Wilding's satirical novel, *Academia Nuts* (2002), suggest that creativity is facilitated rather than taught. If this is true of the traditional classroom setting that Wilding describes, it is equally true of e-learning. Like books, e-learning is a teaching and learning resource that can be put to creative use. E-learning is not in itself creative: Put simply, "Putting a course on the Web does not guarantee [creative learning] … any more than a library on campus does" (Allport, 2001). Rather, e-learning offers a "window of opportunity" for teachers, as facilitators (window cleaners), to scaffold creative learning experiences for their students. In other words, it's not the resource you've got but the way that you use it that counts.

The potential of e-learning is released by the pedagogy that informs its application. Without this, there is a risk of "confusion of technology with education, and tools with learning" (Brabazon, 2002). The purpose of e-learning is to enhance students' creativity and ability to construct their own knowledge. The two projects described in this chapter both harness the creative potential of e-learning by expanding opportunities for high school pupils and university students to become engaged actively in learning beyond the confines of classroom walls. They are both transition projects. The first, Click Around ECU (Edith Cowan University), is an online transition to university project for school-leavers. The originality of Click Around ECU is that it seeks to empower high school pupils to decide for themselves what they want to know about university life through the production of their own web-based, multimedia clips (web-shows). The second project, Careering Ahead in Health Promotion, is a web-based, career-planning program, de-signed for use throughout students' undergraduate studies to enable them to incorpo-rate generic skills into study programs in preparation for graduate transition to employ-ment.

ISSUES, CONTROVERSIES AND PROBLEMS

The transition to university, facilitated by projects such as Click Around ECU, is important because it affects the well being and success of young people. It also has implications for student retention rates. In turn, this affects the nation's purse. A British government report (HEFCE, 1997), for example, estimated the cost to taxpayers of attrition rates in higher education at around ninety million pounds per annum. Needless to say, statistics like this have concentrated the minds of public servants and university management teams on the importance of the transition to university and the enhancement of the first year university experience. In Australia, for example, the Commonwealth Government commissioned projects on the first-year, university experience (McGinnis & James, 1995). The level of academic interest in the transition to university may also be gauged from the fact that a whole edition of the *Journal of Institutional Research* (Vol 9(1), May 2000) was devoted to this topic.

Such literature reveals that the transition to university is a complex process because the experience varies in accordance with students' backgrounds and the nature of the institutions in which they enrol. International students, for example, face particular problems arising from cultural differences; and mature-aged students have transitional needs that differ from those of school leavers. Diversity can give rise to particular problems because "diverse" indicates different, and, very often, unequal. As Elson-Green (1999) reported: "A university education continues to be an elusive dream for some of the most disadvantaged groups in Australian society despite years of equity programs aimed at giving everyone a 'fair chance.' The Equity in Higher Education study … reveals the university system is failing indigenous students and people from rural, isolated and low socioeconomic status (SES) backgrounds." The tyranny of distance in the vast Australian continent gives rise to particular equity and university access issues for rural, remote and indigenous students that appropriate use of e-learning can address.

Strategies to ease the transition to university are many and varied. These include: orientation programs; counselling; academic support; and mentoring. Universities are increasingly using web sites to prepare new students for successful university careers. These have been used in a number of ways as Webb (2001) noted: "While most of the US websites dealing with students' initial transition are based on the premise that staff and students will meet face-to-face in a forthcoming campus-based orientation program, the University of Queensland's http://www.sss.uq.edu.au/isweb/ offers 'stand-alone' information in a questions and answer format . . ." Web-based, transition materials are an important resource. However, the point remains that it is how they are used that counts — and when.

THE CLICK AROUND ECU PROJECT

Most transition strategies have been designed to form part of the first-year university experience. Yet, effective transition to university starts well before enrolment (Pargetter, 2000). The Click Around ECU project assumed this thinking, for it engaged senior high school pupils in a competition to develop web-based, multimedia clips about university life. The competition was organized in a manner that actively engaged students in learning by doing. They were invited to make their own multimedia clips (web-shows) by using material from an existing university web site. In this way pupils were able to give "a personal sense to culturally pre-given meaning structures" (Van Oers & Wardekker, 1999). The aim of the competition was to enhance high school pupils' understanding of university life before enrolment at university. Its specific purpose was to facilitate a sense of control and ownership over the process of transition by creating opportunities for pupils to construct their own knowledge about university life. In this way, the pupils were participating in what Lave and Wenger (1991) called a community of practice, which, according to Herrington and Oliver (2000), "enables the learner to progressively piece together the culture of the group and what it means to be a member."

The project was facilitated by the prior development of the Race Around ECU (RAECU) web site, designed by Interactive Multimedia students of Edith Cowan University. The students were enrolled in a Project Management unit, which required them to find authentic learning opportunities to develop a web site to client specifications and to demonstrate project management skills. A group of these students agreed to design the RAECU web site (http://www.ecu.edu.au/pa/raecu/index.html) to facilitate high school pupils' use of the University's web site and to enhance their confidence and readiness for university. It was organized in terms of questions rather than answers to guide high school pupils to interrogate the material on the Edith Cowan University web site. The "5W,H" questions were deployed as a framework: Who? Where? What? Why? When? How? Ready-made teaching and learning strategies were included to assist schoolteachers in the use of the RAECU site with their classes.

One of the Project Management students, Jack Seddon, incorporated a "web-show" feature in the RAECU web site that enabled high school pupils to investigate, online, aspects of university life and to use this material to produce a multimedia clip about the university. The authoring software used to construct a web-show is Windows Media Tools 4.1, a free-to-download collection of tools including Windows Media Author (http://www.microsoft.com/windows/windowsmedia/technologies/resource/tools.asp).

High school pupils can use this software to combine data, such as images and sound, with Universal Resource Locators (URLs) and scripting commands. This enables them to create interactive, audiovisual files that can take a user to a web site anywhere on the Internet or an intranet. The simplest form of a web-show is constructed on a time-line by adding a sound track (wav file), a URL or a picture file (bmp or jpeg), or a mixture of them. Cue points may then be inserted on the time-line at desired transition times. Each of the cue points can cause the viewer's browser window to jump to a URL. On completion, the developed web-show is saved as a project file with the extension ".AEP." The project file is then compressed to produce a single, web-capable, streaming media file with the extension ".ASP." It may then be linked to a web page. When a user clicks on the link, the web-show will play or stream from a server over the Web and play back on Windows Media Player.

In the first instance, Click Around ECU was run as a pilot project to assess the feasibility of using this technology. A small-scale competition was run between selected high schools in Perth, Australia. Pupils were invited to develop their own web-shows. Staff and students of the University and the high schools closely monitored the process and the product. The Click Around ECU project was funded by Edith Cowan University's Office of Marketing and Public Relations, thereby demonstrating that creative partnerships between non-academic sections of the University, teaching departments and high schools can lead to creative learning experiences for students. The project was designed to take pupils no more than five weeks to complete and, as far as practical, it was integrated into their normal curriculum. Pupils used the Edith Cowan University web site as a resource to gather information relevant to them. A CD ROM (which included all files that needed to be accessed by pupils) was provided as a template for their use. Further, a "web-show demo" was located at www.ecu.edu.au/pa/raecu/Webshow/startdemoshow.html. In addition, each school was supplied with an information pack, which described the project (Hunt et al., 2002).

The outcomes of the Click Around ECU competition revealed that high school pupils enhanced their understanding of interactive multimedia skills and university life. They engaged with the creative processes and went well beyond the basics to produce complex web-shows that incorporated important information about the transition to university. This substantiates Csikszentmihalyi's (1992) idea of "flow," in which, as Herrington and Oliver (2000) explain, "the sense of interest and engagement with a project is not bounded by the restraints of formal exercises and classes." The pupils' learning was frameworked by the rules of the competition so as to allow their creativity to develop in response to the task at hand. The web-shows indicated that high school pupils were attracted to active areas of university life such as sport, and art, drama, dance and music in the Western Australian Academy of Performing Arts (WAAPA@ECU). They touched on matters such as campus location, the application and enrolment processes, accommodation, and the differences in studying between school and university. They used a range of creative devices to engage the attention of their peers. Some web-shows were factual. Others used humour. One group produced an animated character to narrate their show (Edward Cecil Ugenheimer [ECU, Edith Cowan University]: He's a bit of a nerd, but he's a smart nerd and he knows what he's doing . . . sometimes!).

The Click Around ECU project provided creative learning opportunities for high school pupils to construct a story about university life. They expanded their knowledge of the content by choosing their own research focus. They were the constructors of the learning. Pupils involved in this project had to develop effective strategies within the medium in order to be artful storytellers and to engage their audience. They succeeded! Their web-shows were funny and informative and have resulted in web-based resources for on-going use by staff in schools and universities to ease the transition to university.

Was Click Around ECU an effective learning process for high school pupils? Certainly their teachers thought so. They felt that their pupils benefited from working on a real-life task rather than one manufactured by teachers. Further, the pupils worked in a self-directed manner while acquiring multimedia skills as well as transitional knowledge about the University. An important, but seemingly incidental, by-product was that they also learned teamwork. Pupil feedback was also positive. Some indicated that they had changed their minds and now intended to apply to enter university. This was an important outcome in a project that had equity in mind. Some of the schools participating in the Click competition were selected because they are low-transfer schools, sending very few of their pupils to university. The high school pupils also became very conscious of working to non-negotiable deadlines established outside their school. The marriage of technological skills with creativity was something the pupils identified as important. As one said: "I feel confident about the narrative — it's not something we've done before." They also became conscious of the skills that each could bring to the project: "We chose roles we knew we were good at — like, he's good at writing."

The knowledge-construction inherent in the Click Around ECU competition was "a process of experimentation and negotiation in a community of learners" (Van Oers & Wardekker, 1999). In this endeavor, the pupils in the competition engaged in "problem solving, argumentation, use of symbolic tools (signs), and reflective comparison of available (including conventional) solutions [which] ... seem to be essential ingredients for reinventing valuable truths" (Van Oers & Wardekker, 1999). These aptitudes and others, such as working to deadlines, teamwork and writing, are all generic skills necessary to lifelong learning. Such skills are a core feature of the second of the creative e-learning projects described in this chapter.

CAREERING AHEAD IN HEALTH PROMOTION

The project entitled Careering Ahead in Health Promotion is a web-based program designed to link generic, globally transferable skills with graduate career planning. The program exposes university students to:

- the range of occupational groupings that employ public health graduates;
- employers who recruit public health graduates;
- actual job descriptions and selection criteria, in particular generic skills, that students will need to address to be competitive graduates; and
- a range of recruitment and employment patterns including contract positions, tendering options, and non-government, and self-employed, contract positions, along with traditional forms of employment.

It has become increasingly necessary for universities to pay attention to the skills sustaining the employability of their graduates. As the *Times Higher Education Supplement* reported (1998, November 6), "Businesses are not remedial educators. We do not expect young people to come out of education unaware of the world of business and lacking key skills such as communication and teamwork." There is an increasing emphasis on such skills in universities around the world (Dearing, 1997; Commonwealth of Australia, 2002). Known also as generic skills, or graduate attributes, globally transferable skills (Allen, 1991) are relevant to lifelong learning and include: critical thinking, written and oral communication, teamwork, problem solving, managing, and organizing.

In an environment in which universities compete for undergraduate students, and in a context in which university study is increasingly expensive, it is likely that the career success of graduates will become a defining feature of universities. In any case, there may be little choice about linking university study to the graduate attributes required by employers because the political will to produce work-ready graduates is strong: "The changing nature of work is requiring individuals to increase their level of skills and become multi-skilled. To meet these demands, many students are looking for an education that provides a combination of elements of traditional higher education and vocational education" (Commonwealth of Australia, 2002). Careering Ahead in Health Promotion models a way of using e-learning to enhance vocational education and smooth graduate transition to the workforce.

The welcoming page for Careering Ahead in Health Promotion is couched as a series of interview questions that students might expect to face when seeking employment. Students may use these questions to identify gaps in their own learning and experience. These are then linked to courses and units of study that address their identified learning needs. The site comprises seven pages. These include: a welcoming page, and a careers page, which explores where health promotion people work and the skills that are required of them, such as assessing individual and community needs, and planning and developing health programs. One page covers current vacancies. Another links students to the University's Careers Advisory Service and, in particular, any workshops that it might offer. There is a page on professional associations and another on courses. The Web site includes sample selection criteria, and information about the use of online applications for employment. The framework is generic and has broad applicability. The content is subject-specific. This is necessary for two reasons. Firstly, the fields in which students will seek employment are normally confined to their chosen university course. Secondly, in the specific case of health promotion and, more widely, public health, there is limited career advice available within Western Australia.

This online tool encourages students to view their employment search as part of a lifelong learning process. It will enable students to manage their employment direction depending on their area of interest. They can choose to be flexible, aiming at a wide range of employment clusters, or target a specific field of employment. They can thereby prepare themselves for a range of employment patterns and opportunities. The project is still in its developmental stage and has yet to be piloted. However, features of its development illustrate the importance of contextualising e-learning within a pedagogy that facilitates the creative potential of students. Firstly, the web site establishes relevance for students because it encourages them to reflect on their learning needs and to link these to current studies and future employment. Secondly, it engages students with professional associations and enhances opportunities for networking that may facilitate employment prospects. Thirdly, it uses narrative, telling the stories of previous students' graduate employment experiences. Fourthly, and perhaps most importantly, it focuses on generic skills, "Students are expected to play [an] ... active part in learning and the focus [is] ... on the acquisition of skills: expressing opinions, [researching], making connections with various professional practices" (Roelofs & Terwel, 1999). The term "situated learning" is particularly appropriate to the development of this Web site because "[t]he [employment] situation largely determines the structure, content and coherence of the concepts used" (Roelofs & Terwel, 1999).

THE PEDAGOGY

The informing pedagogy of the two transition projects, Click Around ECU and Careering Ahead in Health Promotion, was authentic or situated learning. This means that the projects relied heavily on constructivist learning principles that encourage learners to construct their own meaning for knowledge and information in the learning process. Authentic learning is an eclectic pedagogy that incorporates elements of action learning described by Sandelands (1998) as a form of learning by doing. It focuses on real-life problems and, as Keys (1994) indicated, its aim is to encourage students to ask questions rather than learn answers. It invites students to test ideas and to reflect on outcomes. In this it is similar to problem-based learning, which is "conventionally defined as students learning new knowledge by working on the solution of a defined problem" (Taplin, 2000). According to Herrington and Oliver (2000), the essence of authentic learning may be found in the qualities and features of learning that unite knowing and doing. The eclectic nature of the pedagogy is encapsulated in their nine-point summary of the meaning of authentic or situated learning which:

1.   provides authentic contexts that reflect the way the knowledge will be used in real life;
2.   provides authentic activities;
3.   provides access to expert performances and the modelling of processes;
4.   provides multiple roles and perspectives;
5.   supports the collaborative construction of knowledge;
6.   promotes reflection to enable abstractions to be formed;
7.   promotes articulation to enable tacit knowledge to be made explicit;
8.   provides coaching and scaffolding by the teacher at critical times; and
9.   provides for authentic assessment of learning within the tasks.

Herrington and Oliver's nine dimensions of situated learning accord with what has been called "Knowledge Age" learning practices. Trilling and Hood (1999) noted that in moving from an industrial age to a knowledge age, learning practices have undergone changes to authentic, knowledge-age learning. This transition has been facilitated by e-learning because it enables teachers to move from a directive role to become a facilitator or consultant — the "window cleaner" who sheds light on the processes. Knowledge-age learning moves away from timetabled, scheduled learning to flexible, on-demand learning that is facilitated by e-learning opportunities. The Click Around ECU competition engaged pupils in what Trilling and Hood (1999) described as competitive collaboration and learning that resulted in creative diversity rather than conformity to prescribed norms. Computing was the subject of study because students developed interactive multimedia and computing skills through the projects. It was also the tool for learning that resulted in creative narrative and visual outcomes that included dynamic, multimedia presentations. There were, in fact, two levels of authentic learning taking place in the Click Around ECU project. The aim was to learn about multimedia presentations in an authentic way. At the same time, pupils were engaged in constructing their own knowledge about university life. To accommodate the diversity and creativity of the outcomes of the Click competition, pupils were assessed by experts, mentors and peers. The results were open-ended and each of the four-minute web-shows had different content and tone reflecting the creativity of pupils in self-directed projects.

The Careering Ahead in Health Promotion project is also embedded in authentic learning pedagogy. In particular, it facilitates interaction and socialization with professionals as a critical element in the learning process. This was identified by Oliver et al. (1998) as a core feature of authentic learning. The structure of the web site responds to employer demands for generic skills. "These include the use of appropriate technologies for processing information (Beavan, 1996; Caudron, 1997; Leveson, 1996); verbal, aural and written communication skills (...Jones, 1995; Ward, 1996; team skills (Heskin, 1994); proficiency in solving workplace problems (Heskin, 1994); time management (Mullen, 1997); flexibility (Leveson, 1996); and ability to work under pressure (Cauldron, 1997; Taplin, 2000, p. 279). According to Taplin (2000), the problem-based learning that lies at the heart of Careering Ahead in Health Promotion is "an approach that can enhance the development of all these important skills."

The two projects described in this chapter have been used to illustrate creative uses of e-learning. However, so far, the nature and meaning of creativity has remained uncontested. Yet there are debates about the extent to which creativity can be taught because the uniqueness of the creative process cannot be packaged and described in behavioural objectives. Creativity is sought, not caught, by students in their own struggle to develop meaning. It resonates with "the kind of learning and thinking through which knowledge is transformed into personal understanding that shapes the way we see the world" (Dombey, 1999). E-learning enhances this process by creating classrooms without borders, opportunities for local and global networking and the freedom for students to work in structured and unstructured ways using teachers as facilitators rather than instructors. As Kumar (2002) observed, "The methodology of E-Learning ... employs the principle of distributed cognition and it enables wide interaction disregarding all boundaries in a virtual learning environment. It enables utilisation of existing web sites and promotes development of newer web sites." Both of the projects described in this chapter do exactly that. The Click competition was based on the RAECU and the University web sites, and Careering Ahead in Health Promotion exploits the existing Career Advisory Service web site and the recently developed Edith Cowan University work-based learning web site, known as Work Links (http://www.ecu.edu.au//ssa/worklinks/).

FUTURE DIRECTIONS

The success of Click Around ECU has inspired the project coordinators to consider possible future opportunities for authentic learning about the transition to university. Ideas include extending the competition to rural, remote and indigenous pupils because they remain disadvantaged in terms of access to university. The Click Around ECU concept provides a wonderful opportunity to work with non-metropolitan high school pupils because physical access to campus life is unnecessary in the development of web-shows. Isolated and rural high school pupils can obtain all the information they need from the Web and can communicate with the organizers via bulletin boards. Similar extensions of the concept for use with international students, prior to their arrival in Australia, are under consideration.

The Careering Ahead in Health Promotion project will be incorporated into a wider project on lifelong learning skills. This will include modules on critical thinking, written and oral communication and information technology skills. The aim is to make these available on CD Rom to all incoming first year students in Public Health, with a view to broadening the content to other subject areas after the piloting stage. The beauty of this project is that it will be equally available to internal and external students, the latter comprising a significant proportion of the teaching load at Australian universities. The creativity will lie not just in the students' construction of their own world-view, but also in the flexible manner in which it is planned for inclusion in the curriculum. At this stage, the plan is to allow students to use the CD Rom as an on-demand resource. This fits with the principle of adult learning, that people learn when they need to know. Further, it will be available as a resource for staff to incorporate into existing units or modules of study. Finally, following appropriate accreditation processes, the plan is to incorporate the full meaning of flexible learning by creating opportunities for students to complete a specified number of the modules any time during their university career, for accreditation as an elective unit. This means that the creativity of e-learning lies not only in the opportunities it creates for students, but also in the manner in which it is creatively woven into the fabric of university curricula.

CONCLUSION

There is a risk, when associating e-learning with creativity, of confusion arising between the creativity of online resources and the use of such resources to enhance students' creativity. In other words, fancy packages that serve only to pretty-up the transmission of factual material — infotainment — risk being a "technological travesty" (Wright, 2001), serving only to deliver answers, thereby "de-skilling students." As Reeves (1995) noted, "deeper, richer levels of learning and human development may be better attained via fundamental changes in our pedagogical philosophy rather than by the tinkering of instructional designers with levels of 'ineractivity.'" Both projects described in this chapter adopt this approach and accord with Wright's opinion (2001) that, "[t]he student learning experience online can be empowering, if students are provided with the facilities and tools with which to construct the answers." To reiterate, creativity arises not only from what you've got by way of e-learning resources, but also from how you use it.

ACKNOWLEDGMENTS

I should like to acknowledge the inventiveness and creativity of my partners in both projects: Lorraine Kershaw and Jack Seddon in Click Around ECU, and Julie Howell and Gill Matthews in Careering Ahead in Health Promotion.

REFERENCES

Allen, M. (1991). *Improving the Personal Skills of Graduates: Final Report*. Sheffield: Personal Skills Unit Sheffield University.

Allport, C. (2001). eLearning and our future. *Advocate, 8*(1), 2.

Beavan, S. (1996). Employers want grads who know computers. *Indianapolis Business Journal, 7*(9), 10.

Brabazon, T. (2002, December 4). Why 'consumers' avoid the degree stores. *The Australian*. Excerpt from Brabazon, T. (2002). *Digital Hemlock: Internet Education and the Poisoning of Teaching*. Sydney, Australia: University of New South Wales Press.

Caudron, S. (1997). Hire for attitude: It's who they are that counts. *Workforce, 1,* 20-25.

Commonwealth of Australia. (2002). *Varieties of Learning. The Interface Between Higher Education and Training*. Canberra: Commonwealth Department of Education Science and Training.

Csikszentmihalyi, M. (1992). *Flow: The Psychology of Happiness*. London: Rider.

Dearing Review. (1997). *The National Committee of Inquiry into Higher Education: Higher Education for the 21st Century*. London: HMSO.

Dombey, H. (1999). Use of language across the primary curriculum/Information technology and authentic learning: Realising the potential of computers in the primary classroom. *Cambridge Journal of Education, 29*(1), 145-147.

Elson-Green, J. (1999, March 31-April 6). Equity in higher education confirms inequities. *Campus Review, 5.*

HEFCE. (1997). *Undergraduate non-completion in higher education in England, No. 97/29*. Higher Education Funding Council for England. Available on the World Wide Web: http://www.niss.ac.uk/education/hefce/pub97.

Herrington, J., & Oliver, R. (2000). An instructional design framework for authentic learning environments. *Educational Technology Research and Development, 48*(3), 23-48.

Hunt, L., Kershaw, L., & Seddon, J. (2002). Authentic Transitions: The Click Around ECU On-line Transition to University Program. In A. Goody, J. Herrington & M. Northcote (Eds.), *Quality Conversations. Proceedings of the HERDSA Conference*. Perth: HERDSA. (CD-ROM). Available on the World Wide Web: http://www.herdsa.org.au/.

Jones, E. (1995). *National assessment of college student learning: Identifying college graduates' essential skills in writing, speech and listening, and critical thinking. Final project report*. University Park, PA: National Centre on Postsecondary Teaching, Learning, and Assessment.

Keys, L. (1994). Action learning: Executive development of choice for the 1990s. *Journal of Management Development, 13*(8), 50-56.

Kumar, K. L. (2002). *E-Learning for design education.* Paper presented to the EDUCOM 2000 Conference, Khon Kaen, Thailand. (Unpublished).

Lave, J., & Wenger, E. (1991). *Situated Learning: Legitimate Peripheral Participation.* Cambridge: Cambridge University Press.

Leveson, R. (1996). Can professionals be multi-skilled? *People Management, 2*(17), 36-39.

McInnis, C., & James, R. (1995). *First Year on Campus.* Canberra: AGPS.

Mullen, J. (1997). Graduates deficient in 'soft' skills. *People Management, 3*(22), 18.

Oliver, R., Omari, A., & Herrington, J. (1998). Developing converged learning environments for on and off-campus students using the WWW. In R. Corderoy (Ed.), *Conference Proceedings ASCILITE '98, 529-538.* Wollongong: The University of Wollongong.

Pargetter, R. (2000). Transition: From a school perspective. *Journal of Institutional Research, 9*(1), 14-21.

Reeves, T. (1995). *Reaction to 'interactivity': A forgotten art? Available* on the World Wide Web: itforum@uga.cc.uga.edu.

Roelofs, E., & Terwel, J. (1999). Constructivism and authentic pedagogy: State of the art and recent developments in the Dutch national curriculum in secondary education. *Journal of Curriculum Studies, 31*(2), 201-227.

Sandelands, E. (1998). Creating an online library to support a virtual learning community. *Internet Research: Electronic Networking Applications and Policy, 8*(1), 75-80.

Taplin, M. (2000). Problem-based learning in distance education: Practitioners' beliefs about an action learning project. *Distance Education, 21*(2), 278-299.

Trilling, B., & Hood, P. (1999). Learning, technology and education reform in the knowledge age or 'We're wired, webbed and windowed, now what?' *Educational Technology: The Magazine for Managers of Change in Education, 39*(3), 5-18.

Van Oers, B., & Wardekker, W. (1999). On becoming an authentic learner: Semiotic activity in the early grades. *Journal of Curriculum Studies, 31*(2), 229-249.

Ward, M. (1996). Communication skills most important for new grads. *HR Magazine, 41*(4), 16.

Webb, J. (2001). Using the web to explore issues related to the first year experience. *Higher Education Research and Development, 20*(2), 225-236.

Wilding, M. (2002). *Academia Nuts.* Glebe NSW: Wild and Woolley.

Wright, P. (2001). eLearning emerges. *Advocate, 8*(1), 23.

Chapter IX

Distributed Constructionism through Participatory Design

Panayiotis Zaphiris, City University, UK

Giorgos Zacharia, MIT, USA

Meenakshi Sundaram Rajasekaran, City University, UK

ABSTRACT

We present the implementation of Distributed Constructionism (DC) through a Participatory Design (PD) methodology of an Online Learning community. The students collaborate on the content and functionality development of an online Modern Greek language course, peer review and publish content contributions, and participate in participatory design teams. Participatory design was implemented as a four step process (a) Build bridges with the intended users, (b) Map user needs and suggestions to the system, (c) Develop a prototype, (d) Integrate feedback and continue the iteration. Distributed Constructionism was implemented to enhance the learning experience and community development. Finally Social Network Analysis is employed to quantitatively measure the strength of the online community established and the key role our participatory design team participants played in sustaining this online community.

INTRODUCTION

The contribution of this chapter is the presentation of an empirical study of an online learning community collaborating with the design team of the course under the Participatory Design methodology. We measure the student participation during the different phases of the design process, and the changes in their behavior when new design elements are introduced. We implement the different phases of Participatory Design methodology using a four-stage process: (a) Build bridges with the intended users, (b) Map user needs and suggestions to the system, (c) Develop a prototype, (d) Integrate feedback and continue the iteration. Our participatory design methodology was carried out by following the Distributed Constructionism pedagogical theory, and took advantage of the online and distributed nature of the student community to asynchronously design, implement and study the course. Finally we use Social Network Analysis (SNA) to evaluate the student participation on the online discussion forum. We discover that the students who volunteer to contribute in the participatory design teams and contribute most of the additional material are also the central nodes of the SNA analysis. We conclude that the online discussion board can promote student collaboration and the identification of the key community users who can participate productively in Participation Design activities.

Participatory Design

Participatory design (PD) (often termed the "Scandinavian Challenge") (Bjerknes et al., 1987) refers to a design approach that focuses on the intended user of the service or product, and advocates the active involvement of users throughout the design process. User involvement is seen as critical both because users are the experts in the work practices supported by these technologies and because users ultimately will be the ones creating new practices in response to new technologies (Ellis et al., 1998).

Blomberg and Henderson (1990) characterize the PD approach as advocating three tenets:

- The goal is to improve the quality of life.
- The orientation is collaborative.
- The process is iterative.

Distributed Constructionism

Distributed Constructionism (Resnick, 1996) extends the Constructionism theory (Papert, 1991, 1993) to knowledge building communities, where the online learning community (instead of one student) collaboratively constructs knowledge artifacts (Resnick, 1996). The three major activities of DC, within the context of an online learning community are (Resnick, 1996):

1. Discussing Constructions: Students discuss their constructions during the design, implementation, evaluation and reiteration phases
2. Sharing Constructions: Web-based systems allow students to share their constructions and make them part of the shared knowledge.
3. Collaborating on Constructions: The community can use online communication to collaborate on the design and development of the knowledge artifacts.

The iterative structure of our Participatory Design approach enhanced Distributed Constructionism among the users of the system. The knowledge artifacts contributed to the course, enhanced both the learning experience of the users and the content and functionality of the course itself.

This chapter is structured around four main sections. First, our PD design approach is presented and its linkage to the Distributed Constructionism pedagogical theory specified, then the results of the Social Network Analysis of our course are presented. In the third section the results of a user-centered evaluation of the course are also put forward and the chapter ends with a set of conclusions and suggestions for directions for future research.

DESIGN APPROACH

Our focus has been to design an online learning community around a Computer Aided Language Learning (CALL) course. We believe that online interaction and community would increase users' motivation, commitment and satisfaction with the online course. The Participatory Design methodology blends nicely with our goal. In particular, involving users during system development is thought to lead to greater user commitment, acceptance, usage, and satisfaction with the system (Baroudi et al., 1986).

In the design phase of the online course, we implemented PD as a four-step process (Ellis et al., 1998).

1. *Building bridges with the intended users:*
    This step opened lines of communication between intended users and the development team. Specifically, this step involved the initialization of a multidisciplinary development team, identifying key groups of end users, and creating new methods of communication with users.

    The development team in this project came out of the Kypros-Net (Kypros-Net Inc., 2002) group. Through their involvement in Cyprus and Greece related projects, they had longstanding relations with the intended user community.

    The intended users have been especially people of the Greek Diaspora, travelers to Cyprus and Greece and other Greek speaking areas and people who are generally interested in the Greek culture and language or languages in general. In our case, bridges with the intended users were build through our years of work at providing information about Cyprus through the web pages of Kypros-Net who primarily attracts the same user population as our intended Greek language online course.

2. *Mapping user needs and suggestions to the system:*
    Our conceptual design model has been "to design an effective online Greek language course that can build and sustain an online learning community of students."

    Based on the questions and inquiries we received from our users we tried to match their needs (they wanted an easy to follow, both elementary and advanced course that they could attend at their own pace) with our conceptual design model.

3. *Developing a prototype:*
    The project consists of 105 audio files, which were originally recorded as radio lessons in Modern Greek for English speakers in the 1960s. The lessons were

retrieved from the archives of the Cyprus Broadcasting Corporation, digitized in Real Audio 5.0 format and published online through the course. Although an optional textbook accompanied the original radio lessons, the online lessons were designed as a complete stand-alone course. We used several tools to assist students with the lessons, including an online English-Greek-English dictionary, a Greek spell checker and a web-based discussion board. The discussion boards served as the foundation for creating a community of online students and enhanced the learning experience with Distributed Constructionism.

4.   *Integrating feedback and continuing the cycle:*
Feedback from our users and suggestions are continuously incorporated into our design through a series of additions and corrections. For example, we were asked to add an online notes section and to encode some files again because they were corrupted.

An important element in the participatory design methodology is the direct involvement of the users in all stages of the design process. We kept the users involved by participating in the discussion boards, and sharing with them design and development plans for the course.

COURSE EVOLUTION WITH DISTRIBUTED CONSTRUCTIONISM

The students of the audio courses included people with no knowledge of Greek language, bilingual members of the Greek Diaspora, as well as high-school professors of non-Greek language. These students created an open online community whose collaboration has boosted the learning experience of the whole community. The web-based discussion board has proven to be the most constructive tool for the students' learning experience and the main source of feedback for the maintainers of the project. The experiences shared on the discussion board included tricks and tips on how to record the audio files, installation of Greek fonts, learning methodologies and questions about the Greek language itself that arise from the lessons. The experienced users (some of them were retired teachers of foreign languages) had taken a lead role in the vast majority of the threads on the discussion board, answering most of the questions and encouraging the beginners to study the lessons further. They have also become the communication interface between the maintainers of the project and the community's requests.

At some point, the users started exchanging, through email, written notes taken by the experienced users. They also used the discussion board to announce the availability of their personal notes. This behavior suggests that we must provide (and we did) the users with the capability to post their notes on the project's site.

The students had initiated Distributed Constructionism themselves. The course designers only provided technical support to facilitate the students' construction activities.

Discussing the Constructions

The course designers offered to provide publishing access to the online course to whoever wanted to contribute their material. Five users asked to be given access. As we will see later in the Social Network Analysis of the community, these users also had a central role in the discussion board. Consequently, the five users with the two course designers constituted the Participatory Design team. The PD team solicited contributions from the user community. The users suggested that they should transcribe the audio lessons, and compile verb lists, vocabulary lists, and grammatical notes for each lesson.

Sharing the Constructions

All the user contributions were shared in the common area of the online course. The users members of the PD team regularly posted notices on the discussion board about new material for the course. Also, other less active users chose to offer contributions for the course, by posting on the discussion board, rather than contacting the PD team.

Collaborating on the Constructions

The user members of the PD team did not include any native speakers of Greek. They were all learning the language through the online course, and at that stage, they were primarily dependent on the audio lessons. In order to ensure the quality of the new material before publishing them on the course web site, the user members of the PD team implemented a peer review process. A group of seven users, that included the five central user PD team members, reviewed and corrected all the material before posting them on the web site. Each of the seven users offered to transcribe a number of the 105 Audio lessons, and two of them also offered to provide verb and vocabulary lists. However, all materials were posted in a private area first, reviewed by the seven user members of the PD team, and posted on the web site when the five PD users were satisfied with the quality. Then the two PD course designers, who were both native Greek speakers, would go over the already published material, and make sure that it is correct. Most of the mistakes we had to correct were spelling mistakes, and we rarely had to correct grammatical mistakes.

Two months after the Distributed Constructionism effort started, students of the audio lessons managed to transcribe 81 out of the 105 lessons, correct them through the peer review process among themselves and post them on the project's web site. Six months later, the students had transcribed and peer reviewed all 105 lessons.

The knowledge constructed attracted significant user attention. As we can see from Figure 1, the accesses to the audio lessons, the language tools, and the total access of the message board and the notes pages all kept increasing exponentially. However, once we allowed our users to publish their own notes, there was a dramatic shift of traffic from the message board to the notes pages. In our view this is due to the fact that the users did not need any more to visit the discussion board to find out where other users had posted their notes. All the content was already aggregated and organized in a central location.

The course's popularity is apparent from the fact that the course currently has over 20,000 registered students who actively participate in an online community, which evolved around the course.

Figure 1: Access Statistics for Greek-Online Site

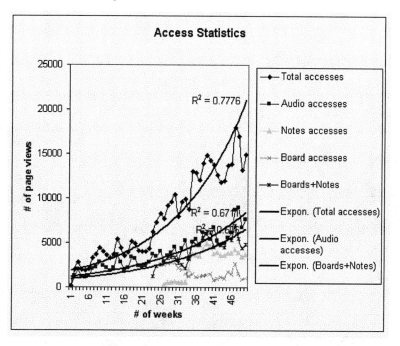

SOCIAL NETWORK ANALYSIS

Social network analysis (SNA) is the study of social relationships between a set of actors (Baroudi et al., 1986). Dekker (2002) enumerates the following four goals of SNA:

- To visualize communication and relationships between people and/or groups through diagrams.
- To study the factors that influence relationships and how they correlate relationships.
- To derive implications of data, like bottlenecks in flow of information.
- Finally, to make recommendations to improve communication and workflow in an organization.

SNA is backed by social sciences and strong mathematical theories like graph theory and matrix algebra (Borgatti, 1999), which makes it applicable to analytical approaches and empirical methods. SNA uses two approaches, namely, ego-centered analysis and whole-network analysis. In ego-centered analysis, the focus is on the individual rather than on the whole network and normally involves only a random sample of network population. Whereas, in whole-network analysis, a survey of full population of network is done, and, hence, facilitates the conceptualization of a complete network. In order to test this study's hypothesis, which involves all members of the online community, the whole-network approach was employed.

SNA uses various concepts to evaluate different network properties (Baroudi et al., 1986), such as: centrality, connectivity and cliques, each of which pertain to particular dimension of the network. This study has employed a few of the important concepts in testing the hypothesis and to reveal any useful implications over the system performance.

Degree Centrality

Degree Centrality assesses the power of an actor (in the online course evaluation an actor is a student) based on the number of alters (other actors) that actor is directly connected to. If an actor receives many ties (relationships), i.e., has a high in-degree, then he is regarded to have "high-prestige" in the network (e.g., Figure 2). Similarly, when an actor makes contact with many alters, i.e., displays high out-degree, then he is regarded to be "highly influential."

Cliques

A clique is a subset of actors in a network who are more closely tied to each other than to the other actors who are not part of the subset.

Many techniques in SNA involve complex and voluminous mathematical calculations. This study has used a GUI based network analysis tool called Netminer for Windows (Netminer, 2002). This tool not only handles large volumes of data and performs complex calculations but also helps in the visualization of the social network structures and positions of actors within the network. The visualization of network is mainly achieved using Sociograms, which are graphs with nodes and lines for actors and ties respectively. The tool also provides numerical data analysis in the form of reports.

SOCIAL NETWORK ANALYSIS RATIONALE

People-intensive social systems like Web-Based Training Systems (WBT) are open-natured and behave unpredictably with their environment. In other words, these

Figure 2: In-Degree Centrality Measure

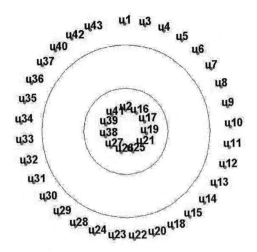

Figure 3: Co-Membership Clique Analysis

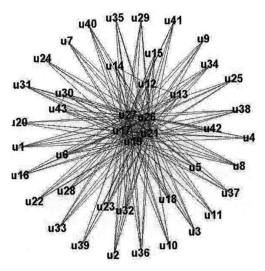

systems are less responsive to well defined scientific methods. Hence a shift in focus from technical to nontechnical approaches like social network analysis (SNA), which is principally used in communication science (Baroudi et al., 1986), is necessary. SNA offers an easy analytical method to monitor and analyze group dynamics, whose results can be translated into implications of social network over the performance and development of the system in consideration (Baroudi et al., 1986; Garton et al., 1999).

Following this, an attempt has been made to evaluate the applicability of SNA as an analytical and empirical method to analyse the interactions within an online community developed through computer mediated communications. This is done by studying the postings made over the discussion board associated with our WBT System by the registered members of the system. Social network analysis helps in identifying useful interaction patterns and relationships among the online community members, whose results are employed to reverse-engineer subsequent system designing and development process.

Furthermore, using SNA techniques, the following hypothesis, which asserts the importance of Participatory Design (PD) methodology, is also tested:

By involving users actively during the design and development phases of a system, a sense of ownership can be cultivated within the users, which consequently will influence them to play key roles in the system. For example, by taking a lead role in building an online community or by using the system extensively.

By testing the above hypothesis one can ensure that up-fronting time and effort in Participatory Design (PD) can be significantly rewarding and consequently motivate system owners to implement PD in the ongoing process of system improvement and maintenance.

Results/Analysis of SNA

For the purpose of SNA, a selection of postings (the collection of initial interactions between the online community members) was subjected to analysis. These postings were carefully examined, categorized and tabulated with details of type of posting made, target of the posting, etc. From the table of postings, information is then transformed in the form of a data set, usable by Netminer for performing SNA. We masked the users' names and email addresses with dummy identities to preserve privacy. In particular, those members who have actively contributed in the participatory design (represented with dummy variables U1, U7, U17, U19, U21, U27, U36 in the analysis that follows) are observed throughout the analysis so as to test the hypothesis.

The community analyzed is comprised of 43 members, out of which five are participatory design team members and two are the course designers. A rigorous analysis has revealed much useful information from which constructive inferences and assertions can be made. An in-degree visualization of the community at scale three (Figure 2) groups three of the five PD team users at the centre, depicting that they have the highest in-degree among seven others, followed by other two at the next level. Similarly, the out-degree centrality analysis at scale three also groups the three PD team members with the others, as having high out-degree. Both of these results clearly depict that the majority of PD team users had large contributions in the online community interactions.

The subgroup analysis to identify the "cliques" present in the network shows (Figure 3) a group of five as those who are present in all of the 35 cliques formed in the network. This can be verified from the cliques table, which lists all the 35 cliques and their participating member list (Table 1). "Cliques" have the strongest notion among all the other subgroup concepts. In order to strengthen the value of these results, a filter of at least 3 interactions was imposed to the above clique analysis.

These results clearly demonstrate that the five actors (three of whom are PD team members) have very strong relationships with every other actor in the network. A strong relationship between two actors is fostered as a result of continued interaction between them.

From the above results, we can deduce that PD activity, which involved users during the design and development phases of a system, has cultivated significant level of interests within the users to make them participate actively in the sustainability and improvement of the system. This stands in support of the initial hypothesis tested.

USER-CENTERED
EVALUATION METHODOLOGY

To further assess the success of our methodology, a series of user evaluation techniques were employed.

Many aspects of usability can best be studied by simply asking the users. This is especially true for issues related to the users' subjective satisfaction and possible anxieties (Nielsen, 1993).

Since the course is highly dependent on user participation, the design team has taken steps in collecting and analyzing user feedback. Evaluation of the course has been, from the beginning, an integral part of our Participatory Design implementation. First,

Table 1: Clique Analysis Report (Each variable under the members column represents a user and each variable under the cliques column represents a clique)

Cliques	Members
K1	(u17, u19, u21, u26, u27 , u12, u13)
K2	(u17, u19, u21, u26, u27 , u12, u14)
K3	(u17, u19, u21, u26, u27 , u12, u15)
K4	(u17, u19, u21, u26, u27 , u7)
K5	(u17, u19, u21, u26, u27 , u8)
K6	(u17, u19, u21, u26, u27 , u9)
K7	(u17, u19, u21, u26, u27 , u10)
K8	(u17, u19, u21, u26, u27 , u11)
K9	(u17, u19, u21, u26, u27 , u6)
K10	(u17, u19, u21, u26, u27 , u16)
K11	(u17, u19, u21, u26, u27 , u1)
K12	(u17, u19, u21, u26, u27 , u18)
K13	(u17, u19, u21, u26, u27 , u2)
K14	(u17, u19, u21, u26, u27 , u20)
K15	(u17, u19, u21, u26, u27 , u3)
K16	(u17, u19, u21, u26, u27 , u22)
K17	(u17, u19, u21, u26, u27 , u23, u32)
K18	(u17, u19, u21, u26, u27 , u24)
K19	(u17, u19, u21, u26, u27 , u25)
K20	(u17, u19, u21, u26, u27 , u4)
K21	(u17, u19, u21, u26, u27 , u5)
K22	(u17, u19, u21, u26, u27 , u28)
K23	(u17, u19, u21, u26, u27 , u29)
K24	(u17, u19, u21, u26, u27 , u30, u43)
K25	(u17, u19, u21, u26, u27 , u31)
K26	(u17, u19, u21, u26, u27 , u33)
K27	(u17, u19, u21, u26, u27 , u34)
K28	(u17, u19, u21, u26, u27 , u35)
K29	(u17, u19, u21, u26, u27 , u36)
K30	(u17, u19, u21, u26, u27 , u37)
K31	(u17, u19, u21, u26, u27 , u38)
K32	(u17, u19, u21, u26, u27 , u39)
K33	(u17, u19, u21, u26, u27 , u40)
K34	(u17, u19, u21, u26, u27 , u41)
K35	(u17, u19, u21, u26, u27 , u42)

Figure 4: Mean User Ratings for the 19 Questions

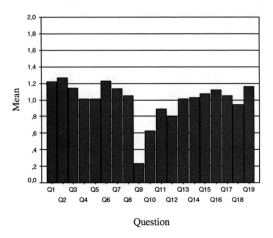

a questionnaire was provided for collecting feedback about the general usability of the course. Secondly, a discussion board was created where users could post their questions and comments. Finally, an email address was provided through which users could contact the design team.

Questionnaire and Discussion Board Postings Evaluation

One hundred and eighty one students, taking the online "Learn Greek Online" course in its first year of implementation, responded to an online questionnaire assessing the overall usability of the course. The questionnaire was based on the Computer System Usability Questionnaire (CSUQ) and was administered through the web-based user interface evaluation with questionnaires system provided online (Perlman, 1999).

CSUQ consists of 19 usability questions to which the respondent was to agree or disagree on a five-point scale, ranging from 2 (Agree) to –2 (Disagree).

Figure 4: Mean User Ratings for the 19 Questions

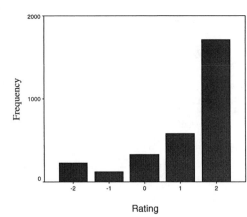

Table 2: Mean User Ratings with Standard Deviation in Parenthesis

	Question	Rating
Q1	Overall, I am satisfied with how easy it is to use this online course.	1.40 (1.14)
Q2	It was simple to use this online course.	1.40 (1.13)
Q3	I can effectively complete my work using this online course.	1.20 (1.22)
Q4	I am able to complete my work quickly using this online course.	1.05 (1.27)
Q5	I am able to efficiently complete my work using this online course.	1.10 (1.24)
Q6	I feel comfortable using this online course.	1.49 (1.07)
Q7	It was easy to learn to use this online course.	1.37 (1.15)
Q8	I believe I became productive quickly using this online course.	1.19 (1.17)
Q9	The online course gives error messages that clearly tell me how to fix problems.	0.13 (1.60)
Q10	Whenever I make a mistake using the online course, I recover easily and quickly.	0.81 (1.29)
Q11	The information (such as help, on screen messages and other documentation) provided with this online course is clear.	0.89 (1.34)
Q12	It is easy to find the information I needed.	0.83 (1.37)
Q13	The information provided for the online course is easy to understand.	1.24 (1.07)
Q14	The information is effective in helping me complete the tasks and scenarios.	1.19 (1.06)
Q15	The organization of information on the online course screens is clear.	1.20 (1.23)
Q16	The interface of this online course is pleasant.	1.30 (1.12)
Q17	I like using the interface of this online course.	1.23 (1.17)
Q18	This online course has all the functions and capabilities I expect it to have.	0.99 (1.30)
Q19	Overall, I am satisfied with this online course.	1.40 (1.06)

Table 2 shows the overall ratings for the online course for the 19 questions. A graphical representation of the results is provided in Figure 4. Next the responses to all questions were combined together and the average overall rating was plotted in Figure 4.

In addition to the questionnaire, we analyzed a total of 371 postings (posted online to the discussion board from December 1998 to March 2000). These are the same postings that were analyzed using SNA in the previous sections.

After a first careful reading of the 371 postings, five main categories were identified: (1) Technical related questions and instructions related to technical questions, (2) Content related issues, like spelling, grammar and syntax, (3) Resources and Notes related postings, (4) Miscellaneous.

Table 3: Frequency of Postings per Subcategory of Usability Issues

Category	Subject	N	%
Tech/Instructions	Problems with needing/installing Greek drivers and fonts	56	15.1
	Problem with/wanting to download lessons	49	13.2
	Problems with installing/using RealPlayer	40	10.8
Content	Questions about vocabulary	28	7.5
	Questions about grammar/spelling	17	4.6
	Questions about dialect	2	0.5
Resources	Questions about availability of text, CDs or including links to web sites	37	10.0
Notes related questions	Online notes	73	19.7
Miscellaneous	Miscellaneous	69	18.6

Then we conducted a more elaborate study and further categorization was performed looking into nine subcategories of the four main categories based on the technical actions necessary to improve on each one of the categories. Table 3 shows the frequency of postings for each subcategory.

In addition to the 19 questions, users were also encouraged to provide feedback by listing up to three of the most positive and up to three of the most negative aspects of the online course.

Analysis of Server Logs

The data described below was taken from the cumulative log file record, a 590-megabyte corpus, for a 30-month period from July 19, 1998, when the learn Greek online project was officially "launched," through December 31, 2000.

These logs, in the extended log file format, keep track of who was visiting the site (unique internet address), when they visited the site, what they requested, how long they looked at each page, where they were before they came to the site, what browser they

Table 4: Access Statistics for the Course: July 19, 1988 to December 31, 2000

Total number of successful hits	3,704,104
Total number of user sessions (visits)	1,256,770
Distinct users	900,481
Average hits per day	4061
Average user sessions per day	1378
Average user session length	0.47 minutes
Average number of documents examined per user	2.55

were using, what country they were from, and more. Log files were analyzed using wusage web log analysis tool (http://www.wusage.com). Table 4 represents the overall access statistics for the 30-month period.

Site Traffic. Traffic to the site peaked following the addition of each new item and any publicity campaign, then tapered off considerably during the late spring and early summer, probably in correspondence with the academic calendar, and then picked up and resumed at about 1,378 user sessions per day (User sessions are defined as a sequence of HTTP requests from a unique user, as determined by internet protocol address. Sessions are considered to have terminated if there are no requests for a 30-minute period.) During the 30-month period, there was an estimated 1,256,770 user sessions, lasting an average of 0.47 minutes with the longest lasting 174 minutes. Sessions were split roughly equally between daytime (8:00 a.m. - 6:00 p.m., user's local time) and evenings (6:00 p.m. - 8:00 a.m., user's local time). There were 46.7% of sessions in the daytime and 53.3% in the evenings.

Requests for Site Features. With respect to features of the site that were accessed, 25.61% of the hits were caused from accesses to the Greek-English-Greek dictionary associated with the course, indicating a substantial usage of this tool by the students of this course or even by visitors that are not regular users of the rest of the items of the online course, this is further supported by the fact that more than 40% of users entered the site through the dictionary section. The main course page attracted 13.71% of the accesses. From the individual audio lessons, it can be observed that lesson one runs high (6.43%) whereas the rest of the lessons received accesses below 1% of the total, this shows to us that a lot of visitors to the Kypros-Net web site show interest in investigating the course (by listening for a few minutes to the first audio file), although they might not be interested in taking the course (for example they might already know enough Greek or they might be interested to know that such a course exists but they don't have time to learn Greek right now, etc.).

Referrer Log Entries. Analysis of the referrer log data suggests that most of the traffic that did not come as a direct result of one of the links on the Kypros-Net other pages arrived at the course web site from a net guide or a search engine. For instance, more than 130,000 accesses came from Yahoo, 13,962 from MSN, 13,346 from Altavista and 8,551 from Google. The keywords that most frequently brought visitors to the site were "Greek dictionary," "Greek language" and "Greek translation," again showing a high popularity for the dictionary of the course.

CONCLUSION

We enhance the learning experience in our WBT by facilitating Distributed Constructionism in the iteration phase of a Participatory Design methodology. Social Network Analysis shows that the PD team members were central on the community discussion board. Questionnaire evaluation shows that the end system received high usability ratings from the users. Therefore Distributed Constructionism enhanced the learning experience of both the PD team and the more passive users.

This is strongly supported from the Social Network Analysis results provided. The students that participated actively in the design of the course also played a central role in the discussion board: answering other students' language questions, helping out students to overcome technical problems and helping them to find other resources to enhance their learning of the Greek language. These observations are in agreement with the underlying goals of Participatory Design, which was an integral part of the development of this specific course.

Furthermore, the results of the analysis of the user questionnaire and the server logs shows that the final product (the course) meets to a very big extent the expectations and needs of the whole user population of this specific course. We believe that the direct involvement of the users in the development of the course helped in designing a more usable course that enhanced the learning of our users and provided them with an enjoyable and rewarding experience.

ACKNOWLEDGMENTS

We want to express our gratitude to our students who devoted valuable time in helping with the development of this course. Without their help this project would have never achieved the success it did.

Finally, we thank the Cyprus Broadcasting Corporation who kindly made the audio files used at the beginning of the development of this course available to us.

REFERENCES

Baroudi, Olsen, & Ives (1986). An empirical study of the impact of user involvement on system usage and information satisfaction. *CACM, 29*(3), 232-238.

Bjerknes, Gro, Pelle Ehn, & Morten Kyng (1987). *Computers and Democracy: A Scandinavian Challenge*. Aldershot: Gower.

Blomberg, J.L., & Henderson, A. (1990). Reflections on participatory design: Lessons from the Trillium Experience. *Proceedings of CHI'90* (pp. 353-359). Seattle, WA: ACM Press.

Borgatti, S. (1999). *What is social network analysis?* Retrieved December 4, 2002 from the World Wide Web: http://www.analytictech.com/networks/whatis.htm.

Dekker, A.H. (2002). A category-theoretic approach to social network analysis. *Proceedings of Computing: The Australasian Theory Symposium* (CATS). Melbourne, Australia: Elsevier Science. Retrieved December 4, 2002 from the World Wide Web: http://members.ozemail.com.au/~dekker/snacat.pdf.

Ellis, R. D., Jankowski, T. B., & Jasper, J. E. (1998). Participatory design of an Internet-based information system for aging services professionals. *The Gerontologist, 38*(6), 743-748.

Garton, L., Haythornwaite, C., & Wellman, B. (1999). Studying on-line social networks. In S. Jones (Ed.), *Doing Internet Research* (pp. 75-105). Thousand Oaks, CA: Sage Publications.

Kypros-Net Inc. (2002). *The world of Cyprus*. Retrieved December 4, 2002 from the World Wide Web: http://www.kypros.org/.

Netminer. (2002). *Netminer for Windows*. Retrieved December 4, 2002 from the World Wide Web: http://www.netminer.com.

Nielsen, J. (1993). *Usability Engineering*. Chestnut Hill, MA: AP Professional.

Papert, S. (1991). Situating construction. In I. Harel & S. Papert (Eds.), *Constructionism* (pp. 1-12). Norwood, NJ: Ablex Publishing.

Papert, S. (1993). *The Children's Machine: Rethinking School in the Age of the Computer*. New York: Basic Books.

Perlman, G. (1999). *Web-based user interface evaluation with questionnaires*. Retrieved December 4, 2002 from the World Wide Web: http://www.acm.org/~perlman/question.html.

Resnick, M. (1996). *Distributed constructionism*. Retrieved December 4, 2002 from the World Wide Web: http://web.media.mit.edu/~mres/papers/Distrib-Construc/Distrib-Construc.html.

Chapter X

Fast Track:
School Based Student
Software Design

Philip Duggan, The Mosslands School, UK

Claude Ghaoui, Liverpool John Moores University, UK

Mike Simco, Liverpool John Moores University, UK

ABSTRACT

Most studies involving students in designing and developing software involve research teams and other professionals outside of the normal school environment. This pilot study demonstrated that involving students in the design and development of software could take place entirely within the school environment. This methodology was called "fast tracking." Students could, and did, play demanding and effective roles in the process of software development. Students were responsible for selecting their own roles in the design process and were assertive in selecting the teaching staff they wanted to work with. The students also proved to be adept at selecting a suitable toolkit for implementing the software. The participating students represented a cross section of the entire ability range. A quantitative analysis of "flow" as an indication of the success of the implementation indicated that middle ability students derived the most educational benefit from using software developed under the fast track approach. Relationships between students and teaching staff exhibited changes in the power structure, which were often difficult to redress outside of the pilot study.

INTRODUCTION

Much of the educational software used in schools is ill suited to the task. Poorly conceived design inhibits the educational progress of the students. Many high profile studies have been undertaken to involve students in the design and development of software, in an attempt to enhance the functionality and usability of the material produced. Critically, many of these studies have attempted to harness the child's perspective on design and utilise the children in a variety of different roles throughout the design cycle (Druin, 1999; Scaife et al., 1997; Jones & Balka, 1998). In the overwhelming majority of cases these studies have relied on the involvement of research teams and professionals outside of the normal school environment. The roles that these outside agencies have undertaken has necessarily been varied but in all cases have caused some disruption to the normal functioning of the school and taken a long period of time to produce a "usable" output.

The aim of this chapter is to develop a new approach, called fast tracking, whereby the involvement of children in the development process can be accelerated using expertise and hardware/software currently available in schools without having to involve external teams of researchers and professionals. The output should be both replicable and transferable. The pilot study arose out of the interest of the Mosslands School for Boys in engaging a group of 20 14-year-old secondary school students and three teachers in the (re)design of science curriculum software. The Mosslands School is situated in Wirral, UK, and has in excess of 1,400 students.

The pilot study was designed to be a small-scale project to be completed in a period of twelve weeks, typically the length of one school term. The objectives of the study were twofold. To investigate the viability of the fast track approach, and to investigate the degree to which students were concentrating (or engaged) when utilising software designed by co-operation with children. Teachers designate this highly desirable state of concentration as being "on task."

The rest of the chapter is broken down into the following sections. The *Background* section examines a theoretical framework for the study. The *Research Description and Methodology Used* section specifies the hypotheses that we were tying to assess. The next three sections describe the work that we actually did. The *Fast Tracking* section develops the theoretical basis for the fast track methodology and considers how it can be assessed. The *Solutions and Recommendations* section relates practical steps involved in implementing the fast track methodology. The *Analysis* section details the results of the quantitative and qualitative data. The *Future Trends* section specifies how we plan to extend the study. The *Conclusion* section summarises the findings of the pilot study.

BACKGROUND

There have been many studies designed to categorise the variety of ways that children can assist in the design of software. Druin's theoretical framework (Druin 2002, 1999) proved invaluable in educating students and teachers in possible methods of including students in the design process. Druin categorises student involvement in software design into four main strands: *users, testers, native informants* and *design partners*. Based on an abstract of this framework let us briefly examine each of these roles and identify some of the more significant studies.

Users

The user role was the earliest form of collaboration and was intended to prove general concepts of software design and better understand the learning process. Some of the most common methods of data collection are *activity observation, user impressions, technological impact* and *work result analysis.*

Activity observation data (data on the observed activities in which students engage) can be collected in a wide variety of formats. These formats include: patterns of activity, and general concerns raised by the user (Burov, 1991; Nicol, 1988); live observations by hidden observers or captured data for later analysis (e.g., Goldman-Segall, 1998; Plowman et al., 1999); and talk, movement, gesture, and machine interaction (Plowman et al., 1999). Researchers can themselves participate in the gathering of data by taking part in the activities of the classroom (e.g., Plowman, 1992), as can teachers (e.g., Koenemann et al., 1999). Qualitative interviews and surveys can be used to collect *user impressions* about their likes, dislikes, interests and difficulties. Interviews can be informal (e.g., Jackson et al., 1998) or more formal, featuring numerical questions (Salzman et al., 1999). The *impact that technology* has on a child's learning can be determined by tests given to children before and after the use of technology. Quantifiable tests are suitable for evaluating subject matter knowledge (Salzman et al., 1999) while qualitative descriptions of children as technology users can be obtained by observing children over an extended period of time (e.g., Blomberg et al., 1993). Data collection can be performed by asking children, teachers and observers to write their thoughts in journals.

Various methodologies exist for *analysing data,* and the precise methodology to be adopted depends upon the nature of the information being sought. Examples of this include measuring the speed at which tasks can be completed (Fell et al., 1994) and the quantity of content questions answered by a child after using technology (Salzman et al., 1999).

The user role has many strengths. The researcher is in control and it is easy to include children into the development process so that research can be accomplished quickly. A large number of comprehensive studies exist in this area. The weaknesses of the user role reflect the essentially passive nature of the role itself. The user has less direct impact on technological changes and therefore little impact on the design process.

Testers

The role of the tester was primarily developed to determine if developing technology meets its design goals and to influence new technologies before release.

When students act as testers, emphasis is placed on the identification of possible areas of confusion, likes and dislikes, the effect of technology on learning outcomes and possible bugs in the software. Potential problem areas of the product are usually scheduled for a heavier testing regimen (Strommen, 1998). The number of children needed during the testing process can vary. In the early stages of prototype development only a few children may be needed for a few hours to highlight the big problems (Loh et al., 1998). Large numbers of testers may generate large amounts of data to be analysed.

The strength of the tester role is that it begins to empower children and it makes changing technology faster than that of the user role. It is also flexible, as testing can be performed outside the environment of the school. However, children don't have an input until later in the design process and the adults tend to make all of the critical decisions.

Native Informants

The role of the informant was designed to raise new issues, confirm assumptions and set developmental directions. Scaife et al. (1997; Scaife & Rogers, 1999) were first to describe the concept of children acting as "informant designers." In this role, the precept is to question *when* children should take part in the design process and make a determination of *any* useful design contributions they could make.

Children can act as informants in numerous ways and at any time the design team believes it needs direction or support. What differs from the user and tester role is *when* these interactions happen and *how* directly they can affect the design of new technology. Low-tech materials, interviews and design feedback on prototypes can all be used continually as methods for informants as long as the materials and methods are appropriate to the age and development of the child. Many of these methods are similar to techniques used when children are in the role of user or tester. The difference is when and how often these techniques are used during the design process.

The informant role empowers children and brings their input into the start of the development. Children and adults work together in a flexible manner that impacts on how technology is shaped and developed. Children are challenged in a positive way throughout the process. However, the decision of when to include the children is still taken by adults and the research flexibility may be difficult to structure. Working with children inevitably takes more time and their suggestions may be unworkable or conflict with the pedagogical goals of the design.

Design Partners

Druin (2002) defines the techniques used in design partnership as a combination of three main strands: the *co-operative design* of Scandinavia (Greenbaum & Kyng, 1991), the *participatory design* of the United States (Schuler & Namioka, 1993), and the *consensus participation* of England (Mumford & Henshall, 1979). The aim of using children as design partners is to encourage children to construct their own paths to knowledge, and to deploy computer tools in a way that can support children as builders, designers and researchers.

Druin's collaborative projects are typical of the size and complexity of the developmental process (2002, 1999). The research method developed in these projects has come to be called *cooperative inquiry*. Although originally designed to bring *adult* users into the design process, methodologies such as *contextual design* utilise interviewing methods to capture user tasks, roles, and design ideas, while *cooperative design* and *participatory design* use brainstorming methods to ask users and designers to sketch out ideas. Cooperative enquiry activities include: *Contextual inquiry* to observe what children do with what technologies they currently have; *participatory design* to hear what children have to say directly by collaborating on the development of "low tech" prototypes; and *technology immersion* to observe what children do with extraordinary amounts of technology (similar to what they might have in the future). Druin (2002) asserts that combination of observation, low-tech prototyping and time-intensive technology use can lead to the development of new technologies. Activity patterns and roles can suggest new design directions. Artifact analysis on low-tech prototypes can suggest new technology features while technology immersion can lead to revision and eventual products. Jones and Balka (1998) and Steyn (2001) extend this metaphor to encourage students to utilise higher tech building blocks and participate in the process of implementation.

The great strength of using children as design partners reflects the fact that children are empowered and the learning process can cause both children and adults to change. Feedback is instant throughout the design process, which informs new design directions and any necessary product revisions. New technology features are easily suggested through the children's experience of design-centred learning. However, team decisions must be negotiated and this can take considerable time, and finding personnel who can work with children may be difficult.

RESEARCH DESCRIPTION AND METHODOLOGY USED

What Are We Trying to Assess?

In simple terms, the essence of the work we carried out can be reduced to the assessment of two hypotheses, which were formulated to determine the validity of the fast track approach and assess the educational benefit of the software output.

Hypothesis 1. The general, or conceptual, hypothesis to test that the fast track approach represents a viable methodology for involving students in the design and implementation of software within a secondary school environment.

Hypothesis 2. The specific directional hypothesis is to test that software developed by the fast track approach is more effective than software developed by teaching staff in keeping students on task.

Why Is This Study Important, and To Whom?

The value of involving external agencies in the design cycle, both in terms of software and knowledge, has been of value in shedding light on the methodology and perception of the role of children in the design process. Many studies involve students as design partners (Druin, 1999; Jones & Balka, 1998). However, research teams usually have their own agenda, which may not coincide with the aims of the school. Teachers would like to be able to replicate this process solely within the secondary educational environment. This is not easily achieved. The design cycle is usually too long and the involvement of external personnel often inculcates an unrealistic design rationale. In many studies, a substantial proportion of the development and implementation relies on software and hardware platforms that are either unavailable in the majority of schools or too expensive to purchase. In addition, the majority of teachers usually do not possess the technical skills to replicate the process of design and implementation once the research teams have left.

What Methodology Did We Use?

The methodology to test Hypothesis 1 was essentially a qualitative design based on using students as full and equal design partners in the redesign of curriculum software.

The methodology to test Hypothesis 2 was essentially a quantitative design. Two similar groups were randomly selected as "matched pairs" by average SAT score in a double blind test to compare flow in untreated and treated software.

All of these considerations will be fully detailed in the following sections.

FAST TRACKING

We define fast tracking as a new methodology of software design and development whereby teachers and children can produce useful outputs solely within the normal school environment.

A natural place to start was to assess the contribution of the involvement of external agencies in the design cycle, and identify those elements which could be adapted and those elements which could be discarded. Of course, any form of fast tracking would inevitably impose its own limitations and constraints when compared to the approach taken by a "full scale" research team. In a sense, the fast track approach is asking children and teachers to adopt and implement some of the capabilities of highly trained personnel in a variety of different areas. However, there are advantages. While children and teachers may not have the expertise possessed by external personnel, they do know the learning environment within which the class operates and they have a keen sense of the germane. In comparing the available methodologies for including students in the design process we needed to ask if the output from a fast track approach would be comparable to the output from a full-scale implementation? This required both a new definition of a full-scale implementation and an examination of a basis for comparison.

For our purposes, it was decided to define a full-scale implementation as any methodology which relied upon research personnel or professional services not usually available in the normal school environment. Note that our definition of a full-scale implementation is not concerned with a determination of the role that students take in the design process. Each of the roles, or a combination of them, could be conducted solely within the school environment or with the involvement of external personnel. Rather, our definition of full-scale implementation speaks to *who* is involved in the design process, *where* it is conducted and *what* resources are available. Given this definition, a variety of qualitative and quantitative comparisons can be attempted. However, many of these comparisons would require teachers to engage in implementing a battery of tests designed to measure usability metrics, or perform a series of observations or interviews. Would teachers even value or see the relevance of such tests once they had been implemented? The time constraints of the pilot study indicated that these would not be suitable approaches. It eventually became clear that the viability of the fast track design process could be determined in both qualitative and quantitative terms by the teachers themselves. In qualitative terms, the feedback and evaluation generated by students and teachers could be analysed to indicate the effectiveness of the design methodology. In quantitative terms, a measurable outcome routinely used by teachers, even though it may not normally be formally assessed, could be used to indicate the effectiveness of the software outcome. It was decided to generate a quantifiable measurement of the degree to which students can be regarded to be "on task" when using software. One visible indication of when a student is on task is where a student exhibits a peculiar state of satisfaction where they are so engaged by certain activities that they seem to "flow" along with it in an almost automatic manner (Rieber, 1996).

Flow: A Measurable Outcome of Being on Task

Csikszentmihalyi's study (1990) relates that flow could be observed when the individual's skills were just sufficient to complete the activities. Individual skills vary, therefore flow is a dynamic quality, which is always a balance between the changing level of skill of the individual and the challenge of the activity. To keep the learner within this flow channel, the changes to the difficulty level should be within context of the skills level of the individual. When a student is on task the student is concentrating and usually does not notice the passage of time, so the student can be said to be experiencing flow. Therefore, it is argued that the degree of flow experienced by the student would be a good general indicator of the ability of the software to keep the student on task. Of course, there are some obvious difficulties in regarding flow as a comprehensive measurement of students being on task. Reiber (1996) observes that the appearance of flow may be indicative of factors completely unrelated to the activities the students are supposed to be engaged in.

Deciding on a suitable method for measuring flow meant that some account had to be taken of differences in student ability. Time by itself would not be a suitable measurement of flow, as more able students may progress through the software more quickly than less able students. Any measurement based purely on time does not compare like with like. A more realistic approach would be for the number of (interface) screens the students accessed before they became distracted to be counted. A screen was defined as all curriculum material examined and all tasks completed. It is argued that this screen measurement is one (but not the only one) possible indicator of the presence of flow. In this way, it was hoped that the non-sequential nature of the software design could be accommodated. The experimental design therefore became a comparative measurement of whether software designed under the fast track approach caused the user to experience significantly more "flow" than software designed by teachers alone.

SOLUTIONS AND RECOMMENDATIONS

It was believed that the conditions under which the pilot study was to be conducted should closely mirror those currently prevalent in British schools, with all the implied constraints in methodology and procedure. All decisions to be made about operating conditions, student selection and methodology originated from data collected under the normal educational and administrative procedures that take place within the school environment. The availability and choice of hardware and software should reflect those available to students and teachers, either in their own school or in institutions to which they would have access. In measuring and evaluating the interaction of students with the software, it was important that teachers should not be expected to adopt sophisticated techniques which would have detracted from the "fast track" nature of the approach.

Experimental Design for Hypothesis 1: To Design or Redesign?

The short time scale of the project meant that it was not feasible to design a piece of software from scratch. Instead, existing software produced by teachers was to be redesigned by the students to make it more usable. This approach had the following advantage in that the curriculum material and pedagogical information were already identified for the students to examine.

Right from the start, it was decided that students should be able to alter the whole structure, navigation, appearance and functionality. In a new approach, they were also to be allowed to alter the curriculum content of the software, subject to teacher approval that the required material covered the essential teaching points. Moreover, in selecting teaching staff, participating students and toolkits, it was decided to develop our own selection criteria rather than rely on those indicated by other studies.

Selecting Staff and Students

Three teachers were selected on the basis of interest rather than expertise. Students were asked which teachers they would like to work with. In all cases, the selected teachers were those identified as teachers who listened, discussed problems with students and were not afraid to accept help from the students themselves.

It was important that participation was not limited to those students regarded as "gifted" or "talented." Anecdotal evidence from teacher observation suggests that "more able" students cope with poorly designed software more easily than students with less ability. This naturally leads to the assumption that more able students might not notice software design features which would cause difficulty or confusion to less able students. Therefore, students were invited to apply from the whole ability spectrum of the year, ranging from the gifted and talented stream to those students "statemented" for special educational needs. In selecting students, the information available to staff included data from Standard Assessment Tasks (SAT's) in English, Mathematics and Science. SAT's are external examinations given to all students in England and Wales to assess capability in the "core" subjects, and this data is usually available to all teachers in schools. It therefore seemed logical that these tests (taken at ages 11 and 14) be used as the basis for student selection. It was not regarded as important that the ability range of the participating students constituted an accurate cross section of the ability range of all students in the year, but it was vital that all ability ranges were represented. In the event, applications were received from students from all sections of the ability range.

Deciding the Student Roles

One important decision was deciding upon the roles that the students would take in the design process. Careful consideration was given to the appropriate role(s), that could be adopted within the available time scale. Common sense decreed that students should be limited to using or testing software in order to fit within the available time. However, it was decided that this approach would be too deterministic and may lead to students being artificially constrained in the roles they wished to take. In the event, it was decided to experiment to investigate if the participating students would be able to select appropriate roles for themselves. It was agreed that students should be able to decide upon the nature of the role(s) and the degree to which they would like to participate. Students and teachers were informed from the beginning of the project that students and staff were to regard each other as full equals in the project. The pilot study was designed to be conducted in three, not necessarily sequential, stages. The stages were designated as:

1.   Team selection, roles and support.
2.   Toolkit selection, design and documentation.
3.   Feedback and evaluation.

Team Selection, Roles and Support

Students were initially asked to take responsibility for a software design and development task from the following list; design, implementation, capture, audio/video production, documentation and training. It was observed that students self-selected their own roles according to their own perceptions of their strengths and weaknesses, although these student perceptions and the roles themselves underwent radical trans-formation. In all cases, the initial student selection of a role was that of a user or tester. As the students gained confidence, several of them began to act as informants and even design partners.

Information on students in the design team with special needs was accessed from the special needs register. This is a database indicating the nature and degree of student disability and concomitant requirements for educational support and is used to brief learning mentors as to the support individual students may need. Learning mentors are staff used to support teachers in classes and provide individual assistance to students with special educational needs. In an attempt to equalise the relationships between students with special educational needs and the other students, the responsibility for requesting support from the learning mentors was given to the individual students. They decided what support they required and when they needed it.

As reported by Druin (2002) and Jones and Balka (1998), there were tensions in the perceived relations between the students and the teachers. Students initially were waiting for instruction and guidance from teachers. However, they soon realised that the teachers involved in the project were not ICT experts. As the project progressed the students adapted to the change in the power structure more easily than did the teachers. Often teachers had to be actively discouraged from attempting to direct the sessions.

Toolkit Selection, Design and Documentation

Selection of the toolkit arose out of the constraints imposed by working within a school environment. Normally, the required functionality of the system indicates the possible range of tools to be used in construction. Within the school environment the reverse situation was the case. The modus operandi became "what can we do with the tools that we have got?" Unlike other projects involving students in the design process, the students were not to be limited to the manipulation of low-tech prototypes (Druin, 2002, 1999; Scaife and Rogers, 1999), but were to be used to undertake the majority of the implementation. Therefore, the student input into the selection of the toolkit was to prove pivotal to the success of the project. Fortunately, initial training for students in basic implementation using Toolbook, Flash and Director was already underway through the multimedia club. Students were trained using paper based and CBT material adapted from introductory training initially written for graduate and post-graduate students in higher education. In its adapted form, it proved to be eminently suitable at the secondary school level. Students became familiar with use of tools, wizards and behaviours, but not familiar with Object Oriented Programming (OO) side of the implementation. From the activities of the multimedia club, students were already familiar with audio and video capture, production and editing. The broad parameters of the software design were outlined to the students and a meeting was held for the students to decide on the most suitable development platform(s) to be adopted. Interestingly, the staff involved in the project had little or no experience in the available authoring platforms and several students took on the task of training the staff and each other.

Jones and Balka (1998) chose a Java based authoring suite while Steyn (2001) encouraged some older students to author in Delphi. However, after consultation with students and teachers, it was decided that Toolbook offered an authoring platform that combined the ability to create building blocks which operated in a similar way to JAVA beans in an authoring environment that was easy to use and supported multimedia elements. The functionality of the project was designed using a set of interdependent and context-independent building blocks coded in ToolBook's own OO language "OpenScript." The building blocks were designed as general purpose utilities that were to be reusable. Building blocks were created in a standardised format that generated dialogue boxes, which asked students to enter the input data as parameters. It was deemed to be a good idea that the output data from the building blocks would be displayed in a dialogue box to the user as a useful form of feedback. Initially the basic building blocks were implemented by the teachers. However, towards the end of the project several students proved to be adept in designing and implementing building blocks of their own, thereby becoming active designers rather than passive users. The students designed a basic template and navigational structure, which was revisited on several occasions in the light of oral feedback sessions.

In a similar manner to Jones and Balka (1998), it was decided that students needed the ability to replicate the metaphor of the design template and building blocks in a non-functional form. The ability to visualise information flow and functionality was regarded as a vital component in inculcating programming expertise in students. Rather than design a new system, it was decided to adopt the SimCHET (an adaptation of PICTIVE) system as devised by Jones and Balka (1998). SimCHET is essentially a diagrammatical technique that gave the students the ability to represent building blocks in an icono-graphic fashion to indicate general functionality, specify visible connections, and specify parameters and functionality. Time constraints meant that for the majority of students the purpose of the SimCHET prototype was not so much an aid to design but a way to document the original system in a useful manner and document the changes in system structure and content. It was interesting to observe that students who were prepared to design on the documentation system were more likely to produce new and innovative design ideas. It was also observed that students taking on the burden of implementing the design tended to adapt their designs towards what the limitations of the software were rather than what they thought would be good design. Figure 1 illustrates an example of typical design issues raised by the students. The original design by the teachers required the students to "drag and drop" the answers on the left onto the correct targets on the right. The students adapted the design so that the user was able to draw a line pointing to the right answer. They added an animated clock to indicate that this question was going to form part of the overall test score. They also simplified the navigation for the less able students by covering the forbidden navigational routes with red crosses, rather than relying on disabled navigation buttons showing a slight change of colour.

Feedback and Evaluation

Students fed back using "open ended" questionnaires and oral feedback sessions compiled by the teachers. The most useful feedback came during sessions where students fed back to each other either individually or in small focus groups. Students felt that in feeding back to each other they were not being judged on their performance. Also, they were able to use their own slang and jargon in a more uninhibited manner. The teachers were instructed to resist the temptation to guide or concentrate the feedback in any specific direction as the lateral thinking of the students generated some very useful insights. Many of the responses were pedagogically related and demonstrated a critical awareness of the constraints and limitations of the developmental platform.

Experimental Design for Hypothesis 2

In measuring flow it was important that we were able to verify that the students were actually on task, and that all curriculum content on each screen was completed. This proved relatively easy to ensure. Each screen generally contained an online activity for the student to attempt that relied upon the curriculum content of the screen for successful completion. A commercially available screen recorder called Camtasia was installed on the curriculum network. The software allowed each student's screen interactions and mouse movements to be recorded as a video file. Camtasia also allowed us to record a continuous commentary by each student as they used the software using a headset. Surprisingly, the students lost awareness that their interactions and commentary were being recorded, and no one questioned why they had to comment on what they were doing out loud. Examination of the interactions, mouse movements and commentary on the video files proved to be a good way of accurately determining the number of screens accessed before distraction set in.

ANALYSIS

Analysing Hypothesis 1

In qualitative terms, student feedback was very interesting and indicated that by the end of the project, roughly one third (nine) of the design team students still regarded their main role as users and testers. Six of the students regarded their role as informants while a further five students regarded their role as co-operative designers and implementers. In a confirmation of Ching's study (1999), oral feedback indicated that students were aware of differences not only in requisite skills of the different members of the group, but also how these skills contributed to the collaborative interactions of the design process. Students cited knowledge and interaction differences in relation to visible skills, like programming, more often than other meta-design skills, such as planning and project monitoring. However, as you may expect, teachers indicated much

Figure 1: An Interactive Quiz Question

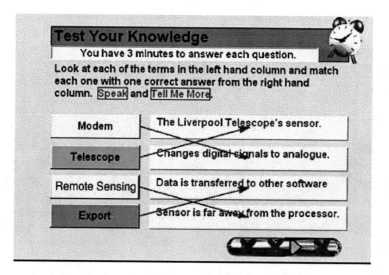

more awareness of their own meta-design skills and expressed confidence in their ability to accurately assess the skills of the students.

Teachers reported enjoying the project and regarded the software as a valuable resource that they would use again. However, all teachers indicated that the fast track process still took up too much curriculum time. Several teachers reported that they had difficulty re-establishing the traditional relationship between students and teachers at other times in the school. This would tend to confirm the observations of Druin (2002) and Jones and Balka (1998) who assert that both children and adults need to negotiate a new "power structure" in which neither adults nor children are completely in charge and identify common goals. Changes in the social and cognitive development of several students and teachers were quite noticeable, although they were not formally evaluated. Several teachers also reported that the experience of seeing some students gaining expertise beyond that attained by the teachers engendered a lack of self-confidence in those teachers.

Analysing Hypothesis 2

We have previously defined flow as the number of screens accessed before a student becomes distracted as a measurement of the student being on task. To quantitatively assess flow, two similar groups, each of 30 students across the ability range, were randomly selected as "matched pairs" by average SAT score in a double blind test. We can now analyse the results.

Generally, the SAT results for each subject are reported as grade points. At the time the pilot study was conducted, the "average" student would normally expect to achieve a grade point average within the range 4.75 to 5.75 across the three subjects. The SAT results for all schools are analysed and displayed on the Internet by the Department for Education and Skills (DFES) so that schools can compare the performance of their own students (DFES, 2003) against national standards.

One member of each pair, chosen randomly from among the two members, was assigned to the control group while the other member was assigned to the experimental group. None of the students knew if they were using the untreated software (software developed solely by staff) or treated software (developed in partnership with students), nor did the teachers chosen to supervise the tests.

The average SAT of the score of the students ranged from 3.75 to 7.00 marks. Each interval represented a score range of 0.37 marks. As far as possible, steps were taken to eliminate sources of experience, participation and instrumentation bias as defined by Tuckman (1999). Of particular concern was the possible effect of bias due to testing. Invalidity often results when the experience of testing students on one piece of software affects subsequent performance of the same students on another piece of software. Therefore, using the same group of students to evaluate both treated and untreated software would have increased the likelihood that any results obtained from the treated software may, in part, have reflected their experience of the untreated software. Although using different students for treated and untreated software raised some concerns as to the equivalence of the groups, the experimental design was regarded as more likely to produce useful results. Group 1 was given the untreated software to use while Group 2 was given the treated software to use. As previously stated, the number of screens each student accessed before they became distracted was analysed using the video files and recorded commentary.

The results were analysed using a *"between-subjects"* two-factor factorial analysis of variance (Tuckman, 1999) with group and average SAT score as independent variables and number of screens accessed (as an indication of flow) as the dependent variable. In a *between-subjects* design, the values of the dependent variable for one group of participants are compared with the values for another, independent group of participants.

Examining the statistical results we can see that there was a significant main effect of the *average SAT score* factor: $F(13,32)=311.807$; $p<0.001$. There was also a significant main effect of the *group* factor: $F(1,32)=60.266$; $p<0.001$. Of more importance there was a significant interaction between *the average SAT score* and the *group*: $F(13,32)=3.479$; $p<0.05$.

Both the *average SAT score* and the *group* were individually significant beyond the 0.001 level, giving a strong indication that the number of screens accessed increased in direct relation to the average SAT score. There was also a strong indication that there was a significant increase in the number of screens accessed in the treated software compared to the untreated software. In other words, in the case of both treated and untreated software the more able students demonstrated more "flow" than the less able students. In addition, in all of the levels *of average SAT score* the students using the treated software experienced more "flow" than students using the untreated software. Both of these results were in line with expected results. However, there was also a significant interaction between the main treatment factors at the 0.05 level, but not the 0.01 level. Clearly the *average SAT score* had different effects upon Group 1 and Group 2. Interestingly, analysis of the results revealed that the most pronounced interaction occurred in *average SAT scores* between 4.00 and 4.67. Interactions within this range were significant at the 0.01 level. This confirms anecdotal evidence from teachers that although there was statistically significant improvement at all *average SAT score* levels between the treated and the untreated software the most educational benefit was gained by middle ability students. It is believed that to a great extent high ability students were able to overcome the difficulties inherent in the design of the software and experience "flow" even when using the untreated software. Lower ability students were still easily distracted even when using the treated software.

FUTURE TRENDS

Students are increasingly critical and discerning consumers of educational software, and they are no longer content to be passive users of technology, they want to become involved at a variety of different levels and have more say in the software that they use. Students' authoring and programming skills often rival or even surpass those of their teachers and they want the chance to implement these skills in a realistic way. They want a sense of *ownership*. This trend will continue and teachers must seek new ways to collaborate with students to utilise their full capability in innovative ways. At the Mosslands School we believe the pilot project represented an effective model to pursue co-operative design within the school environment. We plan to extend the metaphor in several new and exciting ways. Plans are under way to cooperate with the National Schools Observatory of the Astrophysics Research Institute of Liverpool John Moores University in the joint development of curriculum material. Of particular interest in the development, this curriculum material will be the examination of the effect of student involvement in the design process on the development of thinking skills. We hope to be able to identify and map those interaction style which most affect thinking skills and adapt our software designs accordingly.

CONCLUSION

The involvement of students in the design process is a growing phenomenon but it needs to progress in a way that fits within the constraints of normal school life. The increase in complexity and availability of developmental software available on school platforms, and the increasing availability of suitable training material, means that effective procedures can be developed. The pilot study demonstrated that students can be engaged in the development of effective software and that the students are keen to act in a variety of developmental roles, many of which were more demanding than those roles to which students had been constrained in other studies. We hope to have demonstrated that the fast track approach is a viable methodology, which effectively proceeds from more rigorous investigations utilising techniques adapted for use within schools. Quantitative analysis of a measurable quantity, such as flow, provides a good indicator of the success of the implementation to support qualitative feedback from the students. However, fast track projects need to demonstrate their educational worth within a larger context. The future development of similar projects rely not only on the willingness of the teachers and the students, but also on support from schools and government being made available as part of the normal academic cycle. Only if this support is available will designing software become part of many students educational experience.

REFERENCES

Blomberg, J., Giacomi, J., Mosher, A., & Swenton-Wall, P. (1993). Ethnographic field methods and their relation to design. In D. Schuler & A. Namioka (Eds.), *Participatory Design: Principles and Practices* (pp. 123-156). Hillsdale, NJ: Lawrence Erlbaum.

Burov, A. N. (1991). Development of creative abilities of students on the basis of computer technology. *First Moscow International HCI'91 Workshop* (pp. 289-296).

Ching, C. C. (1999). "It's not just programming:" Reflection and the nature of experience in learning through design. In C. Hoadley & J. Roschelle (Eds.), *Proceedings of CSCL 99 Conference* (December 12-15), Stanford University, Palo Alto, California. Mahwah, NJ: Lawrence Erlbaum Associates.

Csikszentmihalyi, M. (1990). *Flow: The Psychology of Optimal Experience.* New York: Harper and Row.

Department For Education and Skills. (2003). Retrieved January 4, 2003 from the World Wide Web: http://www.standards.dfes.gov.uk/performance.

Druin, A. (1999). Cooperative inquiry: Developing new technologies for children with children. *Human Factors in Computing Systems: CHI 99* (pp. 223-230). ACM Press.

Druin, A. (2002). The role of children in the design of new technology. *Behaviour and Information Technology, 21*(1) 1-25.

Fell, H. J., Ferrier, L. J., Delta, H., Peterson, R., Mooraj, Z., & Valleau, M. (1994). Using the Baby-Babble-Blanket for infants with motor problems: An empirical study. *First Annual ACM Conference on Assistive Technologies* (pp. 77-84). ACM Press.

Goldman-Segall, R. (1998). *Points of Viewing Children's Thinking.* Mahwah, NJ: Lawrence Erlbaum Associates.

Greenbaum, J. & Kyng, M. (1991). *Design at Work: Cooperative Design of Computer Systems.* Hillsdale, NJ: Lawrence Erlbaum.

Jackson, S. L., Krajcik, J., & Soloway, E. (1998). The design of learner-adaptable scaffolding in interactive learning environments. *Human Factors in Computing Systems: CHI 98* (pp. 197-194). ACM Press.

Jones, M. L. W. & Balka, E. (1998). *Planning and implementing participant re-design of middle school mathematics software: The second phase of the IPS/PDG/ATIC project* (ATIC-DL Report 98-02).

Koenemann, J., Carroll, J. M., Shaffer, C. A., Rosson, M., & Abrams, M. (1999). Designing collaborative applications for classroom use: The LiNC project. In A. Druin (Ed.), *The Design of Children's Technology.* San Francisco, CA: Morgan Kaufmann.

Loh, B., Radinsky, J., Russell, E., Gomez, L., Reiser, B. J., & Edelson, D. C. (1998). The progress portfolio: Designing reflective tools for a classroom context. *Human Factors in Computing Systems: CHI 98* (pp. 627-634). ACM Press.

Mumford, E. & Henshall, D. (1979). *Designing Participatively: A Participative Approach to Computer Systems Design.* UK: Manchester Business School.

Nicol, A. (1998). Interface design for hyperdata: Models, maps, and cues. *Human Factors Society 32nd Annual Meeting* (pp. 308-312).

Plowman, L. (1992). An ethnographic approach to analyzing navigation and task structure in interactive multimedia: Some design issues for group use. *Conference on People and Computers: HCI'92* (pp. 271-287).

Plowman, L., Luckin, R., Laurillard, D., Stratfold, M., & Taylor, J. (1999). Designing multimedia for learning: Narrative guidance and narrative construction. *Human Factors in Computing Systems: CHI 99* (pp. 310-317). ACM Press.

Rieber, L. P. (1996). Seriously considering play: Designing interactive learning environments based on the blending of microworlds, simulations, and games. *Educational Technology Research and Development, 44*(2), 43-58.

Salzman, M. C., Dede, C., & Loftin, R. B. (1999). VR's frames of reference: A visualization technique for mastering abstract multidimensional information. *Human Factors in Computing Systems: CHI 99* (pp. 489-495). ACM Press.

Scaife, M. & Rogers, Y. (1999). Kids as informants: Telling us what we didn't know or confirming what we knew already. In A. Druin (Ed.), *The Design of Children's Technology*. San Francisco, CA: Morgan Kaufmann.

Scaife, M., Rogers, Y., Aldrich, F., & Davies, M. (1997). Designing for or designing with? Informant design for interactive learning environments. *Human Factors in Computing Systems: CHI 97* (pp. 343-350). ACM Press.

Schuler, D. & Namioka, A. (1993). *Participatory Design: Principles and Practices*. Hillsdale, NJ: Lawrence Erlbaum.

Steyn, D. (2001, April 28). *ITFORUM PAPER #53 - The value of students as part of the design team for educational software.*. Retrieved May 2, 2001 from the World Wide Web: http://it.coe.uga.edu/itforum/home.html.

Strommen, E. (1998). When the interface is a talking dinosaur: Learning across media with Actimates Barney. *Human Factors in Computing Systems: CHI 98* (pp. 288-295). ACM Press.

Tuckman, P. W. (1999). *Conducting Educational Research* (5th ed). Fort Worth, TX: Harcourt Brace.

Chapter XI

E-Learning as a Catalyst for Educational Innovation

Petek Askar, Hacettepe University, Turkey

Ugur Halici, Middle East Technical University, Turkey

ABSTRACT

As a form of distance learning, e-learning has become a major instructional force in the world. In this chapter, initiatives regarding e-learning and its impacts on instructional design, on school management and on the community are described and discussed in order to show different aspects of e-learning environments and their impact on related individuals or institutions. Future trends in e-learning are presented in connection with expected technological improvements and key points needing special care in the development of future e-learning environments are mentioned in the light of diffusion theory.

INTRODUCTION

Most of the discussions related to education are about technological innovations. Indeed as Rogers (1995) stated, we often use the word "innovation" and "technology" as synonyms. A quick analysis of the educational projects all over the world shows us that it is not possible to define a future vision of education without technology, especially e-learning.

E-learning refers to the use of Internet technologies to deliver a broad array of solutions that enhance knowledge and performance (Rosenberg, 2001, p. 28.) E-learning is a form of distance learning which has become a major instructional force in the world. One of the primary goals of higher education institutions today is to start distance education courses and use the World Wide Web (WWW) as an instructional delivery environment.

Besides the technological developments, the last two decades have brought a tremendous increase in knowledge in education, particularly in learning. The emerging views of learning which should be taken into consideration for every learning environment could be stated as follows: Personalized, flexible and coherent (learning is connected to real-life issues); not bounded by physical, geographic or temporal space; rich in information and learning experiences for all learners; committed to increasing different intelligences and learning styles; interconnected and collaborative; fostering interorganizational linkages; engaged in dialogue with community members, accountable to the learner to provide adaptive instructional environments (Marshall, 1997).

WWW is an environment that fits the new paradigm of learning and facilitates "e-learning," which faces a challenge of diffusion. Diffusion is defined by Rogers (1995) as the process by which an innovation is communicated through certain channels over time among the members of a social system. There are four main elements of diffusion: innovation characteristics, communication channels, time and a social system. The innovation characteristics are relative advantage (need), compatibility, complexity, triability and observability.

The initiatives described and discussed in this chapter aim to show different aspects of e-learning environments and their impact on related individuals or institutions:
1.   E-learning and its impact on instructional design
2.   E-learning and its impact on school management
3.   E-learning and its impact on the community

Moreover, such e-learning projects are discussed in terms of diffusion of innovation and educational change in reference to Rogers (1995) and Fullan (1991).

E-LEARNING AND ITS IMPACT ON INSTRUCTIONAL DESIGN

E-learning not only opens up new ways of learning and teaching, but also leads to a new way of thinking and organizing learning content. Collaborations among different stakeholders cause new standards for design of knowledge on the Internet. In traditional computer based instruction, content comes in units called courses. However a new paradigm for designing instruction, grounded in the object oriented notion of computer science, is called "learning objects."

Learning object is defined by the Learning Technology Standards Committee (2002) of the Institute of Electrical and Electronics Engineering (IEEE) as any entity, digital or non-digital, which can be used, reused or referenced during technology-supported learning. The features of learning objects are self-contained, interactive, reusable, and tagged with metadata. By the use of learning objects one can learn just enough, just in time and just for himself/herself.

The idea of educational software as a package is becoming outdated and making way for learning objects as a new way of designing instructional materials. Benefits of learning objects for learners and teachers were described by Shepherd (2000) as:

- Courses can be constructed to meet the individual requirements
- Learning comes in digestible chunks
- Learning is available on a just-in-time basis
- Courses can be customised to suit the needs of different audiences
- Courses can be constructed using components from a wide range of sources
- Components can be reused to meet a range of learning needs

In designing learning objects, the studies on multiple representation of knowledge become important since people have different learning styles and strategies. The association between these two constructs are the main focus of the new instructional design principles. Therefore, the development of learning objects and the way of creating teaching units are well suited for what we call the Information Age.

A representation of knowledge could be decomposed into its parts, where the parts are far from arbitrary. Then they can be used and reused in a great variety of combinations, like a child's set of building blocks. Every combination is meaningful and serves as an instructional whole. Holland (1995) compares building blocks to the features of the human face. The common building blocks are: hair, forehead, eyebrows, eyes, and so on. Any combination is different and may never appear twice. This analogy could be true of e-learning platforms, where learning objects are put together to make up a meaningful whole, which we call instructional materials.

Human-computer interaction is another aspect of the Internet learning environments. Gibbons and Fairweather (1998) identified five attributes that make a computer unique as an instructional medium: (a) dynamic display, (b) ability to accept student input, (c) speed, (d) ability to select, and (e) flawless memory.

An Example: Online Turkish Learning Centre

The goal of this innovative project is to provide a virtual learning environment so that everybody who wants to learn Turkish can have the opportunity to have access to information any time, any place. The intended skills are reading, writing and speaking. The environment was designed and developed by a working team of Turkish language experts (TOMER, Ankara University Turkish and Foreign Languages Research and Application Centre), instructional designers, teachers, experts on Internet based environments, and web engineers (Mobilsoft, a Turkish software and technological company).

The knowledge base of the centre is categorized into three levels:

- *Basic Level* includes basic tenses and simple sentential relation;
- *Intermediate Level* includes verb forms peculiar to Turkish (such as voices) and subordinate structures;
- *Advanced Level* includes syntactic structure of Turkish, textual features and complex grammar structures.

The basic level provides the following skills: meeting people, describing people, telling and asking the time, speaking on the phone, asking and showing the way, expressing feelings (happiness, sadness), asking for help, shopping, and making comparisons.

The intermediate level provides the following skills: talking about past experiences, places visited, activities performed, plans for the future; narrating incidents indirectly; speaking about problems and topics related with occupation; understanding certain jokes and tales; using certain idioms and proverbs, comprehending simple newspaper articles as well as some television and radio programs; describing in detail what one can do, what one's abilities and wishes are.

In the advanced level, learners are supposed to acquire the following skills: reading and discussing news items and articles on any topic; following daily events; trying to find solutions to those problems one is likely to encounter in one's social environment by using Turkish; presenting ones views by talking, writing and discussing on any topic; understanding a film and a novel or poem of a certain level of difficulty and expressing what one understands in written or oral form.

A screen shot of the online Turkish learning environment is shown in Figure 1. In the left column, six modules are listed: Grammar, Listening, Reading, Dictation, Composition and General Exercises. Each module meets clearly defined instructional objectives and consists of self-contained and reusable learning objects for the purpose of developing different skills. The learners can choose whatever they want to learn.

The development principle of each learning object is to use multiple representation rules: real life, textual, graphical, audio and visual representations. In addition, each object includes an exercise for self-assessment and search option for unknown words. The self-assessment allows students to assess their knowledge and get immediate feedback.

Figure 1: A Screen Shot of the Online Turkish Learning Environment

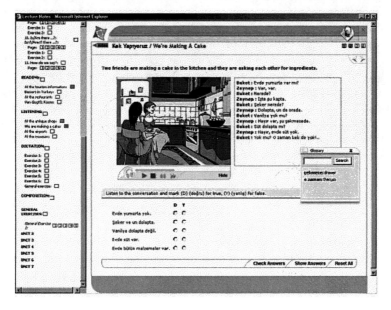

E-LEARNING AND ITS IMPACT
ON SCHOOL MANAGEMENT

For most of the last two decades, technology has been implemented in schools and its potential to change the educational systems has been argued frequently. There are tremendous efforts to encourage the integration of computers and the Internet into schools. However in one of the diffusion studies conducted by Askar and Usluel (2001), two paths to the adoption of computers are presented. One path is related to the use of technology in the school management system whereas the other one is related to the use of technology in the teaching and learning process. For many reasons, the rate of adoption of computers in management applications is quicker than the learning-teaching applications. Indeed the concerns related to use of computers in the teaching-learning process are still at the awareness stage. On the other hand, the need for using computers and Internet for management purposes is more relevant and seems more convenient for the current school system.

Educators assert that the central purpose of school management systems should be to improve instructional program quality. In the light of this idea, a typical configuration of a web-based school management system designed taking this idea into consideration includes administration, assessment and communication. The features are: student enrolment, attendance, registration, test scores, grades and other record keeping tasks, formative and summative evaluation, feedback to parents and teachers about student learning and performance. In addition, new online management systems include item banking capability for adaptive testing and online learning modules.

The web-based platform given below addresses how e-learning affects the management of a school, the roles of teachers and participation of the parents.

An Example: SchoolNet

SchoolNet is a school management system developed for elementary and secondary schools in Turkey. It is an interactive solution to all management aspects of a school. It includes online registration, student information system, item banking, assessment and evaluation. It allows an open interactive environment between students, parents, teachers and administrators. Moreover, an online learning facility is under construction.

SchoolNet has been developed by a multidisciplinary team under the umbrella of an educational institution called YUCE Schools (http://www.yuce.k12.tr) in Turkey. System and software engineers have been working with the teachers, school administrators, and assessment and evaluation experts. The design, development and testing of the environment are implemented in the school. The organizational model of the system provides a realistic environment, which suits the needs of a school. Moreover, it becomes easy to add new features and alternatives.

Every teacher in the school has access to SchoolNet and has an email address. Through SchoolNet, teachers:

- can get information about every student in his/her class,
- have a chance to analyse student performance in other courses or examinations,
- can develop items by using various tools and add items to item banking,
- prepare their own examinations by selecting items from item banking,

- obtain the analysis of examinations from the item bases,
- get announcements from the administration, and
- can communicate online with parents and students online.

To acquire the above skills, teachers have been trained to become computer-literate and to be familiar with the system. Moreover, computers were set up in every teacher's office. Teachers also have access to school network from their home. The school encourages teachers to have a PC at home and to use the facilities of SchoolNet.

Every administrator has an access to the information of the students and the teachers. An administrator can:

- monitor the performance of students,
- analyse the examination results at the instructional objectives level,
- assess which concepts or skills have been achieved and which have not been achieved,
- prepare official letters and announcements,
- inform the teachers, parents and students about recent rules and regulations, and
- prepare timetables for the teachers and the students.

Parents can access the online management system to do the following:

- keep track of the progress of their children,
- get information about all the on-going and future activities of the school,
- communicate with the teachers and administrators anytime, and
- obtain and analyse the examination results on the basis of instructional objectives.

Figure 2: A Screen Shot of an Administrative Message to be Sent to a Parent Through SchoolNet

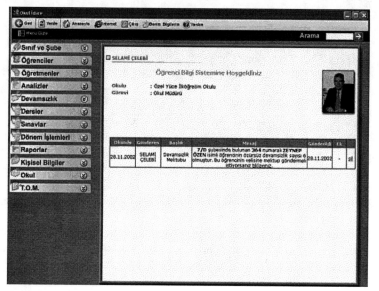

In order to take full advantage of the features of the system, the key factor is the teachers. Therefore, ongoing support for teachers to incorporate it in their daily work is necessary. Thus, teachers have been involved in the design and the development process of the system.

Other critical features of the system include item banking and the test preparation utility. Teachers develop and store their questions with metadata properties, so that every teacher and administrator can easily access, search and use them to prepare their examinations. This increases school efficiency since teachers share their knowledge and work with each other.

Meanwhile, an online learning capability is under construction to give students and teachers access to the learning and instructional materials of their courses, in addition to links to other useful educational portals.

E-LEARNING AND ITS IMPACT ON THE COMMUNITY

The modern world requires individuals and communities to be able to continually develop and utilise different skills and knowledge. There is a growing consensus among OECD countries that modern economies cannot afford a significant number of uneducated people (OECD, 2000). However, education systems throughout the world are ill-equipped to address individual and community learning needs. The existing school system is not flexible for those who for some reasons, left school early.

Distance education is a recognized solution all over the world for bridging the learning and education divide between the educated and poorly educated. It gives people the opportunity to continue their formal education. Despite the initial concerns that distance education might be lower in quality than traditional method of schooling, many forms of distance education are gaining acceptance (Belanger & Jordan, 2000). Therefore distance education is receiving a positive attention from governments as a solution to the educational problem mentioned above.

Also, the trend towards lifelong learning is universal. The transformations taking place in all societies require an increasing participation of individuals, an ability to innovate and solve problems and a capacity to learn and go on learning (Mayor, 1994). Moreover, the term "open learning" is used to lower barriers that stand in the way of individuals and communities wishing to engage in different learning opportunities.

One of the solutions for the above mentioned problems is learning centres, which are flexible learning organizations and which serve the learning needs of the individuals and communities. A school which is well-equipped and organized could be opened during nontraditional school hours. Therefore, schools as learning centres can be critical resources to meet the growing need for distance education students and other community members. However, in highly centralized education systems it is very difficult to organize schools for those other than the registered students. The rules and regulations for conventional school become real barriers for open learning environments.

The project given below addresses a solution for open learning and discusses what e-learning means for the community and how e-learning meets the needs of the community.

An Example: Open Learning Centres

In 1997, Turkey began to implement eight-year compulsory education through parliamentary approval of Law 4306 for Basic Education. Before 1997, compulsory basic education was limited to five years. In parallel to the new structure, to give the chance to students to continue their secondary education, the Open Primary School for years six through eight has been established. Open primary schools are for people who are older than 15 who completed five years of elementary school. Indeed, distance learning opens up new opportunities for students, especially to young women who were excluded from the educational system.

In 1998, the Ministry of National Education, with the collaboration of UNICEF started a project in one of the small towns in Erzurum for young women who enrolled in the Open Primary School. The goal of the centre was to provide distant students with the opportunity to come together, share their knowledge, access different resources and get help from teachers. The centre became an open learning environment for the whole town, not only for students. The need for more information and learning led to the decision to extend the centres to the whole country and keep them open for 24 hours (Adiyaman & Aslan, 2002).

The centres have been established with the help of local organizations, the Ministry of National Education and non-governmental organizations, including foundations.

These centres are equipped with technology that is designed to serve the learning needs of the community. The centres include a communication unit, a multimedia individualized learning unit, computer and Internet rooms, video and television room, areas for group working and discussions, reading and self-study units, guidance and administrative units.

The centres continuously assess the learning needs of the community and accordingly offer short-term courses and organize seminars and conferences. The centres house exhibitions of women's work and are used for group meetings. In addition, field trips to other cities are organised for a variety of purposes such as watching a play, a concert or going to museums.

Figure 3: The Internet Room of a Learning Centre at Van-Muradiye (2001)

Currently the number of learning centres is growing with the help of the local bodies, non-governmental organizations under the guidance of the Ministry of Education. Societies are in search of new models which meet their learning needs. This model is unique since it was developed for the needs of Turkey. However what is common in all these models is the use of technology, especially the Internet, which is an inevitable tool for "Learning Without Frontiers."

FUTURE TRENDS

The interaction between user and computer today is mostly in the form of reading from the display device and writing through the keyboard. Access to e-learning environments is provided through low bandwidth networks, which restricts the amount of information to be transferred and in turn the type of the information, since audiovisual information requires much higher bandwidth with respect to text. There are facilities to search information; however, they are "word" based. The mobile devices are used basically for voice communication and they have not been yet used widely in e-learning environments. E-services are emerging but not matured. Finally and most importantly, only less than 10% of the world population is online (IST WP, 2002).

The technological developments on micro and nano technology are expected to push the limits of miniaturisation and of minimising the costs and power consumption of microelectronic components and micro-systems. Explorations of alternative materials are expected to allow further miniaturisation or organic flexible materials for displays, sensors and actuators so that they can be placed anywhere and can take any shape. The technological developments on interfaces are expected to result in user friendly interfaces which are intuitive, which can interpret speech, vision and touch and which can understand user gestures and various languages. These interfaces are to be coupled with more powerful and flexible knowledge technologies that are semantic-based and context-aware. These kinds of knowledge technologies would allow more effective access to more creative digital content in the next Web generation (IST WP, 2002).

As a result of these advances in technology, it is expected that not only PCs, but all our surroundings will be the interface. Instead of only "writing and reading" in human-computer interaction, all senses are to be used intuitively. Information search will be context-based instead of "word" based. Mobile and wireless devices will be used not only for voice transfer, but for full multimedia. Wide adaptation of services is expected for e-learning, e-health and e-government. Internet is to be used widely (IST WP, 2002).

As information technologies change, open systems and services are to be developed in support of ubiquitous, experiential and contextualised learning and virtual collaborative learning communities, improving the efficiency and cost-effectiveness of learning for individuals and organisations, independent of time, place and pace. Development of advanced digital library services is expected to provide high-bandwidth access to distributed and highly interactive repositories of culture, history and science. Next-generation learning solutions are expected to combine cognitive and knowledge-based approaches with new media having ambient intelligence, virtual and augmented reality, virtual presence and simulation. The school, the library, the local government and local industries are to work together with diverse centres of excellence, supporting and involving pupils, teachers and parents in future advanced "Community Knowledge Networks" (ISTC, 2001).

CONCLUSION

Our current educational system is highly resistant to change. Making a client-based change rather than a technological based one will be the most important innovation to accomplish the educational change. While technology is pushing the limits of e-learning environments, special care should be taken in educational and organisational frameworks. The stakeholders of the systems are students, teachers, principals, learners and the community. Their attitudes, needs, expectations from innovation, its complexity and triability are important issues for the change process. As seen from the examples, every project solves an educational need and develops collaboration with educational community and technology developers.

As stated by ISTC (2001), the educational community needs to be convinced of the potential of new ambient intelligent technologies to provide greater user-friendliness, more efficient service support, user-empowerment, and support for human interactions. Closer collaboration is required between educational researchers and technology developers to create intelligent, "lean-back" systems and applications dedicated to learning needs and processes.

Complexity is another issue to be considered. Rogers (1995) defined complexity as the degree to which innovation is perceived difficult to understand and use. In addition, Fullan (1991) defines complexity as the difficulty and extent of change required of the individuals responsible for implementation. Therefore, there should be an emphasis on simplifying the process of e-learning, while moving from approaches based on knowledge transfer to systems based on the dynamic construction and user-friendly exchange of knowledge among learners, teachers and learning communities.

The educational community, as the end-user of e-learning systems, should be given the opportunity of observing and trying the e-learning systems. Awareness or being informed about the innovation is the key factor for changing negative attitudes or beliefs. It is known that if people see the implementation and results of innovation, they are more likely to adopt them for their usage. Unfortunately, the benefits of e-learning are not well known and well recognized by all relevant stakeholders. Therefore, a comprehensive and systematic awareness campaign is needed to speed up the rate of adoption.

REFERENCES

Adiyaman, Z. & Aslan, M. (2002). *Learning centres*. Ministry of National Education Turkey. Retrieved November 16, 2002 from the World Wide Web: http://www.meb.gov.tr.

Askar P. & Usluel, Y. (2001). Concerns of administrators and teachers in the diffusion of IT in schools: A case study from Turkey. *The 12th International Conference of Society for Information Technology and the Teacher Education*, Orlando, Florida (March 5-10). Available on the World Wide Web: http://www.aace.org/dl/index.cfm/fuseaction/View/paperID/3970.

Belanger, F. & Jordan, D.H. (2000). *Evaluation and Implementation of Distance Learning: Technologies, Tools and Techniques.* London: Idea Group Publishing.

Fullan, M.G. (1991). *The New Meaning of Educational Change.* London: Cassel Educational Limited.

Gibbons, A. & Fairweather, P. (1998). *Computer-Based Instruction: Design and Development.* Englewood Cliffs, NJ: Educational Technology Publications.

Holland, J.H. (1995). *Hidden Order: How Adaptation Builds Complexity.* USA: Perseus Books.

IEEE Learning Technology Standards Committee. (2002). Draft Standard for Learning Object Metadata. Retrieved November 22, 2002 from World Wide Web: http://ltcs.ieee.org/wg12/LOM_1484_12_1_V1_Final_Draft.pdf.

ISTC. (2001). Technology supported learning, ISTC – Information Society Technologies Committee, Final Report from the Working Party on Education and Training, Luxembourg. Report Date October 17, 2001 from the World Wide Web: http://www.proacte.com/downloads/eandt/ISTC-CONsolidated-report-et.DOC.

IST WP. (2002). IST Priority Work programme 2003-2004, Information Society Technologies. Document Date December 17, 2002 from the World Wide Web: http://fp6.cordis.lu/fp6/call_details.cfm?CALL_ID=1.

Marshall, S.P. (1997). Creating sustainable learning communities for the twenty-first century. In F. Hesselbein et al. (Eds.), *The Organization of the Future* (pp. 177-188). San Francisco CA: Jossey-Bass Publishers.

Mayor, F. (1994). Lifelong learning for the 21st century. First Global Conference on Lifelong Learning, Rome, UNESCO, DG/94/39. Retrieved November 17, 2002 from World Wide Web: http://unesdoc.unesco.org/ulis/dgspeechother.html.

OECD/National Centre for Adult Literacy. (2000). *Learning to Bridge the Digital Divide* (Schooling for Tomorrow). France: OECD.

Rogers, E.M. (1995). *Diffusion of Innovations.* New York: The Free Press.

Rosenberg, M.J. (2001). *E-Learning: Strategies for Delivering Knowledge in the Digital Age.* USA: McGraw-Hill.

Shepherd, C. (2000). Objects of interest. Retrieved November 18, 2002 on the World Wide Web: http//www.fastrak-consulting.co.uk/tactix/Features/perfect_etutor.htm.

SECTION II:

MORE ON INTUITIVE, SOCIAL AND INTERNATIONAL ISSUES

Chapter XII

Employing Intelligent and Adaptive Methods for Online Learning

Bernard Mark Garrett, University of British Columbia, Canada

George Roberts, Oxford Brookes University, UK

ABSTRACT

In this chapter, we will explore the potential for employing artificial intelligence and adaptive methods into online learning applications. The existing and newly developing technologies for representing knowledge will be explored and the pedagogic implications for online learning discussed, including examining the roles of intelligent tutoring systems, decision support systems and pedagogic agents. In the wider context, the role of search engines, browsers and virtual learning environments will also be discussed in the context of intelligent systems, and the problems in implementing intelligent web based learning systems in mainstream educational practice.

INTRODUCTION

Individuals working their way through course materials require appropriate feedback and assessment to achieve their desired learning outcomes. Providing such interactions is one of the goals for educational technologists. To be most effective, learning systems must be able to adapt to the user's individual pedagogic needs, provide appropriate sequencing of material and feedback, and use the most suitable examples for the specific learner. Creating systems that can adapt and respond to the individual learner — a machine equivalent of a professional educator for the chosen learning domain — is the subject of this chapter

Educational software falls into different categories according to the place in the educational supply chain to which it is applied: curriculum design, course design and development, learner recruitment and enrolment, course delivery (including learner support and assessment), validation and articulation (Oblinger, 2001). The IEEE Learning Technology Systems Architecture (LTSA) (Figure 1) provides a useful model of the learning technology field.

Oblinger's (2001) higher education supply chain model and the IEEE LTSA enable a complete mapping of educational software applications. For the purposes of this chapter, we will focus on those applications that are directly concerned with learning and teaching (delivery, coaching and evaluation) that have a direct impact upon the learner, and we will address those particularly pertinent to online learning.

Search Engines, Browsers and Virtual Learning Environments

In many education scenarios a significant degree of self-coaching or peer-to-peer coaching is expected and encouraged. Contemporary constructivist pedagogies also encourage the Learner-Teacher/Teacher-Learner paradigm. The LTSA model represents the porous boundary between Learner Entity and Coach by a two-way information flow. Recognising significant bi-directional movement along this axis brings a number of important systems into our discussion.

Figure 1: IEEE Learning Technology Support Architecture

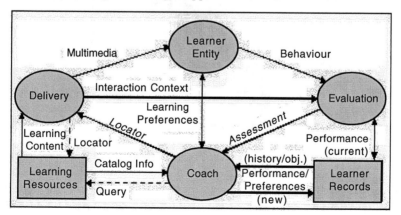

Two key technologies that make up the taken-for-granted background of the online learning experience in fact manifest significant intelligence and adaptivity. Search engines and browsers together may be said to comprise the "common sense" of the Web.

Decker et al. (1999) suggested the World Wide Web (WWW) could be viewed as the largest multimedia database that has ever existed. Its support for retrieval and usage is very limited, however, because its main retrieval services are keyword-based search facilities carried out by different search engines. However search engines are the cornerstone of network intelligence. They not only "recall" information stored in network memory, they perform an important coaching role, directing an inquirer to more or less relevant information, sometimes mimicking the serendipitous human process of juxtaposition of nearly related ideas. All search engines incorporate some AI.

One of the most popular search engines as we write remains Google (http://www.google.com/). There are many reasons for this engine's popularity, but of note for this chapter is Google's modelling of intuitive justification in designing the page ranking (PageRank) algorithms according to which search results are ordered (Brin & Page, 1989). The use of probability distribution and weighted decision criteria is similar to standard multi-criteria decision support tools, and are processes at the heart of many knowledge-based systems. Google's algorithms deliberately model the behaviour of not an expert, but an easily bored novice, a "random surfer," who loses interest rapidly if the results are uninteresting.

While Teoma (http://www.teoma.com/ and http://www.askjeeves.com), and WiseNut (http://www.wisenut.com/corp/pdf/WiseNutWhitePaper.pdf) strive to advance on Google's approach, new engines are taking new directions. The Genetic Algorithms search engine (http://www.optiwater.com/GAsearch/) is an experimental implementation of genetic programming techniques. Currently it only searches for references to genetic algorithms, but the technology could be extended to any domain. The web-enabled Ontology of Software Engineering (WOSE at http://java-emporium.com/WOSE/index.html) asserts that the use of content matching over string matching improves recall and precision in web searching (or in any heterogeneous database).

Where search engines have been designed to guide individual learners, data mining tools using advanced analytical techniques such as neural networks, heuristics, inductive reasoning and fuzzy logic perform a team-coaching role. The learner entity with respect to data mining is often abstracted as the "learning organisation" (Sugumaran & Bose, 1999). Beyond the learning organisation, data mining research aims to create the architecture for an intelligent environment through distributed agents that work cooperatively. Where search engines use ontologies provided by their developers, data-mining applications construct new ontologies from raw data. That is to say — in effect — they learn.

Other recent developments designed to address this issue include Ontobroker and Ontoseek. Ontobroker is an integrated, comprehensive system to extract, reason and generate domain specific metadata (http://ontobroker.aifb.uni-karlsruhe.de/index_ob.html). Borgo et al. (1997) developed Ontoseek to facilitate the retrieval of object-oriented software components. Ontoseek is a system of co-operating intelligent agents. The technology (lexicon-driven information retrieval based on a large linguistic ontology) is, however, applicable to a variety of information sources. More recently, the MALIBU Global Information Gathering Architecture (GIGA) experimental search engine was specifically designed as a research tool (Dent et al., 2001). GIGA uses multiple independent query agents which interact with one another and their search targets independently. Communication between agents takes place by means of agreed domain ontologies, with one overarching ontology (the meta-agent) representing the system as a whole.

As it is easy to overlook search engines as part of the taken-for-granted background to the online learning experience, it is even easier to overlook the browser. However it is the browser that currently makes much adaptivity possible. The process of "bookmarking" sites saves ("remembers") the results of sometimes complex search strategies, and the "history" facility provides another means of individualised cues, helping the learner to "recall" information located last night or last week, which may not have seemed relevant at the time. The use of "cookies," small files that are written to the browser's memory on client machines, enables the browser to recall information about the state of particular sites visited or to remind the web sites of the state of the learner at the learner's last interaction with the site (Netscape, 1999). This feature is particularly important for online learning systems. By interrogating the browser, the online learning system can adapt material to the learner's profile. At the end of a session the learning management system writes a new cookie back to the learner's machine, updating the learner's profile

Intelligent Pedagogic Agents

The use of intelligent pedagogic agents to provide feedback and enhance student interaction with CBL and particularly online systems is a key area for current AI researchers (Seiker, 1994; Lester, Stone, & Stelling, 1999; Chaloupka & Fenton-Kerr, 2000; Whatley & Beer, 2002). As early as 1970, the concept of some sort of an intelligent agent acting as a "butler" for the learner was considered (Negroponte, 1970, cited in Baylor, 2001). Intelligent agents were originally developed and used extensively on the web to perform tasks such as retrieving and delivering information and automating repetitive tasks (Murch & Johnson, 1999). Their use has expanded into a variety of other activities where personalized information retrieval is the goal, and for educational applications their future looks promising.

Intelligent pedagogic agents may be used to support individual learning by offering advice or adapting a study pathway, without it being made explicit to the learner why this advice or change in instructional focus was implemented. They can also be used to support the administration or organisation of learning; for example, personal timetable scheduling or the management of collaborative group work.

Intelligent agents are software systems to provide personalized information that incorporate Expert System technology and often other adaptive technologies such as fuzzy logic or neural networks (Mitaim & Kosko, 1996; Sarma, 1996). There are now a wide variety of programs that have been called "agents," but those that represent intelligent agent functions with a relevance for education are those which:
1. Implement a cognitive function,
2. Perform a mediating role among people and programs,
3. Form the role of an intelligent assistant,
4. Present themselves to use us as believable characters, and
5. Are viewed by users as manifesting intentionality (i.e., having a focused purpose) and exhibiting other aspects of a human mental state. (Baylor, 2001; Bradshaw, 1997)

From the educational perspective, a useful simple description is that intelligent agents are computer programs that simulate human relationships by doing something that another person could otherwise do for you (Seiker, 1994). Chaloupka and Fenton-Kerr (1999) suggest an intelligent agent is a program that makes use of AI approaches to provide timely contextual help or instruction to a learner. They suggest three simple categories of educational intelligent agents:

1.   Simple information retrievers,
2.   Intelligent tutor-guides, and
3.   Pedagogic agents.

Chaloupka and Fenton-Kerr (1999) suggest that pedagogic agents can act autonomously, can communicate with the user, and have some form of anthropomorphic representation. In many intelligent agents an anthropomorphic representation of a human tutor is used to give advice to the student. This style of pedagogic agent is often chosen to facilitate the learning process, as in this context the intelligent agent can be seen as analogous to the role of a human tutor (Garrett & Callear, 2001). The anthropomorphic representation is useful to contextualize the feedback from the system and enhance student interaction with the system (Heitala & Niemirepo, 1998; Lester, Stone, & Stelling, 1999). The anthropomorphic representation now appears to be an effective model for educational intelligent agents (e.g., DESIGN-A-PLANT: Stone & Lester, 1996; VINCENT: Paiva & Machado, 1998; Rickel & Johnson, 1997). Lifelike pedagogic agents present a strong visual presence and may be human or non-human in appearance, for example "Herman the Bug" in a system designed to teach about plant biology (Stone & Lester 1998). Four educational benefits have been identified in using lifelike anthropomorphic representations for intelligent agents:

1.   If the pedagogical agent appears to care about a learner's progress, it will encourage them.
2.   An emotive pedagogical agent that gives appropriate feedback to the learner's progress may help prevent frustration and help prevent loss of interest.
3.   An emotive pedagogical agent may convey enthusiasm for the subject and promote enthusiasm in the learner.
4.   An anthropomorphic agent can make learning more fun and, if the learner enjoys working with the application, they may choose to spend more time using it (and learning).   (Elliott et al., 1999)

Whatley and Beer (2002) have pioneered another use for intelligent agents in supporting online learning. Their work explores the potential for intelligent agents to help students working online develop collaborative group working skills. Computer mediated communication (CMC) tools, such as chat rooms, discussion forums and e-mail, are well-established features to support collaborative working in contemporary managed learning environments (MLEs). Whatley and Beer suggest that an intelligent system is required to advise students which of these many features are appropriate to use at any particular time. They identify several problems seen in traditional student group work including:

•   Knowing who can do which parts of the project
•   Getting group members to agree their responsibilities
•   Problems reaching collective agreement in the group

- Recognizing when extra skills or advice are needed
- Bringing the project together for a successful conclusion

Their solution is the development of the "Guardian" agent, an intelligent agent residing on each of the group member's workstations that autonomously monitors the progress of the group project, suggesting ways in which the students can act to improve the progress of the project as a whole, and also enhance communication between members of the group. The Guardian agent can help students in the planning phase, helping to set ground rules; the implementation phase, ensuring all members contribute; and in the conclusion phase, collating the individual components and preparing the project report. The architecture for the agent involves individual guardian agents operating on students' personal computers, and a server agent residing on a network server. A prototype has been developed using LPA Prolog's Agent Development Kit (LPA, 2000) and has been successfully used to manage the introductions of students in a group-working project and allocate tasks to students. Work is currently ongoing to develop the integration of the Guardian agent into online courseware (Whatley & Beer, 2002).

The development of an intelligent agent that oversees the management of collaborative group working within an online learning environment is a practical reality. From the perspective of most teachers this is likely to represent a highly desirable tool in the support of online learning. It is probable that the use of such agent technology in the market leading virtual learning environments (VLEs) will follow in the near future.

At this stage of development of online learning systems, the role of intelligent agents continues to provide a key research area. Lifelike pedagogical agents seem to hold much promise for online learning environments because they play a central communicative role, and agents that help manage the learning environment are highly desirable. The advantages of these systems for online learning have been clearly highlighted and include the automation of the repetitive tasks of human facilitators in online workshops and the provision of individualised formative advice in asynchronous learning networks (Choonhapong, Bourne, & Olin, 2001). Possibly the flexible nature of interpretation, design and implementation of intelligent agent technology and the success of the anthropomorphic representation in providing an interface with the system have increased their popularity. As with all AI implementations however, they remain complex, requiring a significant investment of time, effort and money to create when compared with non-intelligent systems, therefore those applications that demonstrate a clear commercial advantage to VLE developers are likely to be the first seen in educational practice.

Intelligent and Adaptive Simulation

Intelligent computer-based simulation is proving its value in the simulation of activities where experiential learning is expensive, undesirable or even dangerous. Computer based simulation is also a valuable tool for contemporary problem based learning approaches, particularly in the development of practical skills (Garrett & Callear, 2001). Computer-based simulation has also proved valuable in areas where experiential learning may not be possible due to time, cost or operational constraints, such as in the training of police to respond to bomb threats (Chung & Huda, 1999). Dean and Whitlock (1992) presented a useful classification of types of simulations:

- System facsimile: the training of staff to operate computerised interfaces identical to the real thing under safe conditions.

- Apparatus Operation: the use of computer representations of equipment requiring human manipulation to operate, e.g., a radar simulator for training air traffic controllers.

- Decision-making exercises: large-scale simulation games, such as war games and management exercises.

- Process modelling: demonstrating the effects of all characteristics of a phenomenon in a computerised model, e.g., modelling gravitational fields or molecular structure.

This demonstrates the wide range of applications for computer-based simulation, and many of the more complex modern simulation tools offer complex multifaceted simulations incorporating more than one of these categories. For example, the use of computer-based simulations has been utilised in many areas of health care education, including medical physical assessment (White, 1995), intensive care nursing (Henry & Waltmire, 1992), child health (Lauri, 1992; Krawczak & Bersky, 1995), medical-surgical nursing (Underwood et al., 1997) and midwifery (Woodson, 1997; Lyons et al., 1998). Computer-based simulation can be a valuable tool in the development of practical skills such as clinical decision-making (Garrett & Callear, 2001). In the future the use of intelligent or adaptive simulations holds significant promise for online learning. One example of an early development of online simulation is the University of Iowa's "Virtual Hospital" (http://www.vh.org/) where students can work through simulated clinical presentations. Future developments planned for this initiative include the ability to interact with therapeutic interventions on Virtual Patients.

A practical design for an intelligent simulation has been developed in the School of Health Care, Oxford Brookes University (Garrett & Callear, 2001) and is currently being evaluated. The system architecture provides the basis for an intelligent agent, whilst being relatively quick to produce. The simulation system consists of three modules, a multimedia simulation interface, an expert-assessment system and a searchable domain knowledge base (see Figure 2). Utilising Microsoft Windows help file structures as the domain knowledge base, and coding a relatively simple expert system to model student behaviour and offer appropriate advice with LPA Prolog, a relatively simple architecture has been achieved. The expert system knowledge base is limited to the simulation rather than attempting to model all aspects of the subject domain knowledge, and is used to offer advice to students as they navigate their way around simulations. A simple user-friendly multimedia interface was coded using Borland Delphi with which students access the simulation, and they receive the advice from the expert system via an anthropomorphic representation (the professor) at appropriate times. The system (The Clinical Decision Simulator) simulates clinical environments and allows student nurses to practice their clinical decision-making skills in a safe context.

Although this system was originally developed as a stand-alone application, the architecture is highly appropriate for migration to a web-based context. The development and construction of intelligent online simulation systems is now within the grasp of academics and teachers, rather than IT experts. The latest tools from LPA Prolog can be used to create expert systems and intelligent agents that interface with HTML coded

Figure 2: A Modular Design for an Intelligent Simulation System

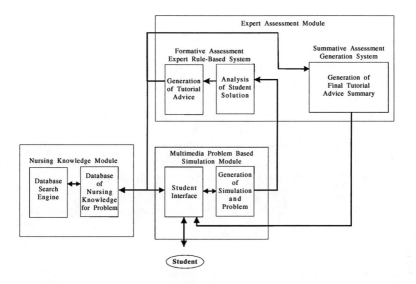

pages, and the current structure of Microsoft Windows help files is already HTML based. Although the construction of such systems requires technical programming expertise, the design and content of such intelligent systems (including the expert knowledge base and rules) can be undertaken by educators.

FUTURE TRENDS

Machine Sentience

Future developments will see advances in knowledge representation and formation, information recall, inference, induction and synthetic personality, and also their integration in hybrid complex adaptable automata.

Mobile Intelligence and Location Based Services

The use of Mobile AI applications is another rapidly expanding field of interest. Roussopoulos et al. (1999) at Stanford University propose a person-level router that meets the following goals:

- Maintain person-to-person reachability,
- Protect the mobile person's privacy,
- Extend easily to new network devices and applications,
- Be deployable without modifying existing infrastructure.

Such location-based services for mobile people have educational implications. Location-based systems induce rules that cause messages to be sent to people or other software systems when certain location events occur.

New recreational applications are emerging that allow multiple players to participate collaboratively but anonymously in proximity to wireless pico-networks. The game controller, an adaptive intelligent system of some sophistication, detects the presence of a player, reads their profile (much like cookies in a browser), matches it to other suitable players or games available within the network, acting much along the lines of the LTSA as coach, delivery process and evaluation (Ben-Ze'ev, 2000).

The application of such location-based systems to teaching and learning is only beginning to find expression.

Current location-based teaching and learning systems are used to facilitate communication by providing alternative means of, for example, connecting to a College LAN, as, for example, in the Reading College Learning Centre (http://www.reading-college.ac.uk), where students can book out an Apple iBook computer using Apple's Airport wireless technology to link up to the College network. Students can log onto their account – and connect to the Internet — from anywhere in the Learning Centre. "M-learning" is being discussed (Quinn, 2000), but applications are restricted to making documents increasingly portable. Academic Advanced Distributed Learning (ADL, 2001) suggests handheld computers and mobile phones are getting more powerful and more pervasive. They are no longer the initial personal digital assistants (PDAs), but tools for collaboration and communication, and even for the delivery of instruction.

Personal Information Agents

Personal Information Agents are beginning to emerge that may have interesting educational application (see MIT Software Agents Group, UMBC Agent Web and Agent Link). Personal Information Agents act as mediators between individuals and the world: the agent acting as a filter, screening information and only allowing the person to see what the agent's induction engine has determined to be useful from long hours observing the person's preferences and behaviour. Such agents will be socially intelligent (Dautenhahn, 1998). Dautenhahn (1998) supposes that relationships that develop between people and their personal information agents will be co-adaptive. Not only will the agent learn the human's preferences, but also agent tools that are behaving socially could influence human conceptions of sociality.

CONCLUSION

AI is also beginning to reach mainstream educational practice and online learning environments, however, the majority of work remains in this experimental and research arena and the value of such approaches remains to be demonstrated effectively. In some ways this is to be expected, as the complexity of knowledge representation is a major obstacle to the development of these systems. AI itself remains a discipline in its infancy with the potential to develop massively. Intelligent applications are beginning to outperform their human counterparts in some specialist areas, proving they can consistently achieve very high quality results. Online education is a very complex area where both the end result and the learning process are important elements, and complex multidimensional ontology's are encountered. Skills-based training is one domain where the application of AI and adaptive technologies is beginning to prove its value, and if

AI can establish its value in online education, then there will be increased investment, more rapid development and the widespread use of AI applications in mainstream educational practice.

As sentient, location-aware information agents emerge from the laboratories and begin to have identifiable persistent existence on the Internet (Coen et al., 2000), some will be acting for commercial interests, some will be acting for personal interests and some will be acting for and against the interest of the state. The questions that arise are fundamental to society, to individual people, and to what it means to be a person. AI, and learning how to work with AI, may be the great educational meta application. Adaptive intelligent systems unify the IEEE Learning Technology Support Architecture (LTSA). They unite people with machines in the Learner Entity, Evaluation, Coach and Delivery Processes. Machines coach and evaluate people who learn, as people coach and evaluate machines that learn. There is no role preserved for one or the other. Adaptive intelligent systems reveal us: human and computer, following Turing and von Neumann, to be universal learning systems, part of life: the universal learning system.

REFERENCES

ADL. (2001). *Academic advanced distributed learning.* Retrieved January 29, 2002 from the World Wide Web: http://www.academiccolab.org/.

Baylor, A. L. (2001). Investigating multiple pedagogical perspectives through MIMIC (Multiple Intelligent Mentors Instructing Collaboratively). *Proceedings of Artificial Intelligence in Education (AI-ED) International Conference*, San Antonio, Texas.

Ben-Ze'ev, Y. (2000). *Pico-Servers and thin clients: A paradigm of providing personal networking experience with Bluetooth.* Retrieved January 29, 2002 from the World Wide Web: http://www.smartm.com/binary/files/personalnetwork.pdf.

Borgo, S., Guarino, N., Masolo, C., & Vetere, G. (1997). Using a large linguistic ontology for internet-based retrieval of object-oriented components. *Proceedings of the Ninth International Conference on Software Engineering and Knowledge Engineering (SEKE '97)* (June 18 - 20) Madrid.

Bradshaw, J. (1997). *Software Agents.* Cambridge, MA: MIT Press.

Brin, S., & Page, L. (1998). *The anatomy of a large-scale hypertextual web search engine.* Retrieved January 22, 2002 from the World Wide Web: http://www7.scu.edu.au/programme/fullpapers/1921/com1921.htm.

Chaloupka, M., & Fenton-Kerr, T. (2000). A holistic view of computer-based learning, development and management. *Proceedings of Association for Learning and Technology Conference* (Alt-C), 1999, Oxford.

Chung, C.A., & Huda, A. (1999). An interactive multimedia training simulator for responding to bomb threats. *Simulation, 1*, 68-77.

Coen, M., Phillips, B., Warshawsky, N., Weisman, L., Peters, S., Gajos, K., Hanssens, N., & Dasgupta, D. (2000). *The Metaglue Software Agent System.* Artificial Intelligence Laboratory, Massachusetts Institute Of Technology. Retrieved January 29, 2002 from the World Wide Web: http://www.ai.mit.edu/research/abstracts/abstracts2001/intelligent-working-spaces/06coen.pdf.

Dautenhahn, K. (1998). The art of designing socially intelligent agents: Science, fiction and the human in the loop. *Applied Artificial Intelligence*, *12*(8).

Dean, C., & Whitlock, Q. (1992). *Handbook of Computer-Based Training* (2nd ed.). London: Kogan Page.

Decker, S., Erdmann, M., Fensel, D., & Studer, R. (1999). Ontobroker: Ontology based access to distributed and semi-structured information. In R. Meersman et al. (Eds.), *Semantic Issues in Multimedia Systems. Proceedings of DS-8* (pp. 351-369). Boston, MA: Kluwer Academic Publisher.

Dent, V., Hall, F., Harris, S., Hay, J., & Martinez, K. (2001). Agent technology concepts in a heterogenous distributed searching environment. *VINE, 1*, 55-63.

Elliott, C.D., Rickel, J., & Lester, J. (1999). Lifelike pedagogical agents and affective computing: An exploratory synthesis. In M. Wooldridge & M. Veloso (Eds.), *Artificial Intelligence Today* (No. 1600 Lecture Notes in Computer Science) (pp. 195-212). Berlin: Springer-Verlag.

Garrett, B.M. (1997). Integrating formative assessment into multimedia simulations for nursing. *Proceedings of ACENDIO 1997: The First European Conference of the Association for Common European Nursing Diagnoses, Interventions and Outcomes*. London: Royal College of Nursing.

Garrett, B.M., & Callear, D.H. (2001). Designing intelligent computer-based simulations: A pragmatic approach. *Association of Learning Technology Journal*, *9*(3), 5-16

Heitala, P., & Niemirepo, T. (1998). The competence of learning companion agents. *The International Journal of Artificial Intelligence in Education, 9*, 178-192.

Henry, S.B., & Waltmire, D. (1992). Computerised clinical simulations: a strategy for staff development in critical care. *American Journal of Critical Care Nursing*, *1*(2), 99-107.

IEEE. (2001). P1484.1/D8, Draft Standard for Learning Technology - Learning Technology System Architecture (LTSA). Retrieved November 16, 2001 from the World Wide Web: http://ltsc.ieee.org/doc/.

Krawczak, J., & Bersky, A.K. (1995). The development of automated client responses to computerized clinical simulation testing. *Computers in Nursing*, *13*(6), 295-300.

Lauri, S. (1992). Using a computer simulation program to assess the decision-making process in child health care. *Computers in Nursing*, *10*(40), 171-177.

Lester, J.C., Stone, B.A., & Stelling, G.D. (1999). Life-like pedagogic agents for mixed-initiative problem solving in constructivist learning environments. *User Modelling and User-Adapted Interaction* (The Netherlands), *1*, 1-43.

Lyons, J., Miller, M., & Milton, J. (1998). Learning with technology: Use of case based physical and computer simulations in professional education. *Contemporary Nurse: A Journal for the Australian Nursing Profession*, *7*(2), 98-102.

MIT Software Agents Group Projects Application Matrix. Retrieved January 29, 2002 from the World Wide Web: http://agents.WWW.media.mit.edu/groups/agents/projects/applications.html.

Mitaim, S., & Kosko, B. (1998). Neural Fuzzy agents for profile learning and adaptive object matching. *Presence: Special Issue on Autonomous Agents, Adapted Behaviours and Distributed Simulations*, *7*(5), 64-69.

Murch, R., & Johnson, T. (1999). *Intelligent Software Agents*. London: Prentice Hall.

Netscape. (1999). *Persistent client state Http cookies*. Retrieved January 28, 2002 from the World Wide Web: http://www.netscape.com/newsref/std/cookie_spec.html.

Oblinger, D. (2001, February 7). *Education technologies and planning in higher education: The US experience.* JISC Technology Watch — Helping to plan for the future of further and higher education. Retrieved January 24, 2002 from the World Wide Web: http://www.jisc.ac.uk/events/01/tech_watch/diana_oblinger.ppt.

Paiva, A., & Machado, I. (1998). Vincent, an autonomous pedagogical agent for on-the-job training. *Proceedings of Intelligent Tutoring Systems Conference.* Berlin: Springer-Verlag.

Quinn, C. (2000, Fall). m-Learning: Mobile, wireless, in-your-pocket learning. *LineZine.* Retrieved January 29, 2002 from the World Wide Web: http://www.linezine.com/2.1/features/cqmmwiyp.htm.

Rickel, J., & Johnson, W.L. (1997). Integrating pedagogical capabilities in a virtual environment agent. *Proceedings of the First International Conference on Autonomous Agents.*

Roussopoulos, M., Maniatis, P., Swierk, E., Lai, K., Appenzeller, G., & Baker, M. (1999). Person-level routing in the Mobile People Architecture. *Proceedings of the USENIX Symposium on Internet Technologies and Systems* (October 1999). Retrieved January 29, 2002 from the World Wide Web: http://mosquitonet.stanford.edu/publications/USITS1999/USITS1999.html.

Sarma, V. (1996). Intelligent agents. *Journal of the IETE, 42*(3), 105-109.

Seiker, T. (1994). Coach: A teaching agent that learns. *Communications of the ACM, 37*(7), 92-99.

Stone, B.A., & Lester, J.C. (1996). Dynamically sequencing an animated pedagogical agent. *Proceedings of the Thirteenth National Conference on Artificial Intelligence* (pp. 424-431).

Sugumaran, V., & Bose, R. (1999). Data analysis and mining environment: A distributed intelligent agent technology application. *Industrial Management and Data Systems, 99*(2), 71-80.

UMBC Agent Web. (2002). Retrieved January 29, 2001 from the World Wide Web: http://agents.umbc.edu/.

Underwood, R., Gamble, R., & Jones, B. (1997). Continuing education for rural based health professionals. Retrieved August 14, 2000 from the World Wide Web: http://www.ruralhealth.org.au/pdf/conedu.pdf.

White, J.E. (1995). Using interactive video to add physical assessment data to computer-based patient simulations in nursing. *Computers in Nursing, 5,* 233-235.

WiseNut. (2001). Search engine white paper. Retrieved January 22, 2002 from the World Wide Web: http://www.wisenut.com/corp/pdf/WiseNutWhitePaper.pdf.

Woodson, S. (1997). *Clinical Simulations in Maternity Nursing 2.* Williams & Wilkins MediSim.

Chapter XIII

Toward Predictive Models for E-Learning:
What Have We Learned So Far?

Maria Alexandra Rentroia-Bonito, Technical University of Lisbon, Portugal

Joaquim Armando Pires Jorge, Technical University of Lisbon, Portugal

ABSTRACT

Currently, developing courseware for e-learning initiatives remains much of a black art. While we are mastering the process of authoring interactive media, we know little about the many factors that affect the e-learning experience. This can drastically limit return on invested efforts for organizations. Indeed, authoring multimedia content is a very expensive endeavor as compared to the traditional approach. A better understanding of the process could yield new approaches and insights to achieve a more ambitious goal: predictive models for e-learning. The reviewed literature highlights a lack of reliable results describing the interplay between e-learning context, web usability, cognitive styles, motivation, learner performance and satisfaction. Clearly, more research is needed to better understand and predict learner performance during an e-learning experience. The expected results of such an integrated approach would assist developers to design better e-learning experiences. This chapter proposes a holistic framework covering the interplay among Business-Process, People and Information-Systems issues. This could serve to guide future research.

Concern for man and his fate must always form the chief interest of all technical endeavors ... Never forget this in the midst of your diagrams and equations

> Albert Einstein
> Quoted in "Science and Values"
> London Times, Jul 1, 85"

INTRODUCTION

The increasing usage of Internet in education raises important questions concerning both its effectiveness and efficiency. Not only we need to know about how effective online training packages are as a knowledge delivery mechanism, but also we need to assess the impact they actually have on supporting new learning processes. However, there is a lack of established models to predict performance and evaluate adequacy of courseware to both the target constituencies and the stated educational or training goals. This can lead to costly investments on creating and maintaining content to develop training packages.

According to the scarce literature and anecdotal evidence, the current crop of e-learning packages, be they internet-based or not, do not seem to provide a satisfying learning experience or serve as a replacement for conventional means of knowledge delivery. Most importantly, they fail to keep learners engaged in learning. This leads to high turnover and yields little value for money for the organizations that have heavily invested in this approach. Some of the most significant barriers identified so far include: (a) a poor match of content structure to learner's cognitive styles, (b) individual perceptions on technology as a hindrance to the learning experience, and (c) a poor organization of content that is ill-suited to hypermedia.

While considerable knowledge from usability seems applicable in this context, we feel that the e-learner experience is considerably different from conventional user experience and has its own richer set of components and associated requirements. Indeed, e-learning experience transcends user experience with the requirements emerging from knowledge acquisition, learning task closure and length of interaction. In addition, there is a need for more theoretical and developmental approaches to improve our understanding of user acceptance and performance factors affecting web-based training programs (Astleitner, 2001). A better understanding of the many factors affecting e-learning performance would allow individuals and organizations to achieve e-learning's much-touted benefits. In so doing, development teams (instructors, courseware developers, web designers, Information Systems, Human Resource process owners, and other professionals) need methods, techniques and tools to evaluate, in advance, which features of web learning packages (design, layout, navigation, content structure and organization) are needed to achieve high learner outcomes, namely performance and satisfaction. To this end, we need to focus on the basis of predictive models to improve learning effectiveness.

This chapter includes four sections. The *Background* presents a proposed e-learning theoretical framework to guide our analysis based upon the reviewed literature. *Key Issues* describes relevant issues arising from proposed e-learning framework. *Potential Solutions and General Recommendations* briefly describes our vision to approach e-learning initiatives. Finally, we present a *Research Outlook*.

BACKGROUND

Individual learning is an active and continuous process. People engage in learning activities in order to obtain key information they need to perform current or new tasks and achieve their goals. In this process, learners are influenced by their context, and individual traits play a differentiator role in acquiring knowledge and developing skills (Bandura, 2000). We can identify some context variables such as availability of learning resources; management support and career opportunities that people value as possibly indirect outcomes of their learning process. Examples of individual traits that may influence the learning experience are learner's cognitive styles, motivation, individual priorities, learning goals, attitudes towards technology, computer self-efficacy, prior experience and knowledge domain (Dillon & Watson, 1996; Holt & Crocker, 2000; Liu & Dean, 1999; Shih & Gamon, 1999; Turcotte & Dufresne, 2000; Walters et al., 2000; Wentling et al., 2000; Welbourne et al., 2000).

If organizations become aware of the interplay between context and individual variables they could achieve a better understanding of the learning experience. This would help improve conditions and achieve expected benefits in terms of competitiveness. Figure 1 conceptually summarizes this interplay.

As seen in Figure 1, within organizational settings, we identify two levels with impact on people performance. At macro-organizational level, key organizational factors, such as business strategies and policies, organizational structures, business process, culture, and leadership styles among others, affect the way people perceive their work environment. Some examples are a shared set of business goals, encouragement towards development of competencies, accessibility to business-related information, mentoring or coaching programs.

At micro-organizational level, we can identify physical, social and technological enablers. Examples of these are ergonomic workplace conditions, clearly stated job tasks, performance goals, clear feedback on performance, good system usability and a support-

Figure 1: Key Macro-Level Factors Influencing Performance (Rentroia-Bonito, 1993)

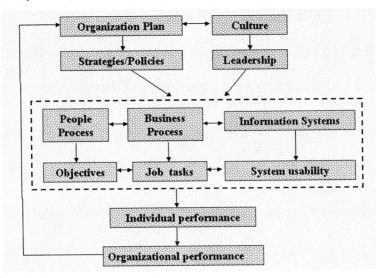

ive work group. At individual level, among many others, two specific traits we consider as influencing individual learning process: cognitive styles and motivation. One important issue is the manner and extent to which these two traits affect learner performance.

Based upon the reviewed literature (Astleitner, 2001; Bandura, 2000; Dillon & Watson, 1996; Dix et al., 1998; Holt & Crocker, 2000; Kim, 2000; Liu & Dean, 1999; Reeves & Nass, 1996; Rentroia-Bonito, 1993; Shih & Gamon, 1999; Strazzo & Wentling, 2001; Turcotte & Dufresne, 2000; Vouk et al., 1999; Walters et al, 2000; Wentling et al., 2000; Welbourne et al., 2000), the external and internal fit (Walker, 1992) among Business strategies, Culture, Human Resource practices, Leadership styles and work context (i.e., physical and technological work conditions surrounding individual job's tasks) affect people's perceptions and, in turn, motivation to engage and perform during a task. We argue that the level of those fits in an e-learning environment is also relevant to e-learners' performance, as shown in Figure 2. The underlying assumption, for this analysis, is that e-learner performance would be mainly affected by motivation and cognitive styles, thus teaching strategies and methods taking into account these two variables could foster positive learning outcomes.

According to Wentling et al. (2000), e-learning involves the acquisition and use of distributed knowledge facilitated by electronic means (e.g., networks, computers, wireless and satellite channels, cellular phones, Personal Digital Assistants, etc.) in a synchronous and/or asynchronous mode. This way, knowledge could be distributed geographically with varied limits of time. The level of effective usage of technology-based instruction would indicate organization readiness to create and sustain the required conditions to succeed at micro-organizational level. In this sense, a holistic approach is needed as a diagnostic and a managerial tool. We think that this framework could lead efforts to design such types of computer-based tools to support development teams, giving them specific information views on diverse aspects of the learning process and outcomes.

E-Learning Framework: A Matter of Fit?

To realize e-learning strategies within an organizational context, we should clarify some key issues that arise at the interface between people and information systems. In

Figure 2: Identified Key Individual Factors Influencing the E-Learning Experience

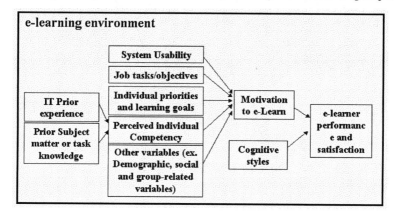

Figure 3: Proposed Three-Entity E-Learning Framework

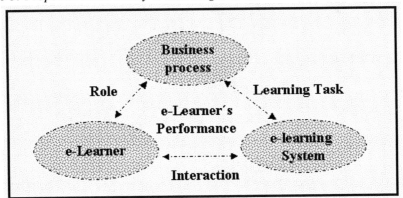

fact, learning systems and people must interact harmoniously in the scope of business processes. This is paramount if we are to articulate business strategies to individual performance when learning. To this end, we propose a framework, as shown in Figure 3, comprising three basic entities: People, Information Systems and Business Processes. These entities instantiate organizational concepts that were described in Figure 1, namely e-Learner, Training Process and e-Learning Systems. Indeed, and contrary to conventional settings, the need for skill development in the workplace should be justified first and assessed last in the context of business practices. Our proposed framework should enable practitioners not only to develop better systems but also to come up with the tools to assess their impact on productivity.

To achieve these we need to identify how the relationships presented in the framework of Figure 3 could improve e-learning experiences. In the proposed framework, arrows connecting elements represent relationships. We suggest three types of relationships: (a) Interaction between people and system, (b) Role played by people during the interaction with systems, and (c) Learning Task to be executed during e-learning experiences by people playing a role when interacting with systems.

Within an e-learning experience, Business Processes provide yardsticks to define educational or training goals and monitor learning outcomes. In this sense, Business Processes frame the interaction between learners and e-learning systems by modeling tasks and taking into consideration roles to be performed by people when interacting. This is three-fold. First, properly designed learning tasks keep individual learning articulated with organizational strategy and goals. Second, roles ascribed to members when e-learning could be as diverse as e-learners, e-instructors, e-speakers, systems and courseware designers, supervisors, reviewers, Human Resource and Information Technology officers, among many others. Third, interaction between e-learners and e-learning systems is characterized by input/output relationship in accordance with Norman's extended model (Dix et al., 1998) and is also shaped by the way people relate to systems. Reeves and Nass' (1996) work suggests that people relate to media as they would relate to real people treating them with affection and courtesy. In the same manner, e-learning systems shape people's perceptions and frame their mental model about potential functioning and usefulness to their activities. Building on these findings, we argue that the more e-learning systems by themselves are: (a) easy to use and learn; (b) "nicely

Figure 4: Proposed Types of E-Learning in Terms of Time and Space

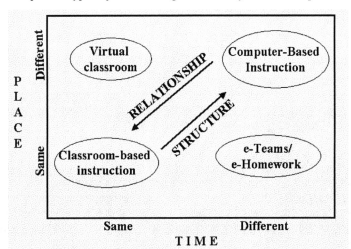

behaved"; and (c) perceived as useful to achieve specific learning goals, the likelier e-learners will engage in the experience.

We propose that all three relationships (Interaction, Role and Learning Tasks) are relevant to e-learning experiences, because each contributes to performance within the defined context. The next section will identify and discuss key issues at the core of our proposed model.

KEY ISSUES

The main issues we identified within the framework presented in the previous section are Structure and Relationship. In what follows, we will explore these two concepts. Figure 4 presents different modes of e-learning regarding the use of technology in education both in terms of distance and time. As technology gets more extensively used for delivery, the need for course structure becomes higher and the relationship between instructor and e-learner is increasingly tenuous. Figure 4 shows this relationship defining three types of e-learning, set apart from conventional classroom instruction. However, we should note that presential instruction increasingly resorts to technology as an auxiliary delivery tool, ranging from humble slide presentations to sophisticated applets and multimedia tools including virtual environments and physically based simulations.

This shows that the use of technology to support learning process requires a much higher level of course structure compared to the classroom-based instruction (Liu & Dean, 1999) to be effective. In addition, current approaches have taken a one-size-fits-all method to provide courseware delivery, regardless of differences in place and time. We cannot argue strongly enough that *delivery needs to be tailored to context* (space and time) in order to: (a) overcome the barriers imposed by structure arising with space-time dimensions, and (b) improve the e-learning experience. We surmise that this needs to be done differently for different students who have different cognitive styles, roles and tasks within organizational context.

Structure Issues

Organizational knowledge is becoming rapidly obsolete in present-day rapidly changing business environment. This obsolescence undermines organizations' ability to adapt and compete. To survive, organizations need to effectively identify and minimize the skill gaps of their workforce. This needs to be done both timely and effectively (Wentling et al., 2000; Strazzo & Wentling, 2001). To achieve just-in-time training, business process must be articulated with appropriate technology and coordinated by a corporate training model. This way, learning will be business-driven and systematically managed. How could this happen? Figure 5 shows training-model phases.

Business Process

Training needs are identified, taking into account work context, business process dynamics, individual tasks/objectives and individual performance improvement areas. Identified skill gaps are the focus to define instructional objectives, design and development of interactive course contents to high quality standards. Defining appropriate goals for training evaluation poses the same requirements both for electronic media and traditional settings. However, as courseware becomes available and distributed through the Internet, quality of service (QoS) becomes an increasingly important factor to e-learner outcomes. At this point, technology becomes another structural issue to contend with.

Technology

The current global market competitive environment imposes high adaptability and productivity levels both on organizations and individuals. Some organizations have responded by adopting web technology as a training delivery platform to reach more participants at lower costs. However, expected results have yet to materialize (Wentling et al., 2000; Strazzo & Wentling, 2001). Findings by Shih and Gamon (1999), Kim (2000), and Turcotte and Dufresne (2000) led us to believe that this perceived shortcoming lies in a poor understanding of the way individuals interact with online learning materials and courseware. Indeed, current research has provided no conclusive evidence on the effects of individual characteristics on web-based learning (Dillon & Watson, 1996; Liu & Dean,

Figure 5: A Model of the Training Process (Goldstein et al., 1991)

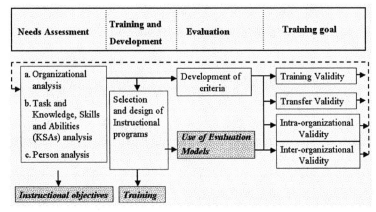

1999; Walters et al., 2000). Further, the lack of holistic approaches and proper tools is identified as one of the major obstacles to the analysis and evaluation of the impact of web-based training on learners. The consequences are users' perceptions of inadequacy of content structure (Astleitner, 2001), which negatively impacts on their motivation to learn and perform. A related proposal to overcome these barriers is exposed by Passerini and Granger (2000). These authors propose a hybrid developmental model integrating both constructivist and objectivist approaches to instructional design of web-courses. This model closely follows an iterative software development cycle. We believe that: (a) studying the interaction between e-learning systems and e-learners' cognitive styles within the business-process context could provide the missing link in such studies, (b) using a similar iterative software-development-cycle approach would make it possible to apply formative tools such as heuristic evaluation, cognitive walkthroughs and learner testing at the module and courseware levels as depicted in Figure 6. In this way, expected e-learner performance would come alongside the metrics suggested by the literature for systematically measuring e-learning progress (Wentling et al., 2000; Dix et al., 1998). We will look more closely into usability and user models in the next two sections.

Usability

Usability is the extent to which a computer system can be used to achieve specified goals with effectiveness, efficiency and satisfaction in a given context to complete a well-defined task (Dix et al., 1998). To develop systems that are both usable and useful we need to evaluate the design at all stages. Ivory et al.'s (2000) findings, working with Internet experts' ratings on information-centric web sites, identified six criteria as highly distinguishing good sites from poorly designed ones. These criteria load on a first factor, in a principal-component analysis, which accounts for 91% of the variance. These criteria are: text cluster count (facilitate scanning), link count (expose the information structure clearly and in turn facilitates information seeking), page size (possibly help users find information faster, but a larger page size, specially with a larger number of images, could potentially degrade download speed), graphics count (used to divide large pages in section or lists), color count (to make display text stand out) and reading complexity (lower scores facilitates information-seeking). These variables predict sites' group membership with 63% accuracy, which means that those usability metrics were capable of predicting experts' judgments distinguishing good from poorly designed web site, with that level of accuracy (Ivory et al., 2000). Later, Ivory et al.'s (2001) work shows that the accuracy level increases to 80%, on average, if the web sites assessment is made within categories (e.g., education, community, living and finance).

User Modeling

User modeling is the knowledge a system has about users, based on users' interactions with the system. Knowledge of both user and task domain should allow intelligent systems to adapt their response to a user's competence level and task needs (Dix et al., 1998). In user modeling, cognitive models (e.g., GOMS, Keystroke-Level Model) are used to predict user performance doing a specific task (e.g., task execution, learning times). We believe one of the main challenges of user modeling is to develop the proper tools to diagnose and monitor learners' performance while: (a) doing simple, ill-structured or complex learning tasks in e-learning contexts, (b) interacting with adaptable systems that allow them control over their experience while providing additional guidance and help (Kules, 2000). This understanding would help developers take into consideration users' expectations into the system design. Perhaps, this may gradually translate into user trust in the system, confidence in the interaction and likely engagement during e-learning experiences.

Having briefly discussed technology-related issues, in the next section we show some relevant evaluation criteria for e-learning.

Evaluation Criteria

As we have seen earlier, Quality of Service (QoS) spans a wide range of criteria ranging from network performance and technical support (Vouk et al., 1999), through quality of content (Fogg et al., 2000; Smith, 1997) to the pedagogical approach (Strazzo & Wentling, 2001). All these are relevant to e-learners' perceived QoS and affect their expectations and outcomes. In fact, QoS is determined by organizational decisions and investment on e-learning strategies. For example, scalability becomes an important issue affecting system architecture, especially when the target population is numerous, disperse and playing diverse roles. Another relevant issue is the time allowed for experts to identify and model key learning tasks and knowledge maps.

To assess the effectiveness of e-learning strategies, we need a comprehensive evaluation toolset, both formative and summative at different levels. Taking a step back, from the standpoint of developers, we can identify in the body of knowledge developed by the Human Computer Interaction (HCI) community different tools to assess courseware development in two dimensions. At the group level, we identify Individuals, Organizations and Society as a whole. In the granularity of structure we can identify four main levels of complexity. Interactive applets comprise the smallest learning unit we care about in this context. At a higher level, we identify modules as self-contained educational units

Figure 6: Potential E-Learning Evaluation Methods and Tools

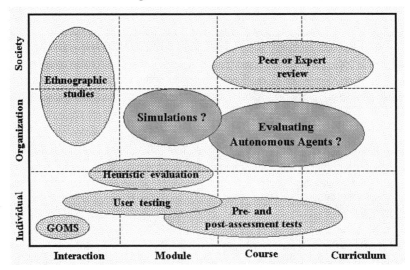

comprising maybe several learning applets. Courses stand for structured sequences of educational units that serve a training purpose or instructional objective. These are usually designed in the context of organizations, whether business or academia. Finally, curricula appear as a highly structured packaging concept addressing complete learning cycles (e.g., academic degrees). These are difficult to find in business contexts and so far have been mostly confined to academia. Figure 6 shows some potential evaluation methods and tools. Many of these still remain research and development issues. Indeed, even academia has only recently begun to take evaluation and performance assessment seriously at the curricular level, let alone Society as a whole (Rentroia-Bonito & Jorge, 2002). Many of the evaluation tools at the individual level come from established research in the Human-Computer Interaction (HCI) community (Dix et al., 1998). However, organizations largely lack a framework (as we have seen before) and a toolset to evaluate process and e-learning performance. We suggest this is an area warranting further research and propose simulations and evaluation agents as two promising methods.

Having discussed structure-related issues, we next focus on relationship as the other key issue for e-learning.

Relationship Issues

Social sciences have identified a construct called cognitive styles as a variable of interest for education related to the human cognition system (Witkin & Goodenough, 1981), which is a key variable in designing an effective system for a particular user group, especially at early stages of the interaction (Dillon & Watson, 1996; Kim, 2000; Liu & Dean, 1999; Turcotte & Dufresne, 2000).

Cognitive Styles

Learning styles are cognitive, affective and physiological characteristics that serve as relatively stable indicators of how learners perceive, think, remember and solve problems (Kim, 2000). This specific individual characteristic is (a) consistent major dimensions of individual differences, and (b) characterized by generality and stability across tasks and over time. They are also relatively independent from traditional measures of general ability and have either positive or negative relationships to motivation and academic achievement depending on the nature of the learning task (Liu & Dean, 1999). Field Dependence-Independence is one of the most widely studied cognitive styles with the broadest application to problems in education (Kim, 2000; Witkin & Goodenough, 1981). However, research results are numerous and mixed, and give no consistent evidence on the relationship between cognitive styles and a learner's performance within a computer-based learning setting (Dillon & Watson, 1996; Shih & Gamon, 1999; Wentling et al., 2000; Walters et al., 2000).

Some research results show that cognitive styles can help explain some usability problems when browsing hypermedia documents (Kim, 2000; Turcotte & Dufresne, 2000). This finding may be translated into the importance of information architecture for the individual learning process. However, are cognitive styles enough to ensure an effective e-learning experience? In the next section, we will look at motivation as a key individual factor to better understand people's behavior when interacting with system during their learning.

Motivation

Motivation is the internal set of processes (both cognitive and behavioral) by which human energy becomes focused on the direction of effort (Welboune et al., 2000). In particular, Shih and Gamon's (1999) findings reveal a significant relationship between students' achievement, motivation and learning strategies. Motivation explains 28% of the variance and learning strategies explain 7% to account for a meager 35% of the variance of students' achievement. But motivation is also affected, among others, by context, system usability (Dix et al., 1998; Reeves & Nass, 1996), and individual-related variables such as cognitive styles, prior experience, perceived self-efficacy, and task knowledge, among others. This requires that development teams should actively involve the different user roles at early stages of system design in order to: (a) get high usability, usefulness, acceptance and usage levels, and (b) highly match specific individual, task and contextual characteristics.

Having discussed some structure and relationship issues for e-learning, in the next section we summarize high-level ideas as potential solutions.

POTENTIAL SOLUTIONS AND GENERAL RECOMMENDATIONS

Currently, people view learning as a product rather than a process. Analyzing e-learner experience holistically leads us to a paradigm shift in dealing with the learning process, especially because it is immersed within interdependent and rapidly evolving contexts (e.g., organizations). In this sense, the major difficulties faced by researchers in further advancing e-learning domain are three-fold. First, researchers need to use large sample sizes in quantitative studies. Second, they should analyze multivariate data in multidisciplinary domains in order to provide significant and comprehensive evidence to this body of knowledge in real settings. Third, they also need more sophisticated tools to represent user and task knowledge adequately.

Further, one of the main challenges for HCI field is to develop theoretical frameworks to predict e-learners' performance based upon holistic views of the learning process. Due to the complexity of such a multidisciplinary effort, and in order to further advance in understanding and benefiting from e-learning initiatives, research efforts should follow the current tendency of business horizontal integration. This would require a community-centric approach to skill development. This is illustrated in Figure 7 by applying Porter's chain-value model as exposed by Laudon and Laudon (2002).

The vision behind this horizontal integration is to constantly pursue usefulness in e-learning initiatives to effectively support people's learning process into a defined context and cost-effectively contribute to their skill development. In this sense, e-learning systems would be a tool for people to use as frequently as they need any kind of information related to their current or would-be tasks. For this to happen, it is required a close e-learner, learning task and e-learning system fit and also a proper knowledge structure or map within the "chain" or "community." To achieve this vision, some research issues acquire even more relevance, especially those related to training and learning evaluation and its impact on individual skill development within specific knowledge domain across involved entities and players. This requires both an active and

Figure 7: Proposed Value Chain Approach to E-Learning

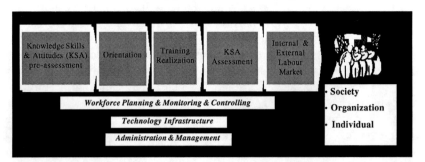

coordinated integration of efforts, information and competencies among the key players (universities, companies, government, research communities, etc.) to achieve a common purpose: skill development at individual, organizational and society levels articulated with defined strategies and policies.

The next section summarizes some of the identified topics in our analysis and sets specific research goals towards this vision.

RESEARCH OUTLOOK

We have discussed relevant aspects of e-learning technology, learning tasks and e-learners fit. The present section identifies some pertinent research issues if we are to develop predictive models for this problem domain.

Learning task-related issues: Learning tasks, user roles and interaction change over time. Which of these changes will impact e-learner performance and satisfaction the most? Do these cause similar effects across users' cognitive styles? How do e-learning initiatives relate to organizational knowledge management? Does the usage of learning materials during task execution differ depending on cognitive style and other individual factors? Does presentation mode (e.g., text, graphics, images, presential lecture) significantly affect performance across cognitive style, user groups? Is there any significant relationship between learning task and user satisfaction during the e-learning experience? Does perceived quality of e-learning experiences vary across user groups, locations, types of training (e.g., technical, language, soft skills), or cultures?

E-learner related issues: What is the critical instructors' set of competencies to enhance the e-learning process? What is the impact of instructors' teaching style on people's motivation, competence and performance level? Is e-learning effective for everybody? Are there usability metrics "universal" across roles, level of technology experience, cognitive styles, job levels, organizational contexts and culture? Should there be different usability measures for different cognitive styles? Does task complexity level mediate a user's perception about usability? Would the initial assigned roles to media by people hold steady throughout the learning process? Or do they change over time motivated by learners' habits?

Interaction related issues: Is there a meaningful relationship between e-learning package interactivity style and e-learner outcomes across different settings (academic, business, classrooms, etc.), user groups, and activities, such as teaching, researching, communicating, studying, etc.? If so, which interactivity elements are more relevant to performance? How does each user profile react to different interactivity styles? To what extent is learner confidence affected by perceived support for privacy, confidentiality and security at the system level? How does user confidence affect e-learning outcomes as compared to the traditional classroom setting? How to cast software agents in the e-learning process as "Personal Assistants" to help: (a) diagnosing performance, (b) keeping students motivated during the learning experience, (c) supporting routine tasks such as grading, sending specific information to students, etc.? Could they be the new "hidden persuaders" (Packard, 1981) to get learners go further into the skill development cycle, overcoming obstacles along the way? Would learners believe software agents when acting like that? Who will be responsible for this "technological persuasion"? Should such concerns be incorporated into a design discipline centered on ethical and deontological roles?

CONCLUSION

In present-day rapid, uncertain and interdependent business environment, e-learning systems could become an important managerial tool. They could help organizations as well as individuals in maximizing their resources when developing required skill levels cost-effectively. The expected benefits for both will lie in the alignment of business strategies to learning outcomes. On one hand, this reduces the financial costs of information and work coordination. On the other hand, it extends the benefits of learning to the integrated value chain, increasing organizational productivity.

We have discussed holistic approaches covering e-learners, e-learning systems and learning task fit while stressing the need for quantitative models. These will allow us to obtain consistent results that contribute to an integrated body of knowledge. In so doing, we believe that a better understanding of the interaction between humans and systems is achievable. A quantitative understanding of the e-learning experience will (a) guide decision makers' efforts in formulating and revising strategies and policies (b) support development teams in designing of e-learning experiences (c) facilitate Human Resource staff to monitor both the skill development process and the e-learning strategy implementation. Furthermore, we need computer-based tools to implement the proposed e-learning framework in real settings by instructors, system designers, courseware developers, HR staff and others. These would allow the developer community to achieve a better understanding of the impact of learning strategies, methodologies and usability features on e-learner outcomes.

Given the current situation, future work should focus on interdisciplinary efforts, gathering diverse research communities (Human Resources, Cognitive Psychology, Organizational Behavior, Education, Human-Computer Interaction, Marketing, among others) to articulate approaches at the macro- and micro-organizational levels. This two-level articulation should address Business-Processes, People and Information-Systems issues. This, in its turn, would improve users' learning experiences and contribute, in a cost-effective manner, to individual and organizational performance.

We have learned that this is a fascinating moment for HCI professionals. Indeed, ongoing research is enriching early-established results and intents for the integration of key individual and contextual factors affecting the learning process in a holistic framework. The objective of this chapter was to propose a preliminary e-learning framework to work towards predictive models. Though there is a huge challenge ahead of us, it may serve as a first step to get there.

REFERENCES

Astleitner, H. (2001). *Web-based instruction and learning: What do we know from experimental research?* Austria: University of Salzburg. Retrieved November 2001 on the World Wide Web: http://rilw.emp.paed.uni-muenchen.de/2001/papers/astleitner.html.

Bandura, A. (2000). Cultivate self-efficacy for personal and organizational effectiveness. In E. A. Locke (Ed.), *Handbook of Principles of Organizational Behavior* (pp. 120-136). Oxford, UK: Blackwell.

Dillon, A., & Watson C. (1996). User analysis in HCI: The historical lesson from Individual Differences research. *International Journal of Human-Computer Studies, 45*(6), 619-637.

Dix, A., Finlay, J., Abowd, G., & Beale, R. (1998). *Human Computer Interaction* (2nd ed.). Prentice Hall Europe.

Fogg, B.J. et al. (2000). *Web Credibility Research: A Method for Online Experiments and Early Study Results.* Stanford University, CA: Persuasive Technology Lab.

Goldstein, I., Braverman, E., & Goldstein, H. (1991). Needs assessment. In K. Wexley (Ed.), *Developing Human Resources* (SHRM – BNA Series 5) (pp. 5-36). Washington, D.C.: The Bureau of National Affairs.

Holt, D., & Crocker, M. (2000). Prior negative experiences: Their impact on computer training outcomes. *Computers & Education, 35*, 295-308.

Ivory, M., Sinha, R., & Hearst, M. (2000). Preliminary findings on quantitative measures for distinguishing highly rates information-centric web pages. *6th Conference on Human factors and the Web.*

Ivory, M., Sinha, R., & Hearst, M. (2001). *Empirically Validated Web Page Design Metrics.* CA: UC Berkeley. ACM SIGCHI'01.

Kim, K. (2000). *Individual differences and information retrieval: Implications on web design.* MO: University of Missouri-Columbia. Retrieved September 2001 on the World Wide Web: http://citeseer.nj.nec.com/update/409393.

Kules, B. (2000). *User modelling for adaptive and adaptable software systems.* MD: Department of Computer Science, University of Maryland. Retrieved September 2001 on the World Wide Web: http://otal.umd.edu/UUGuide/wmk/.

Laudon, K., & Laudon, J. (2002). *Management Information Systems, Organization and Technology in the Network Enterprise (7th ed.).* Prentice Hall.

Liu, Y., & Dean, G. (1999). Cognitive styles and distance education. *Online Journal of Distance Learning Administration, 2*(3).

Packard, V. (1981). *The Hidden Persuaders.* Penguin Books. (Original work published 1957).

Passerini, K., & Granger, M. (2000). A development model for distance learning using the Internet. *Computers & Education, 34*, 1-15.

Reeves, B., & Nass, C. (1996). *The Media Equation: How People Treat Computers, Television, and New Media like Real People and Places*. Cambridge University Press.

Rentroia-Bonito, M. A. (1993). *Exploring the human resources practices, leaders' behaviors and group innovation relationship within a Venezuelan Corporation*. M.Sc. Thesis. Ithaca, NY: School of Industrial and Labor Relations, Cornell University.

Rentroia-Bonito, M. A., & Jorge, J. (2002). *Towards predictive models for e-learning*. Technical Report (v. 1). Lisbon, Portugal: DEI/IST. Retrieved February 2003 on the World Wide Web: http://virtual.inesc.pt/tr/tr-immi-ma-jj-tpmel.html.

Shih, C., & Gamon, J. (1999). *Student learning styles, motivation, learning strategies and achievement in web-based courses*. IA: Department of Curriculum and Instruction, Iowa State University. Retrieved September 2001 on the World Wide Web: http://iccel.wfu.edu/publications/journals/jcel/jcel990305/ccshih.htm.

Smith, A. (1997). Testing the surf: Criteria for evaluating Internet information resources. *The Public-Access Computer Systems Review*, 8(3).

Strazzo, D., & Wentling, T. (2001). *A study of e-learning practices in selected Fortune 100 Companies*. IL: University of Illinois, Urbana-Champaign. Retrieved September 2001 on the World Wide Web: http://learning.ncsa.uiuc.edu/papers/elearnprac.pdf.

Turcotte, S., & Dufresne, A. (2000). *Cognitive style and its implications for navigation strategies*. Computer Research Institute of Montreal, Canada. Retrieved September 2001 on the World Wide Web: http://citeseer.nj.nec.com/cache/papers/cs/11190.

Vouk, M., Bilzer, D., & Klevans, R. (1999). *Workflow and end-user quality of service issues in web-based education*. NC: Department of Computer Science, North Carolina State University. Retrieved September 2001 on the World Wide Web: www.computer.org/tkde/tk1999/k0673abs.htm.

Walker, J. (1992). *Human Resources Strategy*. USA: McGraw-Hill Series in Management (Original work published 1980).

Walters, D., Egret, C., & Cuddihy, E. (2000). *Learning styles and web-based education: A quantitative approach*. Buffalo, NY: Computer Science and Engineering Dept, SUNY. Retrieved September 2001 on the World Wide Web: http://www.cs.buffalo.edu/~egert/papers/CITLS00.pdf.

Welbourne, T., Andrews, S., & Andrews, A. (2000). *Back to basics: Learning about energy and motivation from running on my treadmill*. Retrieved September 2001 on the World Wide Web: http://www.eepulse.com/pdfs/treadmill%20adobe%203.1.01.pdf.

Wentling, T., Waight, C., Gallager, J., La Fleur, J., Wang, C., & Kanfer, A. (2000). *E-learning: A review of literature*. Urbana-Champaign, IL: University of Illinois. Retrieved September 2001 on the World Wide Web: http://learning.ncsa.uiuc.edu/papers/elearnlit.pdf.

Witkin, H., & Goodenough, D. (1981). *Cognitive Styles: Essence and Origins*. New York: Int. University Press.

Chapter XIV

Supporting Informal Interaction in Online Courses

Juan Contreras-Castillo, University of Colima and CICESE, Mexico

Jesús Favela, CICESE, Mexico

Carmen Pérez-Fragoso, Universidad Autónoma de Baja California, Mexico

ABSTRACT

Informal interaction has proven to be useful in supporting collaboration in office and educational environments. Online courses, however, provide limited opportunities for informal interaction, which might put them at a disadvantage when compared with traditional courses. This lack of opportunities could obstruct collaboration among students, a key aspect for successful instruction. To provide students with opportunities for informal interaction, we designed and developed a system named CENTERS. It is an instant messaging and presence awareness system that supports lightweight communications within the group. CENTERS provides awareness of the presence of members of the distributed community and allows them to interact easily and navigate together through the course's materials, share insights, resolve doubts, and collaborate in course related activities. To evaluate the use of CENTERS in an online learning environment, a study was designed to assess interaction from a socio-academic perspective. Results showed that CENTERS helped reduce the students' feelings of isolation and facilitated a greater degree of interpersonal interaction within the course participants.

INTRODUCTION

Distance students and teachers, particularly during online courses, face many interaction difficulties. One of the aggravating factors is that students do not have well defined schedules nor specific places to access course materials and engage in learning activities.

Among others, Blanchard (1989) states that the lack of direct interaction between students and teachers is a severe limitation of distance courses, even if compensated by other benefits. There is ample evidence from studies on traditional learning environments showing that interaction among students and teachers can have an important influence on student performance (Pascarella et al., 1978; Lamport, 1993). The opportunities for interaction during online learning activities are scarce even though their importance has been highlighted (Barnes & Lowery, 1998). This lack of interaction creates important challenges for distance education; one of the points that has to be particularly addressed is the need to alleviate the feelings of isolation experienced by students (Hara & Kling, 1999).

Partial solutions that have been proposed in the literature to address this problem include scheduling face-to-face encounters and telephone calls to maintain personal communication among participants (Harasim et al., 1995). These solutions, however, require additional resources and might be difficult to implement in large distributed groups. Asynchronous and synchronous electronic communication tools play an important role in distance education, allowing interactions among classmates and between students and their teacher without resources external to their learning environment. The main advantages of asynchronous communication tools are flexibility in the continuous communication of the group, and freedom from restrictions of space and time; however, the same asynchrony presents a serious disadvantage in terms of the response time required by the teacher or student to answer the messages (Sherry, 2000). Students' interest might decrease because of these delays while fostering feelings of frustration and loneliness.

In order to alleviate this, we designed, developed and tested a software tool, named CENTERS, meant to encourage and support informal interactions during online courses. The objective of this chapter is to describe this tool and present some preliminary results of its use in four online higher education courses.

BACKGROUND

The affective and social needs of students are of primary importance in both traditional and distance education. According to Yacci (2000) instructional interactivity can be viewed as having two distinct classes of outputs: content learning and affective benefits, although the latter are less well understood. Different authors have stated that the formation and consolidation of online groups — learning communities — apparently transit through the same various stages experienced by traditional students (McDonald & Campbell Gibson, 1998), where the crucial point is to minimize the bridge between feeling themselves outsiders to becoming part of the group (Wegerif, 1998). Establishing rapport and collaboration among students and between students and teacher is thus a key aspect for successful instruction. The first variable in the grid for assessing course interaction developed by Roblyer and Ekhmal (2000) evaluates the course's social rapport-building activities created by the instructor. Based on the works of Gilbert and Moore (1998), they note that social rapport and increased collaboration can lead to greater levels of interaction that address instructional goals.

Research focused on the analysis of online courses' social interaction (Gunawardena & Zittle, 1997; Kanuka & Anderson, 1998) show that social interaction, both among students and between students and teacher, is strongly related to course satisfaction. In a recent study Gunawardena and Duphorne (2000) analysed the association of (a) learner readiness: personal factors that prepare the student for online study, (b) online features: elements that make up the computer conferencing environment, and (c) learning approaches: strategies a student uses to make the conference an effective learning experience. In relation to learner satisfaction they found that online features had the strongest positive correlation and were the best predictor of learner satisfaction, noting the need for technical systems that facilitate the building of an online learning community. One of the problems of traditional social spaces for online learning environments (e.g., online cafeterias, pubs) is that they consist of asynchronous discussion forums and students might feel the need to censor what they write, since their texts might be read by all participants and remain exhibited for the rest of the course.

The role of synchronous electronic communication tools is to provide opportunities for students to receive an answer in almost "real time." Unfortunately, the communication tools used in most online education systems like Blackboard (http://www.blackboard.com), Ariadne (http://ariadne.unil.ch/), and WebCT (http://www.webct.com/), among others, mostly support "formal" or "structured" interaction. By formal or structured, we mean that students have to follow a protocol defined by the teacher (date and time for synchronous interactions, rules and format for the messages, among others). This could lead to an increase in time response and a reduction in conversation fluency. Thus, besides the learner-learner, learner-instructor and learner-content interactions mentioned by Moore (1989), and learner-interface interaction introduced by Hillman et al. (1994), there is a clear need for a less formal and structured type of interaction. By informal we mean the interactions that do not have a defined schedule or place, are spontaneous, not planned and brief, where the topic of the conversation can change during the course of the interaction (Kraut et al., 1990; Whittaker et al., 1997). Studies conducted in face-to-face (FTF) classrooms point towards informal interaction as a potentially significant factor in improving instructional effectiveness, students' performance, and reducing students' attrition rates (Spady, 1970; Pascarella et al., 1978; Lamport, 1993).

Instant messaging and presence awareness (IMP) applications such as Ubique (http://www.ubique.com), ICQ (http://www.icq.com), and Jabber (http://www.jabber.com) provide mechanisms to support informal interaction that could be used in distance learning. They provide users with awareness of the status and availability of other users (online, busy, away, etc.), and allow them to send and receive synchronous and asynchronous messages in a transparent manner (Morán et al., 2001). Even though these tools efficiently support informal interaction, they do not explicitly support web communities, such as those formed specifically by the participants of an online course. Only Ubique addresses this issue, but it lacks the facilities for its integration with the learning materials. In addition, these IMP tools permit the interaction of a larger community, including family and friends, rather than just the students and the teacher participating in the course.

The teacher's role is to promote a feeling of community within the group. To achieve this, the tool should not only be aware of the presence of members of the distributed community but also allow them to interact easily and to navigate together through the course's materials, share insights, resolve doubts, and collaborate in course related activities.

THE CENTERS SYSTEM

Based on the requirements identified in the previous section, we developed a tool named CENTERS (CollaborativE Informal InTERaction System) to allow members of an online course to form a distributed community on the Web. The characteristics of the current implementation of the system include:

1.   The system occupies only a small amount of space on the screen and the user can decide to navigate anonymously if he wishes to do so. This allows for transparent Web navigation without interfering with the current task.
2.   It allows lightweight interactions in the context of online courses. These interactions do not require the additional overhead found even in email or discussion forums.
3.   It displays and updates information about users connected to the site at the same time. When a new user enters the site, all users currently working on the site are notified of his or her presence.
4.   It provides a chat and instant messaging as alternatives for textual communication.
5.   The two communication tools can be used simultaneously. For example, a student can send and receive instant messages from student A whilst having a conversation with student B using the chat. Additionally he can be in two courses at the same time and communicate with colleagues on each one of them using two windows of the browser.
6.   It allows a user to quickly load the page that another student is currently looking at, allowing for synchronous navigation and facilitating the discussion of online material.

For evaluation purposes, CENTERS also:

7.   Stores all user accesses and registers the following data: User name, time, login and logout date, and IP address of the computer from which the connection is made.
8.   Keeps records of date and time of all messages delivered, including the sender and receiver's names.
9.   Keeps a log of acceptance and rejections of chat requests

CENTERS is displayed on the right hand side of the screen. It shows the list of users currently visiting the site. The user can select chat or message. Figure 1 presents an active window during an actual chat session. The sync (synchronise) button permits a student to access the page being viewed by the other student thus permitting synchronous navigation.

Figure 1: Two Online Course Participants Communicate Using CENTERS' Chat Facility

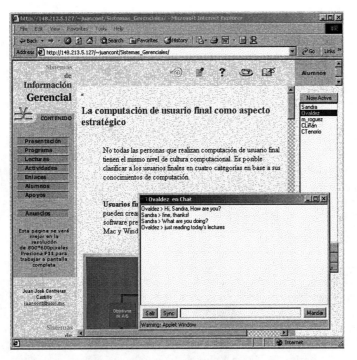

EVALUATION OF CENTERS

To evaluate the use of CENTERS in an online learning environment, we designed a study to assess interaction from a socio-academic perspective. The methodology and some results are as follows:

Forty-three students and two teachers from two Mexican universities, Universidad de Colima (n = 15) and Universidad Autónoma de Baja California (n = 28), participated in the study. These students participated in four different courses: one in Colima and three in Baja California. 56% of the participants were female, and the mean age was 23 years.

Students were invited to participate in the study. The courses were mandatory, but their participation in the experiment was voluntary — 98% accepted. The courses, taught during the spring of 2001, lasted for one semester. At the beginning of each course, students were asked to fill out a questionnaire aimed at obtaining their demographic characteristics, perceived interaction needs, and previous experience with electronic communication tools and distance education courses. It consisted of 23 items. At the end of the course, a second questionnaire was applied specifically to assess the students' impressions and experiences with CENTERS; it consisted of 12 dichotomous, 10 Likert-type and two open-ended questions. The questionnaire was based on a pilot version tested during a previous course (Contreras et al., 2001).

Questionnaire responses were analysed for each group and for the total population. Based on the responses from all students to the final questionnaire, the following results were obtained regarding: interaction opportunities, quality of the interactions, and reactions to awareness of other's presence. Responses were registered using a scale from 1 (lower) to 5 (higher).

When asked, "Compared with a face-to-face course, your opportunities for inter-action with teacher and peers were (higher - equal - lower)?," 80% of students considered that their interaction opportunities with their teacher were equal to those they have in a traditional face-to-face course. A similar question about their interaction opportunities with classmates revealed that 73% of students considered these opportunities to have been equal or higher. Most of the students (95%) answered that they had been able to communicate successfully with their classmates. Additionally, to probe the latter questions, we asked students if the CENTERS system had provided those opportunities for interaction. This question was dichotomous and 72% of students answered yes.

When asked to rate the quality of interaction with teacher and classmates (excellent - medium - bad) the majority of students rated their interaction with classmates and teacher as excellent or good, and only a few (less than 10%), as bad. Sixty-seven percent (67%) of students considered that awareness of others connected to the web site at the same time made them feel accompanied while navigating through course materials and 60% reported that being aware of the presence of others made them feel part of the group attending the same class.

The majority of participants (82%) affirmed that the educational experience using CENTERS was satisfactory and would be willing to take additional online courses using the system. From unstructured interviews we learned that they considered that the educational experience had been enriching when compared with other distance courses they have taken in the past.

From the system's log, Table 1 shows the number of messages exchanged among students and teachers for the four courses considered in the study. On average there were more than 60 messages sent by each student, although some students were much more active.

The number of chat requests accepted and denied during the courses are shown in Table 2. The topics of conversation were classified in six categories based on the content of the messages exchanged. These results are shown in Table 3. The total is slightly higher than the number of accepted chat requests since some conversations involved more than one type of content. For instance, it was not uncommon to begin a conversation socialising, and then proceed to a course related issue or some other theme.

The results show that most of the requests were accepted. The range of exchanges varied from two to 78, not counting four larger outliers. On average, the conversations consisted of 14.55 messages: seven to eight for each participant.

Table 1: Number of Messages Exchanged Among Students and Teachers

	Teachers to students	Students to teachers	Students to students
Messages	349	342	2721

Table 2: Number of Chat Requests Accepted and Denied Among Students and Teachers

	Between students and teachers		Among students	
	Accepted	Rejected	Accepted	Rejected
Chat requests	101	13	271	29

Table 3: Content of Messages Exchanged Using the System's Chat Facility

Content of messages	Number of chat sessions
Social and general themes	135
Class topics: Readings, comments, summaries	65
Final project: Coordination, doubts, documents, meetings	50
Doubts solution: Questions among students and to instructor	40
Technical: Use of the system, other software used and the site	20
Team work:	10
Total	420

What follows is a sample interaction between two students. After establishing social contact, they discussed course related topics and clarified doubts about the use of the system.

User1: good morning
User2: Hi
U1: how are you ...
U2: Good morning
OK and you?]
U1: did you finish the firs reading....
U2: I'm reading it to do my summary
That's what I'm working on
U1: good... it looks like there are some contributions-..
U2: yes
U1: what's Cookson talking about when he refers to systemic systems...
U2: Listen.. to post ... which option is it..? You designed the page and know better than anyone... :)
U1: go to the end of the forums page ... & you'll the POST button just press it and the rest will work like email ...
U2: Is it in the page where the activities are?.. or do I have to link to another?]
U1: its among the electronic forum buttons (the first one: the page with the pencil)

The log of this conversation shows that the general tone of the interaction was informal, casual and friendly. Coinciding with other studies about electronic discourse (Abdullah, 1998), we observed that the students did not worry about grammar, spelling, intonation or punctuation marks. Further analysis of the transcripts, following a discourse analysis approach, could shed light on how this informal use of language may be helping the construction of online learning communities.

DISCUSSION AND CONCLUSION

The students' questionnaire responses regarding the use of CENTERS in their online courses showed that they considered the informal interaction opportunities provided by the system as sufficient to satisfy their needs for interaction with classmates and the teacher. In addition, they considered that the system allowed them to participate in a high number of interactions and that these exchanges helped them to better understand course materials and establish better social relationships with their instructor and classmates. Moreover, they felt that those interactions made them feel part of the group but not closer to their classmates or instructor. Thus, the use of CENTERS in online courses could help reduce the lack of interaction opportunities reported in the literature (Blanchard, 1989; Barnes & Lowery, 1998). In addition, the use of CENTERS facilitates a greater degree of interpersonal interaction in out-of-class discussions (Sherry, 2000), and provides a horizontal communication system (Wegerif, 1998), thereby permitting them greater opportunities for interaction.

Additional comments provided by the students with respect to their interactions in these courses indicate that when they realized that somebody else was accessing the site they often sent messages to socialize with that person. Regarding the teacher, students reported that they often sent messages to greet and welcome him or her, which may have helped the teachers establish a better social presence (Hiltz, 1994; Gunawardena & Zittle, 1997). In addition, the system's records show that the frequency of interaction was greater after a student just entered the site. When he or she received greeting messages from other students, they generally responded. They reported that in many cases these messages worked as a preamble to a course related conversation, and students considered this experience as satisfactory.

These results agree with those reported by Pascarella et al. (1978) and Lamport (1993) for traditional learning environments. They found that the informal interactions that students had with their teachers in some cases influenced them to change the way they approached learning. Moreover, they support Spady's (1970) hypothesis, which states that informal interactions between students and professors have a positive influence on the academic performance of the former.

Among others, Froissart (2000) emphasizes the fundamental role of the variable "loneliness" or "isolation" among the causes for students abandoning distance learning programmes, giving it an even greater importance than poor academic background. The results of the present study indicate that students in these courses felt less isolated than in previous distance courses that they had taken which provided only asynchronous means for interaction. If these results were generalized, this kind of tool could help lower the high attrition rates reported for online courses (Miltiadou & McIsaac, 2000).

Another interesting result is that those students who registered higher levels of interaction indicated a higher level of satisfaction with the course in general, though this was not necessarily due to the use of the system. We consider that students' satisfaction with a course increases when opportunities for interaction with the instructor and classmates are provided; these opportunities, however, do not depend solely on the tools we integrate within the learning environment but on the teacher and classmates' willingness to interact. These results are in agreement with those reported by Hackman and Walker (1990) and Fulford and Zhang (1993) who found that perceived interactions in the classroom influenced students' course satisfaction. The latter authors explain that when there is frequent group participation the students tend to report a high level of satisfaction with their courses, even when individual participation is low. This confirms that the student's level of satisfaction is related to their perception of the overall interactions within a course.

FUTURE TRENDS

Text-based systems that support informal interaction, such as instant messaging systems, have become surprisingly popular in recent years, particularly among teenagers (Grinter & Eldridge, 2001). However, one must keep in mind that very few studies have been conducted to understand the adoption, uses and potential risks of this technology. Recent studies have focused on the use of instant messaging in office environments (Nardi et al., 2001; Herblseb et al., 2002), but none, to our knowledge, deals with learning communities. As their popularity increases, these tools could become as ubiquitous for electronic communication as email is today. This will clearly have an impact in e-education that will be difficult to ignore. Thus, there is a clear need to conduct studies related to the use of informal interaction to support distance education, and for researchers and practitioners to influence the design of these tools.

An important trend in lightweight messaging and awareness systems is to support the user mobility. This is being achieved mostly through the implementation of mobile devices such as handheld computers and mobile telephones. Examples of these include ConNexus (Tang et al., 2001) and Hubbub (Isaacs et al., 2002). Although one might not expect e-learners to access course materials using a telephone or a PDA, given their limited screen size, these applications might be useful for notifying last minute changes or remaining students of upcoming deadlines.

Recently, Morán et al. (2001) have proposed the extension of an instant messaging paradigm to provide awareness of the state of shared resources such as documents. Doc2U, the system that implements this approach, supports the coordination of collaborative writing activities by introducing the concept of document presence. Documents that are shared by a group of colleagues appear in Doc2U as separate entities with their status indicated by names or icons, in a similar fashion as users are announced in traditional instant messaging applications. By extending the notion of user presence to documents and other resources, Doc2U offers new opportunities for casual encounters in a community of co-authors. For instance, when a user notices that a document has been locked, she might decide to send a relevant message or even join her colleague in a synchronous collaborative authoring session. The Doc2U client can also send subtle messages to gain the attention of co-authors. The application of this concept to online courses seems appealing, particularly in courses that might require students to work in small groups to produce shared documents.

An issue that has been raised by critics of instant messaging systems is their scalability. As users become part of a greater number of distributed communities, for example as students of several online courses, it becomes harder to keep in touch with members of all these communities. In CENTERS each course has its own independent display, which can only be used by active course members; however, this could still be a problem if the number of students per course is too large. Studies need to be done to determine what the optimum number of students should be to promote constructive learning. The chat-based system Babble is aimed at supporting large communities of users by displaying an abstract representation of the availability of users based on computer activity (Erickson & Kellog, 2000). This approach, which the authors call social translucence, allows users to "see" one another and make inferences about their activity. Learning communities could use a similar approach, in which the measure of "closeness" with fellow students could be measured using parameters such as the topic one is currently visiting, membership in common team projects, similarity of interests, etc.

Informal interactions often take place in intermittent episodes. One might initiate a conversation with a fellow student and continue the conversation hours later, with little or no need to retrace the initial interaction. Furthermore, one might be engaged in multiple concurrent conversational threads with the same person (Whittaker et al., 1997), which raises the issues of context regeneration and tracking conversational threads. Whittaker argues that people currently exploit the presence of work-related devices (such as papers, drawings, notes, and folders) to help manage the history and context of these intermittent interactions. Computer systems that support informal interaction, and notably instant messaging applications, currently provide little, or no help at all, to "hold the context" of multiple ongoing conversations. ContactMap is a software system that allows users to arrange their individual social networks using a visual map of individual contacts and groups (Nardi et al., 2002). ContactMap enables users to retrieve current or archived information associated with these contacts. This type of facility, integrated in online course material, could allow students keep track of multiple intermittent conversations.

Finally, there are some issues that might discourage participants from using text-based informal interaction systems. The main concern is related to privacy issues. Being aware of the presence of colleagues implies that they are also aware of one's presence. Another issue has to do with the possibility of being easily interrupted. The ease of contact can lead to constant interruptions that disturb the work being done (Czerwinski et al., 2000). This might be an important issue for instructors, since students could have high expectations of teachers' availability, resulting in feelings of frustration if these expectations are not met.

The rapid advances in this field have not permitted the elaboration of pertinent studies to assess the real impact of the incorporation of these new informal interaction systems in the online classroom. More research addressed to exploring the conditions necessary for the formation and consolidation of online learning communities is thus required.

ACKNOWLEDGMENTS

This work was partially supported by the CONACYT scholarship No. 112081 provided to the first author.

REFERENCES

Abdullah, M. H. (1998). *Electronic discourse: Evolving conventions in online academic environments*. ERIC digest. (ERIC Document Reproduction Service No. ED 422 593).

Barnes, F. M., & Lowery, B. R. (1998). Sustaining two-way interaction and communication in distance learning. *Technology Horizons in Education Journal,* 25(8), 65-67.

Blanchard, W. (1989). *Telecourse effectiveness: A research-review update.* (ERIC Document Reproduction Service No. ED 320 554).

Contreras Castillo, J. J., Pérez Fragoso, C., & Favela Vara, J. (2001). Informal interaction in online learning and teaching. In C. Montgomerie & J. Viteli (Eds.), *Proceedings of ED-MEDIA 2001: World Conference on Educational Multimedia, Hypermedia & Telecommunications* (pp. 324-329). Norfolk, VA: AACE.

Czerwinski, M., Cutrell, E., & Horvitz, E. (2000). Instant messaging and interruption: Influence of task type on performance. In C. Paris, N. Ozkan, S. Howard & S. Lu (Eds.), *OZCHI 2000 Conference Proceedings* (pp. 356-361). Sydney, Australia.

Erickson, T., & Kellogg, W. A. (2000). Social translucence: An approach to designing systems that support social Processes. *ACM Transactions on Computer-Human Interaction,* 7(1), 59-83.

Froissart, P. (2000). La formation asisté par Internet. Reseau pédagogique et reseau technique. *MEI "Mediation et information,"* 11, 113-129.

Fulford, C., & Zhang, S. (1993). Perceptions of interaction: The critical predictor in distance education. *American Journal of Distance Education,* 7(3), 8-21.

Gilbert, L., & Moore, D. R. (1998). Building interactivity into web courses: Tools for social and instructional interaction. *Educational Technology,* 38(3), 29-35.

Grinter, R. E., & Eldridge, M. (2001). "y do tngrs luv 2 txt msg?" *Proceedings ECSCW.* Bonn, Germany.

Gunawardena, C. N., & Duphorne, P. (2000). Predictors of learner satisfaction in an academic computer conference. *Distance Education,* 21(1), 101-117.

Gunawardena, C. N., & Zittle, F. J. (1997). Social presence as a predictor of satisfaction within a computer-mediated conferencing environment. *American Journal of Distance Education,* 13(3), 8-26.

Hackman, M. Z., & Walker, K. B. (1990). Instructional communication in the televised classroom: The effects of system design and teacher immediacy on student learning and satisfaction. *Communication Education,* 39, 196-206.

Hara, N., & Kling, R. (1999). Students' frustrations with a web-based distance education course. *First Monday,* 4(12). Retrieved June 2, 2002 on the World Wide Web: http://firstmonday.org/issues/issue4_12/hara/index.html.

Harasim, L., Hiltz, R., Teles, L., & Turoff, M. (1995). *Learning Networks: A Field Guide to Teaching and Learning Online.* Cambridge, MA: The MIT Press.

Herbsleb, J., Boyer, D. G., Handel, M., & Finholt, T. A. (2002). Introducing instant messaging and chat in the workplace. *Proceedings CHI 2002* (pp. 171-178). Minneapolis, MN: ACM Press.

Hillman, D. C., Willis, D. J., & Gunawardena, C. N. (1994). Learner-interface interaction in distance education: An extension of contemporary models and strategies for practitioners. *American Journal of Distance Education,* 8(2), 30-42.

Hiltz, R. (1994). *The Virtual Classroom: Learning Without Limits Via Computer Networks.* Norwood, NJ: Ablex Publishing.

Isaacs, E., Walendowski, A., & Ranganthan, D. (2002). Hubbub: A sound-enhanced mobile instant messenger that supports awareness and opportunistic interactions. *Proceedings CHI 2002* (pp. 179-186). Minneapolis, MN: ACM Press.

Kanuka, H., & Anderson, T. (1998). Online social interchange, discord, and knowledge construction. *Journal of Distance Education*, 13(1), 57-74.

Kraut, R., Fish, R., Root, R., & Chalfonte, B. (1990). Informal communication in organizations: Form, function and technology. In S. Oskamp & S. Spacapan (Eds.), *People Reactions to Technology in Factories, Offices and Aerospace* (pp. 145-199). The Claremont Symposium on Applied Social Psychology. Newbury Park, CA: Sage.

Lamport, M. A. (1993). Student-faculty informal interaction and the effect on college student outcomes: A review of the literature. *Adolescence*, 28(112), 971-990.

McDonald, J., & Campbell Gibson, C. (1998). Interpersonal dynamics and group development in computer conferencing. *American Journal of Distance Education*, 12(1), 7-25.

Miltiadou, M., & McIsaac, M. (2000). *Problems and practical solutions of web-based courses: Lessons learned from three educational institutions.* Paper presented at the 11th International Conference of the Society for Information and Technology & Teacher Education, San Diego, California.

Moore, M. G. (1989). Three types of interaction. *American Journal of Distance Education*, 3(2), 1-6.

Morán, A., Favela, J., Martínez, A., & Decouchant, D. (2001). Document presence notification services for collaborative writing. *7th International Workshop on Groupware, CRIWG2001* (pp. 125-133). Dermstadt, Germany: IEEE Computer Press.

Nardi, B. A., Whittaker, S., & Bradner, E. (2000). Interaction and outeraction: Instant messaging in action. In *Proceedings CSCW 2000* (pp. 79-88). Philadelphia, PA: ACM Press.

Nardi, B. A., Whittaker, S., Isaacs, E., Creech, M., Johnson, J., & Hainsworth, J. (2002). Integrating communication and information through contact map. *Communications of the ACM*, 45(4), 89-95.

Pascarella, E. T., Terenzini, P. T., & Hibel, H. (1978). Student faculty interactional settings and their relationships to predict academic performance. *Journal of Higher Education*, 49, 450-463.

Roblyer, M. D., & Ekhmal, L. (2000). How interactive are YOUR distance courses? A rubric for assessing interaction in distance learning. *Online Journal of Distance Learning Administration*, 3(2). Retrieved June 2, 2002 on the World Wide Web: http://www.westga.edu/~distance/roblyer32.html.

Sherry, L. (2000). The nature and purpose of online discourse: a brief synthesis of current research as related to the web project. *International Journal of Educational Telecommunications*, 6(1), 19-51.

Spady, W. G. (1970). Dropouts from higher education: An interdisciplinary review and synthesis. *Interchange*, 1, 64-85

Tang, J. C., Yankelovich, N., Begole, J., Van Kleek, M., Li, F. & Bhalodia, J. (2001). ConNexus to awarenex: Extending awareness to mobile users. In *Proceedings CHI 2001* (pp. 121-128). Seattle, WA: ACM Press.

Wegerif, R. (1998). The social dimension of asynchronous learning networks. *Journal of Asynchronous Learning Networks*, 2(1), 34-49. Retrieved June 2, 2002 on the World Wide Web: http://www.aln.org/alnweb/journal/vol2_issue1/wegerif.htm.

Whittaker, S., Swanson, G., Kucan, J., & Sidner, C. (1997). Telenotes: Managing light-weight interactions in the desktop. *Transactions on Computer Human Interaction*, 4, 137-168.

Yacci, M. (2000) *Interactivity demystified: A structural definition for distance education and intelligent CBT*. Retrieved June 2, 2002 on the World Wide Web: http://www.it.rit.edu/~may/interactiv8.pdf.

Chapter XV

The Orientation and Disorientation of E-Learners

Bernard Mark Garrett, University of British Columbia, Canada

Richard Francis, Oxford Brookes University, UK

ABSTRACT

In this chapter, we will explore how students may be orientated and disorientated to online learning, examining some of the methods that can be implanted to make life easier for the student and facilitate learning, and also some of the pitfalls to be avoided if students are to study effectively in an online learning environment. The argument is also presented that the disorientation experienced by students in online learning is part of a positive transformative experience leading to greater learner independence.

INTRODUCTION

There are many common elements between online and traditional classes; both have lecturers, student cohorts, course materials and assessments. One of my teaching colleagues recently remarked that the use of web-based materials makes life too easy for students. I would suggest that making learning easier for students is desirable, but although an online environment may offer more flexibility, it also requires more self-direction and self-discipline from the students. The course timetable is often more loosely defined in an online course and students must manage their own learning schedule. There will still be deadlines for assessments but study time will be self managed. Many of the nonverbal mechanisms that teachers use to determine whether students understand the concepts and issues, or if they are having problems such as confusion or frustration, are not available to the online tutor. Therefore, to be successful, online students need to be highly motivated in their studies, and we must consider approaches and mechanisms that will facilitate successful online study and lead to course completion for those students who find the medium more challenging.

Online study can be more demanding of time and energy than traditionally taught classes and demands more specialised study skills. The ability to communicate effectively in writing is crucial, as currently this is the primary medium for communication. Basic computer and more particularly web skills are also important and resolving problems at a distance without the normal support mechanisms that exist in a college or University presents challenges. Online students also need good time management and basic research skills in order to use their study time effectively and find information quickly. They also need to be assertive in order to make their needs known, as again there will be no non-verbal cues for the tutor. As online classes often involve group activity, the ability to work with others is another important skill. Lastly, the ability to be flexible and remain open minded is a key area as adaptability and flexibility are important for online learning, as students are likely to be exposed to some novel, threatening or, at the least, uncomfortable experiences.

Therefore it is essential that designers of online courses take account of these human performance factors and implement appropriate mechanisms that will help students become orientated to this new "virtual" environment. We must pay more attention to this aspect in our course design, as not only do we need to orientate students to new academic material, but also a new way of studying for most of them.

In this chapter, we will explore how students may be orientated and disorientated to online learning, examining some of the methods that can be implanted to make life easier for the student and facilitate learning, and also some of the pitfalls to be avoided if students are to study effectively in an online learning environment.

ENGENDERING STUDENT PARTICIPATION
Motivation

It is possible that the greatest challenge to online learning has nothing to do with technology or the subject involved, but with motivating students. Even with the advantages that learning over the Internet provides, including flexibility with study time and location, those same advantages can provide students with the opportunity for procrastination. Online learning requires self-motivation and independence above and beyond what is required in a traditionally taught course.

Motivation is commonly considered under two categories: extrinsic and intrinsic motivation (Wlodkowski, 1985). Extrinsic motivation involves external driving factors. Typically these include rewards or penalties, such as the results of summative assessment, eligibility for employment, increased pay or grading, or changed contractual status. Intrinsic motivation is the internal drive to learn: the student's personal desire to learn or acquire new knowledge, skills or attitudes. Internally motivated students enjoy learning and achieving results, and participating in the learning process itself. Currently most learners in the context of online learning are intrinsically motivated (Stelzer & Vogelzangs, 2001), although there may be extrinsic factors present as well. Mosley (1984) suggests that most students initially are enthusiastic about computers but that this may decrease as the course progresses. This may be due to a number of factors including isolation, academic workload, social pressures and fear.

Isolation

The individual learner in front of his or her PC may become victim to the demotivating consequences of feeling isolated. Isolation exists as a matter of location (physical) and also psychologically. There are ways in which the effects of isolation can be minimized during an online course. Online activities should be chosen that are intrinsically motivating, to the extent that they engage the student in the process of seeking to solve personally meaningful problems whose outcome is uncertain and whose solutions require skill and effort (Stelzer & Vogelzangs, 2001). Tasks should be neither trivially easy nor completely familiar and tasks involving group collaboration with other online students can help reduce the sense of isolation amongst learners. Online activities that engender a feeling of autonomy, competence and self-determination are ideal as these help with a sense of involvement with the course materials. Therefore, choice in assessment type and negotiation with other learners all help reduce the psychological impact of isolation. Fun and suspense should be introduced to try and create instruction that increases or maintains the initial intrinsic motivation. Motivating communication and interaction when face-to-face contact is not possible may be achieved by integrating synchronous and asynchronous online conferencing, email audio, video mail, virtual rooms, telecommunication (virtual class model) and use of the telephone or fax for additional support. Lastly, the online tutor needs to ensure that he/she is responsive to learner needs (Wlodkowski, 1985).

Social Pressures

There are many social factors that can have an effect on the motivation of learners. Although online learning offers much flexibility, in most cases there are still deadlines, firm due dates and required regular participation. Careful time management is essential to the student's success. Personal circumstances beyond the student's control may hinder students, delaying or preventing them from completing their studies. Therefore adequate support mechanisms must be built into the learning environment that gives the student individual personal tutorial support. Mechanisms that allow students to conveniently contact instructors to let them know what is going on and to make arrangements for making up any assignments or examinations should be employed.

Anxiety and Fear

Initially, students can easily feel like a "newbie" (a person new to the Internet and World Wide Web), or experience a little "technophobia," particularly in mixed ability groups. This will compound any fears they have about their individual academic ability, particularly if they are returning to study after some time. A good way to help minimise these fears is with the use of appropriate preparatory materials and carefully implemented induction and orientation programmes. These need to include plenty of icebreaker and group activities. Being able to personalise other students and staff involved in their studies will help students to feel part of a group and reduce the anxieties associated with isolation.   An introduction to learning about how to use the Internet and World Wide

Web, including search engines, email, web-based discussions and chat rooms, i essential for new users.

Online learning will involve a lot of written communication such as email, discussion postings and formal writing assignments. Students often feel self-conscious about their writing ability. Students can be guided in the use of spell and grammar checking applications that may help support them in this area. These tools and practice within a safe environment, such as a small online tutorial group, can assist the reduction of these anxieties. Tutorial support that includes the reviewing of assignment plans and drafts in the initial phase of an online course can also help here.

> "Arousal describes the general state of excitability of an organism the general level of alertness, responsiveness, wakefulness, or vigilance. ... The optimal level of arousal for our most efficient functioning is an intermediate level." (De Cecco & Crawford, 1974)

Online activities need to avoid either mild or strong stimulation. Boredom is often the reason why learners disengage, whilst on the other extreme, excessive stimulation leads to anxiety and increased emotional stress. In the initial phase of an online course much effort will need to be expended to engage students and a vital part of the strategy to achieve this is the use of effective induction techniques and resources, and provide ongoing support throughout the course.

GROUP DYNAMICS, COHESION AND COMMUNITY OF PURPOSE

It has been suggested that:

> "Learning online represents, for many, the ultimate disorienting dilemma in higher education." (Campbell Gibson, 2000)

For Campbell Gibson, the disorientation experienced by many at the outset of an online learning experience signals the beginning of what Mezirow (1991) describes as a process of transformative learning. The online environment will call into question definitions of teachers, learners and knowledge, what it means to learn both as an individual and as a group, and what it means to have learned. Past values, beliefs and assumptions will be challenged. For many this will represent a disorienting dilemma and provide an opportunity to create new meanings, new perspectives (Mezirow, 1991). How is the learner to be eased through this rite of educational passage? Campbell Gibson suggests a place for this discourse, such as a discussion forum, chatroom or the like. This place is remote from the conduct of scholarly activity in which to lay bare the hopes, fears, struggles, frustrations, and confusion of learning online.

The process of reflection on the learning process and the recognition that one's personal sense of disorientation may be a shared experience can pave the way for the discussion of new roles, responsibilities and strategies for effective and efficient online learning. Learners will have similar issues that they can address in a communal place, such as, for example, identifying what is the least amount of work required to gain a pass grade, or swapping good sources of information for an assignment. Initially learners may express reservations about the value of collaborative and peer communications expressing the attitude:

"Why should I be interested in what my peers have to say?"

We have then a need to encourage learner orientation toward their peers and engender a community of purpose, where the advantages of collaborative learning become apparent.

This can be achieved with the appropriate use of online chat rooms and bulletin boards for individual cohorts of students or tutor groups. There is a need for ground rules and moderation of these forums, at least in the initial induction phase. Getting students to identify their own ground rules for an online discussion forum is a good exercise to initiate such activity.

Tuckman (1965) identified stages of group development and evolution (group forming, storming, norming and performing) and, as we would expect, these can be readily applied to the online learning situation. E-moderation or online facilitation skills are a prerequisite in all these scenarios (Salmon, 2000; after Tuckman, 1965), and these skills cannot be assumed. Salmon presents a useful model of CMC (Computer Mediated Communication), outlining the various stages that online participants typically proceed through during online CMC events.

1.   Access and Motivation: getting connected,
2.   Online Socialisation: getting to know people,
3.   Information exchange: tasks and learning materials,
4.   Knowledge Construction: knowledge construction and collaboration,
5.   Development: reflection and evaluation.

Each of these stages requires participants to master certain technical skills and calls for different e-moderating skills. Typically, participants start at number one and work through to number five, each step building on the last.

One strategy that Salmon (2001) suggests e-moderators may find useful in all forms of CMC is to assign roles to participants in accordance with Edward De Bono's Six Thinking Hats (De Bono, 2001). Each hat represents a point of view or approach to a problem: objective, intuitive, evaluative, logical positive, creative and meta-cognitive. She suggests e-moderators need to:

- deal with lurkers (although initially some lurking — observation without contribution — can be encouraged to build learners confidence)
- have clarity of purpose
- employ creative and eye catching opening messages
- work with the online energy
- use the software to work out what's happening
- have good "process" skills
- explore "lurking" directly
- manage time and complexity
- design creative and flexible online activities
- welcome support & counsel in the online environment

- act as resource guide and a monitor, and
- e-moderate: facilitate knowledge sharing

E-moderation involves watching, listening, weaving and collecting ideas expressed together and summarizing lines of argument. Students need to be encouraged to reflect on the issues raised in the group setting.

If a community of purpose is to be established in an online learning environment, it is important that the members establish their e-voice and e-persona. There needs to be a clear negotiation of roles within the group and an agreed level of tutor intervention.

The purpose of the group should be explicitly identified and involve the collaborative construction of knowledge. However this requires some understanding of how knowledge can be built up collectively on the part of the members.

Example of Role Allocation in a Collaborative Online Group Task

All new teaching staff at Oxford Brookes take the Certificate in Teaching in Higher Education, organised by the Oxford Centre for Staff and Learning Development. The course is taught through a mixed learning mode involving regular face-to-face meetings, at which tutors outline successive discussion themes, interspersed with blended online and face-to-face discussion activities conducted by course participants in multi-disciplinary base groups. The learning artefact for each theme consists of a group presentation summarising the outcomes of the group's collective deliberations. Each course participant is required to produce a portfolio of evidence of the achievement of key learning outcomes. Participation in base group discussions can be cited in evidence for participants' portfolios.

Each base group must organise itself appropriately, which means assigning roles to each of its members. This process may involve a mix of learning modes, typically commencing with a face-to-face, who's-going-to-do-what session. The tutor takes as little part as possible. In one such base group discussion task, analysis of postings to the course bulletin board, combined with interviews with course tutors, reveal that group roles were designated as follows:

- *Discussion leader* — structures the discussion; establishes time frames; delegates responsibilities; sets up discussion topics on the course bulletin board.
- *Researcher(s)* — review the literature; provide a theoretical/conceptual framework for situated learning through individual critical incident reports.
- *Reporter(s)* — relate critical incidents in their professional practice pertinent to the discussion theme, e.g., dealing with student diversity or teaching large classes; link theory to practice.
- *Compiler(s)* — summarise and collate the strands of the discussion into a coherent statement of the group's critical reflections on the discussion theme.
- *Presenter(s)* — present the outcomes of the group's discussions to the larger group.

One great advantage of online discussions over face-to-face seminars is that the process of group collaboration, the social construction of knowledge, can be tracked through the discussion threads. This can greatly assist the tutor in refining and facilitating subsequent runs of the activity.

Problems can arise within any group causing a lack of cohesion and this can easily occur within the context of online learning. A common problem with online discussions or chat rooms is the unjustly maligned lurker. Most learners lurk at some point during a course, as it is an effective strategy for building confidence and for moving in and out of discussions in accordance with their personal learning timescale and needs. Flaming is another area that may result from inadequate empathy for other individuals and flawed cohesiveness with the larger group (King, 1999). Both of these issues can be resolved with an initial agreement on group boundaries and accepted behaviour. There is a clear need to be explicit here, so that all members of the group have a clear understanding of the "rules of engagement" and more importantly feel they have some ownership of these rules. It is important that participants feel that they have a stake in these groups.

Another problem that can arise is the inappropriate posting of messages (or chat) regarding social or non-course related issues. In the course of normal group dynamics, it is expected and desirable that social discourse takes place (especially in the group forming phase). In online learning, however, this needs some form of management and is most easily tackled by setting aside specific social areas (for example a social online café/discussion group, or social chat room). These can also be made private, un-moderated spaces that course leaders and tutors agree to respect as such. Again, these decisions can be agreed when the ground rules for the groups are set, and this needs careful planning in the induction phase of the course.

LEARNER SUPPORT AND INDUCTION

Initially, it is important to create a positive attitude towards the learning situation, the subject and the method. This can be done by creating a good first impression, establishing expectancy for success, creating a positive self-concept for learning (by encouragement and self-control), and by setting clear goals (Wlodkowski, 1985).

The most important aspect of any induction programme is to make sure there is one! It is surprising how often this is neglected and yet this is a key factor for the success of any online course. Online facilitation is a new and developing art and gives the opportunity to empower students to work across great distances. Induction and orientation of students must consider a number of aspects to achieve this:

Structure/Administration

The course induction needs to address:

- Course content, goals and objectives
- Student workload
- Assessment methods and deadlines
- Assessment format and delivery mechanisms
- Background information on the course and support team and contact details
- College/University rules and regulations

Computer/Web Skills

- The Internet and how it developed
- How the Internet works (at a basic level)
- Using the Internet and "netiquette"
- The World Wide Web, web addresses (URLs) and browser use
- What World Wide Web skills will students need to study
- Search tools and skills
- Evaluating web-based information sources
- Introduction to and use of email
- Problems with email
- Synchronous (chat rooms) and asynchronous discussion lists (bulletin boards/ newsgroups)
- File transfer (uploading/downloading and FTP) and file compression
- Navigation tools for the virtual learning environment (VLE)

Student Support and Social Issues

- Where to find help: student services and support (for both on and off-campus learners)
- Health and safety issues (visual display unit guidelines, ergonomics, etc.)
- Discussion of online learning styles/strategies
- Saving money, connection options, working offline, reading online or printing
- Potential Problems and how to find support (medical, social and academic)

A useful strategy to help students orientate to a new course is the use of a frequently asked questions (FAQ) page, which should be based upon previous students' experiences or expected issues when this is not possible. Another useful tool that may help students ensure they have covered all the appropriate materials is a checklist. It is also important during the induction phase to introduce the mechanisms for students' support and set some easy introductory exercises to get students to practice the course technology (send an email, post a bulletin board message, visit a web site, read a welcome message, etc.). These can be combined with appropriate "icebreaker" activities to make this a non-threatening experience for the students.

Tutorial Support and Mentoring

"Distance learning has always favoured the highly motivated, well organised and accomplished learner" (Rowntree, 1995).

To ensure that students are supported and remain motivated we need to ensure that tutor training and development, for student support, and clearly defined support structures for courses and programmes are implemented before students are inducted and tutors take responsibility for online conferences (Salmon & Giles, 1998; Collison et al., 2001; Jonassen et al., 1996).

This ensures that support mechanisms are well integrated and that online tutors are competent computer mediated conference (CMC) practitioners before they need to concentrate on the demanding aspects of helping students to cope with the demands of the course itself (Salmon & Giles, 1998). There are many different views as to what contributes to successful mentoring and even the terminology itself is by no means standardised; the terms mentor, assessor and supervisor being frequently interchanged. One view is that mentoring is a dynamic informal relationship where individuals have choice in the allocation of mentor and the process is concerned with social, academic support and guidance rather than course outcomes and assessment. Mentorship in this context is an intentional, structured nurturing process involving insightful and reflective processes. It is also a supportive process. The role of the mentor as counsellor is also implicit in this approach (Shea, 1992, Parks Daloz & Edelson, 1992). An alternative approach sees the role of guide and support combined with assessor. This may be practical from the perspective of course management but may lead to a conflict of interest, at least from the student's viewpoint (Kerry & Shelton-Mayes, 1995). Mentoring is also linked to coaching, where one person helps another person to release their natural ability to perform, learn and achieve. However, coaching is usually focused on a specific skill or task and is more frequently used in a workplace setting (Parsloe, 1992). Mentoring, in the traditional sense, provides a broader, less specific perspective that gives the student an opportunity to form a developmental relationship with a tutor and gain information from an experienced source. The mentor also helps establish the organizational culture and guide the student in his or her academic development.

From the perspective of student orientation it is essential that the aspects of personal support and guidance are clearly identified and integrated into the online course structure. A key element is the identification of a member of the course team who will act as the student's mentor (individually or in a group). Tutorial support and mentorship can be achieved in an online course in a number of ways including use of the post, email, CMC, the telephone, or even desktop videoconferencing. In some instances face-to-face meetings can be arranged, although this is clearly not possible with widely geographically dispersed students. Schoolnet South Africa (2001) [http://www.school.za/edict/edict/mentor.htm] suggests that to facilitate effective online mentoring, course designers should:

- Use induction workshops to establish parameters of support for learners.
- Use induction workshops to establish confidence in use of support tools.
- Structure online support so that learners are clear in their responsibilities and requirements.
- Structure online course to make allowance for informal online support opportunities.
- Use motivation techniques to encourage participation from learners.
- Design online support opportunities that contribute to the learning process.
- Use techniques for monitoring and assessing learner performances in an integrated and formative way.
- Design the course so that the communication flow between the mentor and learner is regular and appropriate.

These represent sound guidelines for the establishment of online mentoring and if implemented in an online course will provide an effective framework for student support.

INTERFACE DESIGN
Getting Lost in Cyberspace

This phrase has become almost a cliché of the world of instructional design for online learning. Yet the dangers of the nonlinear, hypertextual structure typical of online learning environments are very real to the learner. Among the most commonly reported ones are "disorientation, getting lost in the hyperspace, lack of a sense of size, limits and current position in the whole, difficulties in locating relevant information sources" (e.g., Cunningham et al., 1993; Laurillard, 1993; Armarego & Roy, 2000).

> *"One of the major problems reported with the use of hypermedia as an instructional form when compared to print materials is the orientation of the learner within the learning environment. . . . Disorientation is a problem which is frequently observed in studies of hypermedia users and (one) which significantly limits instructional outcomes . . . Electronic materials can easily conceal much of the information they contain and it is important in the design process to provide the learning with a means to orient and move freely within the information space." Oliver et al. (1996)*

How can instructional design mitigate these disorienting effects? In an article on the use of hypertextual information to support the teaching of law, Warner (2000) compares the way in which a web site can integrate and organize information to the way in which a city map can orient and guide a visitor. Building on this metaphor, he suggests that a well-conceived hypertext provides more than just a means to navigate from point A to point B. Using as an illustration a website on contract law designed to support his own teaching, Warner argues that one of the advantages of hypertext is that the layering and cross-referencing of information into a systematic whole may help to clarify for the learner the immediate structure of the subject.

Clearly, the "conceptual map" of a subject should not be so detailed and complete that it leaves no uncharted territory or room for interpretation. In a comment reminiscent of our colleague's remark at the start of this chapter that the use of web-based materials can make life too easy for students, Warner reflects that "getting a little lost and finding the way out on one's own is a valuable pedagogical experience" (2000). Warner's map metaphor is echoed in the findings of psycholinguistic research which emphasizes the relation between document coherence and information processing (reported by Gladhart, 1998): "A document is coherent if a reader can construct a mental model from it that corresponds to facts and relations in a possible world" (Thüring et al., 1995).

Providing a Cognitive Framework

Instructional design should be couched in a theoretical framework, informed by cognitive learning theory and educational psychology. What does this mean in practice? Warner's point above is that well-conceived hypertextual documents reflect the way in which knowledge is structured by experts within their knowledge domain. However,

Table 1: Performance Support Tools (Sleight, 1997)

Non-Linear Regulation Tasks	Sequencing Instruction	Navigating through the Courseware	Structuring Knowledge
Performance Support Tools	- system map - adaptive advice	- system map - concept map - online help	- notepad - concept map - bookmarking capability

learners may lack the metacognitive strategies necessary to conceptualise this underlying structure in a nonlinear, self-accessed learning environment (Sweany et al., 1996). These problems may be addressed by "training learners to use strategies specific to nonlinear instruction, such as selecting the sequence of instruction, organizing their knowledge, and navigating within the courseware to avoid disorientation" (Sleight, 1997).

Sleight proposes performance support tools to improve self-regulation in nonlinear learning environments (see Table 1).

In a similar vein, Jonassen (1989) offers the following common elements of what he terms "hyperdocument structure" supporting the development of metacognitive learning strategies.

- indexing (online documentation and information databases)
- searching (online documentation and encyclopedias)
- hypermaps (graphic overview of the structure)
- lists (menu that reflect the structure of the document)
- intelligent access to information (expert systems that bridge gaps in user's knowledge)

Beasely and Waugh (1996) also suggest that hypermedia disorientation will decrease and structural knowledge acquisition and retention will increase when the instructional design includes "content structure focusing" activities or "coding elements" (Levy, 1999) which organise the content and focus the learner's attention on the structural aspects of the learning material. It is our experience, for example, as online course designers that much greater detail is required in syllabus specification for online learning than in traditional course syllabuses, particularly in the areas of scheduling, explanation of learning tasks, and explicit statement of learning outcomes.

Appreciation of the tenets of constructivist learning theories is currently considered vital to inform online course design. These stress the social construction of knowledge through collaborative sense-making and the redefinition of the online tutor as orchestrator/facilitator of the collective knowledge building and sharing process (Salmon, 2000). The implications for online course design are that the learner will require purposeful, social interactive learning activities (Siragusa, 2000) explicitly linked to assessed course outcomes, the means by which to gather relevant information and the communication tools necessary to organise the collaborative learning effort, pool and process information and make the meaningful connections which will lead to learning. The course design must also enable the learner to situate new knowledge in relation to personal experience. This implies the need for easy archiving of participation in online discussions for the purposes of self-paced reflection, the provision of discussion summaries weaving together old and new ideas, and the recycling of information and ideas in successive learning activities.

Sometimes, and to an extent paradoxically, it is necessary to return to a more supportive, linear course structure in order to ease the burden of self-orientation on the isolated distance learner. In describing the structure of an online course for healthcare professionals returning to learning, studying at a distance, anxious about their ability to organise their studies and unfamiliar with the use of online learning technology, Winfield et al. (1998) report the success in terms of preserving learner orientation of sequences of "scaffolded" learning activities involving interaction and communication, integrating lectures, case studies, discussion and links to personal clinical experience. As we have seen in the sections on motivation and group dynamics, before assuming a positive learner orientation towards constructivist learning principles, course designers must appreciate that design and use are separate and that learners bring with them epistemic assumptions about the nature and goals of learning, their responsibilities as learners, the status of the expert as knowledge provider or facilitator and the nature of subject knowledge as finite or open-ended.

Course design is by no means the exclusive domain of the tutor and/or instructional designer. As Jonassen et al. (1996) report, the use of students to author web pages or other forms of hypermedia for inclusion in a course's online resources may require them to make high-level connections amongst sources of information.

Finally, the use of online, open-access learning for workplace learning and Continuing Professional Development has led to a trend towards the subdivision of learning content into smaller learning objects or blocks than that of the traditional undergraduate module.

Layout, Navigation and Self-Regulation

The practical nature of the design of the online learning experience has been profoundly influenced by the growing use in Higher Education of integrated learning management software packages, often referred to as Virtual Learning Environments

Figure 1: Brookes Virtual eCourse Template: Homepage, Oxford Brookes University

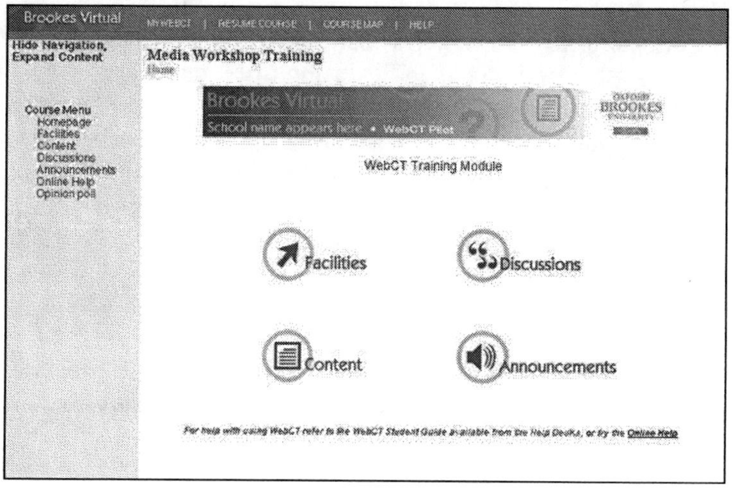

Figure 2: Brookes Virtual eCourse Template: Course Facilities Page, Oxford Brookes University

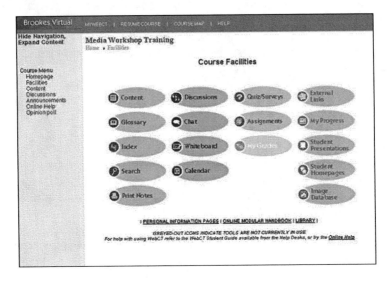

(VLEs). These are tending to be used in replacement of or in conjunction with individual or institutional course websites.

We will illustrate key features of layout, navigation and self-regulation by referring to the implementation of one such VLE at Oxford Brookes University in the UK.

The most obvious feature of this implementation of a VLE is that it adopts a template approach. The template was arrived at after a period of six-months consultation with early academic adopters and has had the benefit of simplifying the staff training and student induction process. A survey of 400 students' reactions to the use of a template confirmed the design team's beliefs that a template aids orientation by guaranteeing consistency across multiple learning modules.

- The **Homepage** groups together the features of the VLE most frequently requested by designers. The inclusion, at the top level, of the discussions and announcements links reflects the designers' belief that the prime usefulness of such a learning environment lies in its ability to improve communications among course participants, thus reducing the risk of alienation and disorientation.

- The **Course facilities** page provides an at-a-glance overview of the sum of available course support tools for any module. The organisational principle behind the use of the facilities page is that of a hub. This reduces the potential of the learners to become disoriented by reducing the number of clicks required to reach a desired tool or resource. The selection and layout of the tools on the screen reflects, through the use of colour-coded columns, their pedagogic purpose and usefulness.

- This VLE (WebCT) provides a personal gateway to their courses (myWebCT), which alerts them to any recent changes to their courses requiring action on their part.

- Contextual online help is provided at all times.

- Learning materials are organised into a table of contents, which provides a visual overview of their structure and sequence. The materials themselves are accompanied by bookmarking and note-taking capabilities for the construction of personal learning paths.

- Designers receive training and guidelines for web page design, including consistent formatting, use of colour, highlighting, indentation, line length, optimal font and font sizes, use of icons, number of links on a page, management of windows, avoidance of scrolling, return paths and accessibility compliancy.

- A navigational aide termed "breadcrumbs" allows the learner to retrace their steps. We would point out that pop-up menus are better for this since they enable forward as well as reverse tracking.

- Student orientation is facilitated by the provision of tracking facilities allowing the learner to monitor their progress through a course and to check their assessment grades.

- Learning activities include mechanisms for frequent and immediate formative feedback by means of self-tests and quizzes.

- High-level links are provided to other important sources of information, such as the electronic library catalogues, online modular handbooks and students' Personal Information Pages. This well illustrates the principle that course information should not be replicated unnecessarily, as this creates potential for discrepancy and thereby learner disorientation.

- External links are grouped separately for independent investigation at will. They also open in a new browser window to prevent the learner from losing their place within the VLE. This does mean, however, that learners must be able to manage multiple open windows.

One potentially negative feature of this style of layout is the use of frames, which can cause disorientation by not always loading correctly when using the browser's navigation buttons.

Information Literacy

How much time do we spend sorting through seemingly endless lists of potentially useful documents on the web?

We may become overwhelmed by the sheer volume of information, disoriented amid the proliferation of hyperlinks from one text to another, distracted from our original quest along the way, unable to assess the quality or even the source of the material we are examining, or to bring our search to a satisfactory conclusion.

"Electronic environments have significantly raised the importance of browsing and selection as information-seeking strategies. From a learning perspective, practicing both the mental discipline of analytical search and the creative exploration of browsing is essential."

Cunningham et al. (1993) argue that although inherently complex, "learning to manage the complexity of hypermedia systems and constructivist learning environments is an essential part of the learning and instructional process," especially in our information age, where "more diverse information is relevant to a wide range of decision making."

It is important, then, that online learning take place within a framework for the discussion and development of information literacy. Conscious attention must be paid to determining how information is to be accessed, understood, evaluated, applied, communicated and created (Marchionini, 1999).

APPROPRIACY OF MEDIA

Online learning resources can take a multitude of forms. This is clearly one of the benefits of learning online, inasmuch as electronic media can cater for a range of learning styles and intelligences (Goleman, 1996; Gardner, 1993; Felder & Silverman, 1988; Hudson, 1967). Information may be presented in many different ways, through text, tables, maps, diagrams, logical notation: the list of traditional media is already long but is greatly extended in the online medium. A web page, for example, may contain, as well as text and images, audio, video, animation, interactive "elements," such as image maps, quizzes, forms, etc., even self-contained applications in the form of "applets." This provides the designer of online learning materials with exciting new ways of conveying ideas and of orienting the learner towards efficient ways of absorbing information and understanding concepts. However, these new media also bring risks: what I find useful and concise as a way of expressing information and ideas may baffle others and vice versa. Furthermore, the use of the range of online media usually brings with it a technological overhead, which can actually get in the way of effective communication of ideas. Finally, there is a temptation to be carried away by one's enthusiasm for a particular technology and to seek a pretext for incorporating it into one's teaching regardless of its "fitness for purpose," i.e., whether it actually fits the learning context; in other words, to seek a problem for solution. Learners may not share this enthusiasm and may question the appropriateness of the technology, or become distracted by it.

It is important, then, to choose learning media that are appropriate in at least four senses. Student orientation to the task will be greatest when the chosen medium is appropriate: (1) to the subject/discipline; (2) to the desired learning outcome; (3) to the physical, social and technical circumstances of the learner; (4) to the preferred learning style of the learner.

1.   **Appropriacy to subject/discipline.** To a student geologist it is entirely appropriate for learning media to make extensive use of images, both still and moving, to identify and highlight geological strata, follow the evolution of a volcanic eruption, or the process of continental shift, for example. An appropriate and easily implemented enhancement of such imagery for learning purposes is to require the learner to pinpoint with their mouse a layer of rock of a specific age, or to calculate the epicentre of an imaginary volcano and locate it on a map. The student is oriented towards the salient information contained in the image and accompanying data and invited to test their understanding of that information. Likewise, business students can be expected to fill out spreadsheets, chemists to manipulate 3D molecular models and language students to listen to recordings of native speakers. Student motivation will be all the greater if exposure to such media in the course of study

Table 2: Meeting Student Learning Needs with Appropriate Use of Technology (Adapted from Learning Technologies and Teaching: Towards a Policy on ICT access and provision. UK Open University)

Student learning need	Appropriate use of online technology
Motivation and orientation	- having access to clear and current information about the course - diagnostic feedback from quizzes early in the course - online group-building activities using discussions or chat

is likely to be viewed as relevant by future employers. What must be kept in perspective is the value placed on different forms of learning (cognitive skills, competencies, etc.) in a given subject/discipline and on the learning products and forms of assessment that are deemed most appropriate for measuring achievement. Electronic learning media may form part either of the process or of the product of learning, and indeed may affect both.

2.   **Appropriacy to desired learning outcome.** As with any aspect of the curriculum, the integration of online media into a course should be designed to achieve explicit learning outcomes, which may be expressed in terms of student learning needs. We have already seen how important motivation and orientation are for the online learner; we must ensure that we make appropriate use of online technology to help meet these fundamental student needs. Table 2 shows three simple suggestions for fostering motivation and orientation.

Though, as we have seen, appropriate use of online media may vary from discipline to discipline, many students' learning needs are common to most disciplines. For example, for each of the following needs, there are corresponding uses of technology that are widely applicable across disciplines (see Table 3).

Table 3: Generic Student Learning Needs (Adapted from Learning Technologies and Teaching: Towards a Policy on ICT access and provision. UK Open University)

Student learning need	Appropriate use of online technology
Skills and procedures	- regular and frequent online quizzes with feedback - using interactive activities using spreadsheets, multimedia, etc.
Developing understanding	- constructing websites which create links between information from a variety of sources - problem-solving exercises, e.g., using databases
Linking theory to practice	- interactive tutorials with feedback - embedded media, simulations, etc.
Practising articulation of ideas	- sharing essays online - threaded discussions

Fitness for Purpose

Assessing the fitness of a technology for the learning purpose for which it is to be used is often a purely practical matter. My students will need to be able to compile and print out the online discussions in which they have taken part because they will have to refer to them in their written assignments. Does my conferencing software permit this? However, it can also entail complex choices and compromises. In courses delivered via a hybrid of online and face-to-face modes, it is common for tutors to wish to make their lecture notes available to students online. They may see this as desirable for a variety of reasons: students gain access to any lectures they may have missed; they can review a lecture, consolidate their understanding of its content and supplement the notes they have taken; they can also revise for examinations. If directed to read the lecture notes in advance of the lecture, students can familiarize themselves with the main points independently of the tutor, thus freeing up the valuable face-to-face contact time for arguably higher-order discussion and extension activities. Online lectures may even replace face-to-face ones. All these are potentially valuable enhancements of the learning experience. However, it is important to consider how the learner is expected to orient him or herself towards the learning content of the material.

Many lecturers use presentation software such as Microsoft PowerPoint™ for their lectures. The resulting slides seldom contain more than an outline of the lecture in question, which is then "fleshed out" by the lecturer. It is a relatively simple matter to distribute PowerPoint slides, either in their original form, or in conversions to html, xml, etc. But how much of the original lecture can be reconstructed in this way by the independent online learner? Is it appropriate to add a written or audio commentary? How may the learner check his or her understanding of the lecture? How can the points made be followed up? Is it appropriate even to seek to replicate the learning experience offered by the lecture or is a shorter, more interactive learning experience more appropriate? If the material is liable to be printed, is it fair to pass the printing costs on to the learner? Misjudgment of such considerations can easily provoke disorientation and frustration in the learner by creating an impression of an impoverishment of the learning experience.

3.   **Appropriacy to the physical, social and technical circumstances of the learner.** There are innumerable ways in which an inappropriate admixture of technology with the external circumstances of the learner can conspire to heighten feelings of isolation and disorientation. A profile of the target learning group needs to be built up by asking a series of questions. What follows is by no means an exhaustive list but will serve to alert the course designer to potential risks. At what times of day will the students be logging on and carrying out their work? What sort of interruptions and distractions will they face? Will they access the course from a private or public location? Does any of the target group suffer from physical or cognitive impairments? What experience of learning with computers do the students have? What technology is available to them? While the cost of computers has fallen dramatically in recent years, they are by no means ubiquitous. Clearly, the prospective learner should not knowingly embark on an online course without access to suitable technology. However, it is the responsibility of course designers to ensure that any material which is to be made available exclusively online, or by electronic means, should be usable on a very modest platform and that the most

basic hardware and software requirements for completion of a course must be made explicit to the learner from before the outset. It may be necessary to include purchase of hardware and/or software in the course fee.

4. **Appropriacy to the preferred learning style of the learner.** As we have seen, online learning materials can enhance the written word with a variety of visual and interactive media. The information-literate society must foster new forms of literacy which go beyond that based on the written word and education must reflect this new emphasis. Clearly, it is not feasible to attempt to provide learning materials in multiple formats to suit the multiple intelligences of the target group of learners. Nevertheless, the online learner can be made aware of how they can take advantage of a media-rich online learning environment in ways that are compatible with their preferred styles of learning.

- Learners may be guided to one of many online questionnaires on multiple intelligences and to discuss the results with their peers. This is an effective ice-breaking activity in the early stages of a course.

- Course design should incorporate opportunities for reflection on the learning process involved in carrying out planned learning activities. This may suggest to the learner alternative ways of organising their learning.

- It should be made clear to the learner to what extent the path through their course content is linear or nonlinear. Frequently online courses merely provide the signposting for the mapping out by the learner of their own learning path.

- There is no need for information to be conveyed through one channel only: video content may have subtitles, or an audio- or text-only alternative. Indeed, codes of practice for accessibility demand that there be a degree of information redundancy in online learning materials.

Where appropriate, learners may be encouraged to make use of digital media such as web pages and multimedia presentations in support of their assessed coursework.

THE VALUE OF MULTIMEDIA

Multimedia computer based learning (CBL) has been seen as one technology that may help to provide a solution to the problem of grasping a large volume of complex material within a short curriculum. Athappily et al. (1994) suggested that integrating multimedia into the training environment would improve effectiveness of training, reduce costs from instructor and participant time, and improve productivity. This remains to be conclusively demonstrated, however, but there are distinct pedagogical advantages in using multimedia to motivate and support learning within specific learning domains. As we have seen, web-based environments are not particularly well suited to large volumes of text-based material. Adding graphics, animation, video and audio to CBL and online learning resources increases the realism of the environment and provides a variety of experience for the students, helping maintain motivation. Audio (sound clips and music) accompanying various elements of a program can be used to give audible cues to certain system events such as receiving advice, or entering a specific area. An exploration of the value that students placed on the video elements of a multimedia CBL application was explored in the evaluation of an application for nurse education. This demonstrated a positive overall preference for video elements in this particular domain (Garrett, 2001). Students were very positive about the value of video in their learning experience, suggesting that it made the simulation a more immersive experience.

Developments in personal computer (PC) technology led to great interest in the potential of interactive multimedia CBL for education in the early 1990s. The availability of CD-ROM drives in PC's increased dramatically at this time. The shipment of CD-ROM drives in 1993 jumped to 6.3 million from 2.5 million in the preceding year (Fritz, 1994), and by 1994 one in five personal computers sold contained both a CD-ROM drive and a sound card (Wilken, 1996). The CD-ROM (and now the DVD-ROM) has become the standardized data storage device for shipping software, and multimedia PCs are now readily available from high street shops. These developments made the use of multimedia computer programs commonplace, and the development of recordable CD drives (CDR) and multimedia authoring software packages have provided educators with the tools to easily develop their own multimedia CBL applications. One area where multimedia CBL has proved its value is in the simulation of activities where experiential learning is expensive, undesirable or even dangerous.

Whilst the early multimedia CBL applications allowed only limited interaction, later developments have focused on giving learners control over their actions and placing them into environments that can be manipulated and interrogated (Harper et al., 1999). An increasing focus upon the pedagogic aspects of multimedia CBL (Benyon et al., 1997) has led to interest in exploiting the potential for intelligent multimedia interfaces. Michael Wilson (1994) discussed the possibility of using multimedia not only to present data stored as images, sound and video on the PC, but also to use intelligent rule-based systems to automatically generate appropriate presentations from retrieved data, and use a variety of specific input modes including natural spoken language.

Web-Based Animation

Simple animation is now fairly commonplace in web-based learning environments. Simple GIF animations can be created and added to web sites to create visual impact. These are established low-bandwidth, "low tech" animations that can be readily viewed in contemporary browsers, without additional software.

In the last five years a range of video/animation playing "plug-ins" for web browsers have also arrived. Many of the early ones served more as a nuisance than a benefit, however, two of the most commonly used web animation formats now use two of the better plug-ins, Macromedia's Shockwave and Flash. Shockwave was created by Macromedia to enable browsers to display Macromedia Director (multimedia) content, whilst Flash (previously named "FutureSplash") incorporates vector-based graphics with animation controls, like zoom, rotate, and gradients. In vector graphics, mathematical equations direct the monitor to display objects of specific colours, shapes and sizes. This creates far smaller files than the alternative raster (or bit-mapped) graphics like GIFs or JPEGs. A typical Flash animation may be ten times smaller than a similar animated GIF. In addition to their small file size and the resulting fast transfer speed, vector graphics are scalable, allowing the zooming in on an image without the loss of sharpness seen in raster graphics. While Director was created for offline programs, Flash was designed to animate banners and to be used on the Web from the start.

Streaming

Another leading graphical/animation format is Apple QuickTime. This is another format that uses a web browser plug-in allowing the user to experience QuickTime animation, audio/music (and MIDI files), video, virtual reality (VR) panoramas and objects directly in a web page. The latest version of Apple QuickTime allows data streaming, working seamlessly within firewall environments and includes free server software.

Streaming is the process of sending media over a network for viewing in real time. Streams can originate from a live source, such as a video camera, a live "web cast," or an audio feed from a radio station, or the source can be a QuickTime movie stored on the server. In either case, the user is not downloading a file when viewing a streamed data source. The data is simply being displayed as it arrives by the plug-in (e.g., Apple's QuickTime or RealNetworks RealVideo). Following streaming, no copy remains on the viewer's hard disk. Creating streaming video is one of the fastest growing web graphics fields. With the new technology available, virtually any user can undertake desktop video production at a reasonable cost.

Network Bandwidth Limitations

All of these multimedia formats discussed above are now in widespread use in education and training, for example in the Oxford University "Virtual Chemistry Laboratory" (http://www.chem.ox.ac.uk/vrchemistry/default.html). However, for online educational systems, the limitations to which multimedia can be used are usually based upon the available network bandwidth. All of the streaming media technologies discussed use codec technology (compression and decompression) to compress the data into the smallest size possible. This inevitably results in some loss of quality (for example small and jerky video clips). In the UK most home network access remains by the public service telephone network (PSTN), whilst in the USA direct cable network access (with higher bandwidth) is more common. As broadband Digital Subscriber Line (DSL) and cable modem access increase, so will the audience for digital video on the Web. In addition to the Internet, many new devices and appliances will be available to distribute web-based materials. We are already beginning to see web-based devices in aeroplanes, in hotel lobbies, on wireless handheld computers and through interactive digital television. This and the current improvements in compressed multimedia formats, such as the latest MPEG-4, ISO/IEC standard developed by MPEG (Moving Picture Experts Group), will ensure an increased use of this medium in online learning environments. The most important aspect of this is undoubtedly image quality, and, without high quality images, video has little value for online learning and becomes a gimmick.

EVALUATION

Another important aspect to consider in the orientation of students to online learning is student involvement and participation in the course design and revision. Online learning is a relatively new discipline, and to ensure that students' learning experiences are assessed and utilized, it is essential that a well thought out evaluation strategies are used and fed into the curriculum revision cycle. The first time an instructor offers an online course, s/he is venturing into the unknown. It is therefore essential that the quality of the learning experience is carefully assessed and that links be made between the resources used, the pedagogy and the course outcomes.

The evaluation of online learning is a complex process. Any evaluation of CBL is concerned with establishing the effectiveness and educational worth of the program being considered. Evaluation studies of CBL in higher education often focus on the comparisons of assessment results and grades (Reeves & Reeves, 1997) rather than the examination of learning experiences and the learning process. The evaluation of the pedagogical design of CBL applications has often been seen as secondary to the evaluation of student performance (Clark, 1994). Many evaluation studies have also been found somewhat inadequate in helping assess the value of CBL in the curriculum. For example, a review of evaluative studies of CBL in nurse education since 1966 revealed that most had significant design faults such as the lack of a control group and small sample size to statistically compare quantitative outcomes (Lewis et al., 2001).

Problems with Evaluating Online Learning

Evaluation is also often confused with assessment, and it has been suggested that many developers of interactive learning applications fail to conduct adequate evaluation, as they rely on inappropriate designs which focus on delivery and outcome assessment rather than examining pedagogical differences (Clark, 1994; Reeves & Reeves, 1997). A review of the literature by Reeves (1995) suggested that major flaws (Table 4) were found in a number of evaluation studies. For example, a model suggested for the evaluation of intelligent tutoring systems by Seidel and Park (1994) suggested a conceptual approach in which the maturity of the technological innovation, technical purposes, processes, and outcome measurements were examined. This illustrates a trend toward focusing on delivery mechanisms and outcomes rather than exploring the nature of pedagogical differences between CBL and traditional approaches. (See Table 4).

In practice it may be impossible to eliminate all the elements outlined by Reeves in any one individual study. For example, an online application may be designed for limited exposure to the user and therefore multiple exposures may be inappropriate if realistic use of the application in an appropriate context is to be achieved.

Multiple Methodological Approaches

Some evaluation studies have taken a combined approach (Reeves & Laffey, 1999; Morris, 1997; Garrett, 2001). For example, Morris in 1997 used interviews, semi-structured questionnaires, audiotapes and pre- and post-exposure testing in the evaluation of a CBL application designed to develop statistical analysis skills. Reeves and Laffey (1999) used both qualitative and quantitative methods including pre- and post-exposure test scores, focus group interviews, email journals, direct observations, and concept mapping to evaluate a CBL delivered undergraduate engineering course. One problem with these multiple method approaches is that they are complex to design, implement, analyze and interpret. Whilst this is certainly true, providing that appropriate tools are used for outcome assessment, and that qualitative data assessment is rigorous, the use of multiple methods should improve the reliability and external validity of the evaluation. In order to minimize measurement flaws and expand the range of assessment strategies for online

Table 4: Major Flaws in Evaluation Studies (Reeves, 1995)

Flaw	Evidence	Remedy
Specification error	The definitions of the primary independent variables (e.g., web based instruction versus lecture)	Complete delineation of the pedagogical dimensions involved in the programmes or products being compared
Lack of linkage to robust theory	Little more than nominal attention to the underlying learning and instructional theories that are relevant to the investigation	Clear grounding of the instructional design of the innovation in robust principles of learning theory
Inadequate treatment implementation	Infrequent (usually single) treatment implementation, often averaging hours or even minutes in duration	Treatments should be optimised over a substantial periods of time before comparisons are initiated
Measurement flaws	Precise measurement of easy to measure variables (e.g., time); insufficient effort to establish the reliability and validity of measures of other variables	A full range of assessment strategies should be employed to "triangulate" even the most difficult to measure variables
Inconsequential outcome measures	A lack of intentionality in the learning context, usually represented by outcome measures that have little or no relevance for the subjects in the study	Participants in studies should have a vested interest in accomplishing the goals and objectives of the program or product being studied
Inadequate sample sizes	Small samples of convenience, e.g., the ubiquitous undergraduate psychology majors	Samples should be of sufficient size to provide sufficient power for statistical inferences
Inappropriate statistical analysis	The use of obscure statistical procedures to tease statistically significant findings out of these data	Educational significance must be considered because statistical significance is often misleading

learning the inclusion of quantitative outcome assessment and qualitative tools is desirable. Such evaluation strategies may include all or any of the following:

- Pre- and post-experience student interviews, outcome tests or questionnaires
- Pre-, mid- and post-exposure interviews with students, staff and technical support personnel
- Student focus groups
- Observations
- Student concept mapping exercises
- Self assessment questionnaires
- Review of materials/pedagogic dimension mapping by peers
- Lecturers' email logs/diaries
- Analysis of achievement, attrition, and log-on, resource usage statistics
- Online questionnaires
- Anonymous evaluation discussion groups

In a recent study (Garrett, 2001) the use of a comparative multiple-method evaluation strategy, although complex, did help provide a comprehensive analysis of learning outcomes and students' experiences and gave a much clearer picture of the students' perceptions of the tools. The qualitative techniques used in this study highlighted some novel findings about students' perceptions of CBL and in particular highlighted the pedagogic value of intelligent agents within the learning environment. A range of qualitative techniques used (including self assessment questionnaires, concept mapping exercises, and focus group interviews) proved effective in achieving a detailed comprehensive evaluation of the complex pedagogic issues surrounding the use of a CBL application. In practical terms it may be difficult to justify the use of such complex evaluation strategies for common use due to the resources required to undertake them. Given a large enough sample and an appropriate domain, however, a multiple method evaluation strategy appears a most effective approach. Such effective evaluation techniques can help obtain the learner's perspective when examining the complex issues of online course design.

Course evaluation can be coordinated by the course leader, but having external academic staff to act as observers provides independent assessment information, and helps disseminate information on online subject delivery to others in the department. The results of an evaluation can be used to ensure that students' experiences are used to maximum benefit in minimizing the disorientation of learners and maximizing motivation and student achievement.

CONCLUSION

Online learning creates many possibilities for increasing flexibility in delivery and providing an added educational value to programmes of study. The very nature of the medium, however, creates many opportunities for students to become disorientated both physically (in their navigation of the virtual learning environment) and psychologically in their adaptation to this medium. Hypertext can facilitate the development of alternative forms of learning such as inquiry-based learning or exploratory and discovery learning. Students can move from one link to another in an enormous global knowledge base, rich with resources in many disciplines. Without carefully planned support in such an environment, however, there is a high risk of user disorientation and dissatisfaction with this mode of study. Furthermore, in many domains this type of learning can represent a significant deviation from more established educational practices where the learning is strongly directed.

We have examined some of the potential pitfalls, and the ways in which we can use these technologies to help students avoid disorientation, and it is clear that the major obstacles to overcome are pedagogical rather than technological. As with any course of study, improper structuring of the content can confuse the learner and lead to disorientation and cognitive overload, as can a lack of appropriate induction and inadequate attention to developing a cohesive community of learners. These aspects are even more important for distance and online learning. If we are to create successful online courses then we must develop a range of new skills in order to facilitate the process effectively. We must be explicit in what we are trying to achieve, that is, essentially to make learning, and the learning process, easier for students using these technologies, and to do so we must pay significant attention to the orientation of the learners if we are to succeed.

REFERENCES

Armarego, J., & Roy, G. G. (2000). Management of a student centred online environment. In A. Herrmann & M.M. Kulski (Eds.), *Flexible Futures in Tertiary Teaching. Proceedings of the 9th Annual Teaching Learning Forum, (February* 2-4). Perth: Curtin University of Technology. Retrieved from the World Wide Web: http://cleo.murdoch.edu.au/confs/tlf/tlf2000/armarego.html.

Athappily, K., Durben, C., & Woods, S. (1994). *Multimedia Computing.* Harrisburg: Reisman.

Beasely, R., & Waugh, M. (1996). The effects of content-structure focusing on learner structural knowledge acquisition, retention, and disorientation in a hypermedia environment. *Journal of Research on Computing in Education,* 28(3).

Benyon, D., Stone, D., & Woodroffe, M. (1997, July). Experience with developing multimedia courseware for the World Wide Web: The need for better tools and a clear pedagogy. *The International Journal of Human-Computer Studies,* 197-118.

Campbell Gibson, C. (2000). The ultimate disorienting dilemma: The online learning community. *Proceeding of the 16th Annual Conference of the Canadian Association of Distance Education,* Québec (May).

Clark, R.E. (1994). Media will never influence learning. *Educational Technology Research and Development,* 42(2), 21-29.

Collison, G., Elbaum, B., Haavind, S., & Tinker, R. (2001). *Facilitating Online Learning: Effective Strategies for Moderators.* Madison: Attwood Publishing.

Cunningham, D. J., Duffy, T. M., & Knuth, R. A. (1993). The textbook of the future. In C. McKnight, A. Dillon & J. Richardson (Eds.), *Hypertext: A Psychological Perspective* (pp. 19-49). Chichester, UK: Ellis Horwood Series in Interactive Information Systems.

De Bono, E. (2001). *Serious creativity*. Retrieved July 29, 2002 from the World Wide Web: http://www.sixhats.com/home.html.

De Cecco, J.P., & Crawford, W.R. (1974). *The Psychology of Learning and Instruction*. Englewood Cliffs, NJ: Prentice Hall.

Felder, R. M., & Silverman, L. K. (1988). Learning and teaching styles in engineering education. *Engineering Education, 78*(7), 674.

Fritz, M. (1994). Video CD, the technology, and the market: Dreaming of a White Book. *CD-ROM Professional, 1*, 18-19.

Gardner, H. (1993). *Multiple Intelligences: The Theory in Practice*. New York: Basic Books.

Garrett, B.M. (2001, September). *The value of an intelligent agent in teaching clinical decision making skills for nursing students* (Ph.D. Thesis). University of Portsmouth, Department of Information Systems.

Gladhart, M. (1998, April). Hypertext. A seminar on cognitive issues related to hypertext and hypermedia. *Cognitive Issues in Technology*. Kansas State University.

Goleman, D. (1996). *Emotional Intelligence: Why It Can Matter More Than IQ*. London: Bloomsbury Publishing.

Harper, B., Hedberg, J.G., & Wright, R. (1999). Designing interactive learning environments: models to incorporate contemporary views of learning. *Proceedings of the Association of Learning Technology (ALT) Conference* (September), Bristol.

Hudson, L. (1967). *Contrary Imaginations: A Psychological Study of the English Schoolboy*. Harmondsworth: Penguin.

Jonassen, D., Davidson, M., Collins, M., Campbell, C., & Haag, B.B. (1995). Constructivism and computer-mediated communication in distance education. *American Journal of Distance Education, 9*(2), 7-25.

Jonassen, D.H. (1989). *Hypertext/Hypermedia*. Englewood Cliffs, NJ: Educational Technology.

Jonassen, D. H., Myers, J. M., & McKillop, A. M. (1996). From constructivism to constructionism: Learning with hypermedia/multimedia rather than from it. In B. G. Wilson (Ed.), *From Constructivist Learning Environments: Case Studies in Instruction al Design*. Englewood Cliffs, NJ: Educational Technology Publications.

Kerry, T., & Shelton Mayes, A. (eds.). (1995). *Issues in Mentoring*. London: The Open University.

King, K. (1999). Group dynamics for the online professor. *Proceedings of Ausweb 99, The Fifth Australian World Wide Web Conference*. Lismore, NSW: Southern Cross University. Available on the World Wide Web: http://ausweb.scu.edu.au/aw99/papers/king/.

Laurillard, D. M. (1993). *Rethinking University Teaching: A Framework for Effective Use of Educational Technology*. London: Routledge.

Learning Technologies and Teaching: Towards a Policy on ICT access and provision. Learning and Teaching Strategy (2002). Learning and Teaching Office, Open University, UK. Retrieved July 29, 2002 from the World Wide Web: http://www2.open.ac.uk/ltto/ltstrategy/index.htm.

Levy, M. (1999). Design processes in CALL. In K. Cameron (Ed.), *CALL Media, Design & Applications*. The Netherlands: Swets & Zeitlinger Publishers.

Lewis, J.L., Davies, R., Jenkins, D., & Tait, M.I. (2001). A review of evaluative studies of computer-based learning in nursing education. *Nurse Education Today, 21*, 26-37.

Marchionini, G. (1999). Educating responsible citizens in the Information Society. *Educational Technology, 39*(2), 17-26.

Mezirow, J. (1991). *Transformative Dimensions of Adult Learning.* San Francisco, CA: Jossey-Bass.

Morris, E.J. (1997). *A formative evaluation study of the program, Link* (Centre for Information Technology in Education Report No.238 ed.). Milton Keynes: The Open University.

Mosley, M.C. (1984). *CAI and Continuing Motivation.* Dallas, TX: Eric Reports ED 243 432.

Oliver, R., Herrington, J., & Omari, A. (1996). Creating effective instructional materials for the World Wide Web. In R. Debreceny & A. Ellis (Eds.), *Proceedings of AusWeb 96: The Second Australian World Wide Web Conference* (pp. 485-492). Lismore, NSW: Southern Cross University Press. Available on the World Wide Web: http://elrond.scam.ecu.edu.au/oliver/docs/96/AUSWEB1d.pdf.

Parks Daloz, L. A., & Edelson, P. J. (1992). Leadership and staff development: A mentorship model. In P. J. Edelson (Ed.), *Rethinking Leadership in Adult and Continuing Education.* New York: Jossey-Bass.

Parsloe, E. (1992). *Coaching, Mentoring and Assessing: A Practical Guide to Developing Competence.* London: Kogan Page

Reeves, T.C. (1995). Questioning the questions of instructional technology research. In M. R. Simenson & M. Anderson (Eds.), *Proceedings of the Annual Conference of the Association for Educational Communications and Technology, Research and Theory Division* (pp. 459-470). Ananheim, CA.

Reeves, T.C., & Laffey, J.M. (1999). Design assessment and evaluation of a problem-based learning environment in undergraduate engineering. *Higher Education Research and Development Journal, 18*(2), 219-232.

Reeves, T.C., & Reeves, P.M. (1997). The effective dimensions of interactive learning on the World Wide Web. In B.H. Khan (Ed.), *Web-Based Instruction* (pp. 59-66). Englewood Cliffs, NJ: Prentice Hall.

Rowntree, D. (1995). Teaching and learning online: A correspondence education for the 21st Century? *British Journal of Educational Technology, 26*, 205-215.

Salmon, G., & Giles, K. (1998). Creating and implementing successful online learning environments: a practitioner perspective. Open University Business School, The Open University, Walton Hall, Milton Keynes, United Kingdom. Retrieved January 20, 2002 from the World Wide Web: http://kurs.nks.no/eurodl/shoen/salmon2/.

Salmon, G. E. (2000). *E-Moderating: The Key to Teaching and Learning Online.* London: Kogan Page.

Salmon, G. E (2001). E-moderation, managing a new language. Net*Working 2001 Conference: From Virtual to Reality. Brisbane, October 2001. Retrieved from the World Wide Web: http://www.chariot.net.au/~michaelc/nw2001/emod_newlang.htm.

Schoolnet South Africa. (2001). Retrieved January 15, 2002 from the World Wide Web: http://www.school.za/edict/edict/mentor.htm.

Seidel, R.J., & Park, O.C. (1994). An historical perspective and a model for evaluation of intelligent tutoring systems. *Journal of Educational Computing Research, 1*, 103-128.

Shea, G. F. (1992). *Mentoring: A Guide to the Basics*. Kogan Page.

Siragusa, L. (2000). Instructional design meets online learning in higher education. *Proceedings of the Western Australian Institute for Educational Research Forum 2000*. Retrieved from the World Wide Web: http://education.curtin.edu.au/waier/forums/2000/siragusa.html.

Sleight, D. (1997). Self-regulated learning during non-linear self-instruction. Educational Psychology, Michigan State University. Retrieved from the World Wide Web: http://www.msu.edu/~sleightd/srl.html.

Stelzer, M., & Vogelzangs, I. (2001). Isolation and motivation in on-line and distance learning courses. University of Twente. Retrieved January 20, 2002 from the World Wide Web: http://www.to.utwente.nl/ism/Online95/Campus/library/online94/chap8/chap8.htm.

Sweany, N., McManus, T., Williams, D., & Tothero, K. (1996). The use of cognitive and metacognitive strategies in a hypermedia environment. *Proceedings of EdMedia*. Boston, Massachusetts (June).

Thüring, M., Hannemann, J., & Haake, J. M. (1995). Hypermedia and cognition: Designing for comprehension. (Designing Hypermedia Applications). *Communications of the ACM, 38*(8), 57(10). Retrieved from the World Wide Web: http://www.cs.uct.ac.za/Courses/CS200W/Resources/HCI/thuring.html.

Tuckman, B. (1965). Developmental sequence in small groups. *Psychological Bulletin, 63*, 384-399.

Virtual Chemistry Laboratory. (n.d.). Department of Chemistry, University of Oxford. Retrieved July 29, 2002 from the World Wide Web: http://www.chem.ox.ac.uk/vrchemistry/default.html.

Warner, R. (2000). *Ford or Cadillac? Distance learning in law schools*. Center for Law and Computers, Chicago-Kent College of Law, Illinois Institute of Technology. Retrieved January 2002 from the World Wide Web: http://www.kentlaw.edu/distancelearning/papers/dlearn.htm.

Wilken, E. (1996). Authoring systems for new media use. *Graphic Arts Monthly, 68*(11), 75.

Wilson, M. (1994). Building intelligent multimedia interfaces. *BCS Multimedia Systems and Applications Conference*, 1-18.

Winfield, W., Mealy, M., & Scheibel, P. (1998). Design considerations for enhancing confidence and participation in web based courses. Distance Learning 1998. *Proceedings of the Annual Conference on Distance Teaching & Learning*, Madison, Wisconsin (Vol. 14, August 5-7).

Wlodkowski, R. J. (1985). *Enhancing Adult Motivation to Learn*. San Francisco, CA: Jossey Bass.

Chapter XVI

Ensuring Usability in International Web-Based E-Learning Systems

Andy Smith, University of Luton, UK

ABSTRACT

E-learning systems cross national borders, are used by people in different cultures, and are applied in culturally different contexts. A number of factors highlight the need to be acutely aware of the role of culture as part of the whole e-learning environment. In mainstream systems development, effective strategies that address cultural issues in both the product *and the* process *of development now often are critical to systems success. In relation to the product of development, cultural differences in signs, meanings, actions, conventions, norms or values, etc., raise new research issues ranging from technical usability to methodological and ethical issues of culture in information systems. In relation to the* process *of development, cultural differences affect the manner in which users are able to participate in design and to act as subjects in evaluation studies. This chapter provides a summary of the main issues within cross-cultural usability with an emphasis on web-based systems. It discusses the application of generic models and theories to the field of e-learning systems and provides an agenda for future research required to ensure usability in international web-based e-learning systems.*

INTERNATIONAL USABLE E-LEARNING SYSTEMS

Web-based systems are now an established channel of communication between a whole variety of organisations and their diverse groups of stakeholders. The Internet makes a global client base accessible to even the smallest organisation. The opportunities for global competitive advantage are considerable. Based on a variety of sources, NUA Internet surveys (NUA, 2002a) estimated that in December 2002 there were 605 million Internet users globally, with the three main regions being North America (183 million), Europe (191 million), and Asia/Pacific (187 million). Whilst projections for the future vary greatly, the Internet offers massive potential in a wide range of fields.

In the domain of e-learning, the emergence of the global information society has led many educational providers in both the public and private sectors to offer their services to a global market. According to the European Centre for the Development of Vocational Training (CEDEFOP) e-learning has the potential to change education and training radically, open new ways of learning and increase the ability of people to acquire new skills (Cedefop, 2002a). This is perhaps most noticeable in the Higher Education sector where many universities now offer open and distance learning programmes to a global student base. E-learning is set to show considerable growth in the coming years. The European e-learning market is predicted to be worth nearly 6 billion U.S. dollars by 2005 (NUA, 2002b), representing a quarter of the European IT training market. In the U.S., 90% of U.S. colleges and universities are predicted to offer some level of e-learning by 2005 (NUA, 2002c).

However, in terms of user perceptions, there is evidence that much needs to be done to improve the quality of e-learning systems. In a recent survey almost two thirds of Europeans rated e-learning as either "fair" or "poor," only one-third as "good," with only one percent "excellent" (Cedefop, 2002b). Ease of use is a key factor in encouraging learners to adopt e-learning styles. Enhancing the usability of e-learning systems includes addressing many traditional aspects of usability and human-computer interaction (HCI) (Smith, 1997). However the success of international e-learning systems is affected by a further range of issues, which relate to cultural differences inherent in the users of such systems. Figure 1 proposes a simple model of how cultural differences may affect the success of international web-based e-learning systems.

Figure 1: Factors Affecting Learning Within Cross-Cultural Web-Based E-Learning Systems

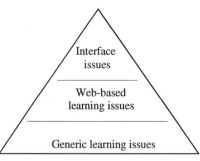

At the deepest level, generic cultural differences in the way in which people actually learn could be considered to be paramount. Hofstede (1986), for example, identifies a range of areas in which differences may influence cross-cultural learning:

1. social position of teachers and learners,
2. relevance of the curriculum (training content),
3. profiles of cognitive abilities between the population from which the teacher and student are drawn,
4. expected patterns of behaviour of teacher/student, and
5. student/student interactions.

The middle level of Figure 1 addresses the ways in which the design of web-based learning systems matches the learning needs of cross-cultural students. Haulmark (2002) discusses the way in which web-based learning requires educators to think differently about their teaching and communication strategies in cross-cultural situations. She addresses changes in the nature of the interaction between teacher and student, and between students themselves.

Both these levels are important for successful international e-learning. However for web-based e-learning systems there is an additional series of concerns that need to be addressed. These relate to the usability of the user interface. Usability (ISO) has been defined in relation the efficiency, effectiveness and satisfaction in which typical users achieve their tasks. Without a usable interface, learners in all cultures will be unable to experience the system at the necessary level of depth that would enable them to appropriately engage in the learning process.

This chapter investigates international issues within the development of usable e-learning systems. It will explore approaches to globalisation on the web, contrast cultural differences in web development and present a limited audit of international e-learning promotional sites. It will move on to present guidelines for the development of international web-based e-learning systems, discuss the problems with user evaluation in such systems and establish an agenda for future research.

INTERNATIONALISATION AND THE WEB

Many organisations are now beginning to realise that, for international web-based systems to be successful, they need to understand and then address the needs of a culturally diverse user base. A survey by World Trade (2000) echoed the view of researchers in cross-cultural usability that the more organisations adapt web-based systems to local markets, the better off they should be. Putting the *"think globally, act locally"* principle into action is not simple but the rewards can be large. The problem is that people differ across regional, linguistic and country boundaries and users' expectations of web-based systems is driven principally by their local cultural perspective. These barriers need to be considered rather than ignored. This means designing and building systems specifically for both global and/or local cross-cultural audiences.

In fact, producing good international software products has always been difficult and there are many examples in the past of IT systems that have failed or caused their users great problems (del Galdo, 1990). Considering both the great expansion in software globalisation offered through the Internet, and the multi-media nature of many web-based systems, effective strategies for design and evaluation that address cross-cultural issues are now often seen to be critical to the success of many applications.

Strategies for Internationalisation

Cultural differences have significance not only for the design itself but also for the process of design. Firstly there is the choice of overall strategy, to develop an international "culturally-free" interface or to provide localised versions. Day (1996) describes three levels of specialisation:

- globalisation, applying an allegedly culture-less standard to be used across different cultures,
- internationalisation, designing base structures for later local customisation,
- localisation, developing specific interfaces to meet particular local markets.

Cultural diversity makes it unrealistic for designers to rely on intuition or personal experience of interface design. However, designing multiple interfaces for different user groups adds significantly to the cost of development. It is important to focus on design characteristics that are sensitive to demographic differences, but it is often not clear what these are. Two broad types of usability issues inherent in international design can be identified. Firstly there are "hard" issues such as language and format conventions. Although important, such issues are not the sole concern here. We are more interested in "soft" issues, those that focus on the ways in which people in different cultures interact with computers. The underpinning cultural and cognitive dimensions of web usability have major implications for international design.

International Usability Evaluation

A key issue in the design of international software systems is affective usability evaluation. There are however huge difficulties in user evaluation for both localisation and internationalisation for multicultural systems development. In relation to *expert/heuristic evaluation*, problems involve the degree to which existing web design guidelines are culturally biased, and how to develop multicultural heuristics. In relation to *user testing*, it is necessary to test with representative local users, but this involves logistical problems and can be both difficult and costly.

International E-Learning Usability

In the e-learning arena, Bourges-Waldegg et al. (1999) describe a pilot study conducted to observe the usability of educational software for teaching mathematics and science. The study led them to identify essential differences between commercial and educational software and to conclude that there are special considerations that should be taken into account when internationalising and localising this type of software. Evers (2002) reported an empirical evaluation of an e-learning website by international user groups and established that differences exist between cultural groups in user interface understanding. Evers also illustrated difficulties in applying usability evaluation techniques within different cultures.

CULTURAL ISSUES IN WEB DEVELOPMENT

There is no lack of theoretical underpinning for cross-cultural usability. However, before summarising some of the key underpinning theories of cultural differences, it is worth emphasising at the outset that there is a lack in explicit demonstration that such theories of culture are actually applicable to, and significant within, the usability of web-based systems. However the author's personal experience of commercial web design and evaluation supports the application of such theory in a general context. Furthermore empirical research is on-going to verify and quantify the effects of such theories (e.g., Smith et al., 2002).

Cross-cultural usability is about making web-based systems an effective means of communication between a global (home) website owner and a local (target) user. Using the Internet to facilitate communication may be a relatively new phenomenon, but in order to fully understand it we need to start by investigating the much wider research area of intercultural communication. Although the roots of intercultural communication can be traced even further back, the anthropologist Edward T. Hall (1959) established the original paradigm. Hall has described culture as a selective screen through which we see the world, and believed that basic differences in the way that members of different cultures perceived reality were responsible for miscommunications of the most fundamental kind. Hall (1976) distinguished cultures on the basis of a way of communicating along a dimension from "high-context" to "low-context." A high-context communication is one in which little has to be said or written because most of the information is either in the physical environment or within the person, while very little is in the coded, explicit part of the message.

Hofstede's Dimensions

In spite of a wide range of research, it is Hofstede's (1991) dimensions of culture that are the most often quoted theories in relation to cross-cultural usability. He conceptualised culture as "programming of the mind" in the sense that certain reactions were more likely in certain cultures than in other ones, based on differences between basic values of the members of different cultures. Hofstede carried out a study of 116,000 IBM employees distributed through 72 countries using 20 languages in 1968 and 1972. The study was based on a rigorous research design and systematic data collection. He proposed that all cultures could be defined through three dimensions:

1. power distance, the degree of emotional dependence between boss and subordinate,
2. collectivism — individualism, integration into cohesive groups versus being expected to look after him/herself,
3. femininity-masculinity, which could be interpreted as toughness versus tenderness.

In addition, he recognised that for Western cultures there was another important dimension:

1. uncertainty avoidance, the extent to which members feel threatened by uncertain or unknown situations and for Eastern cultures,
2. long-term Confucian orientation, which represented a philosophy of life that was prepared to sacrifice short-term results for long-term gain.

Table 1: Example Hofstede Scores

		Power distance	Individualism / collectivism	Masculinity / femininity	Uncertainly avoidance
	Highest	Malaysia 104	USA 91	Japan 95	Greece 112
	Lowest	Austria 11	Guatemala 6	Sweden 5	Singapore 8
USA		40	91	62	46
Japan		54	46	95	92
Belgium		65	75	54	94
United Kingdom		35	89	66	35
India		77	48	56	40
Argentina		49	46	56	86

The great advantage that Hofstede offers to the cross-cultural usability engineer is that through his studies he proposed scores and ratings for each of the dimensions listed above and for a wide range of different countries. Table 1 provides a summary of a selection of countries. Quite large differences can be noticed between countries/ cultures that are geographically quite close. Notice, for example, the large difference between the United Kingdom and Belgium for uncertainty avoidance.

One of the problems with the Hofstede scores is that the data itself could be criticised as being quite old, although Hofstede would claim that culture is quite slow to change. Furthermore, Hofstede's view of culture is often criticised for too closely aligning culture with country. This is particularly true when his ideas are applied to cross-cultural usability. Of course the Hofstede scores apply to the "average" value within each country with individual people ranging on either side. The question here is the extent to which the differences between countries/cultures, as defined by Hofstede, is greater or less than other differences between types of user, irrespective of country/culture. Further discussion and analysis concerning the relevance of Hofstede to cross-cultural usability is included later.

Other Factors

In relation to learning styles, field-dependency is a further factor that varies across cultures (Engelbrecht & Natzel, 1997) and this may also affect cross-cultural usability. Field-independent individuals tend to be more analytical, impose their own structuring more on a situation, and are relatively less passive and global in their behaviour (Ford et al., 1994). Another potentially key dimension is *locus of control* (Rotter, 1966). This factor refers to whether individuals tend to feel that events are the result of their own actions (internal locus) or the effect of the external environment and powerful others (external locus).

BUILDING USABLE
INTERNATIONAL SYSTEMS

As depicted in Figure 2, there are two key issues underpinning usable website development in a global context — *requirements for design* and *strategies for evaluation*

Figure 2: Issues Underpinning International Website Usability

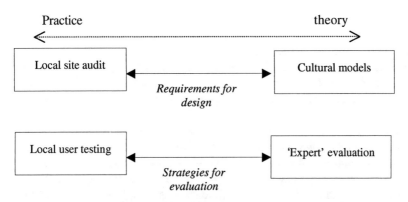

— and that practical approaches to these lie somewhere on scales representing the extremes of theory and practice. For significant international projects it is likely that tools and techniques selected from across both scales will be necessary for affective design.

In relation to cross-cultural usability requirements for a new web-based system, one approach is to undertake local audits to identify the elements that are indigenous to systems in the target culture. The alternative is to predictively apply theoretical models such as Hofstede when proposing designs. The same issues are mirrored in evaluation strategies: either test with real users in the target culture, or evaluate against cross-cultural heuristics. For significant international projects it is likely that tools and techniques selected from across both dimensions will be necessary for affective design.

AN INITIAL AUDIT OF E-LEARNING SYSTEMS

The design of any web-based system is critical to success and to the meanings, both intended and unintended, it may be transmitting. A good place to start when developing web-based system for particular cultural groups is to understand how such systems are built within, and for, the target culture. The first stage should be an audit of local indigenous systems in order to identify typical attractors operating within the culture and domain.

Traditional methods of analysis and design are no longer fully appropriate. Rather, the design of cross-cultural web-based systems is more like creating a film or other mass media for an ill-defined audience. Thus tools used for analysing mass media would be more appropriate here: one such tool is *semiotics*. Semiotics (Peirce, 1953) has been called the "science of signs." More specifically, it is the discipline which connects meaning, meaning making, communication and culture through an understanding of acts of signification. Computer-based *signs,* in this context, include textual cues, images, icons, and sounds.

There are a variety of semiotic discourses and traditions, most noticeably that of Peirce (1953) and Saussure (1974) and there have been various attempts to apply a semiotic framework in the field of IT and HCI (French & Smith, 2000; Anderson, 1990). Semiotics does not recognise that any particular sign is truly "universal." It all rather depends on context: both local and global. Studies have tried to define and quantify the difference between a sign and its meaning (Blankenberger & Hahn, 1991) without much success. This "failure" is not however surprising to semioticians, since it is due to a fundamental semiotic principle: that both the *context of the sign* and the *interpreter of the sign* alter the *meaning* of the sign itself. It is, as a result of this principle, important for local site audits to be undertaken by, or with support from, someone with first-hand experience of the target culture.

Available space here does not allow a full exploration of the cultural characteristics of complex e-learning web-based systems. However, in order to introduce the concept a surface level analysis of three university websites is provided. One problem with an audit of this type is that it is very easy to select sites to support, or otherwise, a certain proposition (for example that Hofstede dimensions are applicable to the design of cross-cultural web-based systems). As a result, the sites were chosen here merely because the name of the university starts with "Lu," as does the University of Luton where the author is based. Such an approach might result in some degree of randomness and impartiality in an incredibly small and statistically insignificant sample. Figure 3 provides the home

Figure 3: University Home pages

University of Luton, UK   University of Lucknow, India

Universidad Nacional de Lujan, Argentina

page of the University of Luton (UK), the University of Lucknow (India), and both the home and main page from the Universidad Nacional de Lujan (Argentina).

Emphasizing again the unscientific nature of this study, and that the aim is merely to explore cultural characteristics of websites, there would seem to be some match between the sites selected and generic cultural characteristics. The University of Luton's website would, for example, seem to embody many of Hofstede's claims about British culture. It is low in power distance (images of people), individualistic (people on their own), high in uncertainty avoidance (quite a complex menu/tabbing system) and masculine (quite stark use of colour and design).

The University of Lucknow would certainly seem to demonstrate the higher degree of power distance evident in Indian society (imposing building representing authority), although Indian users could handle much greater level of complexity in home page navigation, as suggested by its low score for uncertainty avoidance.

In relation to the latter dimension, Argentina has quite high levels of uncertainty avoidance. Certainly this is evident in the home page of the Universidad Nacional de Lujan as it provides merely a "gateway" whereby clicking on the crest of the university gains easy access to the main page. However the main navigation page itself is relatively complex, in contrast to possible expectations. The nature of access via the crest, does however, imply a relatively high level of power distance as suggested by Hofstede.

GUIDELINES FOR DESIGN AND EVALUATION

A wide range of design guidelines for usability are available from many different sources. At the general level, Shneiderman (1992) provides eight "golden rules" for interface design applicable to all interactive devices. In relation to web-based systems much more specific guidance is available (e.g., Nielsen, 2000). Guidance for international and cultural issues is less easy to find, although a number of key sources exist (e.g., del Galdo, 1990, 1996).

The process of internationalisation and localisation of web-based systems involves an analysis of both "hard" and "soft" issues. In this context, a hard issue is one that can be relatively easily addressed through an understanding of routine practice in the target country or culture. A clear example is the use of formats for numeric information such as dates (1/31/02 and 31/1/02 for January 31). Soft issues are more subjective and involve a deep understanding of the target culture. A few key issues are discussed below.

- **Language and language translation.** Language may differ between the home and the target culture. Global systems may adopt the home language and require users to communicate in the home language. In this case, it is necessary to analyse the style and complexity of language used. It may be appropriate to assume that global users have some understanding, but there are a number of areas of difficulty for non-native speakers, such as the level of language complexity and the use of culture-specific meanings, abbreviations, idiomatic expressions, and semi-technical terms. The alternative to assuming that all users can cope with the home language is to translate the system into the target language using the range of professional services that are available. E-learning systems present an additional challenge in the specific field of language learning. Here they may be three languages involved: that of the learning provider, that of the learner and that of the language being learned.

- **Use of colour.** Cross-cultural systems can become confusing, offensive or even dangerous for users if designers are not familiar with the needs of the target culture (Vanka, 1999). Colour semantics differ across cultures and three distinct dimensions are of relevance. Firstly the use of single colours may have specific cultural meanings. White and black, for example, are colours associated respectively with weddings and funerals in the West, but the opposite is true in Asia. Secondly colour combinations and their contrast (e.g., blue/red/black, blue/red/green, etc.) can be significant. Lastly colour saturation can also differ across cultures and business domains.

- **Images and metaphor.** The way in which the system makes use of pictures, icons and other graphic features needs to be analysed for appropriateness and associated meaning in global and local contexts. A metaphor can be a strong tool to aid navigation and information delivery. However the use of metaphors, such as cue-card, cartoon characters, anthropomorphic assistants, and immersive/virtual experience, need to be related to local expectations. Evers et al. (1999) report on the findings of a study that investigated cultural aspects of understanding the website of a virtual campus. Results indicate differences in expectations and understanding due to the users' knowledge of everyday life and real world experience, and suggest that the campus metaphor that was used is not universally transferable.

Generic dimensions of culture can also be applied to develop guidelines for international web design. Marcus and Gould (2000), for example, address Hofstede and

Table 2: Cross-Cultural e-Learning Usability Guidelines

Power distance	
High	Low
Provide a structured access to student learning materials. Focus on the institution and tutors as the source of knowledge and assessment.	Allow student greater flexibility in access to materials. Place emphasis on working together (student and tutor) and attempt to meet individual learner needs.
Femininity/masculinity	
Feminine	Masculine
Design for highly task oriented environment. Gender/family/age distinctions may be blurred. Graphics may be neutral/soft in nature.	Design system for exploration and control. Be aware of traditional gender/family/age distinctions. Graphics may be utilitarian.
Uncertainly avoidance	
High: avoid uncertainty	Low: cope with uncertainty
Keep interface and navigation as simple as possible and provide additional cues (such as colour coding) to support usability. Give emphasis to help systems to provide extra learner support -- particularly task based help.	Less need to support users from failure, complexity and risk are valued by the learner. Provide help focused on information rather than tasks.

present guidance for each of Hofstede's dimensions. The appropriateness of such guidance to the development of usable and acceptable web-based e-learning system needs further research. The issue of collectivism/individualism, for example, raises an interesting conflict between generic cultural characteristics and learning styles. Collectivist cultures might be expected to be more suited to group learning environments, whereas the evidence in countries such as China is the opposite. Haulmark (2002) provides a case study exploring Thai students' perceptions of a web-based distance learning course and how they adapted to more active learning modes. In spite of these words of caution, and specifically not addressing collectivism/individualism, Table 2 shows how Marcus and Gould's guidelines might be simplified and modified to more closely relate to the requirements of usable e-learning web systems. However, it should again be emphasised that the link between Hofstede theories and web usability is largely unproven and that guidelines such as these need rigorous testing and validation.

USER TESTING

User testing is often referred to as the "gold standard" in improving usability because only by studying real people doing real jobs in real environments can we be sure that we will find out what is truly relevant. Of course, for international systems user testing will involve users who are remote from the development team and is therefore potentially difficult and costly. In relation to cross-cultural evaluation of web-based systems, testing within the local culture is generally agreed to be critical in order to assess differences in usability and acceptability. However, cultural differences are not only important for the product of the development process, they can also significantly affect the evaluation process. There are two issues. At the detailed level there is the problem of successfully engaging with users from different cultures within the user testing process itself, whereas at a higher level the whole concept of user-centred design and participation may be difficult for multi-national development teams.

Research into contact between different cultural groups has long recognised the scope for conflict and misunderstandings. Small differences between groups are often exaggerated and distorted to provide a mutually negative image or stereotype based on "us" and "them" differentiation. Bochner (1988) showed that harmonious relations arise when both parties share a super-ordinate goal — a goal that both groups want to attain and neither can attain if they compete. According to Bochner, it should be assumed that individuals will react and try to modify surroundings which cause cross-cultural conflicts.

Contextual Inquiry Evaluation

User evaluation techniques are often based upon the concepts of contextual inquiry (Holtzblatt & Jones, 1993) and are embodied in a variety of methods such as Cooperative Evaluation (Carroll & Mack, 1984) and Developer User Contextual Evaluation (DUCE) (Smith & Dunckley, 2002). The aim is to gain meaningful information about a user's work by empowering the user to pursue their conversation with the evaluator on equal terms.

This type of testing is not always easy in an international context. Usability professionals trying to undertake such techniques in Far Eastern cultures often find that users have particular difficulty. A closely related concept to Hofstede's individualism/ collectivism dimension is Rotter's (1966) locus of control, and this factor could be significant in understanding such difficulties. Locus of control refers to whether individuals tend to feel that events are the result of their own actions (internal locus) or the effect of the external environment and powerful others (external locus). It has been suggested that locus of control influences information-seeking behaviour so that "internals" seek more information in problem solving, although the strength of this behaviour depends very much on the situation. In contrast, when individuals adopt an external approach they cannot generalise or learn effectively.

Remote Evaluation

Advances in web and networking technology are making remote user testing across cultures and remote geographical locations both feasible and lower in cost. The Internet and the Web make it possible to distribute prototypes rapidly at low cost to large numbers of users, linked to groupware technologies such as news groups and e-mail lists. Several researchers (Hilbert & Redmiles, 1998; Hartson et al., 1996) have already noted these opportunities to create remote evaluation systems.

In general, two types of data collection have been used. Firstly the subjective approach can range from user reports and user identified "critical incidents" to question-naires, interviews and ethnographic approaches. Secondly, the objective approach involves automatically collecting data (e.g., counts, sequence and timing of actions) through audio and video recording, conferencing, and automatic software systems. Although objective methods capture detailed feedback information that is difficult to collect by subjective methods, the latter needs one-to-one evaluator-user resources, which makes them resource intensive. A key benefit of the subjective approach is the ability to capture aspects of the users' needs, thought processes and experiences, which are difficult to capture with the objective approach.

In the e-learning environment, Dunckley et al. (2000) describe a low cost remote evaluation method based upon the DUCE technique (Smith & Dunckley, 2002). This is implemented via a "write-along" technique, which captures users' reactions as they experience the system, in contrast to the traditional "speak aloud" method for one-to-one user-evaluator contextual inquiry. Dunckley et al. (2000) show how the method is applied to the remote evaluation of the electronic marking tool of the Open University in the UK by OU tutors. Additionally, Dunckley et al. (2002) extend the technique to include synchronous user-evaluator communication using real-time video conferencing tool, such as Microsoft NetMeeting, again applying the method to the OU electronic marking tool.

In summary, it is clear that cultural differences between the home and target culture affect the process of evaluation. In order to minimise the effect it is necessary to test within the target culture with evaluators who are native to the target culture. Even so the fundamental philosophy of contextual inquiry type methods may not be suitable to some cultures. As in other sections of this paper these issues highlight the need for more research and a greater understanding of international e-learning usability.

CONCLUSION AND FURTHER WORK

E-learning systems cross national borders, are used by people in different cultures, and are applied in culturally different contexts. Although IT researchers and practitioners have long been aware of the challenges of the global market, nevertheless there still are unsolved problems concerning the extent to which culture may affect the usability of the artefacts they produce. Indeed, as Kersten et al. (2000) observe:

> *"There is no solid theory that links software to culture, or the way ideas and values are implemented in software. Such a theory requires and needs to go beyond the consideration of the surface manifestations of culture that have been widely accepted..." (p. 509)*

In relation to cross-cultural web-based e-learning, the situation is even more complex as the learning process itself is also highly affected by differences in culture. Cultural differences are acting in a multi-dimensional environment, both in the design of systems and in the evaluation of systems. Much more research needs to be completed, both in the generic area of cross-cultural usability and in the specific domain of e-learning. The following section sets out a number of issues and research questions. Together they form a loose research agenda for future work.

1. The significance of cultural differences in determining the usability of e-learning systems.
    a. Are the differences between countries/cultures greater or less than the difference between types of user, irrespective of country/culture?
    b. Is the web a truly global phenomenon, operating irrespective of culture? If so, is this also true for e-learning systems?
    c. Is there a "culture of the web" that affects user behaviour in special circumstances by adapting traditional societal culture?
    d. How can the results of empirical studies help answer these questions?
2. The role of generic cultural models in cross-cultural usability.
    a. What evidence is there that such models (e.g., that of Hofstede) are actually significant?
    b. At what levels do they operate? From surface level usability through to deeper learning?
    c. How do we develop systems based on such theories?
3. Guidelines for development.
    a. Are guidelines based upon generic theories of culture to be relied upon to deliver usable international e-learning systems?
    b. How do we refine generic cultural guidelines to produce a meaningful and reliable source for e-learning systems?
4. The role of the international learner in the design process.
    a. How do we avoid cultural bias in requirements elicitation and usability data collection?
    b. How do we localise user-based evaluation methods that address cultural diversity between evaluator and user/learner?
    c. What is the relative effectiveness of remote evaluation systems compared to face-to-face user testing?

5.   Cultural and ethnic diversity within nations.
      a. To what extent are the issues of international systems development mirrored within individual countries with significant ethnic minorities?
      b. How can culturally sensitive systems combat social exclusion in learning?
6.   Modes of learning: individual vs. group learning.
      a. The extent to which web-based e-learning systems can modify traditional modes of learning?
      b. How is group learning best offered to those who would not normally learn in such a manner?

REFERENCES

Andersen, P. B. A. (1990). *Theory of Computer Semiotics*. Cambridge, UK: Cambridge University Press.

Blankenberger, S., & Hahn, K. (1991). Effects of icon design on human-computer interaction. *International Journal of Man-Machine Studies*, *35*, 363-377.

Bochner, S. (1988). *Cultures in Contact*. Oxford, UK: Pergamon Press.

Bourges-Waldegg, P., Moreno, P., & Rojano, T. (1999). Internationalisation and localisation of educational software. In G. Prabhu & E. del Galdo (Eds.), *Designing for Global Markets 1: Proceedings of First International Workshop on the Internationalisation of Products and Systems* (pp. 33-43). Rochester, NY: Backhouse Press.

Carroll, J. M., & Mack, R. L. (1984). Learning to use a word processor: By doing, by thinking, and by knowing. In J. C. Tomas & M. L. Schneider (Eds.), *Human Factors in Computer Systems* (pp. 13-51). Norwood, NJ: Ablex.

Cedefop. (2002a). *E-learning and Training in Europe*. Cedefop. ISBN: 92-896-0106-X

Cedefop. (2002b). *Users' Views on E-Learning*. Cedefop. ISBN: 92-896-0109-4

Day, D. (1996). Cultural bases of interface acceptance: foundations. In M. A. Sasse, R. J. Cunningham & R. L. Winder (Eds.), *People and Computers XI: Proceedings of HCI'96* (pp. 35-47). London: Springer.

del Galdo, E.M. (1990). Internationalisation and translation: Some guidelines for the design of human-computer interfaces. In J. Nielsen (ed.), *Designing User Interfaces for International Use* (pp. 1-10). Amsterdam: Elsevier Science Publishers.

del Galdo, E.M. (1996). Culture and design. In E. M. del Galdo & J. Nielsen (Eds.), *International User Interfaces* (pp. 74-87). New York: John Wiley and Sons.

Dunckley, L., Rapanotti, L., & Hall, J. (2002). Extending low cost remote evaluation with synchronous communication. In X. Faulkner, J. Finlay & F. Detienne (Eds.), *People and Computers XVI: Proceedings of HCI 2002* (pp. 105-120). London: Springer.

Dunckley, L., Taylor, D., Storey, M., & Smith, A. (2000). Low cost remote evaluation for interface prototyping. In S. McDonald, Y. Waern & G. Cockton (Eds.), *People and Computers XIV: Proceedings of HCI 2000* (pp. 389-403). London: Springer.

Engelbrecht, P., & Natzel, S.G. (1997). Cultural variations in cognitive style: Field dependence vs. field independence. *School Psychology International*, *18*(2), 155-164.

Evers, V. (2002). *Cultural aspects of user interface understanding: An empirical evaluation of an e-learning website by international user groups*. Unpublished PhD thesis. Milton Keynes, UK: Open University.

Evers, V., Kukulska-Hulme, A., & Jones, A. (1999). Cross-cultural understanding of interface design: a cross-cultural analysis of icon recognition. In G. Prabhu. & E. del Galdo (Eds.), *Designing for Global Markets 1: Proceedings of First International Workshop on the Internationalisation of Products and Systems* (pp. 173-182). IWIPS.

Ford, N., Wood, F., & Walsh, C. (1994). Cognitive styles and searching. *On-line and CD-ROM Review, 18*(2), 79-86.

French, T., & Smith, A. (2000). Semiotically enhanced web interfaces for shared meanings: Can semiotics help us meet the challenge of cross-cultural HCI design? In D. Day, E. del Galdo & G. Prabhu, (Eds.), *Designing for Global Markets 2: Proceeding of IWIPS 2000* (pp. 23-38). IWIPS.

Hall, E. T. (1959). *The Silent Language*. New York: Doubleday.

Hall, E. T. (1976). *Beyond Culture*. New York. Doubleday.

Hartson, H. R., Castillo, J. C., Kelso, J., & Neale, W. C. (1996). Remote evaluation: The network as an extension of the usability laboratory. In G. van der Veer & B. Nardi, (Eds.), *Proceedings of CHI 96: Human Factors in Computing Systems* (pp. 228-235). ACM Press.

Haulmark, M. (2002). Accommodating cultural differences in a web-based distance education course: a case study. In *Proceedings of Ninth Annual International Distance Education Conference*. Centre for Distance Learning Research. Retrieved December 16, 2002 on the World Wide Web: http://www.cldr.tamu.edu/dec_proceedings.

Hilbert, D. M., & Redmiles, D.F. (1998). An approach to the large-scale collection of application usage data over the Internet. In K. Torii (Ed.), *Proceedings of the 20th International Conference on Software Engineering* (pp. 136-145). IEEE Computer Society Press.

Hofstede, G. (1986). Cultural differences in teaching and learning. *International Journal of Intercultural Relations, 10*, 301-320.

Hofstede, G. (1991). *Cultures and Organizations: Software of the Mind*. Maidenhead, UK: McGraw Hill.

Holtzblatt, K., & Jones, S. (1993). Conducting and analysing a contextual interview. In D. Schuler & A. Namioka (Eds.), *Participatory Design: Principles and Practices* (pp. 177-210). Lawrence Erlbaum Associates.

Kersten, G.E., Matwin, S., Noronha, S., & Kersten, A. (2000). The softwares for cultures and the cultures for software. In *Proceedings of 8th European Conference on Information Systems*, Vienna (pp. 509-514).

Marcus, A., & Gould, E.W. (2000). Crosscurrents: Cultural dimensions and global Web user-interface design. *ACM Interactions, 2*(4), 32-46.

Nielsen, J. (2000). *Designing Web Usability*. Indianapolis, IN: New Riders.

NUA Internet Surveys. (2002a). How many online? Retrieved December 18, 2002 on the World Wide Web: http://www.nua.ie/surveys/how_many_online/index.html.

NUA Internet Surveys. (2002b). E-learning to thrive in Europe. Retrieved December 18, 2002 on the World Wide Web: http://www.nua.ie (full version at http://www.idc.com).

NUA Internet Surveys. (2002c). E-learning gaining strength in US. Retrieved December 18, 2002 on the World Wide Web: http://www.nua.ie (full version at http://www.idc.com).

Peirce, C. (1953). *Collected Papers of Charles Sanders Peirce*. USA: Belnap Press.

Rotter, J. B. (1966). Generalised expectancies for internal versus external control of reinforcement. *Psychological Monograms*, *80*, 1-28.

Saussure, F. (1974). *Course in General Linguistics*. London: Collins Press.

Shneiderman, B. (1992). *Designing the User Interface*. Reading MA: Addison Wesley.

Smith, A. (1997). *Human Computer Factors: A Study of Users and Information Systems*. Maidenhead, UK: McGraw Hill.

Smith, A., & Dunckley, L. (2002). Prototype evaluation and redesign: Structuring the design space through contextual techniques. Interacting with Computers, *16*(6), 821-843.

Smith, A., Chang, Y., & French, T. (2002). eCulture: Quantifying cultural differences in web site usability: Two empirical case studies of Chinese and British users. In *Proceedings of 5ᵗʰ Asia Pacific Conference on Computer-Human Interaction*. Beijing: Science Press.

Vanka, S. (1999). ColorTool: the cross cultural meanings of colour. In G. Prabhu & E. del Galdo (Eds.), *Designing for Global Markets 1: Proceedings of First International Workshop on the Internationalisation of Products and Systems* (pp 33-43). Rochester, NY: Backhouse Press.

World Trade. (2000). Retrieved December 14, 2002 on the World Wide Web: http://www.worldtrademag.com.

Chapter XVII

Knowledge Spaces:
Cultural Education in
the Media Age

Wolfgang Strauss, Fraunhofer Institute for Media Communication, Germany

Monika Fleischmann, Fraunhofer Institute for Media Communication, Germany

Jochen Denzinger, Fraunhofer Institute for Media Communication, Germany

Michael Wolf, Fraunhofer Institute for Media Communication, Germany

Yinlin Li, Fraunhofer Institute for Media Communication, Germany

ABSTRACT

Research into the opportunities offered by electronic media, as regards finding and acquiring knowledge, together with the development of new teaching and learning methods for the field of art and culture is the focus of the work being carried out by the Media Arts Research Studies (MARS) research group at the Fraunhofer Institute for Media Communication. This chapter illustrates the requirements on electronic and digital media concepts in the context of e-learning, using the very latest developments and experience in this sector as examples.

In the broadest sense, the aim is to visualise information and create networked "knowledge spaces" which are accessible to users as new forms of teaching and

learning through play. Experimental methods, tools and interfaces that support communication between the digital and physical spaces and investigate new forms of knowledge retrieval are being developed and tested.

INTRODUCTION
Media-Based Teaching and Learning Concepts

How do people learn? By asking questions and seeking answers, by finding opportunities and making decisions, by processing information and establishing contexts. As in many other sectors, digital media also bring new opportunities for basic and advanced training in the field of art and culture. In contrast to many other sectors, however, the abilities of expression, experimentation and reception are important, since they support the growth of artistic and cultural orientation and the ability to deal with such concepts (Panzini, 1999).

Digital media, information and network technologies have profound implications on the opportunities for communicating and building knowledge, online study and e-learning. For some, the main advantage of online learning is the ability to communicate instructions via the Internet wherever you are, as can be witnessed in numerous popular e-training programs. Others regard the Internet as little more than a wild, untamed data archive. Neither of these groups is making the most of the opportunities available, since the constantly growing "network of networks" offers far more than just that. It creates a space in which learners and teachers can work together to create and depict new forms of knowledge from a universal archive, regardless of the time or place they occupy.

In this sense, the Internet is both an "archive" and a "cultural memory." It is becoming a space for telematic presence and is fulfilling a "globalisation role" that can create a feeling of cultural togetherness — regardless of geographical location (de Kerckhove, 1990).

Because of the lack of suitable methods and tools that provide access to this "complex new world of knowledge," many contemporary e-learning concepts transfer mostly linear, traditional learning and training methods to new, digital media without really exploiting their full potential (Kritzenberger & Herzceg, 2001).

The challenge must be to create constructive and logical frameworks that provide as informative a picture as possible of the extensive collection of data material. In order to be able to understand a large amount of information quickly, this information must first be visualised and contextualised appropriately (Wilson, 2002, p. 761f). In addition to the appropriation of cultural technology for digital media, a "sensory training" is a basic requirement for perception, recognition and learning in order to acquire knowledge (cf., Weibel, 2002). At the same time, the perception of the physical world needs to be included into media-based teaching and learning concepts. Of equal importance are the skills required for social interaction and collaboration, which should not be restricted to a "screen presence."

The MARS Exploratory Media Lab is pursuing the idea of creating networked "knowledge spaces" — telepresent Mixed Reality spaces that are created by overlapping the physical and electronic domains. These are networked places, spaces and tools that are accessed via experimental interfaces, which link the real and virtual environment.

FOUR LEVELS OF
THE KNOWLEDGE SPACE

Four interferential layers of knowledge spaces had been identified by the authors. They build on current research and development work for new forms of teaching and learning at the MARS Exploratory Media Lab and from which the concept of "knowledge spaces" derives.

- The "information space" is primarily where the infrastructural network of a data archive is created. The Internet platform netzspannung.org is introduced.
- The "explorative space" offers knowledge tools that support the intuitive discovery of data. The Semantic map as an explorative browser is introduced.
- The "participation space" is where tangible objects and invisible interfaces provide experimental access to enterable knowledge spaces. The notion of mixed reality is introduced.
- The "mediation space" ultimately focuses on the significance of the social context. A workshop format is introduced.

Information Space: 'netzspannung.org'

The Internet platform "netzspannung.org" provided the basis for the design and development of the technical and structural elements required for a database-backed knowledge platform which supports the homogenous networking of different types of reference sources derived from existing online archives. Of particular significance in this context is the description of data objects (metadata), i.e., the categorised information that makes it possible to locate an object in a database.

Where they are accessible online at all, the main body of existing media culture archives use highly-specialised and proprietary processing systems. To date, these archives have no uniform standard for indexing archive objects with metadata.

In principle, media art — with its specialist needs — requires its own descriptive language, a so-called "media art markup language."

These specific requirements from media art ultimately lead to the model of a "data body," which occupies the digital knowledge space (Figure 1). This data body links itself to all relevant data and maps it, associating itself also with the context of the author or project.

The multimedia online archive "netzspannung.org" locates media art at the intersection of art, science, technology and communication. Topics such as production, distribution, connectivity, collaboration, communication, theory formation, publication, education, archiving and public visibility form the electronic arts community's basic requirements on an Internet platform for media art. These topics had been addressed as the 10 most important issues for the production of media art in the CAT - Communication, Art & Technology — feasibility study of 1998 through an email poll (http://netzspannung.org/journal/issue0/cat-history/en). Individual, curated modules of the "netzspannung.org" platform form the basis for growing data resources and content.

The annual competition to promote new ideas, "digital sparks," is one of the modules that generate high-quality content through a peer review process. The series of "Tele-Lectures" uses broadband streaming and archiving of key lectures to create a

Figure 1: Semantic Structure of a 'Data Body', e.g., Artist's Data-Body or Project Data-Body

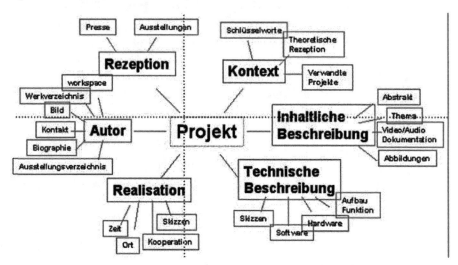

temporarily extended auditorium and a sustained cultural memory. Conferences and workshops are further sources of salient contributions and up-to-date information. For the community, the platform ultimately offers open publication channels, primarily for presentations and discussion. "Netzspannung.org" therefore provides its users with an infrastructure for publishing their own work and also generates its own curated content. It therefore represents a constantly growing, high-quality pool of information belonging to one specific community and is aimed at an audience of professionals and university academics.

After its first year of existence (10/2001 - 10/2002), the bilingual platform contains around 300 projects in the form of media files, texts, images, videos and some 100 hours of recorded talks known as "Tele-Lectures." Over the period of a year, a community has sprung up of around 1,700 registered users of the "netzspannung.org" data pool. Over the last three months, some 22,000 visits were recorded on the site.

The three-layer model of Figure 2 visualizes the architecture of "netzspannung.org" as a distributed community platform. It shows the open, documented interfaces that allow users to implement their projects. The architecture can be understood as a "network operating system." The base is an "Internet hard-disk" that allows the storing of standard formats like XML, but also self-defined data models. The base has an interface that connects to an "application layer." On top of the application layer is an "interface layer" for creating individual skins. The architecture supports various protocols like CORBA, SOAP and HTTP, making it very flexible and offering different layers of complexity or simplicity. Thus, the architecture is attractive for beginners as well as for experienced users.

The aim of future developments is to network "netzspannung.org" with other archives. To achieve this goal from a technical point of view, interfaces will be defined as web services and a "dynamic archive adapter" will be developed. In this context,

Figure 2: Sketch of "netzspannung.org" Platform Architecture

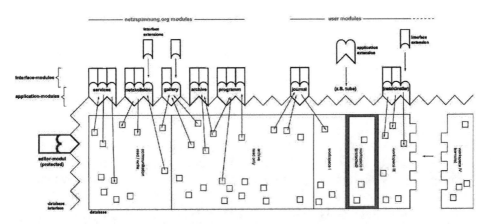

semantic web technologies can be of particular benefit, since they automatically establish a metastructure at semantic level between heterogeneous content and the systematics of different archives.

"Netzspannung.org" then facilitates central access with an interface to a decentral network of various archives and becomes, in the true sense of the word, a portal.

Explorative Space: Knowledge Discovery Tools

Just as large telescopes help astronomers to see the stars, digital cultures need new instruments to be able to see, survey and evaluate the rapidly growing volumes of data.

The "Semantic Map Interface" from "netzspannung.org" represents a "telescope for viewing and evaluating the data cosmos," as astronomer Roger Malina put it at ARTMEDIA 8, held in Paris in October 2002.

"Knowledge discovery tools" — one of which is the "Semantic Map" — are special tools which permit a "bird's eye view" of large volumes of heterogeneous data and facilitate the visualisation of data resources as contextualised information spaces. Because they also support active structuring, preparation and communication, they are also recognition tools.

According to the context in which they are used, three different interfaces have been implemented so far.

- The "Semantic Map" compiles content into clusters and facilitates an explorative navigation of interdisciplinary relationships based on semantic interrelations.
- The "Timeline Interface" arranges content in parallel into various categories and time (x-, y-grid) in order to identify chronological relationships between different fields of content.
- The "Knowledge Explorer" is a more complex tool for communities of experts. Experts can use it to structure data pools, but also create personal knowledge maps and share them with other members of the community who can then tap into uncharted pools of information.

In the next stage of development, the tools will be personalised and made available for use online. The members of "netzspannung.org" can then use these to create personal knowledge maps based on their own content and an information pool they have selected themselves (Novak et al., 2002).

Below, the "Semantic Map" will be described in more detail as an example of knowledge discovery tools.

The "Semantic Map" is an interface, which evaluates and visualises semantic links between individual documents in the "netzspannung.org" database. Interactive visualisation provides an overview of the contexts and relationships between the data. It also gives access to individual documents that are then displayed in separate windows. For the conference entitled "cast01/living in mixed realities" (http://netzspannung.org/ cast01) organised by MARS, the "Semantic Map" serves as an overview of the conference contributions that can be used for research purposes. Figure 3 depicts the map's structure.

1. Each document is represented by a small blue square on the map.
2. Keywords provide information on the content of a cluster.
3. Documents with a greater number of content links are grouped in clusters.
4. The visualisation process is based on the Kohonen Map procedure: It connects all the documents to each other and arranges them in a two-dimensional grid according to their content links (cf., Kohonen, 2001).

Participation Space

The knowledge communication abilities of conventional desktop computers with their GUI interfaces following the WIMP paradigm (Windows, Icons, Menu, Pointing) are extremely limited, since they only take limited account of the person's inherent spatial sense of orientation and are largely unsuitable for collaborative learning on site.

The question of how online archives can be implemented on both metaphoric-virtual and physical-real levels as enterable and tangible knowledge spaces is answered by the Mixed Reality methods developed by MARS for penetrating and over-layering physical and electronic spaces. The "electronic Multi-User Stage Environment" (eMUSE) describes a mixed-reality space continuum in which an enterable audio archive, as an

Figure 3: "Semantic Map" Interface-Layers of Information and Data Processing

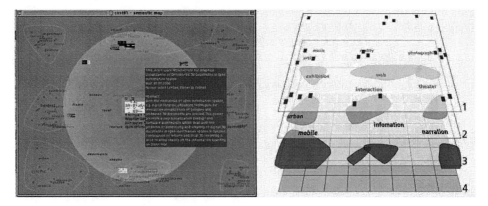

Figure 4: Imagine a Room Furnished with Data

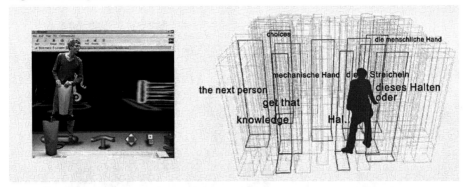

interactive sound space for multiple users, can create the impression of a concert room. The space appears as a room furnished with data (Strauss et al., 1999) (Figure 4).

Mixed Reality Installations

Mixed Reality offers the opportunity of converting 2D information structures into 3D ones. The notion of Mixed Reality was mentioned for the first time in 1994 by Paul Milgram and Fumio Kishino in their paper on Mixed Reality visual displays aiming to enhance the limited research field of Virtual Reality (1994). In contrast to classical, two-dimensional interfaces, users of mixed-reality installations are drawn into the centre of the proceedings. They are not transported into an alien world and morphed into a cyborg with data visors and data gloves, but instead move in a familiar action space with extended electronic functions.

With the performance installation "Murmuring Fields," MARS developed a Mixed Reality audio archive. Data spaces and action spaces are linked via an intuitive interface. In the interactive sound space known as "Murmuring Fields," participants can experience the sound of the virtual space through movement. They experience a space that they "play" with their bodies, as they would an instrument (Fleischmann et al., 2000) (Figure 5).

Based on the eMUSE technology developed in this project, MARS is adapting knowledge tools for the physical space under the title "the enterable knowledge space." In the initial studies, the recipients move over a "Semantic Map" covering the floor, and this now becomes a life-sized, enterable orientation landscape by virtue of the on-screen display (see Figure 6). The data space — now a three-dimensional archive — can be explored by moving through the space and making appropriate gestures. In an interactive, dynamic interchange, content (text, image, video, sound) is selected and depicted in the space.

Tangible Media Learning Objects

The term "'Tangible Media" (Ishii & Ulmer, 1997) describes the linking of physical objects and digital processes. Projects such as "Triangle" (Gorbet et al., 1998) show how computer applications that can only be displayed in a very abstract way on the screen can, when transferred to Tangible Interfaces, approximate more to human behaviour and

Figure 5: Layers of a Mixed Reality-Stage Installation

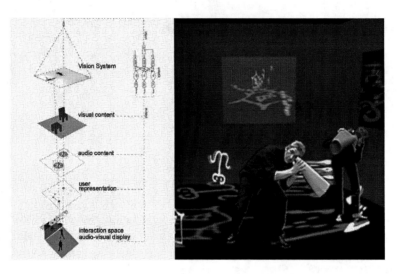

an intuitive understanding of things, thereby making these applications much more useful.

For learning in the pre-literal human development phase, educationalists from Pestalozzi to Montessori encourage learning objects that communicate facts on a concrete, material level. With developments of the MIT, such as "Digital Manipulatives" and computer-enhanced building bricks, etc., pre-school children can learn procedures that previously were regarded as too complex for this age group (Resnick et al., 1998). For the handling, classification and recall of media archive objects such as sound, image and video files, physical representations — i.e., reference objects that make contexts "tangible" in the physical space — can be extremely useful.

In 2002, "Soundgarten," a tangible media learning object that used play and easy-to-understand methods for managing media on a database was created at MARS. "Soundgarten" is a toy for explorative and formative learning using sound (Figure 7). It enables children to create their own sound environments by manipulating physical play

Figure 6: Enterable "Semantic Map" and Gesture Based "Timeline" Interface Control

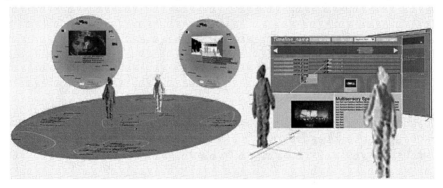

objects. Mushroom-shaped objects represent the individual sounds. Small leaf-shaped and flower-shaped attributes can be attached to these, which then function as filters to change the sound. In the "flowerbed" — or more technically, the base station — the collected sound sequences can be arranged and played through (Wolf, 2002).

As a type of "Lego for sound," it facilitates an explorative game with sounds. By enabling children to design personal sound spaces from variable elements, this promotes their motor, receptive and cognitive skills.

Mediation Space

The process of discovering and developing concepts for knowledge communication in digital cultures must extend beyond simply integrating new technical concepts, and must also investigate the social contexts of teaching and learning. MARS initiates experimental teaching events that examine classical teaching situations. The experiments discussed below using two examples contain cross-university, interdisciplinary and project/action-focused approaches in media culture education. In the classical education system, young people are still being educated using mostly verbally fixed thought and analysis methods. Even though this efficient teaching and learning method continues to be of fundamental significance, current developments in education are showing how important a knowledge of individual skills is in graphic-associative or kinaesthetic thinking in order to be able to exist in the media reality of our society (Svanaes, 1997).

Workshop Titled "I See What You Hear"

The MARS workshop entitled "I see what you hear" is an example of experimental, project-focused learning in heterogeneous workgroups (Figure 8). The participants at the teaching event comprised young people aged between 10 and 15 years, plus art and art therapy students. Working together as equal partners, they developed concepts for kinetic objects. Using the technical principles of the Theremin (http://www.thereminworld.com/) a series of small, interactive exhibition pieces were developed in the workshop. The workshop leaders were chiefly there for moderation purposes. The first stage for the total of eighteen participants involved only the students, who were introduced to the topic over workshops lasting seven days. Then came working groups

Figure 7: Elements of "Soundgarten"

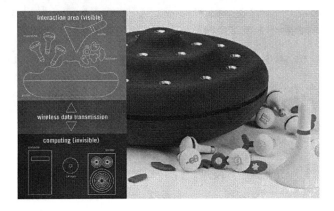

Figure 8: Workshop Activities: I See What You Hear

made up of one young person and one student in the practical part of the workshop. At the end, the results of their work were presented in a public exhibition (http://imk.gmd.de/ich-sehe-was-du-hoerst/reflection_english.html).

The link between practical work and reflection led to a playful and sensory workshop that gave the participants the opportunity to play an active part in designing the workshop content. The various methods of approach used by the groups, whose age and knowledge differed, and the interdisciplinary approach of integrating state-of-the-art information technology into an artistic and playful context gave rise to extremely productive potential for both sides. The bee flies over the flowery meadow which is humming with the sounds of summer and a mouse runs squeaking among the legs of the visitors. The workshop participants share the experience of independently creating the theremin circuit on a circuit board they have soldered themselves — along the lines "Think first, then solder."

Tele-Lectures

Universities are increasingly being faced with tighter budget restrictions. This makes it more difficult to cover interesting topics and bring eminent lecturers on board. The concept of a decentral network of auditoria from different universities is one attempt to address this problem: with "Tele-Lectures," MARS is linking the auditoria of several media and art colleges and universities via broadband Internet streaming to form a single telematic space. A lecture being given in one location is transferred to the auditoria of the other participating universities and moderated there. Discussions then follow. All lectures are also recorded and archived on "netzspannung.org." In contrast to conventional Internet TV broadcasters, the focus of the "Tele-Lectures" lies on the shared experience of live transmissions on the spot and the embedding of content in the context of university teaching.

The further development of the "Tele-Lectures" format focuses on the creation of a feedback channel which facilitates communication between the lecturer and the audience listening at the various locations. In the future, all auditoria will need to have the basic equipment for incoming and outgoing live transmissions. This infrastructure should facilitate an audio-visual exchange between universities that requires as little maintenance as possible and is easy to use. The "Mobile Unit" (Figure 9) of the MARS

Figure 9: Mobile Unit: Web-Cast Production Tool for Real-Time Workflow, Transformation, Capturing of Media Data

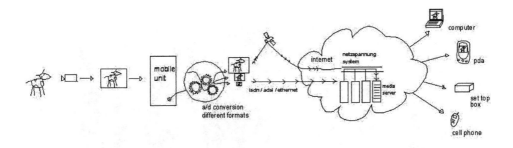

Lab functions as a mobile multimedia streaming laboratory prototype for the mobile classroom (Pfuhl & Peranovic, 2002).

OUTLOOK: MIXED-REALITY LEARNING ENVIRONMENTS

On its current projects, the MARS Exploratory Media Lab is planning to link the layers described in this chapter (information space, explorative space, participation space and mediation space) to form a single knowledge space for media culture education which bridges the digital and physical spaces.

"Mixed Reality Learning Environments" feature a high level of integration where the familiar physical environments and their everyday artefacts are extended by the possibilities of digital information and communication technologies. Concepts such as the "affordances" ("properties of the world that are compatible with and relevant for people's interactions") can be used in order to make electronic functions comprehensible and tangible, and to establish a "direct link between perception and action" (Gaver, 1991). The material and tangible environment with which we are familiar is used in order to facilitate access and interaction on both a cognitive and an emotional level. The structures and behavioural patterns that are linked to the space and the objects that surround us are adopted and expanded.

Alongside technical expertise, there is particular focus in these environments on architects' and product designers' expertise relating to the communication process. Various projects such as the "Designers' Outpost" at the University of Berkeley, to cite a recent example, have focused on these approaches for working environments. Designers' Outpost supports the structuring work of web designers who plan site maps with paper Post-Its, extends these Post-Its electronically and "combines the affordances of

Figure 10: The I2TV System Featuring a Distributed Speech-Play, Based on the Poem "Otto's Mops" by Ernst Jandl

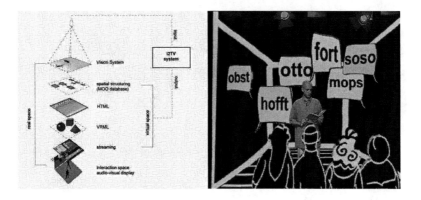

paper and a large physical workspace with the advantages of electronic media to support collaborative information design for the web" (Klemmer & Landay, 2001).

For learning environments, the comprehensive integration of different, heterogeneous media and media formats is as essential as the tactile, comprehensible and material environment. Live streams of audio and video files must also be supported, along with slide-based lectures. The environment must also actively support the creative work of learning groups (cf., e.g., Streitz et al., 1998).

The interactive Internet TV platform "I2TV" developed by MARS is designed as the technical basis for "Mixed Reality Learning Environments" (Figure 10). This platform's system architecture supports connections between different input and output media on-site and online. The I2TV System enables the combination of different levels of content representation, interaction and communication channels based on the situations on-site and online, and depending on bandwidth, input and display devices of individual users using a multi-layered system architecture (Novak et al., 2001).

"Mixed Reality Learning Environments" especially support playful and experimental learning and communicate media expertise as self-referencing content. Different scenarios that are aimed at different age groups are currently being checked out for their feasibility.

Kids' Playground

"Kids' Playground" provides a vehicle for creating and investigating innovative, networked infrastructures for playing, learning and therapeutic purposes. A Mixed Reality playground should offer children participatory and active learning through practical media experience (Figure 11). In workshops, children, students and professionals work together to design new games, mechanisms for supporting play, and interactive playthings. The locomotor system and gestures serve as a basis for interface concepts. The tangible media learning objects serve as ways of trying out new communication and play scenarios and, from the perspective of interactivity and cooperative action, to promote social competence, personal creativity and media expertise (cf., Bobick et al., 1999).

Figure 11: Example of a Mixed Reality Playground

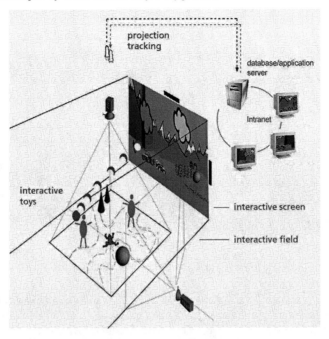

Mixed Reality Classroom

The concept of the "Mixed Reality Classroom" gives online and onsite learners and teachers the opportunity to meet at a specific time, at a specific location, and to generate knowledge in a collaborative way.

The centre of the room is a large board, which is written on with conventional chalk. The content is recorded, digitised and published live on the Internet (cf., Stafford-Fraser & Robinson, 1996; Abowd et al., 1996; Moran et al., 1999; Rojas et al., 2000). Superimposed projections on the board facilitate ad hoc interactions such as annotations, comments and remote publishing. Other projections on the floor or on tables, e.g., those of a personalised "Semantic Map," enable lecturers to navigate through their personal knowledge space in parallel to their lectures and obtain access to personal work-spaces. The classroom functions as a central communication interface. Individual users or groups in different locations can come together and participate. Knowledge maps can be created jointly and exchanged. The "Mixed Reality Classroom" is ideal for linking up multiple universities in shared "Tele-Lectures" (Figure 12).

Online/Onsite Campus

The "Online/Onsite Campus" is aimed at creating a coherent unit of infrastructure and infostructure at universities. Extending beyond the concept of the "Mixed Reality Classroom" (and on a larger scale), the various and extremely heterogeneous aspects of the infrastructure found at a university are linked together. The possibilities include networking stationary kiosk systems and mobile personal devices, publicly accessible

Figure 12: Mixed Reality Classroom Scenarios

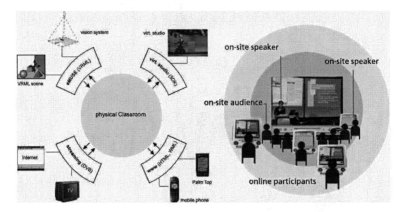

archives and private data resources, collectively used video beamers and personal workstations, in line with the information and action needs of the students and teachers (Figure 13).

A network that spans multiple universities and departments in this manner would also facilitate the interdisciplinary use of resources. It will also be possible to jointly develop approaches and communication concepts for interdisciplinary and media culture content (cf., Carrard & Engeli, 2001; Griswold et al., 2002).

CONCLUSION

The concept of the networked knowledge space is the central theme of this chapter, which presents the work and experiences to date of the MARS research group at the

Figure 13: Distribution and Accessibility of Media Objects (Digital Assets), e.g., the "Tele-Lectures": Wim Wenders on Campus

Fraunhofer Institute for Media Communication. Using the example of the Internet platform "netzspannung.org," a host of infrastructural measures was presented that offer a vehicle for activities in the field of e-learning and media culture education.

The "Knowledge Discovery Tools," with their opportunities for visualising information, the explorative investigation of large volumes of data and the creation of personal knowledge maps, represent a key navigation tool and method for sifting through and visualising the data space.

The limits of two-dimensional user interfaces are increasingly emerging as inadequate. The space that surrounds us, and the objects around us can, however, when given digital capacities, become an extended space — a Mixed Reality environment. The authors believe that the transition to the surrounding space, which becomes an interface, represents a key step towards giving humans the most intuitive access possible to information technologies.

Finally, reference is made to the significance of social contexts for communication concepts, without which learning and teaching is barely possible, even when prefixed with an "e-."

The outlook bundles together the concept of the knowledge space and introduces scenarios for "Mixed Reality Learning Environments" which pick up on all the tendencies mentioned previously - infrastructural measures, smart tools for delivering overviews, the extension of the space that surrounds us (Mixed Reality), and the significance of direct social interaction in groups.

REFERENCES

Abowd, G. et al. (1996). Teaching and learning as multimedia authoring: The classroom 2000 project. In *Proceedings of the Fourth ACM International Conference on Multimedia*, New York (pp. 187-198). New York: ACM Press.

Bobick, A. et al. (1999, August). The KidsRoom: A perceptually-based interactive and immersive story environment. *Presence: Teleoperators and Virtual Environments*, 8(4), 367-391.

Carrard, P., & Engeli, M. (2001). *ETH World Conceptual Competition: Virtual and Physical Presence*. Zuerich, Switzerland: GTA Verlag.

De Kerckhove, D. (1990). Virtuelle Realität für kollektive kognitive Verarbeitung. In G. Hattinger, M. Russel, C. Schöpf, & P. Weibel (Eds.), *Ars Electronica 1990 BAND II – Virtuelle Welten*. Retrieved December 18, 2002: http://www.aec.at/20jahre/archiv/19902/1990b_171.rtf.

Fleischmann, M., Strauss, W., & Novak, J. (2000). Murmuring Fields rehearsals: Building up the mixed reality stage. In R.J. Howlett & L.C. Jain (Eds.), *Proceedings of the Fourth International Conference on Knowledge-Based Intelligent Engineering Systems & Allied Technologies,* August/September 2000 (KES 2000) (Vol. 1, pp. 48-62). Brighton, UK: University of Brighton.

Gaver, W. (1991). Technology affordances. *Proceedings of Conference on Human Factors in Computing Systems*, CHI'91, New Orleans (pp. 79-84). New York: ACM Press.

Gorbet, M., Orth, M., & Ishii, H. (1998). Triangles: Tangible interface for manipulation and exploration of digital information topography. *Proceedings of Conference on Human Factors in Computing Systems*, CHI '98, Los Angeles (pp. 49-56). New York: ACM Press.

Griswold, W. et al. (2002). ActiveCampus: Sustaining educational communities through mobile technology (UCSD CSE technical report, CS2002-0714). La Jolla, CA: Department of Computer Science and Engineering, University of California San Diego.

Ishii, H., & Ullmer, B. (1997). Tangible bits: Towards seamless interfaces between people, bits and atoms. *Proceedings of Conference on Human Factors in Computing Systems*, CHI '97, Atlanta (pp. 234-241). New York: ACM Press.

Klemmer, S., & Landay, J. (2001). *Different strokes for different folks: A fluid toolbelt of paper, walls, and electronic sketching.* Workshop on tools, conceptual frameworks, and empirical studies for early stages of design, CHI '01, Seattle. Retrieved December 18, 2002 on the World Wide Web: http://guir.berkeley.edu/projects/outpost/OutpostCHIWorkshop.pdf.

Kohonen, T. (2001). *Self-Organizing Maps.* Berlin, Heidelberg, New York: Springer.

Kritzenberger, H., & Herzceg, M. (2001). Benutzer- und aufgabenzentrierte Lernumgebungen fuer das WWW. In H. Oberquelle, R. Oppermann, & J. Krause (Eds.), *Mensch und Computer 2001* (225-235). Stuttgart, Leipzig, Wiesbaden: Teubner.

Milgram, P., & Kishino, F. (1994, December). A taxonomy of mixed reality visual displays. *IEICE Transactions on Information Systems* (Special issue on networked reality), *E77-D* (12), 1321-1329.

Moran, T., Saund, E., Van Melle, W., Gujar, A., Fishkin, K., & Harrison, B. (1999). Design and technology for collaborates: Collaborative collages of information on physical walls. *Proceedings of the 12th Annual ACM Symposium on User Interface Software and Technology*, New York (pp. 197-206). New York: ACM Press.

Novak, J. et al. (2002). Augmenting the knowledge bandwidth and connecting heterogeneous expert communities through uncovering tacit knowledge. *Proceedings of 2002 IEEE Workshop on Knowledge Media Networking*, KMN 2002 (pp. 123-129). Kyoto, Japan: IEEE Computer Society Press.

Novak, J., Fleischmann, M., Strauss W., Seibert, C., & Peranovic, P. (2001). I2tv: A mixed reality communication interface. *Proceedings of Contel - 6th International Conference on Telecommunications, 2001* (pp. 237-244). Zagreb: Faculty of Electrical Engineering and Computing, University of Zagreb.

Panzini, K.J. (1999). *Kulturelle Bildung im Medienzeitalter. Materialien zur Bildungsplanung und Forschungsfoerderung* (Heft 77). Bonn: Bund-Laender-Kommisssion fuer Bildungsplanung und Forschungsfoerderung BLK.

Pfuhl, D., & Peranovic, P. (2002). Mobile streaming lab: Leading to a modular learning environment. *Proceedings of the Eighth International Conference on Virtual Systems and Multimedia: Creative Digital Culture*, VSMM 2002, Gyeongju, Korea (September 25-27, pp. 578-584). Seoul, Korea: Kiwissoft

Resnick, M. et al. (1998). Digital manipulatives: new toys to think with. *Proceedings of Conference on Human Factors in Computing Systems*, CHI '98, Los Angeles (pp. 281-287). New York: ACM Press.

Rojas, R., Knipping, L., Raffel, U., & Friedland, G. (2000). Elektronische Kreide: Eine Java-Multimedia-Tafel fuer den Praesenz- und Fernunterricht (Technical Report B-17/2000). Berlin: Institut fuer Informatik, Freie Universitaet Berlin.

Stafford-Fraser, Q., & Robinson, P. (1996). BrightBoard: A video augmented environment. *Proceedings of Conference on Human Factors in Computing Systems*, CHI '96, Vancouver (pp. 134-141). New York: ACM Press.

Strauss, W. et al. (1999). Staging the space of mixed reality: Reconsidering the concept of a multi-user environment. In *Proceedings of the Fourth Symposium on The Virtual Reality Modeling Language*, VRML 99 (February 23-26), Paderborn, Germany (pp. 93-98). New York: ACM Press.

Streitz, N., Konomi, S., & Burkhardt, H. (eds.). (1998). Cooperative buildings: Integrating information, organization and architecture. *Proceedings of the First International Workshop* (CoBuild'98), Darmstadt, Germany. Heidelberg: Springer (Lecture Notes in Computer Science, Vol. 1370).

Svanaes, D. (1997, December). Kinaesthetic thinking: The tacit dimension of interaction design. *Computers in Human Behaviour, 13*(4), 443-463.

Weibel, P. (ed.). (2002). *Vom Tafelbild zum globalen Datenraum. Neue Möglichkeiten der Bildproduktion und bildgebender Verfahren.* Ostfildern: Hatje Cantz.Wilson, S. (2002). *Information Arts: Intersections of Art, Science and Technology.* Cambridge, MA: London: MIT Press.

Wolf, M. (2002). *Soundgarten: A tangible interface that enables children to record, modify and arrange sound samples in a playful way.* University of Applied Sciences Cologne, Koeln International School of Design (Diplomarbeit – unpublished bachelor thesis).

Chapter XVIII

Development and Evaluation of a New HTML Browser Method of Presenting Reading Material for Students with Low Vision

Kazuhito Ujima, Matsuyama School for the Blind, Japan

Koichi Oda, Tokyo Woman's Christian University, Japan

ABSTRACT

Students with low vision or partial sight have a variety of vision needs and their needs are very different from student to student. Provision of suitable reading materials is still a difficult task. What we describe here is a novel method combining web-related technology and recent advancement in vision science. With reading tests by the MNREAD-J reading chart, we obtained parameters defining each student's vision needs. A newly developed software package called the HTML viewer generated a CSS layout data for each student according to the parameters. With this individually adjusted CSS, any web browser displays HTML documents in appropriate way for each student. Textbooks were prepared in HTML format and used with the HTML viewer. Evaluation in real classroom setting showed students were able to use this new method of reading efficiently without a prior knowledge of PC operation.

INTRODUCTION

There is a considerable variety in vision needs of students with low vision. Low vision is defined as vision status where daily living activities such as reading newspapers are difficult even after eye correction is made with spectacles (Faye, 1984). Usually, magnification of print greatly reduces the reading difficulty, but the appropriate print size differs depending on individual's vision needs; for example, one student needs 18 point print whereas the other requires much larger 28 point letters. The variation of vision needs is not confined to the size dimension. For a certain type of low vision, contrast reversal benefits reading, in other words, white text on dark background is more legible than the opposite and usual one (Legge et al., 1986). And, some other type prefers limited field of view for ease of navigation through pages. There are several alternatives in methods of providing reading materials to these students: (1) large print textbooks provided by the government, (2) enlarged copy by Xerox machines, (3) large print materials handwritten by volunteers, (4) normal print with optical reading aids or magnifiers (Zimmerman, 1996), (5) normal print with electronic reading aids such as closed circuit television systems (CCTV). Each method has its advantage and disadvantage, and recent methods are more flexible and adjustable to wider range of needs in general. For example, CCTVs were introduced in 1970s (Goodrich & Sacco, 1996) and are usually capable of changing the magnification power and reversing contrast polarity of text and background. Some models of CCTV show a slit on the screen through which only single text line is displayed at a time in order to make reading easier for persons with a certain type of low vision. Consequently, CCTV "is of particular importance, since it is the only device currently available that can provide variable magnification, good field of view, and variable contrast" (Goodrich & Bailey, 2000).

Not much mentioned in the literature, but simple personal computers (PCs) have introduced very flexible alternatives, such as e-books and web browsers. Although these browsers are not designed specially for the use of users with low vision, they can be very useful. Once reading materials are prepared in PDF or HTML format, which is not very difficult with off-the-shelf software packages, PCs turn into versatile reading aids. Firstly, ordinary web browsers, which one can obtain online free of charge, have a built-in capability to adjust to users' special vision needs, that is, variable text size and adjustable color combination of text and background. Secondly, words wrap around to fit in the web browser window and one does not have to navigate the text horizontally, even with very large text size. This feature makes it much easier to browse enlarged text with web browsers than with the other computerized method. A recent computerized CCTV system scans the printed text and shows optically recognized text on the monitor in the same word-wrap mode (Rosenthal & Williams, 2000). But, wrap-round mode is universal in web browsers and one does not have to have a specialized CCTV for it. Thirdly, hypertext features greatly reduce the burden which persons with low vision experience in navigating through pages. In summary, the computerized alternatives, especially web browsers, have strong advantages in tailoring reading materials for students with a wide range and different types of vision needs.

Even if there are powerful and flexible reading aids, they are useless until they are appropriately adjusted to individual's vision needs. Recent progress in vision science revealed that objective reading measurement is effective in determination of vision needs quantitatively and in predicting the types of reading aids for individuals (Ahn & Legge,

1995). Visual requirements of reading, especially print size and contrast polarity, are easily and precisely measured with the MNREAD reading acuity charts. The MNREAD reading acuity charts were developed by the Low Vision Laboratory of University of Minnesota (Legge et al., 1989). The Japanese version of the MNREAD chart, named MNREAD-J (Oda et al., 1989), was used in this study. A series of simple sentences of fixed length are printed with systematically changing print sizes in the MNREAD charts. Usually letters are printed black on white background, whereas white letters are printed on a black card in the reversed contrast chart. With the MNREAD charts, students are asked to read sentences aloud as fast and precisely as possible and her/his reading time and errors are recorded. Figure 1 shows the typical data plot along with the reading chart. As long as the print size is large enough for an individual, reading speed is fairly constant. This constant reading rate is usually the maximum reading speed (MRS) one can achieve when the condition is good. However when print becomes smaller than a certain size, reading suddenly becomes difficult and its rate rapidly decreases. This certain size is called critical print size (CPS), and is very important in determining appropriate print size for an individual (Mansfield et al., 1996). CPS for persons with low vision is generally larger than usual print size of newspapers and textbooks. This makes persons with low vision disabled to read ordinary texts. In other words, when print size is enlarged up to CPS of a person with low vision, s/he can read any text fluently in her/his maximum reading speed. It should be emphasized that vision needs of each student have to be measured individually and precisely and the environment has to be adjusted according to the needs so that s/he could make full use of their potential abilities. Such objective reading evaluation facilitates determination of vision needs of each student and provides an objective measure to evaluate effectiveness of aids and methods.

Figure 1: Typical Reading Speed Function and Three Parameters Together with the MNREAD-J Reading Chart (Black dots are typical reading speed data plotted at the corresponding print size of the chart.)

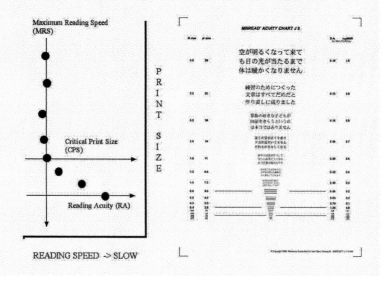

In this chapter, we describe a new method of presenting reading materials for students with low vision, where we combined the web browser with the objective reading evaluation and developed a software package to construct a realistic and integrated way of providing teaching materials in schools for the blind. We first compared students' efficiency in reading and page navigation between large print paper and materials displayed in the web browser window. Then we developed a software package named "HTML viewer" to make full use of HTML technology. Lastly, we evaluated its effectiveness in real teaching situations.

COMPARISON EXPERIMENT

There was a general concern that reading on a PC screen would be not efficient compared to large print on paper. We first tried to find out if reading was slow on screen, and how hyperlinks of HTML could help students navigate through pages.

Method

Thirty pages of different reading materials were prepared. They were taken from primary school textbooks of first through third grade levels and each page had about 100 letters. They were divided into three blocks and one page of table of contents (TOC), listing titles and corresponding page numbers, was added at the beginning of all three blocks. One block of materials were printed on separate sheets of paper and named "paper condition." The second block was displayed on a PC's screen one page at a time with the web browser Microsoft's Internet Explorer and named "HTML condition." The last block was both printed on paper and displayed on the PC's screen for use in practice before the experiment. To eliminate the effect of reading materials' contents, the first block was printed on paper for one half of subjects, and displayed on screen for the other half and the second block vice versa.

Print size was determined for each subject with the MNREAD-J reading acuity test and set equal to CPS on individual basis for both paper and screen. This ensured that sufficient print size was provided in both methods of display. Center-to-center spacing between letters and lines was fixed proportionally to 150% of each subject's print size. The background luminance was 79.3 candle/m^2 on the paper surface and 99.4 candle/m^2 on the CRT screen. The Michaelson contrast of letter against background was more than 70% for both conditions and letters were displayed black on white background.

Subject was first shown a page — not TOC page — and asked to read aloud the material as fast and precisely as possible and reading time and errors were recorded by the experimenter. At the end of each reading material, the title of the next test material was printed. Subject then had to go to the TOC page and find the page number to which s/he moved and repeated the reading. This page navigation time was also recorded. In HTML condition, the TOC page had hyperlinks to material pages and subjects could click the title anchor to move to the next test page. At the bottom line of the test pages there were anchors to the TOC page in HTML condition, but no link was provided directly to the next test page.

Students enrolled in the Matsuyama School for the Blind participated as subjects with consent to the experiment. Subject's profile, such as age, cause of low vision, visual

Table 1: Subjects' Profile in Comparison Experiment

Age	Cause of Low Vision	Acuity (Decimal)	Visual Field Defects	Glare	CPS (logMAR)	PC Experience (yrs)
24	Open Angle Glaucoma, Optic Nerve Atrophy, Severe Myopia and Astigmatism	0.2			1	none
22	Coloboma uveae	0.02	Peripheral	Glare	1.1	10
37	Diabetic Retinopathy and Cataract	0.2	Peripheral	Glare	1	none
50	Hyperopic Astigmatism	0.2	Peripheral	Glare	0.9	none
22	Albinism	0.15		Glare	0.7	10
19	Aphakia	0.15	Peripheral		0.9	5
19	Microphthalmia and Cataract	0.3	Peripheral		1.1	1
19	Aniridia	0.1	Peripheral	Glare	1.1	none
26	Retinitis Pigmentosa	0.2	Peripheral	Glare	0.5	1
32	Macular Degeneration	0.1	Peripheral	Glare	1.1	2
44	Macular Degeneration	0.15	Peripheral	Glare	1.1	20
21	Retinitis Pigmentosa	0.06	Peripheral	Glare	1.18	7

acuity, glare, visual field status, and experience of PC is shown in Table 1. They were all native Japanese and had no additional impairment other than vision. They observed reading materials at 30 cm distance, which was the same distance where the MNREAD-J reading test was administered. The experiment was conducted in a lit classroom and the whole session took about 30 minutes for a subject.

Result and Discussion

Reading speed was calculated as correctly read letters divided by reading time for each page in each condition and for each subject. Average reading speed was 309.1 character/minute with standard deviation of 96.3 character/minute for paper condition, and 301.0 character/minute with standard deviation of 84.2 character/minute for HTML condition. Two-way ANOVA showed no difference in reading speed between paper and

Table 2: Averages and Results of Two-Way ANOVA

a). For Reading Speed

condition	Average	SD(character/minute)
Paper	309.06	96.30
HTML	301.04	84.16

Factor	SS	df	MS	Prob
Condition	386.2	1	386.2	0.590863192 n.s.
Subject	189091.5	11	17190.1	
error	7190.0	11	653.6	
Total	196667.7	23		

b). For Page Navigation Time

condition	Average	SD (second)
Paper	152.49	54.79
HTML	107.56	27.90

Factor	SS	df	MS	Prob
Condition	12113.6	1	12113.6	11.20743501 **
Subject	33473.9	11	3043.1	
error	11889.4	11	1080.9	
Total	57476.9	23		

HTML condition (Table2a). This result shows that once reading material is provided in CPS-sized print, one can read at its best speed regardless of the display media. Also, it is shown that as long as a simple reading task with HTML browsers is concerned, the length of PC use does not make any difference. Detailed look into the individual data implicates that there would be some more to be explained, such as that some of subjects who had glare read faster with paper which was less bright, for we did not use reversed contrast display, i.e., white letters on dark background, for HTML condition.

Page navigation time was determined as time taken by subject from when s/he read the next test material's title up to when s/he reached the target page. Average time was 152.5 seconds with standard deviation of 54.8 seconds for paper condition, and 107.6 seconds with standard deviation of 27.9 seconds for HTML condition. This difference was statistically significant (Table 2b). This difference should be inarguably attributed to the hyperlink's advantage in HTML condition. Students did not have to turn pages to reach the target page in HTML condition. Although this comparison does not look fair, it is evident that the hyperlink feature greatly reduces navigation load for students with low vision.

In summary, reading materials on a PC screen with HTML browsers was as equally efficient as reading traditional large print materials, and navigation was significantly easier with HTML browsers. With cost of adjustment for each student's vision needs in mind, in other words white letters on black background is very costly with paper, and also very large print is not cost effective with paper, the HTML browser method is very promising.

DEVELOPMENT OF THE HTML VIEWER

The largest disadvantage of the HTML method is that the preparation of HTML materials is not easy, especially if we want to develop them to suit students with low vision. However, this disadvantage is not so discouraging. There are more and more materials provided in HTML format on the net, and some word processing software has the capability to save documents in HTML format. Increasing numbers of classic works, scientific findings, journals, newspapers and government documents are published everyday in HTML. There is a separate method called cascading style sheet (CSS) to define layout information, in addition to HTML language. In order to make web documents more accessible, World Wide Web Consortium or W3C (1999) recommends the use of CSS to control layouts. Here we make use of CSS in a more active way. CSS enables the adjustment part for individual students' vision needs maintained and used separately from the reading content information. Once a style sheet is written for a student, it could be used repeatedly with all HTML documents. CSS is usually used to keep related documents uniform in appearance. We use this to make all documents appear equally readable for each student. Hence, if we develop a method to incorporate an individual's vision needs into HTML document via CSS, any simple HTML browser could be used as an individually catered display aid for students with low vision.

The HTML viewer, which we developed, is a collection of software. The core part is a Javascript program to generate a CSS for a student. It works just like a simple CSS written at the beginning of HTML documents. However, it is not a simple CSS program, which is a fixed collection of layout information. We have to prepare different CSS

Figure 2: Relationship of CSS and the HTML Viewer's Core Javascript

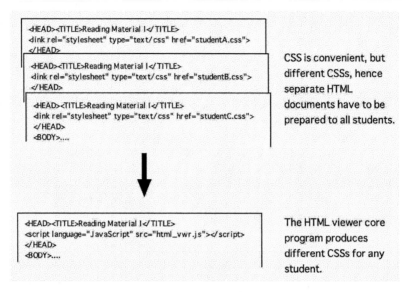

programs for each student and add these different CSS programs to HTML documents every time we present materials to students. Instead of simple CSS, a Javascript program was developed which works for any student. This reduces a great amount of work in preparation of CSS for each student, as a single HTML would suffice for all students (Figure 2).

The core program generates a CSS according to individual student's vision needs and returns the CSS to the browser. So, to the HTML browsers the program looks just like CSS program with the same name, but its content is different when a different student is reading the document. It obtains the individual's vision needs' information via cookie. A separate HTML program was developed to help students save their vision needs information into the HTML browser's cookie. If the core program finds there is no data available, it sets default data into a cookie and produces a CSS according to it. Once a student goes through the adjustment session with the HTML program, appropriate data is placed in the cookie and the core program starts to generate appropriate CSS for her/ him with all HTML materials (Figure 3 and 4). The HTML viewer core program produces CSS description, which specifies: (1) print size, (2) text and background color combination (contrast reversal), (3) letter spacing, (4) line spacing, (5) line length, (6) font style of a HTML document when viewed with HTML browsers. Moreover, we added a feature to the HTML viewer package, which incorporates the MNREAD-J's reading evaluation. This addition reduces the effort of trial and errors in determining the most suitable display layout for a student.

With the HTML viewer package, preparation of reading materials in HTML format became very simple and easy. Simple and minimum markings with HTML tags are sufficient to prepare the reading materials, or one can export a word processor's file into

Figure 3: Diagram of How the Core Program of HTML Viewer Works

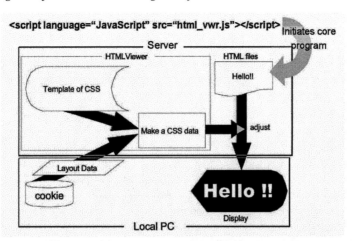

HTML format. Adding the following line in the <HEAD> part of the HTML document makes the core program effective for the document:

<script language="JavaScript" src="html_vwr.js"></script>

The same HTML document could be used by all students with a wide variation of visual needs. In cooperation with teachers in schools for the blind all over Japan, we have started to accumulate HTML materials for teaching. And, thanks to the fact that HTML

Figure 4: User's View of How the HTML Viewer Package Works (Only mode setting page(right) is visible)

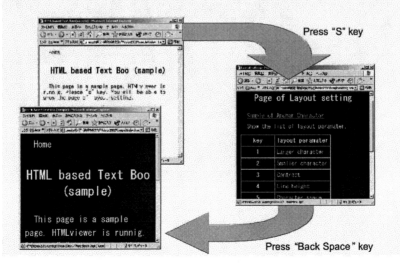

and CSS are text-based technology, even blind teachers are able to make their teaching materials suitable for students with low vision.

FIELD EVALUATION

Previously described comparison experiment revealed that HTML browser method was sufficiently efficient and useful in reading multiple pages of materials. Here we describe how we use the HTML viewer package in the real life classroom and the results of field evaluation. As we have a limited number of applications for the latest version of the HTML viewer, only three cases are reported.

Before the application of the HTML viewer, we evaluated each student's visual needs with the MNREAD-J reading acuity chart and determined CPS and contrast polarity appropriate for each student. Starting with the reading evaluation data as initial settings, we adjusted the display mode of a HTML browser for each student with the HTML viewer package, which included the core Javascript and the setting HTML page. This setting page had an interactive and intuitive interface and was not difficult to work with for novice PC users (Figure 4). Once the setting was done, each student's display mode data was stored in the HTML browser's cookie. Each time s/he used the HTML browser to surf pages of teaching materials, they appeared always in the same suitable way according to the data stored in the cookie. In order to evaluate if the HTML viewer method was truly helping students reading, we measured reading speed of classroom tasks and compared it with result of the initial MNREAD-J's evaluation after two weeks of use (Figure 5).

Case A was a female student in her late 20s with Retinitis Pigmentosa. The visual acuity was 0.1 in right and 0.2 in left eye with black Landolt rings. It was 0.2 in right and

Figure 5: Three Cases of Field Evaluation

0.25 in left eye when white rings were presented on the black background. She had 5 degrees of visual field left in the central retina in both eyes. Her CPS was 18 point at 30 cm and 159.4 character/minute was her maximum reading speed (MRS) in the initial reading evaluation. In setting of the display mode, her best setting turned out to be 28 point in reversed contrast. Two weeks after the introduction of the HTML viewer, her maximum reading speed was 223.9 character/minute. The fact that she had almost no experience in PC use did not prevent her from using the HTML viewer in reading.

Case B was a male student in his late 20s with a brain tumor. His visual acuity was none in right and 0.15 in left eye with black Landolt rings on white background. His left eye had hemianopia in temporal side. Initial reading evaluation with the MNREAD-J showed that his CPS was 28 point at 30 cm and MRS was 141.7 character/minute. In the setting session of the HTML viewer, his best setting was 22 point white letters on black background at observation distance of 20 cm. In two weeks after the introduction of the HTML viewer, his MRS was 141.1 character/minute with the HTML viewer. Although he did not have previous PC experience, his reading efficiency did not decline with the HTML viewer when appropriately adjusted.

Case C is a male student in his 50s with very advanced Retinitis Pigmentosa. His visual acuity was 0.01 in the right eye and none in left eye with white Landolt rings on black background. He had a very severe difficulty in reading print and did not complete the reading evaluation. Fortunately, he was quite fluent in PC operation, and capable to switch from visual interface to audio interface with screen readers. He occasionally used the HTML viewer to visually confirm Chinese characters on the screen, as many Chinese characters share the same sound but have different meanings. The unsuccessful reading evaluation had an effect of encouraging him to change operation modality.

CONCLUSION

Three cases mentioned in the field evaluation let us conclude that our procedure, together with the HTML viewer package, was a successful and efficient alternative of presenting teaching and reading materials in the education for students with low vision. With paper media, large print materials are costly in every resource, including time, money, paper, and manpower. While optical aids and CCTVs make good alternatives, a more advanced and flexible device, a PC equipped with HTML browsers, has been increasingly becoming a very strong alternative. Here, in order to seek for a future possibility, we combine two very promising key components, i.e., objective reading evaluation to determine vision needs of individuals, and the universal display media realized by HTML, CSS, and web browsers. The combination has been successful in real school teaching, although it could be further improved in many ways.

For example, one unsolved problem with this HTML viewer is that you have to add a line of program to every HTML material in order to make the HTML viewer more effective. If we take all materials on the Net into account, it is not realistic to do it by hand. It could be solved easily if we could use transcoding servers. It would be good to have portal sites for readers with special vision needs, which add the line and provide all pages in the HTML viewer format. Another unsolved problem is that adding a line to or altering layout of a document raises the issue of copyright laws.

Whatever the remaining problems are, the method we described here proved that useful technologies are out there and we could make use of them in order to make special education more fruitful. It indicates that two key elements, objective reading evaluation and HTML technology, will make an innovation in education for students with low vision.

ACKNOWLEDGMENTS

This chapter is a continuation of what was presented at "Vision 2002," the 7th International Conference on Low Vision Activity and Participation held in Gothenburg, Sweden, July 2002. Supported by the Grand-in-Aid from the Japanese Ministry of Health, Labor, and Welfare.

REFERENCES

Ahn, S.J., & Legge, G.E. (1995). Psychophysics of reading (XIII). Predictors of magnifier-aided reading speed in low vision. *Vision Research, 35*, 1931-1938.

Faye, E. (1984). *Clinical Low Vision*. New York: Little Brown & Company.

Goodrich, G.L., & Bailey, I.L. (2000). A history of the field of vision rehabilitation for the perspective of low vision. In B. Silverstone, M.A. Lang, B.P. Rosenthal, & E.E. Faye (Eds.), *The Lighthouse Handbook on Vision Impairment and Vision Rehabilitation* (pp. 675-715). New York: Oxford University Press.

Goodrich, G.L., & Sacco, T. (1996). Visual function with high-tech low vision devices. In R.G. Cole & B.P. Rosenthal (Eds.), *Remediation and Management of Low Vision* (pp. 197-210). St. Louis, Missouri: Mosby-Year Book.

Legge, G.E., Ross, J.A., Luebker, A., & LaMay, J.M. (1989). Psychophysics of reading (VIII). The Minnesota low-vision reading test. *Optometry and Vision Science, 66*, 843-853.

Legge, G.E., Rubin, G.S., & Schleske, M.M. (1986). Contrast polarity effects in low vision reading. In G. Woo (Ed.), *Low Vision: Principles and Applications* (pp. 288-307). New York: Springer-Verlag.

Mansfield, J.S., Legge, G.E., & Bane, M.C. (1996). Psychophysics of reading (XV). Font effects in normal and low vision. *Investigative Ophthalmology & Visual Science, 37*, 1492-1501.

Oda, K., Mansfield, J.S, & Legge, G.E. (1998). A new reading chart to prescribe low vision reading aids named MNREAD-J. In *Proceedings of the 7th Convention of the Japanese Association for Rehabilitation of the Visually Impaired* (pp. 157-160).

Rosenthal, B.P., & Williams, D.R. (2000). Devices primarily for people with low vision. In B. Silverstone, M.A. Lang, B.P. Rosenthal, & E.E. Faye (Eds.), *The Lighthouse Handbook on Vision Impairment and Vision Rehabilitation* (pp. 951-981). New York: Oxford University Press.

World Wide Web Consortium. (1999). Web Content Accessibility Guidelines 1.0. Retrieved from the World Wide Web: http://www.w3.org/TR/WCAG10/.

Zimmerman, G.J. (1996). Optics and low vision devices. In A.J. Corn & A.J. Koenig, (Eds.), *Foundation of Low Vision: Clinical and Functional Perspectives* (pp. 115-142). New York: AFB Press.

Chapter XIX

A Sign Language Teaching System Using Sign Language Recognition and Generation Methods

Hirohiko Sagawa, Hitachi, Ltd., Japan

Masaru Takeuchi, Hitachi, Ltd., Japan

ABSTRACT

We have developed a sign language teaching system that uses sign language recognition and generation methods to overcome three problems with current learning materials: a lack of information about non-manual gestures (facial expressions, glances, head movements, etc.), display of gestures from only one or two points of view, and a lack of feedback about the correctness of the learner's gestures. Experimental evaluation by 24 non-hearing-impaired people demonstrated that the system is effective for learning sign language.

INTRODUCTION

Sign language is widely recognized in Japan as an important method of communication for hearing-impaired people. To support the daily life of hearing-impaired people, the number of hearing people who can communicate using sign language has to be increased.

While there are many materials for learning sign language, including textbooks, videotapes and PC software, these materials have three problems. First, they contain little information about non-manual gestures. In sign language, non-manual gestures, such as facial expressions, glances and head movements, are as important as manual gestures. Second, the learners can see the gestures from only one or two points of view. Many learners want to see them from various points of view. Third, the learners get no feedback on the correctness of their own gestures. Learners not only have to study sign language by observing and studying signed gestures, but they also have to practice. The materials should thus give them feedback about correctness of their gestures.

Our group previously developed a sign language recognition method that recognizes Japanese Sign Language (JSL) gestures and translates them into Japanese text (Sagawa et al., 1998; Sagawa & Takeuchi, 2000; Sagawa et al., 2001). Our group also developed a sign language generation method that translates Japanese text into JSL and displays it as a three-dimensional computer graphics (3DCG) animation (Sakiyama et al., 1994; Sakiyama et al., 1996). The sign language recognition method calculates the similarity between the inputted sign language gesture and the gesture data stored in a system. It can also be used to evaluate the correctness of an inputted sign language gesture. The 3DCG animation generated by the sign language generation method enables the gesture to be freely viewed from different perspectives and the size of the CG character in the animation to be freely changed. These features facilitate the learning of sign language.

We have now developed a sign language teaching system that uses the sign language recognition and generation methods to enable effective sign language study. Experimental evaluation by 24 non-hearing-impaired people demonstrated that the developed system is effective for learning sign language.

BACKGROUND

It is now widely recognized in Japan that sign language is an effective method of communication for hearing-impaired people, particularly as they participate more actively in society. Hearing-impaired people often communicate with hearing people through a sign language interpreter because most hearing people cannot understand sign language. However, interpreter support is not always available because the number of interpreters is limited and their services are in great demand. Hearing-impaired people also communicate with hearing people by writing the text on paper and by reading the lip motion of the person talking to them. However, they often have trouble understanding written or spoken language because there are not only differences in the means of expression but also in the grammar between sign language and spoken or written language. Therefore, many hearing-impaired people encounter communication problems in their daily lives.

To facilitate communication between hearing-impaired and hearing people, we have developed a system to automatically translate between Japanese Sign Language and Japanese language. It uses sign language recognition and generation methods we previously developed. The sign language recognition method translates gestures inputted into a computer through a glove-based input device into Japanese sentences. The gesture primitives, such as the hand shape, the palm direction, the linear motion, and the circular motion are detected from the inputted data. The template of a sign language word has been described as a set of gesture primitives, and a word is recognized by integrating the detected primitives based on the template (Sagawa et al., 1998). The meanings of the recognized sign language words are identified, and a Japanese sentence is created by adding appropriate Japanese postpositional particles (Sagawa & Takeuchi, 2000). We have also developed methods for analyzing the representations; they use the spatial relationships and head gestures to recognize the sign language grammar (Sagawa et al., 2001).

The sign language generation method displays a sign language animation using three-dimensional computer graphics (3DCG); it combines the gesture data for sign language words created from the data inputted from the glove-based input device (Sakiyama et al., 1994, 1996). We have also developed a system to edit sign language animations that facilitates their creation (Hitachi, Ltd., 2000). This system stores the gesture data for sign language words and has a table showing the correspondence between the gesture data and Japanese words. The user inputs a sequence of the Japanese words, and the system automatically generates the sign language animation by reading the gesture data corresponding to each word in the sequence. The user can create a natural sign language animation by modifying the generated gesture data and by adding other gestures such as facial expressions and head movements. The newest version of this system can translate Japanese into signed Japanese to support the creation of the sign language animation.

The sign language translation system is still being improved, and it will be many years before it is ready for practical use. However, hearing-impaired people need communication support now.

Another approach to improving communication between hearing-impaired people and hearing people is to increase the number of hearing people who can understand sign language by promoting sign language education. A common way to study sign language is to take a lecture class. However, many people cannot take a lecture class because the number of participants is limited or they do not have the time. So they often study sign language on their own.

There are several types of materials for learning sign language: textbooks, dictionaries, videotapes, and PC software. Many hearing people also use these materials because learning using these materials is easy and does not limit when or where the studying is done. However, there are several problems with learning sign language effectively using these teaching materials.

In this chapter, we will survey existing teaching materials for sign language and discuss why they are problematic for learning sign language. We will focus on PC-based teaching material software and propose a system for effectively studying sign language using our sign language recognition and generation methods. We will also describe the experiment we conducted to evaluate its effectiveness and present some of the results.

SIGN LANGUAGE IN JAPAN

The sign language used in Japan can be classified into three types (Kanda, 1994).
1.   **Signed Japanese.** Sign language words corresponding to Japanese words are signed using manual gestures in the same order as the Japanese words are

represented. The postpositional particles are also shown, either by manual gestures or changes in the shape of the mouth, depending on the circumstances. Signed Japanese is also called SIMCOM (simultaneous communication) because it is represented with Japanese speech. Signed Japanese is linguistically regarded as a simple representation of Japanese, not as sign language.

2. **Japanese Sign Language (JSL).** JSL is used mainly by people with innate hearing impairment to communicate with each other. JSL grammar differs from that of Japanese.

3. **Intermediate Sign Language.** Intermediate sign language is a representation method in which characteristic expressions in JSL are introduced into signed Japanese.

The borders between these types of sign language are not clear-cut, and there is some ambiguity between them. This classification can also be applied to the sign languages used in other countries.

Signed Japanese is easy to learn for hearing people because it is based on Japanese. Therefore, it is often taught in lecture classes. However, signed Japanese is incomplete, and the word usage in signed Japanese often differs from that in JSL. As a result, hearing-impaired people often cannot understand the sign language used by hearing people.

We focus our attention on JSL because our purpose is to develop a sign language teaching system to support communication between hearing-impaired and hearing people.

The characteristics of JSL are as follows:

1. **Continuous gestures.** Sign language sentences are constructed by continuously combining sign language words, as in spoken language.

2. **Multimodal language.** JSL is represented using not only manual gestures but also non-manual gestures such as facial expressions and head movements. The sign language word corresponding to a concept is represented using the manual gestures; the non-manual gestures mainly convey grammatical information.

Figure 1: JSL for "I See a Flying Airplane"

3. **Simultaneous representations.** Two types of sign language words can be simultaneously represented by making independent gestures with each hand. For example, the sentence "I see a flying airplane" can be represented by representing "see" using the right hand and "airplane" using the left hand at the same time, as shown in Figure 1.

4. **Spatial representations.** Spatial relationships between sign language words are often used in typical JSL sentences. For example, in Figure 2(a), the direction of the motion in "speak" is from the position where "he" was represented to the position where "she" was represented. The meaning is "he speaks to her." If the direction of motion is reversed, as shown in Figure 2(b), the meaning becomes "she speaks to him."

The system for teaching JSL has to include functions that teach these characteristics of JSL effectively and easily. Especially important is learning the non-manual gestures and spatial representations used to represent the grammar.

PROBLEMS WITH EXISTING MATERIALS FOR LEARNING SIGN LANGUAGE

Teaching materials generally used to study sign language are textbooks (Kimura & Ichida, 1995), dictionaries (Japanese Federation of the Deaf, 1997; Sternberg, 1994), videotapes (NHK Software Inc., 2001), and software for PCs (IBM Japan, Ltd., 1995; LITEC Co., Ltd., 1996; Higher Learning Systems, Inc., 2000; The Communication Technology Laboratory, 1995). However, textbooks cannot fully display hand motions, which are the key feature of sign language. Videotapes and PC software overcome this problem by showing video images of sign language gestures, enabling the learner to study the natural motion of sign language. However, gestures with movement forward and backward can be hard to understand because many materials show the gestures only from the front. Furthermore, the video images require a lot of storage space, so the number of sign language gestures that can be stored on a videotape or CD-ROM is limited.

PC software using 3DCG animation overcomes these problems (Vcom3D, Inc., 2000). The learner can freely change the direction and size of the CG character in the animation. In addition, more gestures can be included in the material because 3DCG animation requires less storage space than video images.

Figure 2: Examples of Spatial Representation

    (a) "He speaks to her."   (b) "She speaks to him."

PC software using 3DCG animation is thus excellent teaching material for sign language. However, three problems remain.

1. *There is little information about non-manual gestures.*

   In sign language, including JSL, non-manual gestures, such as facial expressions, glances, and head movements, are as important as manual gestures because they often convey grammatical information. While these non-manual gestures are often presented in the illustrations and video images in existing teaching materials, learners have trouble understanding them because the explanations are not complete.

2. *Learners get no feedback on their gestures.*

   Learners study sign language not only by observing and studying signed gestures but also by expressing the gestures by themselves. However, existing teaching materials give the learners no feedback on the correctness of their gestures. For effective learning of sign language, the software should be able to evaluate the learner's gestures and give feedback.

3. *The meaning of a sign language word cannot be searched for based on the gesture used.*

   Beginning sign language learners usually encounter sign language gestures for which they do not know the meaning. Existing teaching materials can search for the sign language word for a word in a written language, but they cannot search for a word in a written language for a sign language gesture.

Previous work has applied a method for recognizing finger spellings to sign language teaching. This system estimates the learner's finger spellings inputted from a glove-based input device and shows a 3DCG animation of the hand gesture to indicate any mistaken part intelligibly (Tabata et al., 1999). However it is difficult to apply this system to the learning of usual sign language because it cannot evaluate motion, which is a key feature of sign language.

We have developed a system for teaching sign language that uses our sign language recognition and generation methods to overcome these problems.

SIGN LANGUAGE TEACHING SYSTEM
System Structure

The structure of the sign language teaching system we have developed is shown in Figure 3, and the components of the system are shown in Figure 4. The sign language recognition part estimates sign language gestures inputted using a glove-based input device. A previously described method (Sagawa & Takeuchi, 2000) is used to evaluate the gestures. In the sign language generation part, sign language animation using 3DCG is generated based on the information stored in the contents for sign language education. The contents for sign language education include information about the conversation in Japanese sign language. The control part controls the sign language recognition part, the sign language generation part, and the display part based on the contents for sign language education and the actions of the learner.

An example screen image of the system is shown in Figure 5. Area (1) is used to display the sign language animation. The buttons and sliders in area (2) are used to start

Figure 3: Structure of Sign Language Teaching System

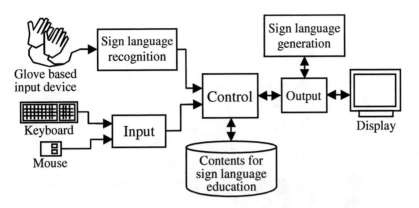

and stop the animation and to change the direction and size of the CG character in the animation. Examples are shown in Figure 6 of changing the direction of the animation. Area (3) in Figure 5 is used to display the information about the sign language sentences that constitutes the conversation in the contents for sign language education. Information about the speaker, the Japanese sentence, the manual gestures, and the non-manual gestures is displayed for each sign language sentence. This information is described in more detail in the next section. Area (4) is used to show a description of the conversation and each sentence. Button (5) is used to display the sign language animation for the conversation. Button (6) is used to start practicing the sign language expressions in a dialog form wearing the glove-based input device. The learner can practice the sign language expression for the sign language sentence or the sign language word that the learner selected by using button (7). Button (8) is used to return to the menu screen. The learner can choose the sentence or the word to be displayed on the screen by using the

Figure 4: Components of Sign Language Teaching System

Figure 5: Example Screen Image of Sign Language Teaching System

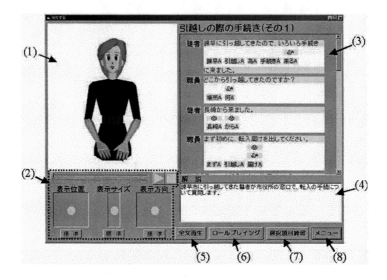

mouse and can view the sign language animation and the explanation for a sentence or a word.

Characteristics

Displaying Information About Manual and Non-Manual Gestures

In this system, a sign language sentence is described as a set of manual and non-manual gestures to enable the student to learn the grammatical expressions in Japanese sign language. The description is in XML, so it can also be used on the Internet. An example description is shown in Figure 7; the tags are defined as follows:

<slsentence> indicates a sign language sentence.

<jsentence> is a Japanese sentence corresponding to the sign language sentence.

<hand> specifies a sequence of sign language words represented by manual gestures.
   Each gesture represents one sign language word.

<hname> indicates the name of a sign language word. The label specified by the attribute
   "id" is used to refer to the word in the description for the sign language sentence.
   The attribute "frame" specifies the number of frames needed to display the
   animation for the sign language word.

<eyebrow> represents a sequence of eyebrow gestures.

<ebname> indicates the name of an eyebrow gesture. The start and end times of the
   gesture are specified as the value of the attribute "pos"; the format is as follows:
      pos="label1:frame1,label2:frame2"
   The "label1:frame1" indicates the start time of the eyebrow gesture, and the
   "label2:frame2" is the end time. The "label1" and "label2" are the labels for the sign
   language words, and the "frame1" and "frame2" are the relative frames from the start
   time of the sign language word.

Figure 6: Example of Changing Perspective of Sign Language Animation

(a) Front view   (b) Right-hand side view

(c) Diagonal left upper view   (d) Diagonal left view

<eye> represents a sequence of eye gestures.
<ename> specifies the name of an eye gesture. The start and end times of the gesture are
     specified in the same way as for the <ebname> tag.
<gesture> represents a sequence of head gestures.
<gname> specifies the name of a head gesture. The start and end times of the gesture
     are specified in the same way as for the <ebname> tag.
<explanation> is the explanation for the sign language sentence.

In addition, there are the <mouth> and <mname> tags to describe mouth gestures.

The data for the sign language words, eyebrow gestures, eye gestures, mouth gestures, and head gestures are expressed as a sequence of motion parameters that are used to operate the 3DCG character. They are stored apart from the description for the sign language sentence and are connected based on the description of the sign language sentence when the animation is generated.

The description for the sign language sentence includes the manual and non-manual gestures and their temporal relationships. This information is displayed as a set of the labels representing the names of the sign language words and of the icons indicating the non-manual gestures in this system, so that the learner can easily understand the relationships between manual and non-manual gestures.

An example display of the information for a sign language sentence is shown in Figure 8. The Japanese sentence means "you should submit a notice of a change of address at the pension section," and the signed words mean "pension," "place,"

Figure 7: Example Description of Sign Language Sentence

```
<slsentence>
<jsentence> どこに行くのですか？ (Where are you going?) </jsentence>
<hand>
  <hname id="hd0" frame="1"> %基本 (home position) </hname>
  <hname id="hd1" frame="4"> %渡り (transition) </hname>
  <hname id="hd2" frame="7"> 場所A (place) </hname>
  <hname id="hd3" frame="4"> %渡り (transition) </hname>
  <hname id="hd4" frame="13"> 何A (what) </hname>
  <hname id="hd5" frame="4"> %渡り (transition) </hname>
  <hname id="hd6" frame="1"> %基本 (home position) </hname>
</hand>
<eyebrow>
  <ebname pos="hd2:0,hd4:12"> ひそめる (knit one's brows) </ebname>
</eyebrow>
<eye>
  <ename pos="hd4:0,hd4:12"> 悲しげ (sad) </ename>
</eye>
<gesture>
  <gname pos="hd4:0,hd4:12"> かしげる(右) (tilt the head to the right) </gname>
</gesture>
<explanation>
行き先を聞く場合の表現です。「場所」「何」という表現で「どこへ？」という意味
になります。
(The signed expression asks the destination. The signed words meaning "place" and "what"
express the word "where".)
</explanation>
</slsentence>
```

"house," "change," and "submit," respectively. The "⬤" icon shows the eyebrow and eye gestures, and the "👌" icon means that the head gesture is expressed.

Synchronization of Animation and Display of Sentence Information

As described above, a sign language sentence is described as a set of manual and non-manual gestures, and the sign language animation is generated based on this description. Therefore, the temporal relationship between each sign language word and the animation can be easily stored when the animation is generated, and it is possible to synchronize the display of the information for a sign language sentence with the sign language animation.

The display color of the label for a sign language word is changed when the animation of the word is being displayed, as shown in Figure 9. The Japanese sentence in Figure 9 means "first, you should submit a notice of a change of address at the citizen section." The display colors for the words "市民A (citizen)," "場所A (place)," "まずA (first)," and "届けA (submit)" are changed when the corresponding animation is shown.

Evaluation of Sign Language Gestures

Each inputted gesture can represent several words, and the sign language recognition method can recognize each one. However, selecting the correct sequence of the words from the recognition result is problematic because the words are not always detected with high accuracy.

Figure 8: Example Display for a Sign Language Sentence

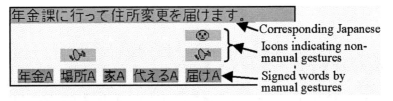

In our sign language teaching system, the sequence of sign language words to be evaluated can be determined in advance. Therefore, the words that constitute the sequence to be estimated are searched for in the recognized words and are output as the estimated result. The steps are as follows.

1. Extract the candidates for each sign language word in the sequence of sign language words to be estimated from the recognition result.
2. Choose one candidate for each sign language word, and create a candidate sequence of the sign language words.
3. Check the temporal relationships between the sign language words in the created candidate sequence, and delete the candidate if the temporal overlap between the sign language words exceeds a threshold or if the order of the sign language words is different from the sequence to be estimated.
4. Calculate the estimated value for the created candidate sequence and store the candidate sequence and the estimated value.

Figure 9: Display of Sign Language Words Synchronized with Animation

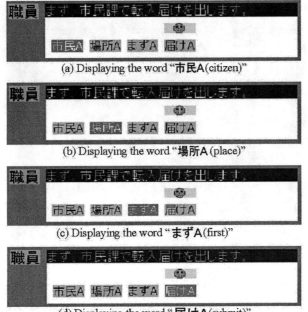

(a) Displaying the word "市民A(citizen)"

(b) Displaying the word "場所A (place)"

(c) Displaying the word "まずA(first)"

(d) Displaying the word "届けA(submit)"

5.   Repeat steps (b) to (d) until there is no other possible candidate for the sequence of the sign language words.
6.   Output the candidate sequence with the highest estimated value.

Figure 10 shows an example estimated result for a sign language gesture by a learner. The results when several sign language sentences were inputted are shown. The estimated value for each sign language sentence and the estimated value for each sign language word in the sentence are displayed. The estimated value for the sentence was calculated by computing the average of the estimated values for the sign language words.

Comparison of Sign Language Gestures Using 3DCG Animation

Learners can judge whether their sign language gestures are correct or not based on the estimated results, as shown in Figure 10. However, this is not sufficient because they cannot understand the problem with their gesture for a word with a low score.

The system solves this problem by synchronously displaying an animation generated from the data for the incorrect gesture and an animation generated from the description of the sign language sentence. It is easy to generate sign language animation from data generated by a glove-based input device (Sakiyama et al., 1994). This enables the learner to study the differences between the incorrect gesture and the correct one in detail.

When displaying these two animations, the gesture for each sign language word has to be displayed simultaneously. The sign language recognition method can output the time range of the sign language word detected from the inputted gesture. The time

Figure 10: Example Evaluation Result for Signed Gestures of Learner

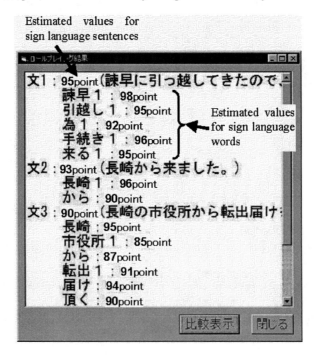

range of a word in an animation generated from the description of the sign language sentence can be stored when the animation is created. Therefore, fitting the word in one animation to a word in the other is easily achieved by expanding or shortening the word in one of the animations based on the time range in the recognition result for the learner's gesture.

Figure 11 illustrates how two animations are synchronized. Figure 11(a) shows the frames and time ranges of the sign language words in the animation generated from the description of the sign language sentence. Figure 11(b) shows those of the recognized words in the animation generated from the data for the gesture inputted by the learner. In Figure 11 (b), the time lengths of recognized words 1b and 3b are longer than those of words 1a and 3a in Figure 11(a). Therefore, the time lengths of 1b and 3b are adjusted to fit 1a and 3a, respectively, by deleting the frames shown as "▤". The frames shown as "■" in Figure 11(c) are inserted because the time length of recognized word 2b in Figure 11(b) is shorter than that of word 2a in Figure 11(a). The transition gestures between the sign language words are adjusted in the same way. Figure 11 shows adjustment by deletion and insertion of frames to simplify the explanation. The time length is actually adjusted by calculating the gesture data between frames.

Figure 12 shows an example display comparing the learner's gesture with the correct gesture. The learner's gesture is displayed on the left, and the correct gesture is displayed on the right. Examples of the sign language words in two animations displayed synchronously are shown in Figure 13.

Reference to Sign Language Word from A Signed Gesture

When sign language learners encounter a sign language word for which they do not know the meaning, it would be helpful if they could look up the meaning of the word based on the gesture. The sign language recognition method can be used to do this.

In a sign language sentence, there are transition gestures between the words and at the start and end of the sentence, even if there is only one word in the sentence. These gestures play a role in detecting the candidate sign language words because the system

Figure 11: Synchronization of Sign Language Animations

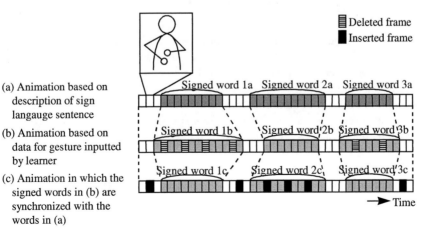

(a) Animation based on description of sign langauge sentence

(b) Animation based on data for gesture inputted by learner

(c) Animation in which the signed words in (b) are synchronized with the words in (a)

Figure 12: Display Comparing Learner's Gesture with Correct Gesture

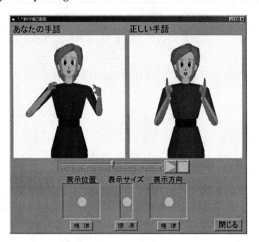

does not know where the word is expressed in the inputted gesture. Therefore, the candidate sign language words detected from the transition gestures must be removed before the sign language recognition method can identify the meaning of the gesture of the sign language word.

Our sign language recognition method divides each inputted gesture into several segments based on the velocity and direction of the manual gesture (Sagawa & Takeuchi, 2000). The last segment is usually a transition gesture when only one sign language word is represented. Therefore, the second segment from the last is the one most likely to contain a sign language word. Accordingly, that segment is weighted the highest, and the values estimated for the recognized sign language words are modified by adding this value. The recognized sign language words are ranked according to the modified estimated values and are output as the search result.

EVALUATION

Method

We evaluated our sign language teaching system experimentally using 24 participants: 15 employees of the Isahaya City Office in Nagasaki Prefecture and nine members of Jumon-Kai, a social welfare organization. The city employees ranged in age from 24 to 36 and had little knowledge of sign language. The members of Jumon-Kai were homemakers ranging in age from 42 to 57 and knew nothing about sign language.

We used three example conversations that are typical of those in a city office. Two hearing-impaired people living in Isahaya provided sample data for the corresponding sign language. The data were used to make the template for the sign language recognition. They also created the sign language animation.

The participants were first given a ten-minute presentation of the usage of the system. They then used the system freely for about ten minutes, following which they answered a simple questionnaire about the system. The questionnaire consisted of 15

Figure 13: Examples of Synchronized Animations

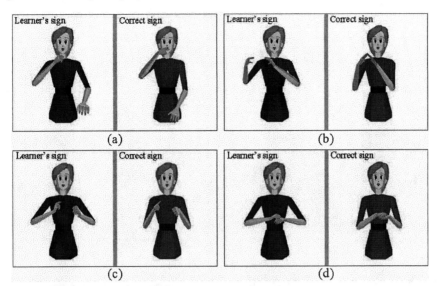

questions about (1) the intelligibility of the sign language animation, (2) the effect of displaying the evaluation result for each sign language gesture, (3) the ease of using the system, and (4) the need for other functions. Most of the questions in (1), (2), and (3) were multiple choices.

Results

Table 1 shows the results of the first three parts of the questionnaire, and Table 2 lists some of the participants' opinions and requests. In Table 1, answers indicating a good impression of the aspect in question were classified as "good," and those indicating a bad impression were classified as "bad." The others were classified as "neutral." The totals for the effect of displaying the evaluation of the signed gesture are greater than the number of participants because they could select several choices for each question. We noted that the number of unanswered questions increased towards the end of the questionnaire, possibly because the participants were getting bored to move on to the next step.

More examples of basic conversations used at the reception counter are required.

DISCUSSION

The overall favorable impression of the participants, as shown in Table 1, indicates that the system we have developed is effective for learning sign language. The participants particularly valued the function that estimates their gestures and displays the estimated result.

The large number of bad impressions of the sign language animation indicates problems related to the configuration of the hands, the depth perception, and the speed

Table 1: Results of Questionnaire

Aspect		Good	Neutral	Bad	Total
Intelligibility of sign language animation	Motion of hand	16	1	7	24
	Figure of hand	12	8	3	23
	Position of hand	13	8	3	24
Effect of displaying evaluation result for each gesture	Displaying the score	32	0	1	33
	Comparison of sign language gestures	31	0	5	36
Ease of using system	Displaying the information of the sign language sentence	11	7	1	19
	Operating the animation	10	4	0	14
	Inputting the sign language gesture	8	5	1	14

of the motion. The hands of the CG character in the current system are small and plain, and the palm is hard to distinguish from the back of the hand. The intelligibility of the animation was also affected by the lighting conditions and the colors of the polygons. It is clear that the hands of the character have to be redesigned, taking these points into consideration. The depth perception was also affected by the same factors. The speed of the animation stored in the system was natural for hearing-impaired people. The animation should be displayed at the natural speed in the sign language teaching system. However, beginning sign language learners felt it was too fast. A function for changing the display speed is thus necessary.

There are also some problems in the comparison of the sign language animations. While two animations can be synchronously displayed in the current system, the system cannot point out the part of the gesture where the estimated value is low. It is thus difficult for the learner to understand the reason for a low estimated value. A function is needed to indicate the differences in values for the parts of the animation. Another problem is that the gesture of the learner cannot be exactly adjusted to the character's body in the animation. The number of sensors thus needs to be increased in order to obtain sufficient data for making the adjustments.

FUTURE TRENDS

In the study of languages, speaking is as important as reading and hearing. Therefore, for example, materials for teaching English that can assess the learner's pronunciation have been developed and put to practical use. The same applies to the study of sign languages because the sign languages differ from the spoken language. Thus, practice representing the sign language gestures is indispensable in sign language learning and teaching.

Table 2: Opinions and Requests from the Subjects

Classification	Opinions and requests
Sign language animation	It is hard to see the motion of the fingers.
	The motion is too fast.
	Depth perception is unclear.
Evaluation of signed gestures	I want to practice the gesture of the word and sentence more easily.
	It is difficult to adjust the system to the learner's body size.
	The comparison of the gestures is hard to understand.
Contents	It is better to display the meaning with the animation.
	More examples of basic conversations used at the reception counter are required.

Learners can correct their sign language gestures with the guidance of a teacher or a hearing-impaired person in a lecture class or in a sign language circle. They cannot correct their gestures when studying sign language on their own using existing teaching materials. Therefore, providing a function for assessing a learner's gestures and giving feedback on them is important.

The quality of support for hearing-impaired people in Japan is no better than it is in most other countries, and it will be a big problem in the future. The proposed teaching system aims to solve this problem.

From the viewpoint of the sign language recognition method, the recognition accuracy in the teaching system does not need to be as high as that required in a system for translating sign language into spoken language. In a translation system, the sign language recognition method can be used to search for the gesture most similar to the gesture inputted by a user from among many gestures stored in advance. Increasing the number of stored gestures reduces recognition accuracy because there are more similar gestures, making it more difficult to distinguish one gesture from another. Therefore, the sign language recognition method needs high recognition accuracy when it is used in a translation system.

In our sign language teaching system, on the other hand, the gesture to be estimated can be determined in advance. Therefore, only the difference between the inputted gesture and the gesture to be estimated needs to be calculated. This means that the current method for recognizing sign language can provide enough information for learners to check whether their gestures are correct or not, even though the accuracy of the current recognition method is not sufficient for it to be used in a sign language translation system.

For these reasons, our sign language teaching system is an indispensable application of the sign language recognition method.

CONCLUSION

We have developed a sign language teaching system that uses sign language recognition and generation methods. Experimental evaluation showed that functions based on these methods effectively improve the learning of Japanese sign language.

We plan to improve the sign language animation to make it easier for learners to understand the gestures. We also plan to add other functions, such as game playing, to make studying more fun.

The sign language recognition method in the current system can estimate only manual gestures, so the user cannot practice expressions using non-manual gestures. We intend to enhance the method to enable it to recognize sign language expressions with non-manual gestures,

We also plan to investigate the use of cheaper input devices because the glove-based input device we used is expensive, and the price of the system must be reasonable if it is to be marketable worldwide. We will focus on input devices using other types of sensors and/or a video camera to detect the hand configuration and position.

ACKNOWLEDGMENTS

We thank the staff of Jumon-kai, the social welfare organization in Isahaya City and the staff at the Isahaya City Office for helping with the evaluation.

This research was supported by the New Energy and Industrial Technology Development Organization (NEDO) in Japan.

REFERENCES

Higher Learning Systems, Inc. (2000). *Sign language for everyone*. Retrieved from the World Wide Web: http://www.higherlearning.com/signlang.html.

Hitachi, Ltd. (2000). *P-Channel: Sign language animation software Mimehand II.* Retrieved from the World Wide Web: http://www.hitachi.co.jp/ Prod/comp/app/ shuwa/.

IBM Japan, Ltd. (1995). *Everybody's Sign Language* [in Japanese].

Japanese Federation of the Deaf. (1997). *Japanese-Sign Language Dictionary* [in Japanese].

Kanda, K. (1994). *Lecture on sign language study*. Tokyo: Fukumura Publication's Inc. [in Japanese].

Kimura, H., & Ichida, Y. (1995). *First Sign Language*. Tokyo: Nihonbungeisha [in Japanese].

LITEC Co., Ltd. (1996). *Sign Language Master the Introduction* (Light version) [in Japanese].

NHK Software Inc. (2001). *Sign Language for Everyone* [in Japanese].

Sagawa, H., & Takeuchi, M., (2000). A method for recognizing a sequence of sign language words represented in a Japanese sign language sentence. *Proceedings of the Fourth International Conference on Automatic Face and Gesture Recognition* (FG2000) (pp. 434-439). Grenoble, CA: IEEE Computer Society.

Sagawa, H., Koizumi, A., & Takeuchi, M. (2001). A recognition method of Japanese sign language sentences based on head movements. In *Poster Sessions: Abridged Proceedings HCI International 2001* (pp. 84-86). New Orleans: Lawrence Erlbaum Associates, Inc.

Sagawa, H., Takeuchi, M., & Ohki, M. (1998). Methods to describe and recognize sign language based on gesture components represented by symbols and numerical values. *Knowledge-Based Systems*, *10*(5), 287-294.

Sakiyama, T., Oohira, E., Sagawa, H., Ooki, M., & Ikeda, H. (1996). A generation method for real-time sign language animation. Transactions of IEICE, J79-D-II(2), 182-190 [in Japanese].

Sakiyama, T., Sagawa, H., Oohira, E., Ikeda, H., & Ooki, M. (1994). A generation method of sign language animation using time sequential data. *Proceedings of the 20th Annual Meeting of the Japanese Federation of the Deaf* (pp. 69-72). Tokyo, Saitama: Japanese Association of Sign Linguistics [in Japanese].

Chapter XX

Precursors to
Web-Based Methodologies:
Lessons We Can Learn from
Teaching Machines,
Automatic Tutoring Devices
and Learning Hierarchies

Robert S. Owen, Texas A&M University-Texarkana, USA

Bosede Aworuwa, Texas A&M University-Texarkana, USA

ABSTRACT

Many of us are using the World Wide Web in ways that are similar to the teaching machines and automatic tutoring devices of the 1950-1960s, yet we are moving ahead without building upon a base of knowledge that already exists from that era. This chapter reviews the basic ideas of the original automatic teaching and tutoring machines of those two decades — a linear programmed learning model and a programmed branching model — and compares these to hypermedia methods that are now enabled via web technology. Some classic ideas in assessing the cognitive and affective learning outcomes of teaching — somewhat analogous to usability issues of utility and likability — are reviewed. Greater emphasis on considering the educational outcomes is advocated when we use new online teaching technologies in programmed instruction.

INTRODUCTION AND BACKGROUND

With the rapid advances in technology in the last few years, it is important that we explore the use of technology in education. The mechanical and computerized teaching machines and automatic tutoring machines of the 1950-1960s experienced a natural death, perhaps in part because they were so expensive and cumbersome (except in programmed textbook form), prohibiting large-scale implementation. The Web and hypermedia-based dynamic HTML now gives us the same programmable capabilities as the programmed instruction devices of the 1950-1960s. However, it has additionally provided us with much more flexibility, much greater standardization in programming methods, much lower cost, and infinitely greater distribution across the Internet with lower barriers to participation than we had even with the rise of PC use in the 1980s. Given the current ease and low cost of both developing online programmed instruction methods by the teacher and using these methods by the learner, it is only natural that so many of us have begun to experiment with the use of these methods. Programmed instruction methods were abandoned in the early 1970s before a full assessment of their pedagogical value, and we now have the opportunity to pick up where we left off in the 1960s.

Unfortunately, our increased use of various modes of technology in teaching since the 1960s has been technology-led, rather than theory-led, and has rarely addressed issues of the effectiveness of the chosen technology in achieving some particular outcome with regard to student learning and achievement (cf., Fernald & Jordan, 1991; Jones & Paolucci, 1999; Ravenscroft, 2001; Seidel & Park, 1994; Tergan 1997; Wang & Sleeman, 1993; Zane & Frazer, 1992). For example, Zane and Frazer (1992) conducted a study in which the producers of 95 educational software programs were asked to supply "any evaluative data, research findings, or field-test results" concerning educational outcomes and usability issues, and no company provided reference to any empirical documentation of these issues.

With regard to the educational outcomes of online programmed methods of instruction, particular interest in the present chapter is in the hierarchical cognitive and affective outcome factors proposed in a body of work that has come to be known as "Bloom's Taxonomy" (A Committee of College and University Examiners, 1956; Krathwohl et al., 1964), an idea that was gaining in research interest at a time when the programmed instruction methods of teaching machines and automatic tutoring devices were being abandoned. The present authors hope to revitalize interest in programmed instruction designs that use the *linear programmed* methods of Skinner (e.g., 1954, 1958) and the *programmed branching* methods of Crowder (e.g., 1959, 1963) because they are so closely analogous to designs that are easily used in web-based hypermedia technology. We hope to revitalize attention to the cognitive and affective learning outcome domains of the "Bloom's Taxonomy" because these propose a hierarchical structure that might help us to think about what we might gain or lose in educational outcomes as we shift between traditional classroom instruction and web-based programmed instruction applications. The measure of "learning outcomes" is somewhat analogous to the measure of "usability," where "cognitive outcomes" might be somewhat related to the idea of "utility," and "affective outcomes" might be related to the idea of "likability."

LINEAR PROGRAMMED AND PROGRAMMED BRANCHING MACHINES

One key feature that web-based hypermedia learning methods have in common with the automatic teaching and tutoring machines of Skinner and of Crowder is that they can provide automatic feedback. This can be feedback for the sake of the professor, as in measuring study-time distributions (Taraban et al., 1999), study space navigation behavior (Ellis et al., 1998; Schroeder & Grabowski, 1995), or automated grading (Stockburger, 1999), but automatic feedback can also be used for the sake of the student. Many web sites associated with textbooks, for example, provide "radio button" style practice exams in which the student clicks on a button next to answers associated with multiple choice questions and then after taking the exam, receives a numerical score or a listing of correct answers for incorrect choices.

Research has found that the provision of minimal feedback, in the form of knowledge of results or knowledge of the correct response, results in superior learning over the provision of no feedback (Lalley, 1998), and this is very easy to provide through a web browser. An issue in considering methods of online programmed instruction, however, is the nature of this feedback. A shortcoming of the radio-button exams of many textbook sites is that they merely test students on material studied before the exam. The sorts of machines described below, however, incorporate immediate feedback with principles of learning that allow the machine to teach new material. Although a radio-button style of exam provides feedback, an even better method might be *adaptive feedback* in which the application provides elaboration based upon the student's decisions or choices (Mory, 1994). Below we will consider two basic types of machine models, one which provides feedback in the form of reinforcement, and one which provides feedback which is adaptive to the learner's response.

Skinner's Teaching Machine: Linear Programmed Instruction and Operant Conditioning

A classic "low tech" example of linear programmed instruction is the psychology textbook of Holland and Skinner (1961), which asked the student a question on one page, and then asked the student to turn the page to find the answer and a new question:

> "A doctor taps your knee (patellar tendon) with
> a rubber hammer to test your _____."

The student thinks or writes down the answer, turns the page to find the correct answer, "reflexes," and is then asked another question:

> "If your reflexes are normal, your leg _____
> to the tap on the knee with a slight kick (the
> so-called knee jerk)."

Skinner believed that such programmed textbooks caused learning through *operant conditioning*, whereby questions or statements are arranged in *frames*, and the student receives *reinforcement* for a correct answer on each sequential frame (cf., Cook, 1961; Skinner, 1954, 1958). According to operant conditioning, learning is expected to occur when the student receives positive feedback associated with finding that s/he had formulated the correct answer. With hypermedia computer systems, such as is possible with web browsers, the operant conditioning of the structured, sequential, linear, Skinner-type programmed text can easily be implemented by substituting a hyperlink to another frame (web page) wherever the instructions above ask the student to turn the page.

Crowder's Automatic Tutoring Machine: Programmed Branching and Learning from Mistakes

Pressey (1963), a predecessor of Skinner in the use of teaching machines, was critical of the operant conditioning approach of Skinner, arguing that a student can learn not only from knowing a correct answer, but can also learn to discriminate from making mistakes. Crowder (e.g., 1959, 1963), a contemporary of Skinner, also argued against Skinner's approach, since students only saw correct answers even though people are expected to make mistakes. Crowder distinguished the *automatic tutoring device* from the Skinner-type *teaching machine*, proposing that the automatic tutoring device is more flexible in allowing the student to receive an explanation when making an error. The idea is that when the student makes a choice in a multiple-choice question, the teaching device should provide feedback that is relevant to the choice that was made by the student. Crowder (1959, pp. 110-111) provides an example of how this idea could be used in a book:

"In the multiplication of 3 x 4 = 12, the
*number 12 is called the **product** and the*
numbers 3 and 4 are called the

*Page 15 **quotients.***
*Page 29 **factors.***
*Page 43 **powers.***

"The correctional material that appears on [page 43 of the scrambled text]
reads as follows:

"Your answer was 'powers.'
We'll get to powers of numbers
pretty soon, but we're not there yet.
The numbers that are multiplied to-
gether to form a product are called
'factors,' not 'powers.' Now return
to page 1 and choose the right
answer."

Note that Crowder's method, too, could be easily implemented on a hypertext system, where the student clicks on a hypertext answer that links her/him to an explanation. Owen (1999b) describes the use of HTML dropdown menus to provide tailored feedback on questions following an online case study.

Levels of Learning

Crowder's approach works in a *branching* manner in which both correct and incorrect answers lead to an explanation that is tailored to the student's thinking at the time the choice was made. Whether or not the student made a correct choice in the answer, s/he is provided with feedback that is presumed to be useful in learning to discriminate between right and wrong answers. Skinner's approach, on the other hand, works in a step-by-step *linear* manner, whereby the student *emits* correct answers to be *reinforced*. The student learns merely to recite the correct response to a particular question or statement. Textbook publisher's web sites that provide radio-button style practice multiple choice exams, if intended to be tools for learning, could be argued as being a step *below* the operant conditioning approach of Skinner, providing feedback on *all* answers only after *all* questions have been answered, without even the potential benefit of operant conditioning.

The above discussion suggests that different systems or methods of teaching will lead to qualitatively different learning outcomes. In one method, a student takes a multiple choice practice exam and receives feedback only with regard to which of many answers were correct after taking the entire exam; some learning could be expected. However, we would expect that feedback at the time that each answer choice is made, identifying the correct answer, would be qualitatively better from a learning perspective. From a theoretical perspective, this second method provides reinforcement at each frame, thereby causing the student to learn, say, definitions and lists through operant conditioning.

Although Skinner's method of linear programmed instruction presumably has greater value, Crowder's branching method has been argued to be qualitatively better in that it teaches the student greater insights into relationships by providing an explanation for both wrong and right answers. That is, there would seem to be a hierarchical ordering to the sort of learning that is possible by these three methods, with Crowder's method presumably providing a "higher order" of cognitive learning than Skinner's, and Skinner's providing "higher order" of cognitive learning than the radio button exams of textbook web sites. We do not mean to imply here, however, that one level in a hierarchy is necessarily better. A student's cognitive age or stage in the learning process might cause a "lower order" mode of learning to be more appropriate.

COGNITIVE AND AFFECTIVE HIERARCHIES OF LEARNING OUTCOMES

Many ideas have been proposed with regard to a hierarchical perspective on learning, the most well known being "Bloom's Taxonomy" (A Committee of College and University Examiners, 1956). This idea proposes that the objectives of learning lie on a continuous, cumulative, hierarchical continuum, with the major steps in the hierarchy being knowledge, comprehension, application, analysis, and synthesis. The idea that there can exist an ordered, cumulative hierarchy has resulted in much controversy and criticism with regard to validity (see, for example, a discussion by Furst, 1981, one of the "Bloom's Taxonomy" authors). The authors of Bloom's Taxonomy, however, never made any claims about its theoretical underpinnings (cf., Kreitzer & Madaus, 1994), but it has had enough appeal, at least on face validity, to form the basis of discussion for the outcomes of learning (e.g., Clabaugh et al., 1995; Green, 1997; Stearns & Crespy, 1995).

Discussions of Bloom's Taxonomy tend to rely exclusively on Part I of a work that is generally bound as *two* parts. Part I focuses on the "cognitive domain" of learning and it is what is meant when reference is made to "Bloom's Taxonomy." Part II (Krathwohl et al., 1964), written several years later and largely ignored in the literature, focuses on the "affective domain" of learning. (A Part III on the psychomotor domain was also proposed in the original Part I, but was apparently never written or published.) As with Bloom's Taxonomy (of the cognitive behavioral outcomes of learning), the affective taxonomy proposes a cumulative, linear ordering that could be subjected to the same philosophical arguments regarding validity. Indeed, the Part II authors themselves raised this issue in noting that it is difficult to place some of the sub-elements above or below others. Nonetheless, the taxonomy of the affective outcomes of learning, like the cognitive taxonomy, has value in evoking discussion of such issues in learning, regardless of its validity as a model in the whole. Table 1 summarizes the cognitive and affective domains.

Table 1: Cognitive and Affective Domains

The Cognitive Domain	The Affective Domain
The taxonomy of the cognitive domain (A Committee of College and University Examiners 1956) can be summarized as follows: 1) *Knowledge:* knowledge of specifics of terminology and facts; knowledge of ways and means of dealing with specifics; knowledge of the universals and abstractions in a field. 2) *Comprehension:* translation and paraphrasing; interpretation; extrapolation. 3) *Application:* the use of abstractions in particular situations. 4) *Analysis:* identification of elements in a communication; analysis of the relationships between elements of a communication; systematic arrangement and structuring of a communication. 5) *Synthesis:* production of a unique communication; production of a plan or proposed set of operations; derivation of a set of abstract relations. 6) *Evaluation:* judgment in terms of internal evidence; judgment in terms of external criteria.	The taxonomy of the affective domain (Krathwohl, Bloom, & Masia 1964) can be summarized as follows: 1) *Receiving (Attending):* awareness of ideas; a willingness to receive ideas while suspending judgment; control of attention. 2) *Responding:* involvement or commitment to a subject, activity, or idea; acquiescence or willingness to comply in responding; satisfaction in responding. 3) *Valuing:* feeling that a thing, phenomenon, or behavior has worth; acceptance of a value; preference for a value; motivation to act out a behavior. 4) *Organization:* the organization of multiple values into a system; the determination of the interrelationships among multiple values; the determination of dominant and pervasive values. 5) *Characterization by a Value or Value Complex:* the generalization of a value system to a person such that it is now pervasive in their behaviors; the integration of beliefs, ideas, and attitudes into a total philosophy or worldview.

Note that the idea of this hierarchy is not that one method is better because it reaches a higher level of cognitive learning, but that it is merely better suited for achieving some level of cognitive learning. Some students, for example, might not be ready or willing to learn to "understand" an idea beyond the knowledge of key words, definitions, or lists, and forcing them to think about issues might prove to be frustrating. Learning facts and comprehending relationships is merely part of a *cognitive* mental process; having a *willingness* or desire to learn is part of an *affective* state. Unfortunately, many researchers throughout the years have noted a neglect for any *systematic* research of issues of affect as an enabling state for learning and as a behavioral outcome of learning (cf., Bloom et al., 1971, Ch. 10; Gable & Roberts, 1973; Hopkins, 1998, Ch. 11; Laforgia, 1988; Nahl-Jakobovits & Jakobovits, 1993; O'Donnell et al., 1987; Popham, 1994).

Perhaps because of a focus on cognitive, rather than affective, issues in learning, the Skinner approach to programmed instruction had been abandoned by 1970 (cf., Kulhavy & Wagner, 1993). Since many of the machine-assisted methods that we are attempting to use with hypertext-based systems on the web resemble the programmed learning methods of Skinner and the automatic tutoring methods of Crowder, it seems that we should attempt to understand how these methods work, from a pedagogical perspective, lest we repeat the history that has seen an abandonment of the earlier-machine assisted methods. In order to study the effects of machine-assisted learning, as when we provide students with web-based exercises, we must consider the affective behavioral outcomes as well as the cognitive behavioral outcomes. The student who is asked to use methods based on Crowder's branching ideas might become frustrated (an affective state) by the level of thought that is required, but might find the more simple positive reinforcement that is provided with linear approach of Skinner to be more rewarding and enjoyable (an affective state), thereby better stimulating the student toward a greater desire to study the lesson materials.

CASE EXAMPLE A

One of the present authors posted a web-based multiple choice practice exam using drop down menus for the answer choices. The exam is posted on the web site as the *first* link above a list of links to topic readings. The idea is that this exercise is not a test of material that is already learned, but that it is a test in which learning occurs. A learner who is *racing*, or not carefully reading the questions and therefore prone to error (cf., Crosbie & Kelly, 1994), would be expected to choose the most intuitive choice. Learners click on a choice from the list of HTML dropdown menus, and upon clicking an incorrect choice, the menu box drops to explain the conditions under which the answer would be correct, but why the chosen answer would not always be the correct choice. The authors hypothesize that when a learner is surprised at the explanation for what seemed intuitively to be a good answer, s/he would pause momentarily to reflect on the issues raised in the explanation and to encode this into memory in a personally meaningful way.

From a learning perspective, this method is presumably more effective than a radio-button style of exam that only provides feedback after the student has answered all questions. Unlike the linear programming of Skinner's approach, in which students receive reinforcement that leads to the learning of key words and such, the Crowder programmed branching approach allowed and even encouraged students to make mistakes that would cause them to think about a variety of issues. Regardless of whether or not the exercise causes cognitive learning, the exercise appears to generate student interest in the course. (It is shown in class on the first day when the syllabus is distributed, and students seem to enjoy the "tricks" of the first few questions that are demonstrated in class.) From the developer's perspective, creation of dropdown menus requires nothing more than simple HTML code in contrast with CGI programming to save, sum, and report the scores on a radio-button style exam. Indeed, an application was written and posted online (not posted at this time) which automatically generated the HTML for dropdown multiple choice exams (Owen, 1999a).

Following student interest in this pre-learning exam, an online case was developed using the dropdown menu method. In a business class case discussion, students are led through a discussion that is somewhat choreographed. That is, the professor knows *a priori* what sorts of mistakes and controversy and gray areas will enter into a class discussion. So an online case study was written with a series of questions after the case. These questions were again designed after the Crowder idea of programmed branching, where wrong answers are provided with a thought-provoking explanation; in a case study, wrong answers are desired because they are opportunities for learning. The actual case is described in Owen (1990b); the point here is that an online interactive case discussion can be automatically moderated with an individual student, whereby the professor asks a series of questions and provides guidance for answers that are not always or are not entirely correct. Since the instruction is somewhat personalized to the student's responses, then this case could be considered as a form of automated tutoring.

CASE EXAMPLE B

One of the present authors posted a web-based make-up exercise in 1996 for the sake of students who had done poorly on an exam involving forecasting problems. In quantitative problem solving, the student can make procedural mistakes that are repeated throughout the problem (as with the repetitions of exponential smoothing forecasting), and the only way for the student to unlearn incorrect procedures is to be shown the correct procedures at the point that they are making the mistake. The online interactive, programmed (JavaScript) make-up exercise required that the student go through a series of forecasting problems that stopped the student at the time that a mistake in procedure was made; the program provided a hint as to the correct procedure and would not permit the student to continue to another step in the exercise until the correct problem set-up was entered at the current step of the problem. Upon completion of the entire series of problems, the program gave the student a unique receipt, which was submitted to the professor in return for extra credit on the exam.

A survey of these students indicated that they felt that the make-up exercise was enjoyable and useful (an affective outcome), and that they believed that they would have done much better on the exam had this exercise been available as a practice exercise prior to the exam. In subsequent semesters, the exercise was assigned as required homework prior to the exam, and surveys of students indicated that they, too, believed the exercise to be a valuable learning tool before they took the exam. In all cases, students were told that the programming required to maintain the exercise was not worth the professor's effort to maintain for future classes unless students believed it to be useful, and that they were therefore encouraged to be honest in expressing a negative opinion on the anonymous, voluntary survey. Although most students returned the surveys, and although the overwhelming majority expressed a presumably unbiased opinion that the exercise was a useful learning tool, exam scores suggested that these students were still performing no better than students from previous semesters.

This seems to suggest that the exercise was a failure from a cognitive learning perspective (that is, it provided no improvement in exam scores). However, we must note that students who did the exercise were forced to work through a series of problems to completion, and, importantly, to do so *correctly*. In working through these problems, the students presumably learned an *appreciation* of how different forecasting methods work, and this appreciation might be something that stays with the student long after the completion of the course. The point of teaching quantitative forecasting methods in the course was not with the expectation that students would forever remember the mechanical mathematical procedures, but that they would gain an understanding for how these work and would gain an appreciation for how and when these methods are used. The long-term *affective* benefits of using the online exercise might be more important than the immediately apparent *cognitive* benefits, and such an exercise might be able to provide these benefits in a way that in-class teaching cannot.

HYPERMEDIA AND THE WEB

In applying structured, closed, linear and branching programmed instruction methods of the teaching machines to hypermedia-based systems, we are providing hyperlinks, which take the student to some known place in an order that we determine *a priori*. Much of the course work that we are posting on the Web, however, is much less structured, providing the student with a more random-access sort of environment. For example, in using real-world class consulting projects, one of the present authors allows students to find and post useful web resources on a common class web space. Class members individually do an environmental scan by surfing the Web for useful resources, and then post links to their findings, for course credit, at the course web space for the rest of the class to use. In this use of the hypermedia capabilities of the Web, there is very little structure in contrast to the automatic teaching devices. It is analogous to sending students to the library to wander around at will, asking them to throw interesting books on a particular table for the rest of the class (and the class client) to browse.

Unfortunately, such unstructured uses of hypermedia, as when lists of links are provided to students, can lead to very special problems that would confound the study of learning outcomes, mostly falling under the general umbrella of "lost in hyperspace" problems (Astleitner & Leutner, 1995; Chen et al., 1997; Tergan, 1997). "Lost in hyperspace" problems arise when the student becomes overloaded with too much information, gets lost in a sea of information and loses sight of the objectives of an assignment, or otherwise becomes disoriented in a random-access, unstructured environment. Because of such problems, the closed-loop structure of the programmed instruction methods of the classic teaching machines and the structure of ideas of the cognitive and affective hierarchies of the behavioral outcomes of learning are advocated here as the starting points for studying the qualitative values of online programmed instruction methods.

CONCLUSION

This chapter has reviewed the basic ideas of the *linear programmed learning* model of Skinner and of the *programmed branching* model of Crowder in the hopes that we will consider the different ways that hypermedia models can be designed. This chapter has also reviewed the idea of *hierarchies of learning* from the perspective of the Cognitive Domain ("Bloom's taxonomy") and the Affective Domain, ideas from the 1960s. Although these concepts do not have a monopoly on good ideas, and they have been criticized for their lack of any testing for validity, they are at least as well developed as any alternative ideas with regard to face validity. The use of the concept of learning hierarchies is advocated because it provides us with a way to compare the qualities, or categories of usefulness, of different types of instruction — an important issue that could help us to understand or at least predict what we are getting in return for our investment into technology-based instruction. Although the present authors currently have only anecdotal rather than empirical evidence as to the learning outcomes of a handful of online programmed instruction applications, at least these designs originated from the perspective of learning objectives rather than being technology driven.

REFERENCES

A Committee of College and University Examiners. (1956). *Taxonomy of Educational Objectives, the Classification of Educational Goals, Handbook I: Cognitive Domain.* New York: David McKay Company.

Astleitner, H., & Leutner, D. (1995). Learning strategies for unstructured hypermedia - A framework for theory, research, and practice. *Journal of Educational Computing Research, 13*(4), 387-400.

Bloom, B.S., Hastings, T., & Madaus, G.F. (1971). Evaluation techniques for affective objectives. In B.S. Bloom, T. J. Hastings, & G.F. Madaus (Eds.), *Handbook on Formative and Summative Evaluation of Student Learning* (pp. 225-245). New York: McGraw-Hill Book Company.

Chen, B., Wang, H., Proctor, R.W., & Salvendy, G. (1997). A human-centered approach for designing World Wide Web browsers. *Behavioral Research Methods, Instruments, & Computers, 29*(2), 172-179.

Clabaugh, Jr., M.G., Forges, J.L., & Clabaugh, J.P. (1995, Fall). Bloom's cognitive domain theory: A basis for developing higher levels of critical thinking skills in reconstructing a professional selling course. *Journal of Marketing Education*, 25-34.

Cook, D.L. (1961). Teaching machine terms: A glossary. *Audiovisual Instruction, 6*, 152-153.

Crosbie, J., & Kelly, G. (1994). Effects of imposed feedback delays in programmed instruction. *Journal of Applied Behavior Analysis, 27*, 483-491.

Crowder, N.A. (1959). Automatic tutoring by means of intrinsic programming. In E. Galanter (Ed.), *Automatic Teaching: The State of the Art* (pp. 109-116). New York: John Wiley & Sons.

Crowder, N.A. (1963). On the differences between linear and intrinsic programming. *Phi Delta Kappan* (March). Reprinted in J.P. DeCecco (Ed.), *Educational Technology* (pp. 142-152). New York: Holt, Rinehart, and Wilson.

Ellis, R.D., Jankowski, T.B., Jasper, J.E., & Tharuvai, B.S. (1998). Listener: A tool for client-side investigation of hypermedia navigation behavior. *Behavior Research Methods, Instruments, & Computers, 30*(4), 573-582.

Fernald, P.S., & Jordan, E.A. (1991). Programmed instruction versus standard text in introductory psychology. *Teaching of Psychology, 18*(4), 205-211.

Furst, E.J. (1981, Winter). Bloom's taxonomy of educational objectives for the cognitive domain: Philosophical and educational issues. *Review of Educational Research, 51,* 441-453.

Gable, R.K., & Roberts, A.D. (1973). Affective and cognitive correlates of classroom achievement: Research for the counselor. Paper presented at the American Educational Research Association Convention, (February 26-March 1). New Orleans. ERIC document no. ED 074 430.

Green, D.H. (1997, Summer). Student-generated exams: Testing and learning. *Journal of Marketing Education,* 43-53.

Holland, J.G., & Skinner, B.F. (1961). *The Analysis of Behavior.* New York: McGraw-Hill Book Company.

Hopkins, K.D. (1998). *Educational and Psychological Measurement and Evaluation* (8th ed.). Boston, MA: Allyn and Bacon.

Jones, T.H., & Paolucci, R. (1999). Research framework and dimensions for evaluating the effectiveness of educational technology systems on learning outcomes. *Journal of Research on Computing in Education, 32*(1), 17-27.

Krathwohl, D.R., Bloom, B.S., & Masia, B. (1964). *Taxonomy of Educational Objectives, The Classification of Educational Goals, Handbook II: The Affective Domain.* New York: David McKay Company.

Kreitzer, A.E., & Madaus, G.F. (1994). Empirical investigations of the hierarchical structure of the taxonomy. In L.W. Anderson & L.A. Sonsick (Eds.), *Bloom's Taxonomy: A Forty-Year Retrospective* (pp. 64-81). Chicago, IL: The University of Chicago Press.

Kulhavy, R.W., & Wagner, W. (1993). Feedback in programmed instruction: Historical context and implications for practice. In J.V. Dempsey & G.C. Sales (Eds.), *Interactive Instruction and Feedback* (pp. 3-20). Englewood Cliffs, NJ: Educational Technology Publications.

Laforgia, J. (1988). The affective domain related to science education and its evaluation. *Science Education, 72*(4), 407-421.

Lalley, J.P. (1998). Comparison of text and video as forms of feedback during computer assisted learning. *Journal of Educational Computing Research, 18*(4), 323-338.

Mory, E. (1994). Adaptive feedback in computer-based instruction: Response certitude on performance, feedback-study time, and efficiency. *Journal of Educational Computing Research, 11*(3), 263-290.

Nahl-Jakobovits, D., & Jakobovits, L.A. (1993, Spring). Bibliographic instructional design for information literacy: Integrating affective and cognitive objectives, *Research Strategies,* 73-88.

O'Donnell, A.M., Dansereau, D.F., Hall, R.H., & Rocklin, T.R. (1987). Cognitive, social/ affective, and metacognitive outcomes of scripted cooperative learning. *Journal of Educational Psychology, 79*(4), 431-437.

Owen, R.S. (1999a). An application for generating interactive exercises on the web. In Elizabeth O. Sullivan (Ed.), *Proceedings of the Eighth Annual SUNY FACT*

Conference on Instructional Technologies (pp. 66-69). System Administration, State University of New York.

Owen, R.S. (1999b). Using programmed branching to automate interactive cases on the web. *Marketing Education Review, 9*(3), 41-60.

Popham, W. J. (1994). Educational assessment's lurking lacuna: The measurement of affect. *Education and Urban Society, 26*(4), 404-416.

Pressey, S. L. (1963). Teaching machine (and learning theory) crisis. *Journal of Applied Psychology, 47*, 1-6.

Ravenscroft, A. (2001). Designing e-learning interactions in the 21st century: Revisiting and rethinking the role of theory. *European Journal of Education, 36*(2).

Schroeder, E.E., & Grabowski, B.L. (1995). Patterns of exploration and learning with hypermedia. *Journal of Educational Computing Research, 13*(4), 313-335.

Seidel, R.J., & Park, O. (1994). An historical perspective and a model for evaluation of intelligent tutoring systems. *Journal of Computing Research, 10*(2), 103-128.

Skinner, B.F. (1954). The science of learning and the art of teaching. *Harvard Educational Review, 24*(2). Reprinted in A.A. Lumsdaine & R. Blasser (Eds.), *Teaching Machines and Programmed Learning* (pp. 99-113). Washington, DC: National Education Association.

Skinner, B.F. (1958, October 24). Teaching machines. *Science, 128*, 969-977.

Stearns, J.M., & Crespy, C.T. (1995, Summer). Learning hierarchies and the marketing curriculum: A proposal for a second course in marketing. *Journal of Marketing Education*, 20-32.

Stockburger, D.W. (1999). Automated grading of homework assignments and tests in introductory and intermediate statistics courses using active server pages. *Behavior Research Methods, Instruments, & Computers, 31*(2), 252-262.

Taraban, R., Maki, E.S., & Rynearson, K. (1999). Measuring study time distributions: implications for designing computer-based courses. *Behavior Research Methods, Instruments, & Computers, 31*(2), 263-269.

Tergan, S. (1997). Conceptual and methodological shortcomings in hypertext/hypermedia design and research. *Journal of Educational and Computing Research, 16*(3), 209-235.

Wang, S., & Sleeman, P.J. (1993). Computer-assisted instruction effectiveness ...A brief review of the research. *International Journal of Instructional Media, 20*(4), 333-439.

Zane, T., & Frazer, C.G. (1992). The extent to which software developers validate their claims. *Journal of Research on Computing in Education, 24*(3), 410-420.

About the Authors

Claude Ghaoui is a senior lecturer in Computer Systems (since 1995) at the School of Computing and Mathematical Sciences, Liverpool John Moores University, UK. Her research interests and expertise are mainly in Human Computer Interaction, Multimedia Technology and their innovative applications in education. From 1991-1995, she worked at the Computer Science Department of Liverpool University as a publishing director of an active R&D group of 25 staff. Prior to that, she worked at IBM and at Kuwait University. She passionately promotes innovative IT for the provision of flexible learning. She has numerous publications and has organized a number of international workshops and sessions since 1994. She is UK correspondent for EUROMICRO (1998-2003), and has served on program committees for several international HCI/multimedia conferences. She is an advisor (since 2000) for University.Net, which promotes online learning, research and innovation. She co-edited a book, *Medical Multimedia* (1995), and published a book, *Usability of Online Learning Programs* (2003, Idea Group Publishing).

*   *   *

Petek Askar is a professor of Computer Education and Instructional Technology at Hacettepe University (Turkey) where she teaches and conducts research on Diffusion of Technology, Distance Learning, and Development and Evaluation of Educational Software. She has been involved in various projects on computers in education and Distance Learning in Turkey. She is the head of the working group for the dissemination of the European Computer Driving Licence in Turkey. She has publications in several journals, both in Turkish and in English. For more information, visit: http://www.ebit.hacettepe.edu.tr/akademik/PetekAskar.shtml.

Bosede Aworuwa is associate professor and program director, Instructional Technology, at Texas A&M University-Texarkana, USA. She has a PhD in Educational Systems Development from Michigan State University. Her areas of interest include issues of teaching and learning with technology, Instructional Design, and Professional Development. She has worked extensively with both pre-service and in-service teachers on ways to effectively use technology to promote the achievement of educational objectives. She has been a project co-director and a project coordinator on grants sponsored by the U.S. Department of Education.

Véronique Baudin is research engineer at LAAS-CNRS in France. Her PhD thesis in Production Control was obtained in 1980 at Toulouse University (France). She has developed several software environments (production control, discrete events simulation using Petri Nets) used by academic and industrial partners. Since 1992, she has worked in projects related to High Speed Collaborative Multimedia Systems. She has been involved in several French (CESAME, technical control and co-management of TOPASE, @IRS++) and European (CANET, GCAP) projects, where application domains were either Co-design or E-training. She is now developing the PLATINE platform inside the IST Lab@Future project and promoting it with industrial partners.

Juan Contreras-Castillo is a professor-researcher at the University of Colima in Colima, Mexico, and doctoral student at CICESE in Ensenada, Mexico. He holds an MS in Computer Sciences from CICESE and a BSc from the University of Colima. He collaborates in the Distance Learning Program at his university. His research focus is on the analysis of interactions in online courses and software developments to support them.

Industrial designer, **Jochen Denzinger**, joined the MARS Exploratory Media Lab (Denmark) team in February 2002 and works in the domain of Interaction and Interface Design. In the team, he is concerned with all aspects of Human Computer Interaction, especially Mixed Reality and Ambient Media. From 1997 to 2000, Jochen worked for the IPSI (Integrated Publication and Information Systems Institute) of the former GMD in Darmstadt on topics as CSCW and Augmented Environments — application domain was the office of the future. He has also worked as a freelance designer, and was a researcher at "Hochschule fuer Gestaltung Offenbach am Main." Currently, he is working on his PhD thesis on the subject of Design and Ubiquitous Computing.

Khalil Drira received an Engineering degree and an MS (DEA) in Computer Science from INPT (National Polytechnic Institute of Toulouse) in 1988, and a PhD in Computer Science from UPS (University Paul Sabatier Toulouse) in 1992. Since 1992, he has been Chargé de Recherche CNRS, a full-time research position at the National Center for Scientific Research of France. He is or has been involved in several national and international projects in the field of distributed and concurrent communicating systems. He is the author of more than 80 regular and invited papers in international conferences and journals.

Philip Duggan is a full time secondary school teacher. He is currently head of Information and Communication Technology at The Mosslands School, a comprehensive school for boys near Liverpool, UK. He has a keen interest in involving his students in the design of curriculum software and runs a number of innovative pilot schemes in the school. Philip also lectures on a part time basis to post-graduate students at Liverpool Hope University College, where he specializes in Web and User Interface Design and supervises dissertations. As a keen astronomer, he is a member of the Advisory Body to the National Schools Observatory, a robotically controlled telescope on the island of La Palma. This telescope can be controlled over the Internet by school students. He is currently studying for his doctorate at Liverpool John Moores University. His research area is the investigation of the effect of User Interface Design on the development of thinking skills.

Jesús Favela is a professor at CICESE in Ensenada, Mexico, where he leads the Collaborative Systems Laboratory. He holds a BSc from UNAM (1987), and an MSc (1989) and PhD (1993) in Computer-Aided Engineering from MIT, where he worked as a research assistant in the Intelligent Engineering Systems Laboratory. His research interests include Computer Supported Cooperative Work, Multimedia Information Retrieval and Software Engineering.

Monika Fleischmann, a research artist and scientist, is head of the Media Arts Research Studies Department (MARS) Exploratory Media Lab at Fraunhofer Institute for Media Communication, Sankt Augustin, Germany. Her multidisciplinary background — Computer Graphics, Art, Play and Drama, Fashion Design — has made her an expert in the world of art and media technology. Fleischmann's artistic work, in partnership with Wolfgang Strauss, has been exhibited and awarded widely throughout the world at Ars Electronica - Linz, ZKM - Karlsruhe, Nagoya Science Museum, SIGGRAPH USA, ICC Tokyo, Imagina - Monte Carlo, Centre Pompidou Paris, Haus der Kunst Munich, etc.

Richard Francis, MA (Cantab.), MA (B'Ham), DTEFLA. Richard joined Oxford Brookes University (UK) as a Learning Technologist in 1999. In 2000, he became head of Media Workshop, an e-learning consultancy unit coordinating online learning development at the University. Richard's background is in Linguistics and Language Teaching. His teaching career began in Rome in 1978. Between 1982 and 1996 he worked for the British Council in Italy, Poland and Slovenia and taught at the Universities of Bologna and Trieste. In 1996, he returned to the UK to work at the University of East Anglia. He is experienced in Online and Computer Assisted Language Learning and has published extensively in this area. Richard can be reached at rafrancis@brookes.ac.uk.

Bernard Mark Garrett, PhD, BA (Honors), P.G.C.E.A., R.G.N., R.N.T. Bernard Garrett is an assistant professor at the University of British Columbia, School of Nursing, Canada. He has a range of teaching and clinical experience from medical and renal nursing practice in Hampshire and Oxford in the UK. Prior to his current appointment he was a principal lecturer at Oxford Brookes University (UK) and the lecturer practitioner for the Oxford Kidney Unit. His research interests are in the application of AI techniques in education, and use of Resource Based Learning to support clinical education. To contact Garrett: bmgarrett@brookes.ac.uk.

Ugur Halici is a professor of the Electrical and Electronics Engineering Department of the Middle East Technical University in Turkey. She is the head of the Computer Vision and Intelligent Systems Research Laboratory in the same department. She has been involved in various projects on Computer Vision, Intelligent Systems, and Human-computer Interaction, and has publications in several journals, books and conferences. To contact Halici: http://vision1.eee.metu.edu.tr/~halici/.

Associate professor **Lynne Hunt**, PhD, is associate dean (Teaching and Learning) in the Faculty of Communications, Health and Science, Edith Cowan University (ECU), Perth, Australia, and teaches in the Centre for Public Health. She is the recipient of three ECU awards for teaching excellence and the 2002 Australian Award for University Teaching in the Social Science category. She won the 2002 Prime Minister's Award for Australian University Teacher of the Year. She publishes in the fields of Women's Health and Tertiary Teaching and received the 2002 Merit Award for Best Paper on Authentic Learning from the Higher Education Research and Development Society of Australasia.

W.A. Janvier, BSc (Honors), graduated at Liverpool John Moores University (LJMU) (UK) in 2000 reading Computer Science. His current post-graduate PhD research program is "An AI-based Model to Support Distance Learning," where his initial research concentrated on Distance Learning Tools and Intelligent Tutoring Systems. He is currently researching the Learner's Communication Preference, Learning Styles and Neurolinguistic Programming with a view to combining these into a generic Distance Learning Interactive Intelligent system called WISDeM (Web Intelligent Student Distance-education Model). Prior to studying at LJMU, Bill, for many years, ran a dress manufacturing and finance business, then he joined the Life Industry, where he was in management until he retired. He was a licensed Seminar Speaker for both Allied Dunbar and J. Rothschild Assurance.

Joanna Jedrzejowicz holds a PhD in Computer Science. She works as a professor in the Institute of Mathematics, University of Gdansk, Poland. She has published widely in computer science conferences and journals. Her research interests include Theoretical Computer Science and Computer-based Learning. She conducted research and was a co-author of a project and implementation of a computer-based system for teaching the theory of automata and formal languages — the system is still used for teaching and research.

Joaquim Armando Pires Jorge, Instituto Superior Técnico (IST/UTL), Lisbon, Portugal, teaches Computer Graphics and User Interfaces at IST/UTL. He received his PhD and MSc in Computer Science from Rensselaer Polytechnic Institute, Troy, NY, USA, in 1995 and a BSEE from IST/UTL. He is head of the Cooperative Virtual Environments Lab at INESC. A co-chair of EUROGRAPHICS'98, which took place in Lisbon, he served as proposal evaluator for the ITR program of the National Science Foundation in 2000-2003 and EU's IST (Fifth framework program) INFO2000, EUREKA and related consultation meetings. He has served on program committees of many international conferences. A member of the Editorial Advisory Board of Computers & Graphics (Elsevier) and Computer Graphics Forum Journals, he has published more than 70 refereed journal and conference papers.

Athanasis Karoulis has a BSc in Mathematics from the Aristotle University of Thessaloniki (Greece), a degree in Educational Technologies from the University of Macedonia

(Greece), a degree in Open and Distance Learning from the Greek Open University, an MSc in Information Systems from the University of Macedonia (Greece), and a PhD in Informatics, in the domain of Human-Computer Interaction, from the Aristotle University of Thessaloniki, Greece. He is currently active as an instructor in educational technologies for secondary education, as a multimedia and web project manager and as a researcher in the domains of HCI and Distance Learning, regarding the application of new technologies at the Department of Informatics at Aristotle University. He is author of two books and co-author of another five, which are published in Greece, and he has managed more than six multimedia projects. His scientific interests concern Human-Computer Interaction, Multimedia and Web design, Educational Technologies and Distance Learning.

Mizue Kayama received her DrE degree from the Graduate School of Information Systems, the University of Electro-Communications in 2000. Presently, she is a lecturer at Senshu University, School of Network and Information, Japan. Her research fields are Artificial Intelligence in education, Knowledge Management at educational context and E-learning. Currently, she is a member of ISO/IEC JTC1 SC36 (Learning Technology) WG2 (Collaborative Technologies).

Martin Christof Kindsmüller, Dipl.-Inf. Dipl.-Psych., studied Computer Science, Psychology and Media Arts and Sciences at Berlin University of Technology (TUB), Karlsruhe University of Technology (UKA), and Massachusetts Institute of Technology (MIT), Media Laboratory. He holds master's degrees in Computer Science and Psychology from TUB and is currently working at the TUB Center for Human-Machine-Systems (HMS). Being a member of MoDyS-Research Group, he is working on different interdisciplinary projects within the group's focus (methods of user modeling in dynamic human-machine-systems).

Alexander Künzer received an MS (Dipl.-Inform.) in Computer Science from Aachen University, Germany. In parallel to academics, he worked for a German software company and was responsible for the development of software products for one-to-one marketing. In 2000, he joined the research team "User-Centered Design of Information and Communication Systems" at the Institute of Industrial Engineering and Ergonomics at Aachen University. His current work as a research assistant is concerned with modeling user intentions in Human-Computer Interaction; interface agents as well as genetic algorithms. He developed a web-based shared workspace to support different cooperation tasks.

Sandro Leuchter studied information science at TU Berlin and gained professional experience at the GMD in Bonn, Germany. Since October 2000, he is a member of the ZMMS MoDyS Research Group. He works on User Modeling in Cognitive Architectures, on the application of model-based user adaptive algorithms and has special interests in Software Engineering in innovative human computer applications.

Yinlin Li works as research scientist at MARS–Exploratory Media Lab – the Media Arts Research Studies department at Fraunhofer Institute for Media Communication, Sankt Augustin, Germany, since April 2001. His research focus is human-centred, body-free

Human Machine Interaction (HCI) and ambient intelligence technologies. He received his PH.D diploma in the area of electronic engineering at Peking institute of technology, china in 2000 and then worked until March 2001 in mobile phone research centre of China Electronics Co. to develop the baseband chipsets of the 3rd generation mobile phone (WCDMA).

Jun Munemori was born in 1955. He received BE and ME degrees in Electrical Engineering from Nagoya Institute of Technology, Nagoya, Japan, a DE in Electrical and Electrical Communication Engineering from Tohoku University, Sendai, Japan, in 1979, 1981, and 1984, respectively. He worked for the Mitsubishi Electric Corp., Kagoshima University, and Osaka University. He is currently a professor of Department of Design and Information Sciences at Wakayama University, Japan. His interests are Groupware, Human Interface, and Neurophysiology. He received IPSJ SIG Research Award, IPSJ Best Paper Award, and IEEE CE Japan Chapter Young Best Paper Award in 1997, 1998, 2002, respectively. He is a member of IEEE, ACM, IPSJ and IEICE.

Koichi Oda graduated from the Graduate School of Human Sciences at the Tokyo University. He was a researcher at the Japanese National Institute of Special Education in 1984. He spent nine months in the Psychology Department at New York University as a visiting scholar (1987) and, since then, he has started to apply vision science to the field of education and rehabilitation of persons with low vision. He moved to Tokyo Woman's Christian University in 1992 and serves as a board-of-trustee member for the Japanese Society of Low Vision Research and Rehabilitation and for the Vision Society of Japan.

Toshio Okamoto received the DrE degree from Tokyo Institute of Technology in 1988. He is professor at the University of Electro-Communications, Graduate School of Information Systems, Japan. His research fields are Theoretical and Application Studies/ Design of Artificial Intelligence Models for ITSs, Computer Supported Collaborative Learning System, and Collaborative Memory and Knowledge Management, particularly curriculum development/evaluation of IT-education in the Internet environment. He is a president of the Japanese Society for Information and System in Education and a member of the millennium project on IT-education under Japanese government. He was a chairman of ICCE99 and a chairman of the program committee of IEEE-ICALT2001. He is a convener of ISO/IEC JTC1 SC36 (Learning Technology), WG2 (Collaborative Technologies).

Robert S. Owen is an assistant professor of Marketing at Texas A&M University-Texarkana, USA. He has a PhD in Marketing from Ohio State University and has a technical background in the field of measurement. His primary area of interest is in issues of attention and attention measurement. His work on consumer information overload is cited in consumer psychology textbooks. His published work also includes issues of Machine-Assisted Learning and Diffusion of Innovation.

Carmen Pérez-Fragoso, is a researcher at the Institute of Educational Research and Development at the Universidad Autónoma de Baja California in Mexico, and doctoral student at the Institute of Communications and Media at the Université Stendhal in Grenoble 3, France. She holds an MEd degree from the University of Manchester and a

DESS in Distance Education from the Universities UNAM - Paris II. She collaborates in the Online Teachers' Training Programme and coordinates the Programme of Open and Distance Education at her university. Her research focuses on the analysis of interactions and the assessment of online courses.

Andreas Pombortsis received a BS in Physics and an MS in Electronics and Communications (both from the University of Thessaloniki), and a Diploma Degree in Electrical Engineering from the Technical University of Thessaloniki. In 1987 he received a PhD in Computer Science from the University of Thessaloniki, Greece. Currently, he is professor in the Department of Informatics, Aristotle University of Thessaloniki, Greece. His research interests include Computer Architecture, Parallel and Distributed Computer Systems, and Multimedia Systems.

Meenakshi Sundaram Rajasekaran recently finished his MSc in Business Systems Analysis and Design program of City University, London. His thesis was on Social Network Analysis of Computer Mediated Communication and E-learning.

Maria Alexandra Rentroia-Bonito works as a business consultant in Lisbon, Portugal. She received an MSc in Industrial and Labor Relations, minoring in Organizational Behavior from Cornell University, Ithaca, NY (1993), and an MBA from Catholic University "Andres Bello," and a bachelor's degree in Systems Engineering from IUPLCM, both in Caracas, Venezuela. During the last 18 years, she has worked as HR manager, consultant, trainer and analyst within several Human Resources Departments, mainly in multinational companies. She is currently pursuing her PhD in Human-Computer Interaction at DEI/IST in Lisbon.

George Roberts, MPhil, MEd, BA. George Roberts is a learning technologist with experience ranging from E-learning Development to Community-outreach Education for adults returning to learn. He is currently development manager of Brookes Online, an initiative of Oxford Brookes University, UK, that aims to create the institutional and technical environment within which technology-assisted off-campus programs can flourish. Before Brookes, he was with the College of Petroleum and Energy Studies where he developed Distance Learning courses and other CPD programs across a range of disciplines in corporate, industrial and educational contexts. He conducted training needs analysis, training market surveys and institutional capacity development studies in Russia, Azerbaijan and Kazakhstan. In his career he has also developed and taught community-based courses for the WEA, Cowley Community Education Committee and the PEP in Oxford, Reading and Newbury, and taught English at Temple University, Philadelphia, USA. To contact Roberts: groberts@brookes.ac.uk.

Kerstin Röse, Prof. Dr.Ing. Dipl.Psych, studied Psychology at the Humboldt University Berlin and earned a PhD in Engineering at the University of Kaiserslautern, Germany. She started her work as a consultant and HMI researcher in 1996 at the Institute for Production Automation, Department of Mechanical Engineering at the University Kaiserslautern. In 1998, the Center for Human-Machine-Interaction (HMI) at the University of Kaiserslautern was founded by Professor Dr.-Ing. D. Zühlke. There she worked as leader of the HMI group (99-02) and manager (01-02). In 2002, she became an assistant professor for User-centered Product Development at the TU Kaiserslautern, with a special focus on intercultural and contextual product design.

Hirohiko Sagawa received a master's degree in Information Engineering from the University of Tokyo in 1991. Since joining Hitachi, Ltd. (Japan) in 1991, he has researched and developed Sign Language Recognition and Generation Methods and Systems. He is currently a senior researcher in the Hitachi's Central Research Laboratory, focusing on Pattern Recognition, Natural Language Processing, and Human Interfaces. He is a member of Information Processing Society of Japan, the Human Interface Society, and the Japanese Association of Sign Linguistics.

As a practicing ICT teacher, **Mike Simco** developed an experiential approach to his teaching based around the practical application of new technologies in the classroom. Pupil motivation lies at the heart of learning and Mike has developed many innovative teaching strategies. Currently, he is leading the development of an exciting educational project, the National Schools' Observatory, based at the Astrophysics Research Institute of Liverpool John Moores University, UK. The aim of the project is to stimulate learning across a range of National Curriculum subjects by providing schools with the opportunity to access and use the University's multi-million pound research astronomical telescope sited in the Canary Isles.

Andy Smith is a reader in HCI and is director of the Centre for Software Internationalisation at the University of Luton in the UK, which provides a focus for usability in a global context. He is author of *Human Computer Factors*, published by McGraw-Hill, and has authored a wide range of academic papers. He jointly proposed the LUCID interface design methods, which aims to optimize, as opposed to iteratively improve, usability. He is also technical director of Optimum-Web Ltd., a usability consultancy based in Central London, which provides expert and user-based usability, accessibility and internationalization services to a range of public and private sector organizations. He is an executive committee member of the British HCI Group and is currently managing a European Union funded project supporting the development of usability in India.

Wolfgang Strauss studied Architecture and has held teaching positions in Interactive Media Art. In 1988, he was a co-founder of Art+Com, Berlin. His artistic work — produced with his partner Monika Fleischmann — was awarded the Golden Nica of Ars Electronica and is exhibited worldwide. Since 1997, he has been co-directing the MARS Exploratory Media Lab at the Fraunhofer Institute for Media Communication in Sankt Augustin, Bonn. His recent work is about Intuitive Interface Environments related to the human body and digital media space. "With digitization, the field of architecture extends: we must build the exterior, but also electronic interior, spaces to create the aesthetics of a new eco-system."

Masaru Takeuchi received a master's degree in System Science from the Tokyo Institute of Technology in 1986. He joined the Advanced Research Laboratory, Hitachi, Ltd. (Japan) in 1986. Since moving to Hitachi's Central Research Laboratory in 1995, he has worked on Graph Theory, Pattern Recognition, Genetic Algorithms, and Sign Language Translation Systems. He is now a senior researcher and a member of the Institute of Electronics, Information and Communication Engineers and the Society of Instrument and Control Engineers.

Ioannis Tarnanas has a BSc in Psychology from the Aristotle University of Thessaloniki, Greece. He has a MSc in Human Centre Computer Systems from Sussex University, UK, with Distinction and Honour. He has a scholarship of excellence for postgraduate studies, Aristotle University of Thessaloniki, Greece. He is currently a PhD candidate in "Virtual Reality Systems for Psychology and Training." He is the project leader and a scientific responsible for a three-year funded project from the Greek Secretarial for Research and Technology about "The Use of Artificial Environments in Crisis Management and Affect Regulation for Kids." He is also member of PIE (Psychophysiology in Ergonomics task force), part of the International Ergonomics Association *IEA*, of the EU funded "VR Research Network of Excellence," of the Greek Alzheimer and similar disorders company, of the American Biographical company research board of advisors in Human-Computer Interaction and the Cambridge Biographical Company Vice Consul in Psychology. His scientific interests concern Virtual Reality Systems in education and psychology, Human-Computer Interaction, Cognitive Ergonomics, Ubiquitous Computing and Assistive Technologies.

Saïd Tazi is assistant professor in Computer Science at Université des Sciences Sociales, Toulouse, France. His research focuses on Interactive Systems, including technologically mediated communication especially with documents. His affiliation was with the LIHS laboratory (Laboratoire d'Interaction Homme Systèmes) until December 2002, where he conducted a team working on development of formalisms, methods and software that provide: a way of reasoning formally about the effectiveness of writing communication; an explicit representation of use that connect content and expression; and help to reduce cognitive charge for writers and readers. This research was applied to industrial and academic projects, such as commercial aircraft documentation, and pedagogical documents. He is integrating with the LAAS-CNRS Laboratory in January 2003, to participate to E-learning projects with the "Communications Software" team.

Immediately after graduating from the School for Teachers of Acupuncture and Physical Therapy (1994), **Kazuhito Ujima** became a teacher in the Matsuyama School for the Blind, Japan. He spent a year at the Japanese National Institute of Special Education as an in-service trainee in 2000 and initiated projects related to the application of web and information technologies in teaching students with low vision. He recently received several awards for his outstanding practice.

Leon Urbas, after his PhD-study on using simulators and the Internet for operator training in chemical plants (TU Berlin), joined a leading global player in fine chemistry. With three years experience on industrial work in Data Driven Process Modeling, Process Optimization, Engineering of Process Information Systems and Management of Automation Projects, he went back to university in October 2000 to lead a junior research group, sponsored by VolkswagenStiftung, working on interdisciplinary methods for and applications of user modelling in complex, dynamic human-machine-systems.

Thierry Villemur is maître de conférences at the Institut Universitaire de Technologie of Toulouse University, France, and belongs to the "Communications Software" group of LAAS-CNRS (France). His research topics include Computer Supported Collaborative Work, Synchronous E-learning Platforms, Multimedia Groupware Applications, and Formal Design of Collaboration Services and Protocols. He participated in several French (CESAME, TOPASE, CAMERA), and European (DSE) projects. With K. Drira, he has co-edited a book, *Cooperative Environments for Distributed System Engineering*. He is now working in the European IST Lab@Future project to define a generic augmented reality and collaborative platform for future e-learning applications.

Michael Wolf works at MARS Exploratory Media Lab, the Media Arts Research Studies Department at Fraunhofer Institute for Media Communication, Sankt Augustin, Germany, since April 2002. After having finished a three-year diploma in Communication Design at Krefeld, Germany, he studied Interface Design and Product Design at the University of Applied Sciences in Cologne — Koeln International School of Design. His research at MARS-Lab focuses on tangible media, i.e., smart toys and interactive playing and learning environments. He has won several design awards.

Takashi Yoshino was born in 1969. He received BE and ME degrees in Electrical Engineering from Kagoshima University, Kagoshima, Japan, in 1992 and 1994 respectively. He received a PhD in Information Science from Tohoku University, Sendai, Japan, in 2001. In 1995, he joined the Department of Electrical and Electronics Engineering, Kagoshima University. He is currently a research associate of Department of Design and Information Sciences at Wakayama University, Japan. His interests are Groupware, Mobile Computing and Human Computer Interface. He is a member of IEEE, ACM, IPSJ, and IEICE.

Giorgos Zacharia is founder and chief scientist of Open Ratings, Inc. (ORI), where he leads Research and Development. Giorgos is also a PhD student in Computer Science at the Center for Biological and Computational Learning of the MIT Artificial Intelligence Laboratory, USA. His research at MIT focuses on Statistical Learning Theory. Giorgos holds an MS from the MIT Media Laboratory, where he was a Telecom Italia Fellow in the Software Agents Group, a BS in Mathematics, and a BS in Computer Science with a minor in Economics from MIT as an undergraduate Fulbright Scholar.

Panayiotis Zaphiris is a lecturer at the Centre for Human-Computer Interaction Design, School of Informatics of City University, London. Before joining City University, he was a researcher at the Institute of Gerontology at Wayne State University, from where he got a PhD in Industrial Engineering specializing in Human Computer Interaction (HCI). His research interests lie in HCI with an emphasis in issues related to the elderly and people with disabilities. He is also interested in Web Usability, Mathematical Modeling of Browsing Behavior in hierarchical online Information Systems, Online Communities, E-learning and Social Network Analysis.

Index

NEW Titles
from Information Science Publishing

- **Instructional Design in the Real World: A View from the Trenches**
  Anne-Marie Armstrong
  ISBN: 1-59140-150-X: eISBN 1-59140-151-8, © 2004
- **Personal Web Usage in the Workplace: A Guide to Effective Human Resources Management**
  Murugan Anandarajan & Claire Simmers
  ISBN: 1-59140-148-8; eISBN 1-59140-149-6, © 2004
- **Social, Ethical and Policy Implications of Information Technology**
  Linda L. Brennan & Victoria Johnson
  ISBN: 1-59140-168-2; eISBN 1-59140-169-0, © 2004
- **Readings in Virtual Research Ethics: Issues and Controversies**
  Elizabeth A. Buchanan
  ISBN: 1-59140-152-6; eISBN 1-59140-153-4, © 2004
- **E-ffective Writing for e-Learning Environments**
  Katy Campbell
  ISBN: 1-59140-124-0; eISBN 1-59140-125-9, © 2004
- **Development and Management of Virtual Schools: Issues and Trends**
  Catherine Cavanaugh
  ISBN: 1-59140-154-2; eISBN 1-59140-155-0, © 2004
- **The Distance Education Evolution: Issues and Case Studies**
  Dominique Monolescu, Catherine Schifter & Linda Greenwood
  ISBN: 1-59140-120-8; eISBN 1-59140-121-6, © 2004
- **Distance Learning and University Effectiveness: Changing Educational Paradigms for Online Learning**
  Caroline Howard, Karen Schenk & Richard Discenza
  ISBN: 1-59140-178-X; eISBN 1-59140-179-8, © 2004
- **Managing Psychological Factors in Information Systems Work: An Orientation to Emotional Intelligence**
  Eugene Kaluzniacky
  ISBN: 1-59140-198-4; eISBN 1-59140-199-2, © 2004
- **Developing an Online Curriculum: Technologies and Techniques**
  Lynnette R. Porter
  ISBN: 1-59140-136-4; eISBN 1-59140-137-2, © 2004
- **Online Collaborative Learning: Theory and Practice**
  Tim S. Roberts
  ISBN: 1-59140-174-7; eISBN 1-59140-175-5, © 2004

Excellent additions to your institution's library! Recommend these titles to your librarian!

To receive a copy of the Idea Group Inc. catalog, please contact 1/717-533-8845, fax 1/717-533-8661,or visit the IGI Online Bookstore at: http://www.idea-group.com!

Note: All IGI books are also available as ebooks on netlibrary.com as well as other ebook sources. Contact Ms. Carrie Skovrinskie at <cskovrinskie@idea-group.com> to receive a complete list of sources where you can obtain ebook information or IGP titles.

Designing Instruction for Technology-Enhanced Learning

Patricia Rogers
Bemidji State University, USA

When faced with the challenge of designing instruction for technology-enhanced education, many good teachers find great difficulty in connecting pedagogy with technology. While following instructional design practices can help, most teachers are either unfamiliar with the field or are unable to translate the formal design process for use in their own classroom. *Designing Instruction for Technology Enhanced Learning* is focused on the practical application of instructional design practices for teachers at all levels, and is intended to help the reader "walk through" designing instruction for e-learning.

The goal of *Designing Instruction for Technology Enhanced Learning* is to pool the expertise of many practitioners and instructional designers and to present that information in such a way that teachers will have useful and relevant references and guidance for using technology to enhance teaching and learning, rather than simply adding technology to prepared lectures. The chapters, taken together, make the connection between intended learning outcomes, teachings strategies, and instructional media.

ISBN 1-930708-28-9 (h/c) • US$74.95 • 286 pages • Copyright © 2002

"Most often, when forced to use new technologies in teaching, teachers will default to a technology-enhanced lecture method, rather than take advantage of the variety of media characteristics that expand the teaching and learning experience."
–Patricia Rogers, Bemidji State University, USA

It's Easy to Order! Order online at www.idea-group.com or call our toll-free hotline at 1-800-345-4332!
Mon-Fri 8:30 am-5:00 pm (est) or fax 24 hours a day 717/533-8661

Idea Group Publishing

Hershey • London • Melbourne • Singapore • Beijing

An excellent addition to your library